ANABAPTIST WORLD USA

D0167305

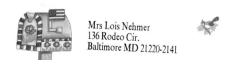

Mrs Lois Nehmer
136 Rodeo Cir.
Baltimore MD 21220-2141

ANABAPTIST WORLD USA

Donald B. Kraybill
C. Nelson Hostetter

Herald
Press

Scottdale, Pennsylvania
Waterloo, Ontario

um-
the

Library of Congress Cataloging-in-Publication Data
Kraybill, Donald B.
    Anabaptist world USA / Donald B. Kraybill, C. Nelson Hostetter.
    p. cm.
    Includes bibliographical references and index.
    ISBN 0-8361-9163-3 (alk. paper)
        1. Anabaptists—United States. 2. Anabaptists—United States—Statistics.
    I. Hostetter, C. Nelson, 1923- II. Title.
BX4933.U6 K73 2001
289.7'73—dc21

                                                                        2001024423

The paper used in this publication is recycled and meets the minimum requirements of American National Standard for Information Sciences—Permanence of Paper for Printed Library Materials, ANSI Z39.48-1984.

Unless otherwise noted, Scripture is from the *New Revised Standard Version Bible,* copyright 1989 by the Division of Christian Education of the National Council of the Churches of Christ in the USA, and is used by permission.

Sections of chapters 5 and 7 are adapted by permission from Donald B. Kraybill and Carl F. Bowman, *On the Backroad to Heaven: Old Order Hutterites, Mennonites, Amish, and Brethren*, chapters 4 and 2 (respectively), © 2001, The Johns Hopkins University Press, Baltimore, Md. Reprinted with permission of The Johns Hopkins University Press.

Some sections of C. Nelson Hostetter's *Anabaptist-Mennonites Nationwide USA* (1997) are adapted by permission of Masthof Press.

Photos are credited on the pages where they appear.

Figures were designed by Linda Eberly.

ANABAPTIST WORLD USA
Copyright © 2001 by Herald Press, Scottdale, Pa. 15683
    Released simultaneously in Canada by Herald Press,
    Waterloo, Ont. N2L 6H7. All rights reserved
International Standard Book Number: 0-8361-9163-3
Library of Congress Catalog Card Number: 2001024423
Printed in the United States of America
Cover and book design by Merrill R. Miller

10 09 08 07 06 05 04 03 02   10 9 8 7 6 5 4 3 2

To order or request information, please call 1-800-759-4447 (individuals);
1-800-245-7894 (trade). Website: www.mph.org

To

Harold S. Bender, Donald F. Durnbaugh, and John A. Hostetler,
our mentors in the study of Anabaptist communities

CONTENTS

FIGURES
AND TABLES

FOREWORDS

The authors have brought together much excellent and helpful data, both statistical and expressed in prose. More remarkably, they have done it in a way that is pleasing to read, use, and extract. It is full of information, yet does not read like a census report. It is useful as a reference work, but it may well find its way also to people's bedside stands. That is no mean accomplishment.

On the whole Kraybill and Hostetter have introduced the basic common issues of the Anabaptist-derived faith (or faiths) very well, very palatably, very succinctly. Without having to confront heavy theology, readers get a good introduction to what the Anabaptist movement and tradition is about. In a way their discussion is elementary, but really in its own way it starts readers also on the road to the profound.

Admirably, the authors have done their work largely by cool description. The tone is not at all partisan or judgmental. Of course, no author escapes making some judgment. They made the judgment to be respectfully descriptive. A fine judgment!
—*Theron F. Schlabach, Professor of History, Goshen College*

Place this one next to the *Martyrs Mirror,* but within easy reach. This twenty-first-century reference on the Anabaptist World USA is sure to become the standard authority on the four major "tribes" of the movement. This comprehensive work is far more than a church directory or a catalog of resources, though it is that. Provocative, fresh essays examine current issues against the backdrop of history to probe substantial questions for the future.
—*Lee Snyder, President, Bluffton College*

This excellent resource will prove invaluable for that rapidly increasing number of persons belonging to or having interest in the expanding family of churches known as Anabaptist. Once commonly used as a pejorative epithet, *Anabaptist* is now understood as a positive and distinguishing hallmark among groups belonging to a common church tradition. In turn, Anabaptist bodies, collectively, are recognized as an influential component of world Christianity. Kraybill and Hostetter provide concise descriptions of the four major Anabaptist groupings—Amish, Brethren, Hutterite, and Mennonite—explain how they are alike and how different, and provide helpful lists of detailed information, never before available.
—*Donald F. Durnbaugh, Editor,* The Brethren Encyclopedia

Kraybill and Hostetter provide a geographical, cultural, and churchly map of more than sixty related groups. The data alone makes this a unique and indispensable resource. The interpretive framework enlarges the perspective, sharpens self-understanding, and extends public awareness.

—*John A. Lapp, Executive Secretary Emeritus, Mennonite Central Committee*

Interpretative essays, definitions, charts, a Directory of Congregations, and much more make this the indispensable guide through the maze of the Anabaptist World in the United States. Both those inside and those outside the traditions will find here a rich source of information and knowledge.

—*E. Morris Sider, Editor,* Brethren in Christ History and Life

Anabaptist World USA will be an invaluable resource not only for Anabaptists but for all of those who continue to be attracted to the extraordinary world the Anabaptists have made. Small in numbers though they may be, the Christian witness the Anabaptists make will surely be essential for all churches as we rediscover the significance of discipleship.

—*Stanley M. Hauerwas, Gilbert T. Rowe Professor of Theological Ethics, Duke University*

This meticulously researched, conveniently organized handbook summarizes membership data for more than sixty groups within Amish, Brethren, Hutterite, and Mennonite fellowships in the United States. This in itself is a major accomplishment—one that will serve as a benchmark at the dawn of a new century for later studies. But more than merely listing names and numbers, the volume offers a lively historical survey of each major group and cogent summaries of distinctive beliefs and practices. An indispensable reference work that belongs in every church library and pastor's study.

—*John D. Roth, Editor,* Mennonite Quarterly Review

Donald Kraybill and C. Nelson Hostetter have combined their passions to add greatly to the store of knowledge in the broad sweep of Anabaptist expression in the United States today. Their broad strokes provide a readable summary that offers an introduction to first-time inquirers, as well as to those who come from one form of Anabaptism but remain uninformed about the other types.

—*James Schrag, Executive Director Designate, Mennonite Church USA*

This work is a major contribution to Anabaptist studies. The interpretative essays are informative and thought-provoking, as well as a pleasure to read. Many readers will also appreciate the newly compiled directories and statistical information. At last all major Anabaptist communities—from Old Order Amish and Hutterites to mainstream Brethren and Mennonites—have a resource that affirms their common spiritual heritage while pointing out the tremendous diversity in beliefs and practices.

—*David B. Eller, Director, The Young Center for Anabaptist and Pietist Studies, Elizabethtown College*

The book will be an indispensable addition to any collection of Anabaptist studies and to any reader who is also a member of any of the sixty groups described within. The essays, charts, graphs, and names will save scholars hours of time and provide an inclusive snapshot of this part of the Radical Reformation nearly five hundred years after its beginning.

—*Shirley H. Showalter, President, Goshen College*

I have wished for a resource like this for a long time! At last we have a reliable guide to the complexities of Anabaptist life and witness in the United States.

—*Richard J. Mouw, President and Professor of Christian Philosophy, Fuller Theological Seminary*

PREFACE

The religious landscape of American society sparkles with diversity. Indeed, religious freedom and the pluralism it has spawned are trademarks of the American experiment. Scattered among the mosaic of hundreds of American religious groups, dozens of Anabaptist communities add their own distinctive hue. Despite their common theological roots, these communities sport a remarkable diversity of their own that we explore in the following pages.

Anabaptist World USA is a first-time effort to assemble all the pieces of the Anabaptist puzzle in the United States. It provides a turn-of-the-century snapshot of the groups that identify with the Anabaptist Movement of sixteenth-century Europe through direct lineage or intentional affirmation. The maze of Anabaptist communities involves some sixty different groups. Our compilation will assist insiders and outsiders alike to better understand where the various groups fit in the larger puzzle of Anabaptist life. Moreover, we hope the project will also serve as a useful benchmark for future studies of Anabaptist communities throughout the twenty-first century.

Our work builds on a previous book, Anabaptist-Mennonites Nationwide USA, which C. Nelson Hostetter compiled in 1997. *Anabaptist World USA* updates all the membership estimates and includes Brethren groups as well as Hutterite colonies. Our entire study is grounded on a database of some 5,500 congregations scattered across forty-seven states as well as Puerto Rico and the District of Columbia. The membership and population estimates reflect the state of Anabaptist communities in the United States at end of the year 2000.

In sixteenth-century Europe, the nickname *Anabaptist* identified people who were twice baptized, once as infants and later as adults. Thus strictly speaking, few present-day Anabaptists are literal Anabaptists by rebaptism. Even the early Anabaptists did not consider themselves Anabaptists; they regarded their adult baptism as their one and only true baptism. Over the decades the term *Anabaptist* has taken on a broader meaning that designates the theological tradition flowing from the sixteenth-century Anabaptist Movement as well as the communities that have formed in its wake. In this broader sense, we use the term to denote both an Anabaptist heritage and a theological identity. Specifically, we focus on what we have called four tribes of Anabaptists: Amish, Brethren, Hutterites, and Mennonites. We call them tribes, not in a technical anthropological sense, but as a convenient way to designate four clusters of Anabaptist groups that have emerged over time.

Some of the groups in the Anabaptist World have direct historical ties to the early Anabaptists, and others are more tangential. Hutterites and Mennonites, for example, are descendants of the sixteenth-century

Anabaptists, but many of the Brethren groups were shaped by both Radical Pietism and Anabaptism, nearly two centuries after the initial Anabaptist Movement. When considering what groups to include, we have erred on the side of inclusivity. We have counted groups with a direct and continuing connection to sixteenth-century Anabaptism as well as those that actively identify with Anabaptist theology. If a group carries the name Amish, Brethren, Hutterite, or Mennonite, or if its leaders consider it "Anabaptist," we have included it. Our definition of *Anabaptist* focuses on formal church bodies and thus misses many "hidden" Anabaptists in other religious communities who identify with Anabaptism but who are not formally members of an Anabaptist church.

The Brethren in our story trace their roots to the German Baptist Brethren that formed in Schwarzenau, Germany, in 1708. We have not included other groups carrying the Brethren name—Evangelical United Brethren and Plymouth Brethren—but not linked to the Schwarzenau Brethren. Moreover, we have not included the Baptists, the Church of Christ, the Church of God (Anderson), the Disciples of Christ, the Missionary Church, the Moravians, the Quakers, and other groups that share some similarities with many Anabaptist communities. Also missing are one-time Anabaptist congregations and groups that have deliberately shed their Anabaptist identity, even though they may once have had direct historical ties. A discussion of the selection procedures and a listing of all the groups appears in sections A and B of the Resources (see Contents).

We use the term *world* to refer to the entire social sphere of Anabaptism in the United States. There are *many* Anabaptist Worlds—Asian, African, Canadian, and so forth. This project focuses specifically on one of the many worlds—Anabaptist communities in the United States. We have assembled the contemporary Anabaptist puzzle in the United States but have not told the Anabaptist story, for there are dozens of Anabaptist stories. Each of the sixty some groups we have identified has its own intriguing story.

Some of the groups under the Anabaptist canopy do not interact with each other and some actually know little if anything about each other; yet others cooperate on a regular basis. Some churches are on the fringe of the Anabaptist World; others stand in the center. In other words, several communities in this book have a marginal Anabaptist identity; for others, Anabaptism is central to their historical and theological self-understanding. Some of the churches, for example, are deeply committed to peacemaking; others see nonresistance and nonviolence as rather peripheral to their faith.

We do not provide historical case studies or social analyses of the groups because those are available elsewhere. We have not tested sociological theories, developed new conceptual interpretations, or traced historical changes. This is not a historical, sociological, or theological study. Historians may gasp at our sweeping historical overviews, sociologists will likely shudder at our broad generalizations, and theologians may tremble at our scant discussion of the doctrinal and ethical formulations undergirding Anabaptist life. Our modest, but challenging task was to assemble the pieces of a complicated puzzle on a small board in a concise fashion. In part 2 we have compiled some Resources for those who want to explore a particular group or topic in greater depth.

One of our challenges was to determine what constitutes a group. Using the arbitrary standard of two or more affiliated congregations with a total membership of at least 250, we have identified some sixty different groups. Large ones like the Church of the Brethren count more than 137,000 members. Some of the smaller groups have only a few congregations and claim less than 1,000 members. In addition, there are many loose affiliations and small independent congregations. We use the term *denomination* sparingly because some congregations are connected in loose fellowships that are not exactly denominations in the technical sense. The term *affiliation* refers to a cluster of congregations that relate with each other even though they may not always share identical beliefs and practices or have a centralized organization. Some of the networks of more conservative groups prefer to be known as *fellow-ships* rather than denominations or affiliations. Throughout the book, we typically use the term *congregation* for local units of worship, even though the Amish call theirs "church districts" and the Hutterites call theirs "colonies."

Approximately 537,000 adult members participate in the life of some 5,500 congregations. If we include children and unbaptized participants, the total population swells to an estimated 861,000. We systematically make a distinction between baptized adult members and the total population of a group because the differences are often substantial. In Old Order communities, for example, the number of unbaptized children and youth typically exceeds the number of members, yielding a total population more than twice the size of the membership.

In conviction and habit, Anabaptist communities stretch across a wide cultural and religious spectrum. Some are rural separatists with conservative worldviews and lifestyles. At the other end of the spectrum are cosmopolitan, urban congregations that have assimilated into mainstream culture. Some Anabaptists drive horse-drawn carriages, read by lantern light, and go to one-room schools; others participate in public life as stockbrokers, physicians, politicians, and corporate executives. Until mid-twentieth century, many of the Anabaptist communities in the United States had strong strains of German, Swiss, or Russian ethnicity. Today, however, African-American, Asian-American, Latino-American, and Native American congregations in the Anabaptist fold speak more than a dozen different languages.

As noted above, we have clustered all the groups into four Anabaptist tribes: Amish, Brethren, Hutterite, and Mennonite. The tribal clusters are based on the name, historical influences, and present-day characteristics of the groups. In some cases where groups are linked to two tribes, we had to make arbitrary judgments. For example, we placed Amish Mennonite groups in the Amish tribe because they have come from Amish roots and continue to use the name. We counted the Brethren in Christ groups with the Brethren tribe despite their affiliation with some Mennonite organizations. We included Charity Christian Fellowship and The Apostolic Christian Church of America in the Mennonite tribe, even though they do not carry the name *Mennonite*, because they share many similarities with conservative Mennonite groups.

The tribal placement of each group is shown in section B of the Resources. In later discussions of each group, as well as in section A of the Resources, we give our reasons for placing various groups with a particular tribe.

In addition to sorting by tribe, we also classified groups by their cultural assimilation, placing them into three conceptual bins: *traditional, transitional,* and *transformational.* Few groups fit one category perfectly; some groups indeed straddle the categories or tilt one way or the other. Moreover, we are not suggesting that all groups move in the same direction or go through the same steps of development as they change. Each group has its own story, with a variety of unpredictable twists and turns. Nevertheless, the three conceptual categories help to tease out key differences and clarify an otherwise complicated and confusing maze. Chapter 4 provides a more thorough discussion of the three types of groups.

The task of fitting the pieces of the Anabaptist puzzle together was challenging, and we offer several disclaimers. The membership estimates and population estimates are just that: *estimates.* We sought authoritative written and verbal sources whenever possible, but our numerical counts should be seen as reasonable estimates, not hard facts. Many of the Old Order groups do not keep individual membership statistics, so we had to rely on selective samples and the best insights of knowledgeable informants. The membership rolls of some congregations include people who have been inactive for years. In contrast, some growing congregations have more Sunday worship participants than their official membership rolls suggest.

The population estimates we made also required assumptions about family size and the age of baptism. Hence, though we provide numerical summaries that may *appear* to be precise, they should always be seen for what they are—informed estimates. See section A of the Resources for a discussion of our methods.

The Anabaptist World in the United States is changing and dynamic as new congregations hatch and others die every day. This project offers a turn-of-the-century snapshot of an Anabaptist World in flux. Although we have tried to be comprehensive and accurate in our enumeration of congregations in the United States, we realize that we may have missed some groups or congregations. For that we apologize. We welcome corrections, suggestions, and updates, so that revised editions may accurately reflect the changing patterns of Anabaptist life in the United States.

The book is divided into three parts: part 1 is a series of Interpretative Essays, part 2 provides Resources related to the various groups, and part 3 consists of a Directory of Anabaptist congregations in the United States. For those who want to test their knowledge of Anabaptist groups, we have also created a fifty-item quiz that is posted on the website of Herald Press at www.mph.org/books/anabaptistworld.htm.

Over the years, we have both served in a variety of different Anabaptist settings and bring an ecumenical Anabaptist perspective to the project. Our purpose is not to applaud or judge particular groups, but to simply assemble the puzzle. We have tried to be evenhanded and fair in our presentation, yet the length of text devoted to each group is not proportionate to its size. For example, we devote an overview chapter to both the Hutterite and Mennonite tribes despite their considerable difference in size. Space limitations made it impossible to mention every group or program in the text, so we beg your forbearance if we missed your favorite one.

As ecumenical Anabaptists, we hope that all of these communities of faith will flourish. We hope they will find new ways to work together and learn from each other. We do not dream of a great day when they will all be one, but we do envision a growing spirit of respect and understanding that will lead to more and better cooperation within the Anabaptist family of faith. We trust that this modest project will contribute to that end.

—*Donald B. Kraybill*
—*C. Nelson Hostetter*

ACKNOWLEDGMENTS

In countless ways, dozens of people have contributed time and support to this project. We are especially grateful to the many leaders of small churches and independent conferences who have provided C. Nelson Hostetter with membership statistics on their congregations during his many phone calls and trips across the country. To those who kindly granted interviews amid their busy schedules, we also offer our sincere thanks.

We owe an enormous debt to two colleagues who were especially generous with their help and counsel: Stephen Scott and Steven M. Nolt. Steve Scott patiently helped us identify some of the smaller groups often missing from formal directories and secluded from the public eye. Steve Nolt provided helpful resources and bibliographic suggestions. We thank both of them for finding time in their busy schedules to study an earlier draft of the manuscript and to offer critical feedback that has improved the accuracy of our text.

Our colleagues Donald F. Durnbaugh, John A. Lapp, Theron F. Schlabach, James Schrag, and E. Morris Sider provided critical feedback and suggestions that substantially improved the text. We are also indebted to David Eller for wise counsel and for providing resources at the Young Center for Anabaptist and Pietist Studies, which he directs at Elizabethtown (Pa.) College.

Our research team at Messiah College (Grantham, Pa.) deserves special kudos for excellent cooperation and support in the face of short deadlines. Research assistant, Mark Lacher, who assisted us at every turn, created, organized, and manipulated the database of 5,500 congregations. His superb work and careful attention to detail produced the printouts essential for our writing. Richard Dent, director of Information Technology Systems, and his staff provided valuable technical expertise in creating the database. Krista Malick performed a variety of support services for the database, gathered and verified information, and checked and rechecked the consistency of our text. Esther Hostetter provided computer support services throughout the project. Michele Gómez, our administrative assistant, coordinated many aspects of the project and key-stroked numerous revisions in a tireless and pleasant fashion.

Without this team's endless devotion, buoyant spirit, and excellent cooperation, the project would remain unfinished. We are also grateful for the helpful critique of our manuscript by David Weaver-Zercher, director of the Sider Institute for Anabaptist, Pietist, and Wesleyan Studies at Messiah College, as well as for ongoing support from the Sider Institute.

We are thankful for the excellent work of Linda Eberly, who created the graphics that grace the pages of this book. For this project, Lois Ann Mast of Masthof Press kindly granted us permission to adapt some sections of C. Nelson Hostetter's previous book, *Anabaptist-Mennonites Nationwide USA*.

Without the financial support of many people, the project would have been impossible. We extend our sincere gratitude to those who have provided generous financial assistance as well as friendly support and interest. Specifically, we thank the following contributors: Milton and Ann Good, Jobie E. Riley, Martin and Mary Lee Spangler, Edgar and Gladys Stoesz, Paul and Arlene Witman, as well as several other anonymous donors.

Finally, it has been a pleasure to work with Herald Press editor S. David Garber, who along with his team coordinated the publication of *Anabaptist World USA* in a very short period of time. We are blessed to have so many fine associates and colleagues who have helped us in a multitude of ways. Moreover, we have also enjoyed working together as our partnership grew through the many phases of the project.

—*Donald B. Kraybill*
—*C. Nelson Hostetter*

Part 1
Interpretative Essays

Chapter 1

ANABAPTIST BEGINNINGS

I highly esteem all that accords
with the Word of God.
—*Elisabeth Dirks, 1549, when interrogated as an Anabaptist teacher. She
was tortured with thumbscrews and eventually drowned in a bag.*[1]

ANABAPTIST REFORMERS

The Anabaptist story begins in January 1525 in Zurich, Switzerland, when a group of young radicals secretly baptized each other in the home of Felix Manz. Such an event today would hardly provoke a stir. But in sixteenth-century Europe, baptizing an adult was a defiant act of civil disobedience, a capital crime that triggered execution. The simple baptisms in Zurich helped to ignite the Anabaptist Movement during the early years of the Protestant Reformation. The young reformers were soon nicknamed *Anabaptists*, meaning rebaptizers, because they had already been baptized as infants in the Catholic Church.[2] They contended, however, that their adult baptism was their one and only true baptism.

The Anabaptist Movement had been brewing for several years. Martin Luther had already launched the Protestant Reformation in 1517 when he nailed his ninety-five theses to the door of the Wittenberg Church in Germany. At that time Germany was not a unified state but a patchwork of some three hundred political units—states, cities, and territories ruled by different princes and monarchs. Between 1524 and 1526, a Peasants' War in several regions of western Europe had left a hundred thousand bloody casualties; peasants were venting their frustrations against political, economic, and religious oppression. The swirling forces of religious reformation and social unrest rapidly unraveled the centuries-old bonds that had wrapped church, society, and state into a single social package. Village and countryside were rife with change and social turmoil.

The young reformers in Zurich were students of the local Protestant pastor, Ulrich Zwingli, a leading voice in the Reformation. Impatient with Zwingli's slow pace of reform, the dissidents for several years had been meeting for Bible study. They argued that Christian practices should rest solely on Scripture, not on church tradition and civic custom. Calling for a sharper break from Catholic traditions and a cleaner separation between church and civil government, they refused to baptize their babies, raised questions about the mass, scorned the use of images, and criticized the morality of church officials.

After spirited consultations with the Zurich city council, the young renegades rebaptized each other. They contended that baptism should be conferred only on an adult who had made a voluntary decision to follow the teachings of Jesus. Although adult baptism became the public symbol of the Anabaptist Movement, the deeper issue was one of authority. Where did ultimate authority rest? Did government officials have the right to interpret and prescribe a Christian practice, such as infant baptism, or was the Bible the sole and final authority for the Christian church? The answer was clear in the minds of the rebaptizers. For them, Scripture and the voice of the Spirit were the ultimate authorities. They felt compelled to obey the teachings of Christ, even if such obedience would bring the executioner's sword.

The Anabaptists refused to baptize infants, swear oaths of allegiance, and follow the dictates of established tradition; their refusals incensed political and religious authorities. The name *Anabaptist* became a dirty word for a dangerous movement that threatened to upend many political and religious patterns. The young reformers shook the pillars of civil authority because infant baptism conferred membership into both Catholic and Protestant Churches. It also granted automatic citizenship that gave civil authorities the power to tax and conscript. The Anabaptists turned their backs on traditional Catholic teaching, evolving Protestant doctrine, and the laws of the Zurich city council. As young upstarts, they followed their own interpretation of Scripture, the words of Jesus, and the prompting of the Holy Spirit.

Anabaptist convictions tore asunder the threads that had woven social, religious, economic, and political interests into a single fabric over the centuries. Civil authorities, as well as Protestant and Catholic leaders, were not about to be mocked by a motley group of young radicals.

Leaders of the new movement were promptly arrested, imprisoned, and banned from several cities and regions. Within four months of the first rebaptism, the first Anabaptist was killed for sedition, and the "heretics" began to flee for their lives. Within two years, in a public spectacle, Felix Manz was drowned in the Limmat River, flowing through Zurich. Meetings were often held in secret and secluded places to avoid detection.

Propelled by persecution and missionary zeal, Anabaptism mushroomed in many areas of Europe. Anabaptist preachers and sympathizers sprang up in various cities and villages—in Moravia, Germany, and the Netherlands in the early days of the movement.

With many centers of activity and different flavors of Anabaptism, the movement attracted a host of people with divergent religious views. Some Anabaptists were mystics and spiritualists; others expected the imminent return of Christ and the end of the world. Some were pacifists and others were violent anarchists. Still others emphasized daily obedience to Jesus' teachings and the importance of building a church of committed believers.

Thousands of Anabaptists were executed by cruel and torturous tactics. Civil authorities even commissioned special hunters to search for Anabaptist heretics. When they were caught, many met a martyr's death. Thousands were tortured, branded, burned, drowned, imprisoned, and sometimes dismembered. Even today, stories of the harsh persecution can be found in the *Martyrs Mirror*, a book of some 1,100 pages that chronicles the bloody carnage.[3] As the persecution waxed and waned, Anabaptists found refuge in Moravia, Alsace, the Palatinate, the Netherlands, Poland, and eventually in the Ukraine and North America. After the enthusiasm of the first decades cooled and the fringe groups faded, the surviving Anabaptist communities developed stable rhythms of congregational life and practice.

For the most part, Anabaptists accepted the historic creeds of the Christian church. Along with Protestant Reformers, they emphasized the authority of the Scripture, salvation by grace through faith, and the priesthood of all believers. In addition, the Anabaptists accented the work of the Holy Spirit, a life of obedient discipleship, the practical fruits of conversion in daily life, accountability to a body of believers, adult (or believers) baptism, the rejection of oaths and violence, and in some cases, social separation from the larger society.[4] An early statement of the Swiss Brethren in 1527 summarized some of their convictions.[5] This confession of faith

The site on the Limmat River in Zurich where the Anabaptist Felix Manz was drowned for his beliefs in 1527. Photo by Jan Gleysteen

emphasizes, among other issues, the authority of the New Testament as a guide for everyday life and highlights:

Adult (or believers) baptism
The church as a covenant community
Literal obedience to the teachings of Christ
The refusal to swear oaths
The rejection of violence
Social separation from the evil world
The exclusion of errant members from communion

One scholar has argued that the core of the Anabaptist vision contained three distinctive features: (1) a radical obedience to the teachings and example of Christ that transforms the behavior of individual believers; (2) a new concept of the church as a voluntary body of believers, accountable to one another and separate from the larger world; and (3) an ethic of love that rejects violence in all spheres of human life.[6] In recent years, Anabaptist theology has sometimes been called a "third way" that is neither Protestant nor Catholic, a third way that blends evangelical spirituality with social justice.[7]

THE HUTTERITES

Faced with bitter persecution—imprisonment, torture, and execution—many Anabaptists fled eastward to safe havens of tolerance in Moravia, in present-day Czech Republic. Beginning in 1527, Moravia became a sanctuary for Anabaptists and other "heretics" for several years. Anabaptists of diverse persuasions congregated in the Moravian town of Nickolsburg, where they enjoyed protection under the shadow of a sympathetic lord.

The seeds of the Hutterite Movement sprouted in this town amid a dispute between several factions of Anabaptists over pacifism, the use of the sword, and the payment of war taxes for civil protection. The members of one subgroup were nicknamed *Stäbler*, people of the staff, because they carried a staff rather than a sword. Various disagreements led a group of some two hundred *Stäbler* to leave Nickolsburg in the spring of 1528 and head for safety in Austerlitz, another Moravian town. Faced with the challenge of moving such a large group, leaders urged their followers to spread their possessions on cloaks on the ground and share them freely with others, in the spirit of the early church as depicted in Acts (2:42-47; 4:32-37).[8]

In Austerlitz, several groups of Anabaptists began practicing community of goods—sharing material goods in the spirit of the apostolic church. However, dissension within and between the various groups over leadership and how to organize a communal church led to turmoil. Jakob Hutter, an Anabaptist pastor in Tyrol, east of Zurich, visited Austerlitz in 1529. Impressed with the commitment and willingness of believers to practice community of goods, he returned for yearly visits and lived there briefly from 1534 to 1535. During that time he assumed leadership of one of the communal groups that eventually carried his name.

Facing renewed persecution, Hutter fled from Moravia in 1535. Within a year he was captured, tortured, and burned alive after brandy was poured over his bruised body in Innsbruck, Austria. Although Jakob Hutter's leadership helped to define the Hutterite Movement, Peter Riedemann wrote their primary confession of faith in prison (1540-42).[9] His lengthy confession of faith and many of his hymns continue to inspire Hutterite convictions today. Riedemann eventually escaped from prison and served as one of several Hutterite leaders until his death in 1556.

The early years of Hutterite history were filled with tumult from leadership quarrels, rivalries with other groups, frequent migration, and intense persecution. According to the Hutterite *Chronicle,* more than two thousand Hutterites gave their lives for the sake of their faith, and others were taken as slaves. The most cruel means of torture were used: burning, branding, chopping bodies into quarters, drowning, and starvation in dungeons. Despite the many waves of brutality and migration, the Hutterite commitment to community of goods and their identity as a distinctive people survived against incredible odds. After 1553, they enjoyed more peaceful times and a "golden period" from 1565 to 1592, when some one hundred *Bruderhofs* (villages) flourished.[10]

All of that ended abruptly in 1593. In the following three decades, war, persecution, and the plague killed many of them. In 1621 alone, over a third of the members died of the plague. Seeking safety and religious refuge, and often on the verge of extinction, they migrated frequently, spending time in Hungary, Transylvania, Romania, and Austria. In 1770 the Hutterites moved to Russia and then in the early 1800s relocated again within Russia to several villages northeast of the Black Sea. By 1819, for various reasons, they even abandoned their religious trademark, community of goods.

Some forty years later, in 1859, preacher Michael Waldner, a blacksmith, had a dream that led to the revival of communal sharing among a subgroup acknowledging his leadership. His people (*Leut*) became known as the *Schmiedeleut*, the blacksmith's people. A year later, in 1860, another preacher, Darius Walter, reestablished community of goods among his followers, who were dubbed the *Dariusleut.* Other Hutterites continued to practice voluntary mutual aid, but not a formal community of goods. When they immigrated to the United States in the 1870s, a third subgroup under the leadership of Jacob Wipf also renewed the practice of communal living. Wipf was a teacher, a *Lehrer*, and his followers became known as the *Lehrerleut.*

A fourth contingent of Hutterites that came to the United States never revived communal living and became known as noncolony people or simply as *Prairieleut*, the prairie people. The Prairieleut eventually joined some of the neighboring Mennonite groups in the Dakotas.[11]

THE MENNONITES

Anabaptists emerged in several areas of Europe in the first decade of the movement. Many leaders traveled as evangelists from one region to another. Without central leadership or a consensus on theological issues, a variety of voices carried the banner of Anabaptism. Centers of Anabaptist activity emerged in Switzerland, Moravia, South Germany, and Austria, as well as in North Germany and the Netherlands. Some of the initial adherents were young university students, scholars, and ex-priests, but Anabaptism soon became a grassroots movement.

Around 1530, Anabaptism surfaced in the Netherlands under the teaching of Melchior Hoffman, an apocalyptic preacher who expected Christ to return promptly and institute a New Jerusalem on earth. Inspired by such preaching, a group of radical Anabaptists occupied the city of Münster in February 1534 and gave its populace a stark choice: flee or be rebaptized. The anarchists held the city for about sixteen months until it fell in a bloodbath in 1535. This sad debacle tarnished the word *Anabaptist;* it also frightened political and religious leaders in other regions, who tried harder than ever to extinguish the flames of Anabaptism.

Menno Simons, a Dutch Catholic priest ordained in 1524, had growing sympathies for Anabaptist convictions. He watched from the sidelines for several years, then joined the movement in 1536. He soon became a powerful and moderating voice in the Netherlands and beyond. Menno was a gifted leader and writer who developed a following among some of the Dutch Anabaptists. By 1542 civil authorities were offering a sizable sum of money for anyone who captured him; but despite his frequent traveling and speaking, he was never arrested. As early as 1545, the followers of Menno were called *Mennists*, and by 1550 they were the dominant group of Anabaptists in North Germany and Holland.[12]

In time, Anabaptists in regions beyond Holland, who were influenced by Menno's writing and thought, also become known as Mennists or Mennonites. In Switzerland, however, the Anabaptists were simply known as Swiss Brethren for many years. Ironically, years later the Anabaptist Church in Holland, Menno's home, did not take his name but simply called itself *Doopsgezinde,* baptist-minded. Meanwhile, Anabaptists in other areas carried the Mennonite name as they migrated to Prussia, Russia, and eventually to North America. Unlike the Hutterites and Amish, whose names reflect the influence of a leader over a particular group, many Anabaptist groups from different origins eventually assumed the Mennonite label.

THE AMISH

The relentless persecution in Switzerland drove many Anabaptists to remote mountainous areas, where they could more easily elude authorities. As the persecution dwindled, many Anabaptists turned to farming; over the generations their religious fervor mellowed as congregational life developed routine patterns. Renewed persecution near Bern, Switzerland, in the 1660s spurred some Anabaptists to head northward to more tolerant areas along the Rhine River. By the late 1600s, clusters of Swiss Anabaptists had emigrated from Switzerland to the Alsace region of present-day France, west of the Rhine River. In the early 1690s, a controversy erupted among some of

After escaping from prison, Anabaptist Dirk Willems rescued his captor. He was recaptured and burned at the stake in Asperen, The Netherlands, in 1569.
Courtesy of Lancaster Mennonite Historical Society

the Alsatian immigrants as well as among factions back in Switzerland. The quarrel came to a head in 1693 and gave birth to the Amish Church.

The *Amish* take their name from Jakob Ammann, a Swiss Anabaptist leader who moved to the Alsace to escape persecution. Banned from Switzerland by civil authorities, Ammann was considered a "roving arch-Anabaptist." He was a recent convert who, according to civil authorities, had become "infected" by the Anabaptist sect.[13] In the 1690s, Ammann called for change and renewal in church life.

Ammann proposed holding communion twice a year rather than annually, the traditional Swiss Anabaptist pattern. Following the lead of Anabaptists in Holland, he argued that foot washing should be observed literally in the communion service, in obedience to Christ's command. Other issues—the excommunication of liars, the role of church discipline, and the salvation of Anabaptist sympathizers—also hovered over the dispute. Many of Ammann's proposed reforms reflected early Swiss Anabaptist teaching as well as practices advocated by Menno Simons. Thus the formation of the Amish Movement, in some ways, was an effort for church renewal.

The decisive issue that polarized the debate, however, was the shunning of excommunicated members. Following the teaching of Menno Simons, Ammann taught that expelled members should not only be banned from holy communion but they also should be shunned in daily life. Many Swiss Anabaptist congregations excluded wayward members from communion but did not ostracize them socially. Cultural and regional factors, as well as personality conflicts, amplified the theological differences. However, disagreements over shunning drove the final wedge between various clusters of both Swiss and Alsatian Anabaptists in 1693.[14]

The emergence of the Amish created a permanent division among Swiss and Alsatian Anabaptists. Although dress styles were not the catalyst for the schism, they gradually became distinctive among the Amish, encouraged perhaps because Ammann was a tailor. Ammann also taught against trimming beards, rebuked those with fashionable dress, and administered a strict discipline in his congregations. The Amish were sometimes called "hook-and-eyers" because they considered buttons too ostentatious; Mennonites by contrast were sometimes nicknamed "button people."

Ammann left no books and only a few letters for his followers. For theological guidance, the Amish rely primarily on Anabaptist literature written before Ammann's time. Thus, Swiss Anabaptism originating in Zurich in 1525, had two branches after 1693: Amish and Mennonite. Nourished by a common heritage, Amish and Mennonite life has flowed in separate streams since the division.[15]

THE BRETHREN

The Brethren formed in central Germany about fifteen years after the emergence of the Amish. Strictly speaking, the Brethren are not an organic offshoot of sixteenth-century Anabaptism, but they are directly linked to the Anabaptist story. Influenced by both Radical Pietism and Anabaptism, the Brethren Movement began in 1708 in the German village of Schwarzenau.

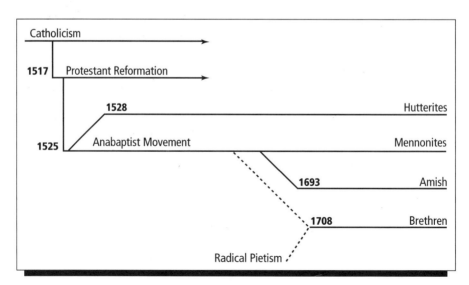

FIGURE 1.1 European Roots of the Hutterites, Mennonites, Amish, and Brethren

Although they were grounded in Radical Pietism, they embraced many beliefs of the early Anabaptists and the Mennonites with whom they often associated: adult baptism, the separation of church and state, pacifism, and church discipline. Alexander Mack Sr. was the leader of the first Brethren, who eventually became known in the United States as *German Baptist Brethren* or simply *Dunkers* or *Dunkards* by outsiders because they baptized, "dunked" by immersion.[16]

By 1700 there were three official churches in German territories— Catholic, Lutheran, and Reformed. Despite the Anabaptist call for a free church, unregulated by the state, the official religion in each of the many German territories followed the preference of the ruler or prince. As political fortunes bounced back and forth, so did the official religion of the region, sometimes shifting frequently. The official churches were controlled by the state and funded with taxes. Nearly two hundred years after the Protestant Reformation, church life, according to its critics, consisted of hollow dogma and sterile ritual. Despite bitter competition with each other, the official churches nevertheless collaborated with civic authorities to suppress dissident views and critics.

Reacting to what they considered a barren and spiritless life in the state churches, a Pietist Movement emerged within both the Reformed and Lutheran churches in the late 1600s. Lay members, gathering in small groups called conventicles for Bible study and discussion, advocated reforms within the state churches. Impatient with the pace of change, the *Radical Pietists* were sometimes called *Separatists* because they called for a complete separation from the official churches. They contended that genuine piety and love flowed through the Holy Spirit, not through outward symbols, sacraments, and rituals. The Pietists emphasized the importance of love in all human relationships. Indeed, the celebration of a Love Feast became an important feature in the life of many churches with Pietist roots. The importance of a loving spirit in human relationships and in the corporate life of the church continues to shape the ethos of Brethren groups today.

The Brethren Movement began with the rebaptism of eight adults in the Eder River in 1708. The group selected a person by lot to baptize Alexander Mack Sr., the leader, who then baptized his baptizer and six other adults by trine immersion. News of the illegal baptisms brought immediate harassment and persecution. Mack was banned from several regions for conducting secret baptisms. Facing persecution and imprisonment, the Brethren spread into other areas, including Krefeld, a German town near the Dutch border. Here they interacted with Mennonites who had been granted tolerance in the area and persuaded some of the Mennonites to join the Brethren Movement. Inspired by the convictions and practices of the *early* Anabaptists, the Brethren thought their Mennonite neighbors had "deteriorated" and "strayed" from the teachings of the original Anabaptist Movement that had formed some 175 years earlier.[17]

Except for immersion baptism and the Love Feast, many of the beliefs and practices of the Brethren harmonized with Anabaptist views as well as

The Eder River in Schwarzenau, Germany, site of Brethren baptisms in 1708.
Photo by Jan Gleysteen

Mennonite practice. Common themes underscored by the Brethren included biblicism, discipleship, obedience, the recovery of the apostolic church, nonresistance, mutual aid, church discipline, and nonconformity to the larger society. The first Brethren baptisms in the Eder River signaled a rejection of the religious individualism of Radical Pietism, which had sparked their spiritual awakening. While Brethren sought to maintain the deep and almost mystical spirituality of Pietism, they added understandings of community discernment, discipline, and accountability typical of their Anabaptist neighbors.

NEW WORLD DEPARTURES

A few Mennonites arrived in the Americas by 1683, and others came in several waves in the eighteenth and nineteenth centuries. Unlike the Mennonites, the Brethren spent little time in Europe. They began sailing to North America in 1719, a decade after their beginning. By 1729 most of the Brethren had fled persecution in Europe to seek religious freedom and economic opportunity in North America. The first sizeable group of Amish anchored in Philadelphia on the *Charming Nancy* in 1737. Later Amish migrations came in the mid 1700s and early 1800s.

Philadelphia became the port of preference for Amish, Brethren, and Mennonite immigrants. Many of them resided briefly in the village of Germantown, north of the city. Later they often lived in the same areas of Virginia, Ohio, and Indiana as they fanned out from eastern Pennsylvania.

Hutterites and Mennonites living in Russia began arriving in the United States in the 1870s, much later than the earlier immigrants. Bypassing the eastern Anabaptist settlements, the Hutterites went directly to Dakota territory. Mennonites of Russian origin settled in Dakota Territory, Kansas, Minnesota, Nebraska, Oklahoma, and in Manitoba, Canada.

Today the Mennonites are the only group with continuous churches remaining in Europe. Virtually all the Brethren had migrated by 1740. The final Amish migrations came in the 1850s, and their last congregation in Europe closed in 1937. The Hutterites have no remaining communities in Europe today. In recent years several Anabaptist groups from the United States have begun mission programs in various European countries.

The Anabaptists of the sixteenth century, along with their Hutterite, Mennonite, Amish, and Brethren descendants, were ahead of their times in many ways. Their convictions have shaped understandings that eventually came to be taken for granted in the modern world. Some of their contributions included the notion of a "free" church—independent from state control, the freedom of individual conscience in religious practice, respect for the voluntary decisions of adults in religious matters, mutual accountability within a visible Christian body, the importance of peacemaking, and the power of suffering and nonviolent resistance to overcome evil.

For these views, once considered heretical and seditious, thousands of believers suffered cruel persecution and sacrificed their lives and families. Anabaptist calls for faithful obedience to the way of Christ, practiced with the counsel of fellow believers, formed the legacy of what came to be called the *believers church*, which the heirs of the Anabaptists brought to North America.[18]

In the following chapters, we profile the Anabaptist communities in the United States at the turn of the twenty-first century. We also examine some common convictions that undergird Anabaptist life today as well as some of the fractures that divide it. We delineate in greater detail the various groups and their place within the various tribes of the Anabaptist World. Throughout the remainder of the book, the order of presentation is simply alphabetical—Amish, Brethren, Hutterite, and Mennonite. We begin by taking a gigantic step over several centuries of history to survey the contemporary Anabaptist communities in the United States today.

Chapter 2

CONTEMPORARY COMMUNITIES

> We have a truly unique phenomenon in Philadelphia with twenty-two
> urban congregations comprised of eleven language groups.
> —*Mennonite Bishop Freeman Miller*[1]

TRIBES, GROUPS, AND BODIES

In the United States, the immigrant Anabaptist communities grew and expanded during the nineteenth and twentieth centuries. Today Anabaptists number about 537,000 members in some sixty groups and more than 5,500 congregations. Counting children and adults, the total population likely tops 860,000 persons. These numbers pertain only to the United States and do not include Canada, where sizeable numbers of Mennonites and Hutterites also reside as well as some Amish and Brethren in Christ. Anabaptist congregations are found in Puerto Rico, the District of Columbia, and all of the states except New Hampshire, Nevada, and Rhode Island.

Table 2.1 shows the size of the four Anabaptist tribes in the United States. Considering adult members only, Amish groups account for about 16 percent of the Anabaptist World, with nearly 87,000 members in 1,439 con-

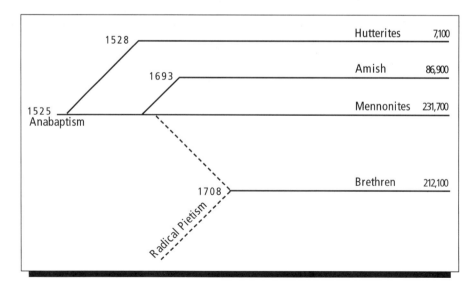

FIGURE 2.1 Historical Lineage and Adult Membership in the United States

TABLE 2.1
Congregations, Membership, and Population of the Four Anabaptist Tribes

TRIBE	CONGREGATIONS		MEMBERSHIP		POPULATION	
	N	%	N	%	N	%
Amish	1,439	26.0	86,894	16.2	192,248	22.3
Brethren	1,812	32.7	211,752	39.4	293,360	34.1
Hutterite	125	2.2	7,090	1.3	15,624	1.8
Mennonite	2,163	39.1	231,696	43.1	360,249	41.8
TOTALS	5,539	100.0	537,432	100.0	861,481	100.0

N = Number   % = percent

gregations. This tally does not include the twenty-four Amish congregations in Ontario, Canada. Brethren groups numbering some 212,000 adults make up about 39 percent of the Anabaptist orbit. The Hutterite groups compose the smallest tribe, with about 7,000 adults in 125 colonies in the United States. Organized in more than 2,100 congregations and nearly forty groups, Mennonites with almost 232,000 adult members, account for nearly 43 percent of the Anabaptist membership.

The Anabaptist World is filled with many small affiliations, fellowships, and independent congregations. Thus one of the challenges of describing Anabaptist communities involves defining the specifications of a group. For the purposes of this project, we have defined a group as two or more affiliated congregations with a combined membership of at least 250 members. Bodies not meeting this criterion were considered small independent congregations. For example, we considered the following as independent congregations rather than a group: a single congregation with 600 members or a network of three congregations with 200 members.

If a body met the standard of having 250 members and two affiliated congregations, we counted it as a group. For example, the Old Order Nebraska Amish with fourteen congregations and some 700 members qualified as a group. On the other hand, we considered the Conservative Baptist

TABLE 2.2
Number of Groups, Independent Congregations, and Regional Bodies by Tribe

SOCIAL CLUSTERS	AMISH	BRETHREN	HUTTERITE	MENNONITE	TOTAL
Groups 250-1,000	3	3	1	18	25
Groups 1,000-5,000	6	2	3	11	22
Groups 5,000 +	2	5	0	9	16
Total Groups	11	10	4	38	63
Independent Congregations	16	21	0	172	209
Regional Bodies/Districts	0	30	0	47	77

Note: Groups have two or more affiliated congregations and a total membership of 250 or more. We classified bodies not meeting both criteria as small independent congregations. The count of eleven groups for the Amish underestimates their number of groups because we have not identified several affiliations. A listing of all the groups appears in section B of the Resources.

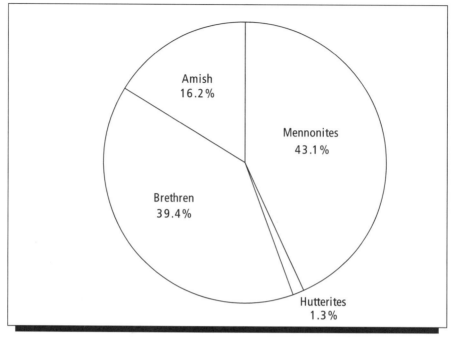

FIGURE 2.2 Adult Membership of Anabaptist Groups in the United States

Brethren, with two affiliated congregations and 135 members, as two independent congregations.

Using these criteria as guidelines, we identified eleven Amish groups, ten Brethren groups, four Hutterite groups, and thirty-eight Mennonite groups, making a total of sixty-three groups in the Anabaptist orbit.[2] Adding small independent congregations (209) and various regional districts and conferences (77) the total number of bodies likely tops 350. Some of the groups are large denominations, such as the Church of the Brethren with 137,000 members. Other groups are small bodies or affiliations with fewer than 1,000 members, such as the Evangelical Mennonite Brethren with four congregations and 455 members.

MAJOR GROUPS

As shown in table 2.3, the eleven largest groups have about 456,000 members and make up nearly 85 percent of the Anabaptist membership in the United States. Smaller groups and independent congregations with about 81,000 members and 1,124 congregations claim the remaining 15 percent of the Anabaptist pie. The likely formation of the Mennonite Church USA in 2002—a merger of the Mennonite Church and the General Conference Mennonite Church—will make the new body the largest Mennonite group. At the conclusion of the merger, the two largest bodies will likely be the Church of the Brethren with 137,000 members and the Mennonite Church USA with possibly 120,000 members. Together these two bodies would claim about 48 percent of the Anabaptist pie.[3] Today the Mennonite Church and the Church of the Brethren hold about 43 percent of the adult Anabaptist membership in the United States.

CONGREGATION SIZE

Congregations range in size from small house churches of less than a dozen members to the 1,900-member Grace Brethren Church in Columbus, Ohio. If a prize for size is fitting in an Anabaptist World, the Grace Brethren congregation in Columbus claims the gold, as shown in table 2.4. On the other hand, if the last shall indeed be first, the prize will have to be shared by three small mission congregations that each list two members: a Mennonite mission in Anaheim, California, the Mennonite Fountain of Life congregation in Puerto Rico, and the Mennonite Fellowship in Brookings, South Dakota. They barely meet the biblical benchmark of being a place "where two or more are gathered in [Jesus'] name." However, if the truly last shall be first, then the prize goes to some twenty mission outposts that report no members to date. Meanwhile, the Amish are handicapped in any contest that prizes big congregations because the size of their homes restricts the number that can gather for worship.

Generally speaking, congregations are small. Only seventy-seven of the 5,500 congregations have more than 500 members, and only nine congregations have more than 1,000 members. As shown in table 2.5, when all

TABLE 2.3 Groups Above 10,000 by Size of Membership

CHURCH BODY	CONGREGATIONS	MEMBERSHIP	PERCENT
Church of the Brethren[a]	1,071	137,037	25.5
Mennonite Church[b]	871	92,157	17.1
Old Order Amish Groups[c]	1,237	73,609	13.7
Grace Brethren, Fellowship of	261	32,046	6.0
General Conference Mennonite Church[d]	179	27,507	5.1
Mennonite Brethren	168	22,777	4.2
Brethren in Christ	196	20,043	3.7
Old Order Mennonite Groups[e]	127	16,478	3.1
Church of God in Christ Mennonite (Holdeman)	111	12,152	2.3
Apostolic Christian Church of America	79	12,113	2.3
The Brethren Church	115	10,641	2.0
Smaller Groups, Independent Congregations	1,124	80,872	15.0
TOTALS	5,539	537,432	100.0

[a] Includes 31 congregations and 2,536 members in congregations with dual affiliations.
[b] Includes 140 congregations and 13,490 members in congregations with a dual affiliation with the General Conference Mennonite Church and eleven congregations (396 members) with other dual affiliations. Membership of Mennonite congregations with Mennonite Conference and General Conference dual affiliation were allocated 2/3 to the Mennonite Church and 1/3 to the General Conference Mennonite Church.
[c] Includes all Old Order Amish groups.
[d] Includes 70 congregations and 6,745 members having a dual affiliation with the Mennonite Church.
[e] Includes all Old Order Mennonite Groups.

TABLE 2.4 Ten Largest Congregations by Location and Size

NAME OF CONGREGATION	LOCATION	MEMBERSHIP
Columbus Grace Brethren	Columbus, Ohio	1,920
Cornerstone Mennonite Church	Harrisonburg, Virginia	1,244
Long Beach Grace Brethren	Long Beach, California	1,228
Reedley Mennonite Brethren	Reedley, California	1,200
Bethesda Mennonite Church	Henderson, Nebraska	1,131
First Mennonite Church	Berne, Indiana	1,119
College Mennonite Church	Goshen, Indiana	1,063
Frederick Church of the Brethren	Frederick, Maryland	1,058
Calvary Community (Mennonite) Church	Hampton, Virginia	1,040
Carlisle Brethren in Christ	Carlisle, Pennsylvania	920

TABLE 2.5 Congregational Size by Tribe in Percent

SIZE	AMISH	BRETHREN	HUTTERITE	MENNONITE	TOTAL
0-75	96.7	48.6	96.0	56.0	74.3
76-150	2.4*	28.2	0	22.5	13.2
151-300	0.9*	15.5	4.0	15.1	8.9
301-500	0	5.6	0	4.6	2.6
501-1,000	0	1.9	0	1.5	0.9
1,000+	0	0.2	0	0.3	0.1
Totals	100%	100%	100%	100%	100%
TOTALS (N)	1,439	1,812	125	2,163	5,539

* Congregations with more than seventy-five members are typically Amish Mennonite or Beachy Amish congregations.

groups are combined, 96 percent of the 5,500 congregations have fewer than 300 members. Congregational size varies by tribal affiliation. Because the Amish meet in their homes for worship, their congregations divide as they grow. Amish Church districts vary in size in different regions of the country; on average they have about sixty members per district.

Membership in Hutterite colonies varies by affiliation but averages about fifty-seven adults per colony across the different groups. The typical congregational size among Mennonite groups hovers around 105 members. The largest congregations are found among the Brethren groups, with congregations across the nation averaging 120 members. In general, small congregations are typical with 99 percent of the 5,500 congregations having fewer than 500 members, as shown in table 2.5.

NATIONAL PROFILE

About 52 percent (279,000) of the members live in the three states of Pennsylvania, Ohio, and Indiana, as shown in table 2.6. Pennsylvania, home to 28 percent of the national membership, holds the lion's share of Anabaptist communities. Four out of five adult members live in one of the ten states displayed in table 2.6; the remaining 20 percent of members are scattered across thirty-seven other states. The three states with the smallest

Anabaptist populations have less than 200 members each: Maine (155), Wyoming (110), and Utah (43).

NAMES AND IDENTITY

The diversity of the Anabaptist World is reflected in the names of local congregations. Many of them use the name of the local town, such as Fairview Mennonite in Fairview, Michigan. Dozens of congregations in towns and cities use "First" in their name, such as First Church of the Brethren in Phoenix, Arizona. More than 200 congregations have a non-

TABLE 2.6 Anabaptist Membership in the Top Ten States

STATE	CONGREGATIONS	MEMBERSHIP	PERCENT
Pennsylvania	1,284	146,419	27.2
Ohio	788	76,916	14.3
Indiana	568	55,379	10.3
Virginia	308	39,081	7.3
Kansas	169	25,971	4.8
California	201	22,893	4.3
Illinois	182	22,199	4.1
Maryland	133	16,094	3.0
Iowa	124	10,840	2.0
Michigan	176	9,976	1.9
Other states (37)	1,606	111,664	20.8
TOTALS	5,539	537,432	100.0

Note: Ranked by adult membership that does not include unbaptized children. A membership summary for each state appears in section F of the Resources.

Old Order Mennonites congregate outside a meetinghouse on Sunday morning.
Photo by Dennis Hughes

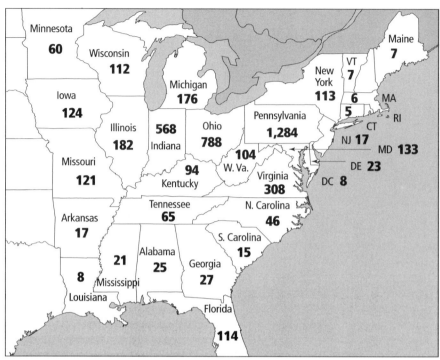

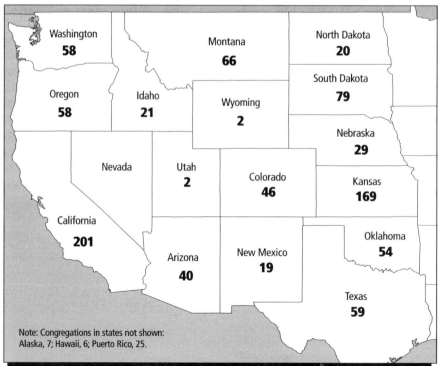

Note: Congregations in states not shown:
Alaska, 7; Hawaii, 6; Puerto Rico, 25.

FIGURE 2.3 Distribution of Anabaptist Congregations in the United States

The facilities of this Church of the Brethren reflect the size of some of the larger congregations.
Photo by Daniel Rodriguez

English language or identity embedded in their name. Dozens of others have a multiethnic membership even though it may not be evident in their name. Numerous congregations employ biblical images in their names: Prince of Peace, Peace, Hope, Grace, Faith, Agape, Shalom, and Jubilee. In Kankakee, Illinois, members of a Mennonite Church unapologetically couch their mission in their name: they are People for Reconciliation.

Out in the countryside, congregational names have a different cast: Shady Lawn, Strawberry, Happy Hollow, and Greasewood. In the Western states, visitors have the choice of attending the Spirit in the Desert congregation in Arizona, but if the preaching there is too dry, they can quench their thirst at the Agua Viva congregation in California. Among Hutterite colonies, nature prevails with names like Big Sky, Big Rock, Thunderbird, and Grass Ranch.

Anabaptist golf enthusiasts may want to visit the Teegarden First Brethren Church in Plymouth, Indiana, and touring snowbirds will certainly not want to miss the Tourist Mennonite Church in Sarasota, Florida. In the winter months, Sarasota hosts a microcosm of Anabaptist life as members of upscale to downscale groups flock to Florida to frolic in the sun. However, those seeking a better beach may need to fly to Hawaii and join the Ke Ola Hou Grace Brethren Church on Ewa Beach.

Seekers with a thirst may want to explore the New Wine Fellowship in Bourbon, Indiana. Better yet, they can try the seven Amish congregations in Winesburg, Ohio: Winesburg West, Winesburg Northwest, Northeast, and so on. Still thirsty? Try the Vineyard Community Brethren Church in Franklin, Ohio. Young women searching for a spouse may want to visit the Bachelor Run congregation of the Old German Baptist Brethren at Flora, Indiana.

The Amish are so down to earth that their district names frequently reference local landmarks. In Ohio, there is Walnut Creek and Apple Creek; if one is not satisfied, what about Sugarcreek? As Amish districts grow, they divide and often add a north or west to the name; indeed, there are actually *six* Walnut Creek districts and *six* Apple Creek districts, north, east, northeast, and so on. Sometimes it becomes confusing. For example, an Amish district near Shipshewana, Indiana, is called East Shipshewana West; just up the road is the North Middle Shipshewana district. If that is too complicated, seek clarity at the Tokahookaadi Church of the Brethren in Cuba, New Mexico. Overcome with anxiety from too many choices? Flee to the City of Refuge Mennonite Church in Vineland, New Jersey.

Because historically Brethren baptized by immersion in local creeks, they would often name their congregations for their favorite baptismal site. In Pennsylvania, Brethren congregations carry many creek names: Yellow Creek, Upper Conewago, Big Swatara, Spring Creek, Chiques, Codorus, Conestoga, Dunnings Creek, Indian Creek, and James Creek, to note but a few of the dozens of Brethren congregations named for flowing water. For those worried about drowning during baptism, there are other Brethren options: they can join the Welsh Run, Sugar Run, Spring Run, Bear Run, or better yet, the Dry Run congregation, where they would surely face less danger during a triple immersion.

Mennonites of Swiss German stock typically baptized by pouring or sprinkling, so they had little need for flowing water. Hence, many Mennonite communities, at least in Pennsylvania, named their congregations for families: Gehmans, Gingerichs, Erismans, Bosslers, Goods,

The multiethnic leadership team of the Philadelphia Mennonite churches. Photo by Robert Zeitler

Mellingers, and Habeckers, to name but a few that carry a family label.

Those who find the German ethnicity too thick and somber can head eastward to Philadelphia. If they bypass the Brethren and Mennonite congregations at Germantown, they can worship with the Vietnamese Mennonite Church, La Communidad de Amor, or the Ethiopian Evangelical Fellowship. If overburdened with choice and hungry for grace, they can head to Malden, Massachusetts, and join the Chinese Grace Mennonite Church, or better yet, go to Boston and worship with the Chinese *Saving Grace* congregation. Still searching and seeking for paradise? Visit the Paradise Mennonite Church in Paradise, Pennsylvania. If these havens fail to satisfy, head for heaven or check the Directory of Congregations at the back of this book for some 5,000 other Anabaptist options.

Chapter 3

COMMON CONVICTIONS

No one can truly know Christ
except one who follows him in life.
—*Hans Denck, 1526*

MEMORIES

Members of the sixty different groups in the Anabaptist World would gladly disagree on many issues. Hutterites might bemoan the private property amassed by individuals in the other tribes. The Grace Brethren may fear that the Amish are not properly saved. Horse-and-buggy driving Mennonites might worry that progressive Mennos are driving their Volvos down the road to perdition. And the Old German Baptist Brethren would readily explain the proper mode of baptism to any Amish who would be kind enough to listen. Members of these groups would happily debate dozens of differences in belief and practice among themselves. Indeed, some of the groups will shun members of other groups over points of doctrine and practice. Nevertheless, these communities of faith do claim a common heritage and a similar theological identity.

Despite their endless differences, what convictions do they share in common? The most widely shared thread is their historical memory, their affirmation of an Anabaptist heritage. However, the strength and affirmation of that memory varies greatly. Among more traditional groups—especially the Amish and the Hutterites—stories of Anabaptist martyrs remain alive in songs from the *Ausbund* hymnal and reports in *Martyrs Mirror* and the great Hutterite *Chronicle*. For many other groups as well, the Anabaptist story inspires congregational life and multiple forms of witness in the larger world.

Some groups work hard to recall their past, but others have largely lost the memories. In some cases, groups bearing a Brethren or Mennonite name worry that their heritage and their identity will impede evangelistic efforts. Local congregations sometimes drop their denominational name and use a more generic tag like Faith Community Church. Nevertheless, the collective memory of an Anabaptist past—both strong and weak—provides some common ground for members today. But beyond the remembered past, what, if anything, do these groups claim in common?

The following nine themes, flowing from their Anabaptist heritage, continue to shape the identity of many of these groups today. These themes are not necessarily unique to Anabaptist groups. After all, these are Christian convictions that are also embraced by many other churches and denominations. Nevertheless, many Anabaptist groups have underlined these commitments in special ways in their life and practice. These themes emerge from three sources: (1) convictions of some of the early Anabaptists, (2) commitments that have solidified over the centuries in Anabaptist communities, and (3) ideals that stir Anabaptist passions today. Despite irregular and inconsistent practice over the years and across the groups, these understandings continue to inspire and define the Anabaptist World today.[1]

CHRISTOCENTRIC BIBLICISM

The early Anabaptists insisted that the authority of Scripture should transcend the mandates of the state and the dictates of religious custom. The origin of the Anabaptist Movement actually pivoted on the question of scriptural authority. Did Scripture or the Zurich city council have the last word in matters of faith and practice? In many locations, early Anabaptists spoke with great zeal because of their supreme confidence in the authority of the Scripture. Their appeal to Scripture focused on the words and teachings of Jesus. They had a Christocentric canon: Jesus became the key for interpreting the rest of Scripture.

One scholar has shown that many of the Mennonite confessions of faith focus first on the New Testament, then on the Gospels, then on Matthew, and then on the Sermon on the Mount within Matthew.[2] The Anabaptists did read and use the Old Testament, but they appealed to Jesus as the final norm of revelation. They appealed, not so much to the doctrinal Christ of church history, but more to the teachings and life of the Jesus of the Gospels.

Early Mennonite leader Menno Simons anchored his teaching on 1 Corinthians 3:11, "For no one can lay any foundation other than the one that has been laid; that foundation is Jesus Christ." The Church of the Brethren, accentuating its noncreedal stance, says it has "no creed except the New Testament." Its mission statement proclaims that Brethren are "continuing the work of Jesus, simply, peacefully, together." The Scripture readings in the annual Amish lectionary typically include only New Testament texts. Various Anabaptist groups will argue about the meaning and application of a particular passage of Scripture, but when they are true to their heritage, they affirm a Christocentric view of Scripture that makes it their highest authority for doctrine and practice.

The courage of the early Anabaptists to claim that the words of Jesus trumped *all* the other authorities was the radical step that led to the formation of a "free church"—free from government control. Such a church based its authority solely on the Scripture, especially on the New Testament and the words of Jesus.

BELIEVERS BAPTISM

The very word *Anabaptist* (rebaptizer) signals the centrality of adult baptism in this theological tradition. The refusal to baptize infants and the courage to baptize adults were public acts of defiance that sparked the Anabaptist Movement in 1525 as well as the counter-response of brutal persecution and martyrdom. Believers baptism underscored the authority of

Scripture over state edict; it also signaled a major shift in understanding the nature of Christian faith and experience. For the Anabaptists, genuine conversion meant a voluntary, adult decision to follow Jesus coupled with a full awareness of the social consequences that often brought martyrdom.

Religious faith was not something to be imposed or coerced. In the Anabaptist view, faith rested on the voluntary decision of adults who had been touched by God's grace and who through the power of the Holy Spirit, repented of their sins and sought to live new lives graced with the fruits of the Spirit. These understandings are also shared by a variety of denominations beyond Anabaptist circles that have participated in a series of Believers Church Conferences, which began in 1967.[3]

Some groups in the Anabaptist World will debate the proper mode of baptism. Many Brethren groups and the Mennonite Brethren baptize by immersion; Mennonites, Amish, and Hutterites typically baptize by pouring. Nevertheless, the commitment to a believers baptism remains strong. All the groups continue to baptize adults. In several groups, two issues have prompted discussion in recent years: the age of baptism and the acceptance of adult members baptized as infants in other churches.

Churches influenced by American Evangelicalism and child evangelism have sometimes baptized children as young as six years old, which critics argue is surely not adult baptism. Some Anabaptist groups face the dilemma of how to affirm the faith development of young children and keep them in the flock if baptism is delayed until the teenage years. Most youth are baptized between the ages of twelve and sixteen. Among some Old Order groups, the age tends to be higher, sixteen to twenty-two. The Amish underscore the integrity of adult baptism by waiting until the late teens or early twenties, even if they lose some youth in the process.

Various Anabaptist congregations have also struggled with how to receive prospective members who were baptized as infants in other religious traditions. Most congregations in the Anabaptist World require rebaptism. The Church of the Brethren gives local congregations the option of receiving as new members those earlier baptized as infants if they affirm their faith, even without rebaptism. In several denominations, this has been a contentious issue for some congregations. Believers baptism has implications for congregational life because members make a deliberate decision to join the family of faith, live according to the standards of a local body of believers, and participate in mutual admonition and counsel.

DISCIPLESHIP

What does it mean to follow Jesus in daily life? That pivotal question shapes Anabaptist theology and practice. In both the sixteenth and eighteenth centuries, Anabaptists and Pietists were reacting against what many considered the sterile orthodoxy of the state churches. They criticized the vain repetition of creeds without a corresponding change in daily behavior. They were incensed by priests and theologians who assented to pious dogma but lived lives of sinful hypocrisy.

A Hispanic Mennonite pastor baptizes a new believer in North Carolina. Photo by Dale D. Gehman

Consequently, the Anabaptist spirit has always focused on practice rather than creed, on daily discipleship rather than systematic theology.[4] The question of obedience is central. Are you willing to become a disciple of Jesus, to take up your cross and follow him daily (Luke 9:23) in concrete and practical ways? Are you willing to love enemies, to go the second mile, to forgive, to serve the needy, and to suffer the consequences of such obedience? The words of a hymn penned by Alexander Mack Sr., founder of the Brethren, ask believers to "Count well the cost." Are you willing to risk reputation, self, and wealth for Christ the Lord?[5] The Brethren in Christ consider "following Jesus in wholehearted obedience" as one of the core values of their denominational calling today.[6]

Present-day Anabaptists sometimes make distinctions among *creed, confession*, and *doctrine*. Mennonites, for example, have written many confessions of faith, and various groups speak of "doctrines." However, because of their noncreedal roots, some Brethren groups are uncomfortable with formal confessions of faith.

The early Anabaptists emphasized the importance of surrendering all selfish interests by yielding to the will of God. This theme of yieldedness, *Gelassenheit,* continues to permeate Anabaptist thinking, especially within Old Order circles. Some Mennonites and Brethren were attracted to Dietrich Bonhoeffer's notion of "costly discipleship" because it recaptured the spirit of this aspect of the Anabaptist tradition. In any event, the concept of discipleship permeates the Anabaptist heritage and focuses on the fruits of righteousness—the practical expressions of faith in daily behavior and social relationships. In response to the question, "What is a living faith?" an early Anabaptist catechism responds, "One that produces the fruits of the Spirit and works through love, Gal. 5."[7] Some critics have charged that discipleship merely leads to "empty works of self-righteousness," but to Anabaptist thinking, faith without fruit is sterile.

CHURCH AS COMMUNITY

The Anabaptists argued that genuine disciples of Jesus would gather in a visible church for mutual edification, support, and accountability. The restitution of the apostolic church—with all of its concrete social meanings—was central to Anabaptist understandings of the church.[8] The early Anabaptists were incensed by the state churches, which allowed nominal church membership without active participation in congregational life. Instead, the Anabaptists expected adult believers to give and receive admonition. They argued that Jesus and Heaven had given the church authority to "bind and loose" on earth—to make and enforce decisions about its moral order by following the procedures outlined in Matthew 18:15-20. In their view, these guidelines should regulate the patterns of accountability in the corporate life of the church.

This concrete and social understanding of the nature of the church was central to the Anabaptist Movement. It led to the development of collective standards of behavior, to procedures of discipline and excommunication, and in some cases to shunning members who reneged on their baptismal promises or refused to heed churchly counsel. The underlying assumption was simple: the collective wisdom of the church superseded the freedom and rights of the individual. Members were expected to yield to the corporate body, to maintain the harmony, peace, and witness of Christ's body in the world. Over the years most Anabaptist congregations have developed various self-examination procedures and rituals prior to celebrating the Lord's Supper. These rituals reinforce the accountability of members to the congregation and enable the communion service to be a celebration of communal solidarity and unity.[9]

This view of the church as a discerning community, with mutual accountability, sometimes clashed with mystical, spiritualized, and individualistic interpretations of the Scriptures. The emphasis on a visible church also led some groups to promote external symbols such as dress and to draw sharp boundaries of separation from the larger world. By underscoring the collective authority of the church and calling for self-denial, some Amish and

Mennonite groups cultivated the values of personal surrender and humility.

Although most of the churches in the Anabaptist World would endorse this view of the church as a visible body, they practice it in many different ways. The more traditional groups continue to emphasize boundaries and will excommunicate those who step across the lines. By contrast, other churches tend to focus on the center, the core of faith, rather than on the boundaries separating them from the world and from each other. More assimilated congregations rarely if ever excommunicate members, partly because they have no clear standards for membership and partly because they emphasize grace and acceptance rather than discipline and accountability. Some Brethren groups, nurtured by their Pietist heritage, give special attention to the importance of loving relationships in the life of the church. In any event, viewing the church as a concrete social community, marked by mutual accountability, is central and fundamental to the Anabaptist legacy.

MUTUAL AID

A spin-off from this theological understanding of the church is the social dimension of community. Over the centuries, Anabaptists have understood the church as a social community as well as a spiritual body. Participants were members one of another who shared in common meals, work, and play. They often lived near each other and shared community life as well as spiritual experience. Social and spiritual often blended without distinction in the rhythms of daily life. In the Anabaptist view, it takes a community to produce a believer. Mature Christian faith is formed and honed by active participation in a local body of believers.

One practical expression of both the spiritual and social dimension of the church is mutual aid. Recent scholarship has shown that among the Swiss Brethren, voluntary sharing of goods for needy members was the norm.[10] However, in Hutterite communities sharing material goods became the expected standard. In other early Anabaptist congregations, the practice of mutual aid in times of disaster, distress, and special need was simply taken for granted. Much of the aid was spontaneous, or at least it appeared that way, because it was so deeply woven into the fabric of the church.

The Amish barn raising, romanticized in many accounts, continues today as a profound expression of care within the Christian community. Spontaneous forms of mutual aid continue in virtually all congregations in the Anabaptist World: assistance with moving, childcare, elder care, medical care, and other special needs. Many other Christian groups, of course, practice mutual aid as well, but it has become a distinctive trademark of Anabaptist communities because of their view of the corporate nature of the church.

More institutionalized forms of mutual aid emerged in the twentieth century: regional Anabaptist aid societies provide automobile, fire, and health insurance. Large national organizations such as Mennonite Mutual Aid and the Mutual Aid Association of the Church of the Brethren offer a wide variety of aid and insurance to church members across the nation.

PEACEMAKING

Not all Anabaptists were peaceful in the first decade of the movement, but by 1540 many Anabaptist groups had embraced an ethic of nonresistant love. Following Jesus' instructions to love enemies and not to resist evil-doers, the Anabaptists practiced a nonresistant love that rejected the use of force and violence in human relations; in short, they were willing to suffer in the face of injustice. They understood that this was the way of the cross, the way of Jesus in the face of torture. The emphasis on biblical nonresistance led many Anabaptists to reject military service. Hence, Christian pacifism has become a distinctive earmark of the Anabaptist heritage. For some, nonresistance also meant rejecting any coercive action—litigation, membership in labor unions, and aggressive political activities.

The pacifist convictions of North American Anabaptist groups were tested in the Revolutionary War, the Civil War, and especially in World War I. In 1935, representatives of Brethren, Mennonite, and Quaker groups gathered in Kansas to declare their opposition to war and form an alliance of Historic Peace Churches. These churches warmly welcomed the opportunity for conscientious objectors to perform alternative service during World War II. During the war, many persons from Anabaptist churches served in Civilian Public Service programs, but not all—some entered noncombatant service, and others joined the regular armed forces.

For many Amish and Mennonites, the emphasis on nonresistance led to an ethic of separation and social withdrawal. However, involvement in the

A representative of a Christian Peacemaker Team discusses a conflict with a Mexican Army major. Christian Peacemaker Team Photo

Civil Rights Movement and protests of the Vietnam War in the mid-twentieth century prodded many mainstream Anabaptists toward more activist forms of peacemaking.[11] Although all the groups under the Anabaptist canopy today affirm the importance of peacemaking, the centrality of it in their theology and practice varies widely. For some, it constitutes their core understanding of Christian faith; for others, it is peripheral. For some groups, peacemaking means quiet nonresistance to evil; for others, it means assertive peacemaking in the face of injustice.

Some of the more traditional groups excommunicate members who enter military service. Other Anabaptist churches discourage military service but do not discipline members who join. Still others make conscientious objection a matter of individual conscience despite formal denominational declarations. A few groups rarely speak of peace at all.[12] In contrast, some traditional groups forbid litigation, yet members of more mainstream churches work as lawyers and readily hire legal help to defend personal or corporate interests. In some groups the historic commitment to nonresistance has been transformed into active programs of conflict mediation, social transformation, and social justice. For example, Christian Peacemaker Teams, supported by various Brethren and Mennonite groups, train volunteers to intervene in volatile situations of conflict around the world.

SERVICE MINISTRIES

Anabaptist churches have become known for a host of service ministries, from relief and refugee work abroad to disaster service at home, from victim-offender programs to foster care, and from disability programs to elder care. Responding to Jesus' command to love the neighbor, Anabaptist churches have pioneered work in disability services, mental health, health care, and many other forms of social service. Some of the traditional groups are less active in these areas, but even many Old Order groups in some regions of the country actively support projects of the Mennonite Central Committee, Mennonite Disaster Service, and Christian Aid Ministries.

The Brethren and the Mennonites invested considerable financial and human resources in the reconstruction of Europe after World War II through Brethren Service and the PAX (Peace) Program respectively. In the last half of the twentieth century, Mennonite Voluntary Service and Brethren Volunteer Service placed hundreds of young people in service ministries around the world. Mennonites and Brethren in Christ support the Mennonite Central Committee (MCC), a major international relief and service agency with an annual budget of $70 million and some 900 volunteers and staff in fifty-six countries. The Brethren Service Center in New Windsor, Maryland, coordinates many service activities for the Church of the Brethren. In addition, dozens of smaller regional service agencies extend a cup of cold water in the name of Christ to needy people around the globe.

Disaster relief auctions and sales have been a major means of raising funds for international refugee and aid projects. Regardless of their theology or political views, Anabaptists from Old Order to mainstream groups enthusiastically support disaster and relief auctions by donating goods and time. Since 1957, hundreds of Mennonite Central Committee-sponsored auctions have raised millions for disaster and relief activities. In 1999 alone, forty-one sales raised $4.8 million. One annual Brethren Disaster Relief Auction alone has raised some $5.5 million since 1977.[13] The commitment and willingness to serve needy neighbors far and near varies from congregation to congregation. Nevertheless, concern for the needy and a commitment to service persists across all sectors of the Anabaptist World.

CHURCH AS COUNTERCULTURE

Radical discipleship mixed with a conviction that the church is a visible body producing a countercultural understanding of the church. The church, in the Anabaptist mind, should develop a distinctive culture—values and practices—that reflect the gospel and teachings of Jesus. Such a counterculture will often challenge the values of the larger society. At the beginning of the Anabaptist Movement, two related factors enhanced this view: the Anabaptist critique of the established church and the devastating persecution. These realities, combined with Anabaptist understandings of the nature of the church, galvanized the conviction that the church was a counterculture that should stand apart from the larger society and challenge its values.

Over the generations, this notion of nonconformity or separation from the world has played itself out in various ways in different social settings. Some Anabaptist groups withdrew into quiet ethnic enclaves; others became rigidly sectarian. Still others tried to transform the world through business and politics. Some engaged in missionary activity to save souls; still others pursued social justice activities as a means of social transformation.

The Anabaptist groups that emphasized separation from the world often talked of "nonconformity" to the world and developed special standards of dress and other social restrictions. Many of the Anabaptist groups in the United States emphasized nonconformity in the late-nineteenth and early-twentieth centuries. However, in the face of growing pressures from modernization, industrialization, and urbanization, a good number of them progressively relaxed their standards of separation in the twentieth century. Yet many traditional Anabaptist groups continue to emphasize separation from the world through plain clothing, constraints on social activities, and limits on technology as a witness to their faith.

The early Anabaptists were ardent missionaries. However, the major Mennonite and Brethren bodies did not become actively involved in evangelism and missionary work until the last decades of the nineteenth century. Missionary activity grew rapidly in the first half of the twentieth century and expanded the Anabaptist family around the globe. Mission agencies and activities have waxed and waned, depending on the enthusiasm and priorities of particular churches. Today some denominations have vigorous outreach and church-planting programs, while others do not. The traditional Old Order communities generally do not engage in missionary work.

Some of the mainstream Mennonite and Brethren groups have more pas-

Brethren Service worker Mildred Long (standing) supervises a Vienna soup kitchen for refugees in 1948. Photo by J. Henry Long

sion for peace and social justice programs than for evangelistic endeavors. Nevertheless, in varied settings around the globe, Anabaptist missionaries emphasize a "third way"—a wholistic approach that blends spiritual ministry with social justice, physical care, and economic development. Outside of North America and as a result of Anabaptist missionary efforts, more than a million converts to the Christian faith are members of Anabaptist-related churches.[14]

Despite many different expressions and applications, Anabaptist communities contend that a believers church should be a transforming counter-culture that gives a witness in the larger society. In the Anabaptist World, distinctive subcultures based on the teachings of Jesus and other Scripture have taken many forms: from communal living to engaging in mission activities, and from wearing plain clothing to advocating for peace and justice on behalf of the gospel. These various forms of witness, each in their own way, give testimony to the lordship of Christ in the daily lives of individuals and congregations.

LORDSHIP OF CHRIST

Another theme of distinction woven throughout the experience of many Anabaptist groups is an affirmation of the lordship of Christ over all the principalities and powers, including civil government.[15] Though the phrase "the lordship of Christ" came into parlance in the mid-twentieth century, Anabaptists from the beginning of the movement have affirmed their allegiance to Christ over any loyalties to governments and national bodies. Migrations, persecution, pacifism, and international service have helped to foster an international ethos that emphasizes the global nature of the kingdom of God over the seductive appeal of nationalism and patriotism. In some ways, Anabaptists have been more concerned about social boundaries than political borders.[16]

In the United States, many Anabaptist groups have been cautious about giving undue allegiance to the flag and mixing "God and country" together in a civil religion that promotes nationalism in the name of God. Anabaptist groups, for example, are less likely to have flags in their church sanctuaries and private church-related schools.[17] When Anabaptists are true to their biblical heritage, they proclaim an international kingdom of God that transcends national borders, loyalties, and symbols.

In summary, across the generations and spanning different cultural settings, Anabaptist congregations have stressed the importance of a Christocentric biblicism, believers baptism, discipleship, church as community, mutual aid, peacemaking, service ministries, the church as a counterculture, and the lordship of Christ. These nine themes constitute common commitments that crisscross the Anabaptist World today. Anabaptists may have difficulty agreeing on how to apply some of these convictions; but members of all stripes and tribes have little difficulty rallying around disaster and relief auctions and sales that reach out to the needy of the world. On first blush, these groups may appear to have little in common, but beneath the surface these themes form the bedrock of Anabaptist commitments.

The heirs of the Anabaptists live in a dramatically different world today than the world of their sixteenth-century religious ancestors. In the United States, church and state are separate, individual conscience is respected, and adults can freely participate in any religious body of their choice. Hence, a pivotal and enduring question for members and congregations in the United States is how to best translate their Anabaptist convictions in such a different postmodern world. In other words, what does it mean to be faithful Anabaptist Christians in the context of a pluralistic post-Christian society?

Chapter 4

DIVISION AND DIVERSITY

Good wood splits well.
—*Ira Landis, Mennonite historian*

SCHISM

Despite the bedrock of common convictions, Anabaptist communities have many divisions. The depth and intensity of convictions often incite division. As noted before, some sixty groups can be identified, and many of them have fewer than a thousand members. Although all four tribes have splinter groups, the Mennonites and Amish have been the most divisive. One scholar recently studied more than 208 conflicts within several Mennonite groups alone![1] A lay Mennonite historian, trying to put the best spin on all the fractures, once remarked, "Good wood splits well."

Though some voices in the Anabaptist World decry all the divisions, separations sometimes spur renewal and spiritual revitalization. Conflicts may even bring positive fruits: stronger solidarity within groups, sharper group identities, clearer boundaries, and revitalized commitments. Schism and division, albeit painful, reflect the fact that people care deeply enough about their convictions to make hard decisions that may lead to separation. In the end, a world of strong commitments and separations may be more desirable than a wishy-washy world of spineless beliefs.

Many of the breaches in the Anabaptist family have been amicable, but others have been bitter. Some arise from sincere differences of heartfelt convictions, others from personality clashes, family squabbles, and power plays by dominant leaders. Different cultural, ethnic, and historical traditions also add ingredients for schism. Social groups typically balance the competing interests of various sectors of their membership. But after a breach, the social equilibrium is lost, and the opposing factions solidify more firmly. The conservative flank digs its traditional roots even deeper, and the progressive crowd accelerates at a faster pace because it no longer needs to placate the conservatives. In any event, Anabaptist communities have not been immune to schism.

Why do peaceful people quarrel? Why do they squabble among themselves? How do peaceloving groups become embroiled in conflict? There are many reasons; an obvious, however trite one, is that these people are indeed people. Like other humans, they become annoyed, greedy, stubborn, and sometimes find it difficult to forgive. Human factors always hover over conflict. In addition to social forces, some theological factors within the Anabaptist legacy itself may make these communities especially prone to split. The following five themes within the heritage may provide a breeding ground for conflict.

Discipleship. The accent on discipleship can be a catalyst for division because it gives more importance to practice than to doctrine. Some divisions have emphasized doctrine, but many have focused on practical applications of faith related to dress, the use of technology, and relations with the outside world. A focus on the practical expression of faith in daily living can easily lead to squabbles over where to draw the lines of distinction in the sands of righteousness. Discipleship calls attention to social ethics and the integrity of daily life; yet it also can foster a literalism that may lead to division.

A Visible Church. A related factor within the Anabaptist tradition is the view of the church as a visible expression of the body of Christ with the power to loose and to bind, to make moral decisions with external consequences (Matt. 18:15-20). This weighty view of the church means that faith commitments take on corporate expressions in visible ways. Viewing the church as a concrete community means that members must find ways to live together and not merely give lip service to doctrinal precepts. Some Anabaptist communities believe that churches should have clear signs of membership and clean lines of separation from the larger society if they are to be a counterculture with a credible witness.

Moreover, granting the church moral authority to make decisions that will be engraved—bound and loosed—in heaven, is a heavy matter. Consequently, debates over where the lines should be, what visible signs are appropriate, how Scripture should be interpreted, and who should decide— such debates can foment conflict and sometimes schism.

The Kingdom Now. The Anabaptist focus on the Sermon on the Mount sometimes cultivates a form of perfectionism. For those who seek to practice the ethics of the Sermon on the Mount, the kingdom of God is inaugurated now in the corporate life of the church and continues until its final consummation at the end of the ages. Jesus urged his disciples, "Be perfect, therefore, as your heavenly Father is perfect" (Matt. 5:48). This desire for perfection and the assumption that the kingdom has already begun within the body of Christ, raise the stakes and stir the emotions in ways that can easily fuel the fires of conflict.

Communal Authority. Anabaptists contend that when adults confess, "Jesus is Lord" (1 Cor. 12:3), they become part of a corporate church body and must yield themselves to its collective wisdom and standards. Anabaptists do not merely worship and fellowship together; they *covenant* to live together, according to common norms. The church and its covenant become a higher authority than individual conscience. Divisions sometimes emerge because some individuals are not able or willing to abide by what they may consider the tyrannical rule of elders.

Issues revolving around communal authority became more pronounced in the twentieth century as some groups absorbed the values of modern individualism, with its emphasis on personal freedom and choice. Brethren groups, shaped by Pietism, have tended to respect individual conscience on some matters more than some Mennonite and Amish groups that have stressed the communal authority of the church. Groups with roots in Pietism, with its accent on love, have been less likely to splinter, at least in recent years.[2]

Church Polity. Another factor involved with division is church polity, in particular the degree of central authority versus congregational authority. Groups with centralized authority that try to keep uniform standards may experience greater division as they try to enforce them across a diverse constituency. Anabaptist polity has emphasized both congregational and regional (conference or district) governance. Some Mennonite bodies with regional conferences have struggled with division as they tried to enforce standards across a wide body of members. On the other hand, congregational governance can also lead to division when independent congregations and strong (or even autocratic) leaders chart their own course of action.

In addition to these five themes, a variety of social, cultural, and economic factors—education, occupation, migration, lifestyle, race, nationality, and ethnicity—help to pry groups apart. Differences along these lines often make it harder to unite and easier to divide. However, these factors are not always the culprits because some divisions occur among rather homogeneous groups as well.

In any event, even the most diplomatic divisions are unhappy moments. Nevertheless, they often reflect sincere attempts to follow Jesus in daily life and to maintain the purity of the body of Christ in visible ways. Theologian Paul Tillich once reportedly said that *reformation* is the key Protestant principle. Some divisions have been sincere attempts to revitalize and reform the spiritual life and vitality of Anabaptist communities. Others have been the result of obstinate and cantankerous people. Despite the propensity to divide, there are many fine examples of union, merger, and cooperation in the Anabaptist World as well.[3]

DIVERSITY

Anabaptist groups span a wide social spectrum. Some Anabaptists read by gas lights, while others surf on the World Wide Web (www). Some members live without credit cards; others work as stockbrokers. Thousands study in one-room schools; others teach at Harvard University. Some are recent immigrants from Asia and others claim nine generations of German stock. Some are gay and some are straight, some are black and some are white. This is truly a diverse company of souls that for one reason or another has gathered under the Anabaptist canopy.

Social analysts have used a variety of concepts to describe differences between groups. The term *acculturation* is often used to describe the extent to which a minority group has absorbed the values of the larger culture. Similarly, *assimilation* signals how much a small group has merged into the social networks and organizations of the dominant society.[4] Despite this classical distinction, we use the term *assimilation* throughout the book to refer to *both* the cultural and social blending of Anabaptist communities into the larger society.

We have used three concepts—*traditional, transitional,* and *transformational*—to indicate three degrees of assimilation.[5] The triple breakdown of traditional, transitional, and transformational groups highlights a group's relationship to the larger society. We need to stress that these are broad categories and may not fit a particular group perfectly, but they do help to clarify differences and identify common themes.

In general, *traditional* groups concentrate on preserving religious and cultural traditions and make little effort to engage the dominant culture. At

TABLE 4.1
Typical Traits of Traditional, Transitional, and Transformational Groups[a]

Traditional Groups	• Use horse-drawn transportation
	• Speak a special dialect
	• Consider themselves Old Order
	• Selectively use technology
	• Preserve older forms of religious ritual
	• Emphasize traditional practices
	• Practice nonresistance
	• Accept the collective authority of the church
	• Wear plain clothing
Transitional Groups	• Encourage individual religious experience
	• Emphasize rational, formal, written doctrine
	• Engage in evangelism[b]
	• Use technology except television
	• Forbid divorce[c]
	• Forbid the ordination of women[c]
	• Discourage higher education[c]
	• Ordain lay pastors[c]
	• Practice nonresistance
	• Wear plain clothing
Transformational Groups	• Support higher education
	• Engage in diverse forms of ministry
	• Hold professional jobs
	• Hire professional, salaried pastors
	• Widely use forms of technology
	• Involved in peacemaking and social justice
	• Accept individualism
	• Participate in mainstream cultural activities
	• Operate large church organizations
	• Participate in local, state, and national politics

[a] A specific group may not necessarily exhibit all the traits of a particular category.
[b] Applies also to many transformational groups.
[c] These traits apply to traditional groups as well.

the other end of the spectrum, *transformational* groups seek to change or transform the larger world. The *transitional* groups lie somewhere in between, trying to maintain their traditions, yet trying to reach out as well.

We must stress several key points. This is not a simple linear model where each group, over time, marches along the same line from traditional to transitional and eventually ends up transforming the world. Some groups may stay in the traditional slot for decades; other groups may move in the opposite direction, becoming *more* traditional rather than less. Nevertheless, the forces of history generally tend to pull groups away from their traditional moorings. If a group starts moving too quickly, a splinter group may peel off in order to preserve some endangered traditions.

Finally, there are many shades of difference within each category. Some transformer groups, for example, are actively involved in evangelizing, others focus more on peace and justice, and still others are interested in transforming the arts.

TRADITIONAL GROUPS

Communities in this category exhibit at least *one* of the following four characteristics: they consider themselves an Old Order group, they speak a German dialect,[6] they forbid private ownership of automobiles, or they vigorously preserve old rituals and patterns of the church. A group like the Old Order Amish fits all four criteria. The Old German Baptist Brethren only meet the first and fourth. About 20 percent (107,000) of the Anabaptist membership in the United States carries the traditional banner.

The social practices and family life of traditional groups tend to follow older patterns as well. Traditional groups emphasize the moral authority of the church over the individual, they are predominately rural but not neces-

Old German Baptist Brethren greet each other with a holy kiss at their Annual Conference.
Photo courtesy
Roanoke Times

sarily agricultural, they typically are satisfied with an eighth-grade education, and they do not engage in evangelism. With large families, these groups normally grow through biological reproduction and raising children who claim the faith for themselves, rather than through missions. In many ways, the larger society is irrelevant to them. They are more interested in preserving social and religious practices than in changing the larger world. Tradition looms large among these people. They use technology cautiously and selectively. With little bureaucracy, traditional groups emphasize informal social relationships. They value fellowship above policy and prefer oral over written communication.

Some of the groups under the traditional banner include the Old German Baptist Brethren, the Old Order Amish, the Hutterites, the Groffdale Conference Mennonites, and the Weaverland Conference Mennonites. The Amish, Hutterites, and Groffdale Mennonites speak a non-English (Germanic) dialect and forbid private automobiles. The Hutterites use the latest productive technology but read sixteenth-century sermons in Old German during their worship services. The Old German Baptist Brethren and the Weaverland Conference Mennonites own automobiles and use English in their worship services, but they both consider themselves Old Order groups and emphasize the preservation of older forms of worship and ritual. All these groups forbid television and entertainment technology.

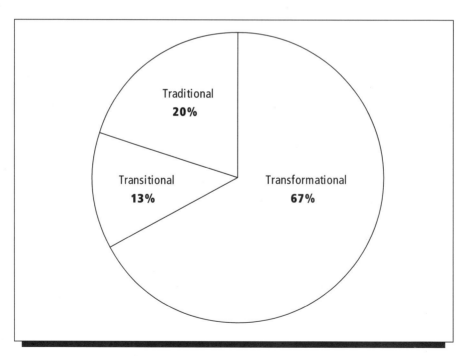

FIGURE 4.1 Anabaptist Membership by Type of Assimilation

Members of a conservative Mennonite family at the dinner table. Photo by Kevin & Bethany Shank/Dogwood Ridge Photography

TRANSITIONAL GROUPS

In broad strokes, the transitional groups come from two directions. Some are leaving Old Order roots, and others have pulled away from transformational groups in order to preserve more traditional standards. Roughly 13 percent (70,000) of the Anabaptist World membership stands on transitional ground.

The transitional groups speak English and own automobiles, but they still emphasize separation from the world. These groups require their members, especially women, to wear clothing that distinguishes them from the larger society. Although transitional groups share a conservative worldview with traditional groups, they tend to interact more with the outside world and are more likely to engage in mission activities. Transitional groups emphasize individual salvation and individual religious experience more than traditional groups. In short, they are more individualistic in their faith and encourage personal, subjective experience. They also take a more formal and rational approach to religious faith, and they are more likely to emphasize doctrine and write their beliefs than traditional groups.

Transitional groups have Sunday schools, youth meetings, and formal programs of Christian education such as Bible schools and Bible institutes. Their church buildings tend to be fairly plain, and they generally do not use musical instruments in worship. Ministers are usually selected by nominees drawing lots or are elected from within the local congregation; they do not have professional training or receive a salary.

Transitional churches use the latest productive technology, but typically forbid television; however, many of them selectively use the World Wide Web. Many members complete high school, but higher education is often discouraged. Members of these groups tend to support private church schools at both the elementary and secondary levels. Virtually all of these groups forbid divorce, the ordination of women, military service, and holding political office. Like the more traditional groups, these churches will excommunicate members who violate their standards.

Examples of transitional groups include the Dunkard Brethren, the Beachy Amish, the Eastern Pennsylvania Mennonite Church, and many of the independent Mennonite conferences. All of these groups feel internal pressures to lower their standards and accommodate to the larger society. Yet some of them, like the Eastern Pennsylvania Mennonite Church, have actually become more conservative—for example, making ownership of radios a test of membership.[7] Many of these transitional groups engage in mission and service programs with an entrepreneurial spirit. They give greater freedom to individuals while still trying to keep them within the moral order of the church. They seek to change the world through mission efforts without discarding their distinctive plain dress.[8]

TRANSFORMATIONAL GROUPS

Plain dress creates a big divide between many of the transitional and transformational groups. When groups change from plain clothing to the clothing worn by the surrounding culture, they lose their public identity and visibility as a distinctive group. The change from plain dress is one visible and clear signal of assimilation into the broader society.[9] Transformational groups are eager to engage, to transform the larger culture in a variety of ways; many of them would say that plain clothing simply hinders their

Members of the Pasadena (California) Mennonite Church singing during worship.
Photo by Tom Price

efforts of evangelism and witness.

These groups pursue various avenues of transformation: personal evangelism, church planting, overseas mission work, prison ministries, international relief and development, social justice, peacemaking, and conflict mediation. Members of transformational groups work in a wide array of jobs as farmers, surgeons, mechanics, nurses, lawyers, educators, carpenters, therapists, stockbrokers, managers, and business owners. Most members of these groups have televisions and use the World Wide Web as well as other forms of mass media. About two-thirds (360,000) of the adult Anabaptists in the United States are in the transformational camp.

Transformational groups show many expressions of Christian faith and piety. They usually grant individual conscience priority over the collective authority of the church. Reflecting the plurality of modern culture, these groups differ on a host of issues, such as the ordination of women, homosexuality, abortion, capital punishment, political involvement, and peacemaking. Some groups are ardent evangelicals; others accent peacemaking and social justice. Still other churches try to weave all these strands together.

Many transforming congregations have a paid professional staff of pastors, musicians, Christian educators, and youth leaders. Many church buildings of these groups are modern facilities equipped with well-appointed sanctuaries, fellowship halls, and multiple-purpose gymnasiums; however, in rural areas this is not always the case. Transformational groups also tend to develop national programs and organizations with bureaucratic features: publishing houses, mission boards, colleges, service agencies.

The larger denominational groups fit under the transformational banner: the Brethren in Christ, the Brethren Church, the Church of the Brethren, the Fellowship of Grace Brethren Churches, the Mennonite Brethren, the General Conference Mennonite Church, and the Mennonite Church. These groups seek to transform the larger world through various modes of witness, ranging from evangelism to soup kitchens, from racism workshops to mental health programs, from television ads to nonviolent civil disobedience, and from shelters for victims of domestic violence to holding political office. Members of transformational groups have a sense of civic responsibility in the larger society and sometimes participate in the political process by voting and holding office.[10]

There are fundamental differences between the traditional and transformational groups: *divergent* worldviews and different understandings of the self, of salvation, and of the nature of the church itself. In the traditional arena, progress and change are suspect. The Old Order worldview accents the past and values tradition as much as change; it often cherishes the wisdom of the past even more than the insights of science. By contrast, transformer groups welcome change, innovation, and planning for the future; they applaud science, experts, strategic planning, and organizational efficiency at every turn. Traditional groups, on the other hand, have not absorbed all the assumptions and values of modernity that transformational groups tend to take for granted.

The transforming groups accent the individual—individual conscience, choice, and freedom. Many of them emphasize personal salvation, personal Bible study, and personal evangelism. By contrast, traditional groups focus more on the communal dimensions of salvation, place more restrictions on the individual, and grant greater authority to the church. Among traditional people, the community rather than the individual is the primary agent of moral authority. Across the spectrum from traditional to transitional, the cardinal issue is one of moral authority. Who holds the key to moral authority? The group or the individual or some mix of both? Are individuals free to follow their conscience and make their own decisions about dress, divorce, abortion, killing, television, and financial investments? Or does the church speak for heaven on these matters?

Different understandings of the mission of the church in the world also stretch across the traditional-transformational spectrum. Some transformers contend that the church should provide a witness to the world that challenges its depravity and transforms society through the spiritual regeneration of individuals. Aggressive programs of evangelism seek to bring individuals to Christ and incorporate them into the life of the church. Other transformers focus on changing sinful social structures and policies that perpetuate economic injustice, racism, sexism, and poverty. Still others want to transform the broader culture through creative contributions in the arts, mental health professions, and civic endeavors. Regardless of mode, the transformationalists share the conviction that the good news of the gospel should induce transformation, whether at the individual level, sociocultural level, or both.

The traditionalists, on the other hand, argue that their communities are a beacon on a hill, a light to the world. Their first priority is to live faithfully within their community in ways that give witness to their faith. They will reach out to help needy neighbors who face disaster; yet in their view, the primary mission of the church is to faithfully practice the gospel in daily life. A pure church, unstained and unspotted by worldly contamination, is the best and most enduring witness to the larger world. Thus, Old Order

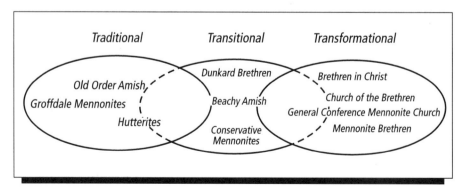

FIGURE 4.2 Selected Groups by Type of Assimilation

communities have little interest in trying to be relevant to the world or in trying to discern the most effective strategy for witness; instead, they seek to live faithfully in community, leaving the effectiveness of their witness in the hands of God.

In the last half of the twentieth century, one of the great ironies is that groups like the Old Order Amish have attracted enormous public attention without any attempts to evangelize. Transformers, however, might argue that stirring the curiosity of tourists may be interesting but have little impact in transforming the world for Jesus Christ.

THE ANABAPTIST ESCALATOR

Members of more traditional groups often talk of "Low" (conservative) and "High" (progressive) congregations and denominations. "High" churches are more progressive in the Anabaptist World, more assimilated into the surrounding culture. In areas of the country thick with Anabaptist groups, some members of so-called low churches will ride the Anabaptist escalator to greater freedom in a nearby so-called high church.[11] This may happen within an affiliation when members switch congregations or when they trade groups, such as moving from the Old German Baptist Brethren to the Church of the Brethren. It also happens between tribes, when a Hutterite, for example, joins the Mennonites.

Switching tribes or affiliations often occurs through marriage or around the time of marriage, when a young couple decides their church affiliation. Others occasionally ride the escalator to a new church home later in life as well. The growing mobility and professional involvements of members in transformational churches encourage switching, but it's not always upward. Sometimes dissatisfied members step down to a more conservative congregation or affiliation, and some people merely step sideways when they switch affiliations.

Consider some examples: Horse-and-buggy-driving Mennonites sometimes worry that their youth will step up a notch and join a car-driving Old Order Mennonite Church. Car-driving Old Order Mennonites fear that their discontents will join an assimilated Mennonite group. In Holmes County, Ohio, Old Order Amish youth sometimes move up to the New Order Amish; in turn, New Order youth may join the Beachy Amish, who currently offer three choices on the Holmes County Anabaptist menu. Moreover, the Beachy Amish worry that they will lose members to a mainstream Mennonite Church or, Menno forbid, a Brethren Church.

In some areas, Mennonite pastors fear that if they mute their evangelical pitch, they will lose members to the Grace Brethren or the Brethren in Christ; or if they are too evangelical, they will lose sheep to the Church of the Brethren. Pastors and denominational leaders sometimes feel pulled from both sides in this Anabaptist tug of war that uses a pacifist rope.

The traditional communities often serve an important feeder function for many of the mainstream groups. Youth who find Old Order ways too stifling often leave and help to replenish the stock and provide leadership in a higher church group. Dropouts from Old Order Mennonite and Amish groups, for example, have helped to feed the growth of the Mennonite Church. Moreover, numerous Mennonite church leaders have come from Old Order roots. The Church of the Brethren is more handicapped in this regard because it has a much smaller Old Order contingent.

There are people who would like to switch tribes or groups but cannot do so for whatever reason—Old Order Amish with a New Order heart, or Brethren in Christ with a Mennonite heart, and so on. In any event, exiles from traditional churches have helped to feed the growth and the leadership pool of many transformational Anabaptist churches.

COMING AND GOING

People who are switching churches generally tend to circulate within Anabaptist circles, but not always. Sometimes members of more traditional groups, seeking greater freedom for spiritual expression, leave Anabaptism completely and join a charismatic, independent, or fundamentalist church. In the upper hemisphere of the Anabaptist World, members of transformer groups may leave for an Episcopalian or Presbyterian fold; others may even stray completely out of Christian pastures.

There are many types of exits from Anabaptist churches. In some cases, members are excommunicated and leave with bitter memories. Others exit voluntarily for a variety of reasons such as lack of nearby Anabaptist churches, unhappiness with certain aspects of practice or doctrine, the preference of a spouse, or the erosion of their faith. For whatever reason, these *exiles* leave the flock and lose their love for the Anabaptist faith.

By contrast, there are also *ethnic* Anabaptists on the fringes, people who do not participate in a local congregation and yet share the Anabaptist spirit and vision. Many of these ethnic Anabaptists grew up in an Anabaptist family but, for various reasons, find it difficult to affirm the faith. Nevertheless, they enjoy the lovely quilts, relief sales, or poetry of Anabaptist writers. These bystanders affirm the culture but not the heartfelt faith of their birthright community. This is the last step on the ecclesiastical escalator for some children of transformer churches.

Other birthright Anabaptists leave the church through marriage to join Methodist, Baptist, or Episcopalian congregations, and yet remain *closet* Anabaptists in their new church family.

Standing at the edge of the Anabaptist tent are also many *sympathizers,* people in other religious traditions who for one reason or another have developed an appreciation for Anabaptism. These friendly cheerleaders, such as Stanley Hauerwas, are somewhat akin to the sympathetic half-Anabaptists of earlier Anabaptist times.[12] These friends of the Anabaptist family support and promote the Anabaptist cause in ecumenical, academic, and theological circles, but they are not practicing members of Anabaptist congregations.

Finally, there are many *transplants* in the Anabaptist World who have joined the community for many reasons, some through marriage, others by evangelism, and still others, upon leaving other denominations, because they were attracted by particular practices or beliefs. Relatively few outsiders have joined the Hutterites and Amish. Probably fewer than a dozen Hutterites and less than a hundred Amish are first-generation converts from the outside. The transitional groups welcome transplants through various outreach programs. However, the bulk of newcomers to the Anabaptist family have joined transformational churches through a variety of service, mission, and outreach programs.

Churches can only grow two ways: by making converts or by making babies and raising them to claim the faith for themselves. For the traditional and transitional groups, the primary source of growth is their own children; for the transformational churches, growth comes mostly from converts. Groups who lose many of their children and win few converts, will in time, of course, diminish or even die.

In the next four chapters, we explore each of the tribes: Amish, Brethren, Hutterite, and Mennonite in greater detail. We begin with the Amish, a tribe that has enjoyed spectacular growth in the twentieth century through what some have called biological evangelism.

Chapter 5

THE AMISH

> Our children are our most important crop.
> —*Amish farmer*

AMISH BRANCHES

With the rise of tourism and generous media coverage, the prominence of the Amish spiraled upward in the last half of the twentieth century.[1] Although they often find themselves in the public spotlight, the Amish prefer to live quiet, undisturbed lives. Unlike the Hutterites, but similar to the Brethren and Mennonites, the Amish own private property. They live alongside non-Amish neighbors in small villages and farming communities in some thirty-three states, mostly in the mid-Atlantic and Midwestern regions of the country.

The word *Amish* evokes images of buggies, bonnets, and beards. At first blush, the Amish appear to be pressed from the same cultural cookie cutter. In fact, however, the Amish World overflows with complexity because their congregational autonomy creates endless variations at the local level. Two Amish authors confessed, "It is impossible to find two Amish church districts, new or old, that are exactly the same."[2] Congregational autonomy and sincere convictions have produced a colorful quiltwork of subgroups.

In broad strokes, there are four major branches within the Amish tribe: Old Order (73,600 members), New Order (3,960), Beachy Amish (7,370), and Amish Mennonite (1,960), each with their own subgroups as shown in table 5.1. Combined together, the four types of Amish have 1,439 congregations with about 86,900 members. The Old Order Amish account for 86 percent of the Amish World.

None of the four major clusters are organized in a formal way at the national level, but their congregations often associate in informal ways. In general, the Old Orders are the largest and most traditional of the four Amish branches. New Orders are smaller in number and more progressive in their understandings of faith. Both Old Order and New Order groups use horse-drawn transportation; the Beachy Amish and Amish Mennonites use motor vehicles. The Beachy Amish and Amish Mennonites tap public electricity, worship in meetinghouses, engage in evangelism, and have fewer restrictions on plain dress. There are considerable differences in the forms of piety and religious expression between the various groups.

The Amish have a congregational polity that places considerable authority in the local congregation. They shy away from centralized structures and prefer to speak of fellowships rather than formal organizations, or even regional conferences. When groups are in harmony with each other on church practices and standards, they permit their ministers to exchange preaching assignments. Clusters of congregations with similar practices are sometimes called an affiliation and usually are considered "in fellowship" with each other. Sometimes a distinction is made between simply exchanging preachers and sharing in communion services, with the latter considered a deeper level of fellowship.

TABLE 5.1 Congregations, Membership, and Population of Amish Groups

AMISH BODY	CONGREGATIONS		MEMBERSHIP		POPULATION	
	N	%	N	%	N	%
Old Order Amish	1,237	86.0	73,609	84.6	165,620	86.2
Beachy Amish	103	7.1	7,365	8.5	13,993	7.3
New Order Amish	70	4.8	3,961	4.6	8,913	4.6
Amish Mennonite	29	2.1	1,959	2.3	3,722	1.9
Total	1,439	100.0	86,894	100.0	192,248	100.0

Note: Excludes Canadian Amish church districts

The word *order* derives from the German word *Ordnung*, meaning the discipline or standards of behavior held by a particular group. Old Ordnung groups follow older and more traditional practices; New Ordnung people are more change-minded in both their religious life and social practice. The Old Order label emerged in the 1860s and 1870s when sizeable clusters of Amish in some communities formed more progressive Amish Mennonite churches. The conservers, about one third of the Amish at that time, wanted to preserve more traditional ways and became known as the Old Order Amish. The more progressive Amish Mennonites eventually joined mainstream Mennonite churches.[3]

Across the country, a number of practices typically signal traditional sentiments. In general, the more conservative the group, the longer the beard, the wider the hat brim, the darker the color of clothing, the larger the head covering for women, the slower the singing in church, the longer the sermons, the greater the use of Pennsylvania German, and the more traditional the technology. Many Amish talk about low and high church districts. Low districts adhere to a more traditional old Ordnung; High districts are more progressive, higher on the ladder of cultural assimilation.

OLD ORDER AMISH GROUPS

Most of the 1,200 congregations under the Old Order tent simply consider themselves Amish or Old Order Amish. There are, however, a few distinctive Old Order subgroups that merit special mention. The so-called Swiss Amish of Allen and Adams Counties, Indiana, were late immigrants to the United States; they went directly to the Midwest from Europe in the 1850s. Their Swiss dialect as well as some of their social and religious practices differ from the Amish who speak Pennsylvania German and trace their roots to earlier migrations. There are several subgroups within the Swiss ethnic enclave.

Several different subgroups of Old Order Amish reside in the Big Valley of Mifflin County, Pennsylvania. Typically, subgroups take a name associated in some way with an early leader. The Byler Group, formed in 1849, is distinguished among other things by their yellow-top buggies. A Renno group that emerged in 1863 carries the distinction of asking men to wear only one suspender. One of the most conservative groups are the so-called Nebraska Amish, who in 1881 organized also in Mifflin County, through the help of a bishop living in Nebraska at the time. Extremely conservative in lifestyle, dress, and technology, the Nebraska Amish, with three subgroups, are noted for their white-topped buggies. Mifflin County has the unique distinction of having among its Old Order subgroups three different-colored carriage tops: white, yellow, and brown.

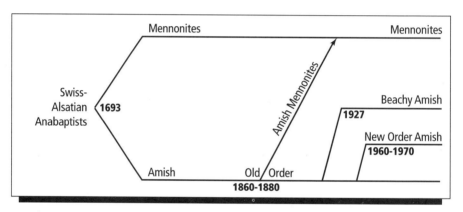

FIGURE 5.1 Formation of Amish Groups

The Holmes County, Ohio, area hosts the largest Amish settlement in the world, with more than 180 church districts. It has also spawned a number of subgroups. The Swartzentruber group, named for several of its leaders, emerged there in 1913. Holding a strict interpretation of shunning, the Swartzentrubers have become legendary for their stubborn traditionalism in many social and religious practices. Along with the Nebraska group, they reflect the more conservative flank of Old Order sentiments. In 1932 a division within the Swartzentruber group resulted in a new affiliation known as the Troyer Amish. Today the Troyer group has districts located in several states.[4] Another subgroup emerged in Holmes County in 1952 and became known as the Andy Weaver group. This affiliation is generally more conservative than many of the other Old Order districts in Ohio.

These are some of the more noteworthy subgroups that congregate under the Old Order Amish canopy. Factors distinguishing some of the subgroups are differences over the interpretation and application of shunning (*Meidung*) as well as acceptable forms of technology.

NEW ORDER AMISH

Another stream of Amish life developed in Holmes County, Ohio, in the 1960s. Forming over the course of a decade, New Order Amish held Bible studies for youth, set stricter guidelines for courtship, emphasized a more individual understanding of salvation, and were more flexible with the use of technology. Today New Order congregations are found in thirteen states, but the majority remain in Ohio. Various subaffiliations have developed within the New Order fold, yielding a diversity of religious and social practices.[5]

The New Order groups in Holmes County continue to use horse-and-buggy transportation but most have rubber on their carriage wheels. They use electric from generators for power tools but do not have electric lights in their homes. About half the districts have telephones in their homes. New Order men usually have trimmed beards and shorter hair, and the women wear brighter colors than Old Orders. The New Orders are more likely to have Sunday school, youth Bible studies, and participate in outreach projects. More accepting of change, New Orders encourage a more individual experience of salvation and are more likely to engage in missionary work than the Old Orders.

A network of New Order churches in several states has more flexible church standards than the major group based in Holmes County. The more progressive branch uses tractors for fieldwork and also for local transportation. Most of them have electricity and telephones in their homes. Moreover,

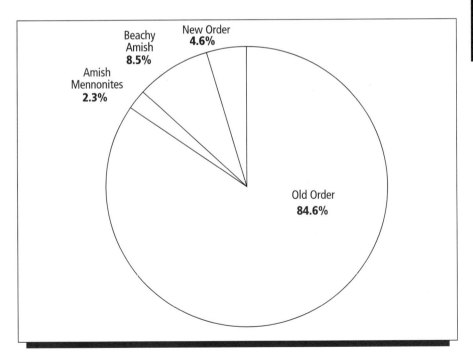

FIGURE 5.2 Adult Membership of Amish Groups

some of the congregations hold their worship services in meetinghouses.

A third cluster, known as the New Order Fellowship Churches separated from the New Order Amish in Holmes County in 1985-86 over some doctrinal issues. The Fellowship Churches have a more evangelical, almost charismatic understanding of faith. Their church standards are less strict than the main New Order group. They use tractors for fieldwork and for local transportation on the road. They also use public utility electricity for power and light. According to their leaders, they emphasize a heartfelt experience more than rules and regulations. The New Order Fellowship Churches are less enthusiastic about their Amish roots than many of the other New Order churches.

BEACHY AMISH

The Beachy Amish emerged in the 1920s in Pennsylvania, with roots in both Somerset and Lancaster Counties.[6] In the course of the twentieth century, a number of groups in other parts of the country also began to fellowship with the Beachy Amish. Sometimes called the Beachy Amish Mennonite Fellowship, the group derives its name from an early leader, Bishop Moses Beachy. It views itself as a fellowship rather than a conference or denomination with a centralized structure. Congregations associated with the Beachy Amish are found in twenty-two states, with strong concentrations in Indiana, Ohio, and Pennsylvania.

The Beachy Amish drive cars, install electricity, use telephones in their homes, own computers, and dress less plain than the Old and New Order groups. Beachy congregations are active in mission and evangelistic efforts, have Sunday schools, use church buildings and in general take a more evangelistic approach to spiritual life. There are several subaffiliations within the Beachy family of faith.[7]

AMISH MENNONITES

Some groups that leave traditional Amish ways call themselves Amish Mennonite, signaling their move in a progressive Mennonite direction and also reclaiming the Mennonite part of their heritage that predated Amish origins in 1693. Many of the congregations that left the Amish in the 1860s and 1870s were known as Amish Mennonites for many years and eventually merged with a Mennonite group. Over the past fifty years, some of the congregations that left the Old or New Order Amish fold have also claimed the Amish Mennonite label. Although not fully embracing a mainstream Mennonite identity, these people are similar to the Beachy Amish in their use of cars, electricity, telephones, and meetinghouses, and in their emphasis on evangelistic work. Skeptical of centralized programs operated by the church, they support many privately operated mission and service efforts.[8]

OLD ORDER IDENTITY AND DIVERSITY

Beards, bonnets, and buggies are distinctive symbols of separation that carve deep contours between the Old Order Amish and the larger society.

These public symbols provide easy recognition of Amish persons and imprint an indelible identity on the minds of members. Moreover, Old Order practices generate a strong sense of community, solidarity, and identity in Amish life.

At least ten badges of identity are shared by most Old Order Amish across the states: (1) horse-and-buggy transportation, (2) the use of horses and mules for fieldwork,[9] (3) plain dress in many variations, (4) a beard and shaven upper lip for men, (5) a prayer cap for women, (6) the Pennsylvania German dialect, (7) worship in homes, (8) eight grades of schooling, (9) the rejection of electricity from public utility lines, and (10) a taboo on the ownership of televisions and computers. These symbols of solidarity circumscribe the Old Order Amish World, mark it off from the larger society, and bridle the forces of social assimilation.[10]

There are other distinctives of Amish life as well; what is remarkable is that these badges of separation have been preserved without a national body to coordinate the more than 1,200 Old Order congregations. The tangible symbols of separation have served the Amish well by carving out a distinctive public identity and satisfying the social-psychological needs of their members. Differences between various subgroups are often camouflaged by the visible symbols that provide a united public front.

Beneath the surface of Amish life, many differences abound. A deeper look reveals divergent practices within and between many groups. Some affiliations forbid milking machines; others depend on them. Mechanical

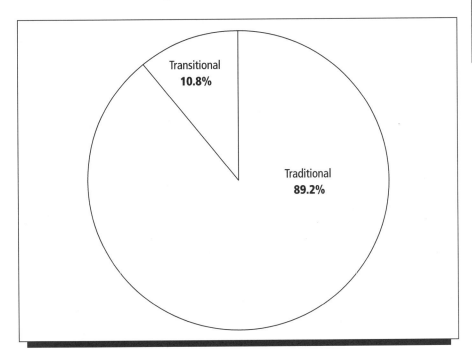

FIGURE 5.3 Amish Membership by Type of Assimilation

hay balers, pulled by horses across some Amish fields, are taboo in others. Prescribed buggy tops are gray or black in many affiliations but white or yellow in others. Buttons on clothing, banished in some groups, are accepted in the more progressive ones. Gas refrigerators are welcomed by some groups but forbidden by others. The dead are embalmed in most Amish communities but not in every settlement.

Because moral authority resides in the local church district, practices can vary between congregations, even within the same affiliation. Some bishops permit telephones in small shops, but others do not. Artificial insemination of livestock is acceptable in one district but not in another. In some communities, most of the men are farmers, but in other regions the majority of adult men work in small shops and industries. In the Nappanee and Elkhart-Lagrange settlements of Indiana, many Amish people work in large rural factories owned by non-Amish. Endless diversity with dozens of distinctions thrives behind the common badges of identity that appear on the front stage of Amish life.

VALUES AND ORDER

Several core values distinguish the Amish from mainstream culture. Unlike American culture that prizes individual choice and rights, the Amish highlight the welfare of the community over the individual. Members are expected to submit and yield to the collective wisdom of the church. Submission is a cardinal value, and so the Amish prize humility, modesty, and obedience. Pride is considered a sin that can disturb the common life. Hence, they frown upon photographs of individuals and other activities that call attention to the self. The Amish also emphasize separation from the world—avoidance of some of the values and practices of the larger society. The principle of separation regulates many of their customs, including their use of technology. The church is viewed as a redemptive community that stands apart from the broader culture.

Tradition looms large in Amish culture and guides many of the decisions of the church. The Old Order Amish emphasize both *oldness* and *orderliness*. Amish life and practice is regulated by the Ordnung of each congregation. Typically unwritten, the Ordnung embodies the behavioral expectations that shape Amish life. It carries prescriptions related to dress: women are to wear prayer caps and men to wear beards. It has proscriptions: do not own a television, hold a driver's license, or attend high school. The Ordnung covers a broad spectrum of Amish life, ranging from attire to technology, and from education to transportation. Children learn the ways of the Ordnung at an early age by observing adults and receiving parental instruction. Church leaders occasionally revise the understandings of the Ordnung as special issues emerge and new forms of technology arise.

SOCIAL ORGANIZATION

The *extended family* and the *church district* form the basic building blocks of Amish society. Amish parents typically raise about seven children,

Amish pupils head for home from their nearby school. Photo by Richard Rinehold

but ten or more is not uncommon. More than half the population is under eighteen years of age. An Amish person will often have seventy-five or more first cousins, and a typical grandmother will easily count more than thirty-five grandchildren. Members of the extended family usually live nearby, perhaps just across the field, down the lane, or beyond the hill. Youth grow up in this thicket of family relations where, as one Amish woman put it, "Everyone knows everyone else's business." One is rarely alone but always embedded in a network of support in time of need and disaster. The elderly retire at home, usually in a small apartment attached to a larger house.

Twenty to forty families constitute a *church district* or congregation. The geographical boundaries of this basic unit are marked by roads and streams or other natural borders. Members must participate in the district in which they live. A district's geographic size varies with the density of the Amish population. In smaller districts, families can walk to church services; other districts may be several miles wide. As districts grow, they divide.

Typically, a bishop, two preachers, and a deacon share leadership responsibilities in each congregation. None of the leaders receive formal education or payment for their services. The bishop, as spiritual elder, officiates at baptisms, weddings, communions, funerals, ordinations, and membership meetings. The church district is the hub of Amish life, with church, club, family, and precinct all wrapped up into a neighborhood parish. Periodic meetings of ordained leaders in some settlements link the districts into a loose federation.

Amish society is remarkably informal. Without a centralized national office, a symbolic national leader, or an annual convention, the tentacles of bureaucracy are rare. Apart from one-room schools, a modest publishing operation, and a few historical libraries, formal organizations do not exist. The one exception is a loosely organized National Amish Steering Committee that has representatives in each state. This body provides a common voice for dealing with government agencies and legal issues.[11] Regional committees in various areas coordinate activities related to schools, mutual aid, and historical interests, but typical bureaucratic organizations are simply absent. The conventional marks of social status—education, income, occupation, and consumer goods—are also less evident in Amish society.

RELIGIOUS PRACTICE

Worship services convene in Old Order Amish homes every other Sunday. Depending on the district's size, a group of 150 or more gather for worship, including friends from other districts who have a "no-church Sunday." They meet in a farmhouse, the basement of a home, or in a shop or barn—underscoring the integration of worship with daily life. A fellowship meal at noon and informal visiting follow the three-hour morning service.

A plain, simple, and unwritten liturgy revolves around congregational singing, prayer, and two sermons. Without the aid of organs, offerings, candles, crosses, robes, or flowers, members yield themselves to God in the spirit of humility. The congregation sings from the *Ausbund,* a hymnal of German songs that lacks musical notations and dates back to the sixteenth-century Anabaptists. The tunes, passed across the generations by memory, are sung in unison without any musical accompaniment. The slow, chant-like cadence creates a sixteenth-century mood. A single song may stretch over twenty minutes. Extemporaneous sermons, preached in the Pennsylvania German dialect, recount biblical stories as well as lessons from

Members of an Amish church district gather at one of their homes for worship.
Photo by Dennis Hughes

daily life. Preachers exhort members to be obedient to Amish ways and abstain from worldly vice.

Baptism typically occurs between the ages of sixteen and twenty-two, later than in most Anabaptist churches. Before baptism, the candidates are instructed in the eighteen articles of faith from the Dordrecht Confession of Faith, an old Anabaptist confession written in the Netherlands in 1632. These same articles of faith also guide some of the more conservative Mennonite groups. Baptism is a pivotal moment in the life of Amish youth because it signifies, not only a confession of Christian faith, but also a pledge to uphold the Ordnung of the church for the rest of their lives. Young men promise to serve as ministers if ever called by the congregation through use of the lot.

Because adult baptism is central to Amish theology, they respect the integrity of each individual's decision about baptism. Those who accept baptism but later renege on their vows will face excommunication and shunning. However, people who reject baptism and drift away from the community can relate to their family and friends without the stigma of shunning.

GROWTH AND EXPANSION

Despite their tenacity for traditional ways, the Amish have thrived in the most technologically advanced society of all time. Around 1900, Amish adults numbered about 5,000. Now scattered across thirty-three states, the four Amish branches number about 190,000 children and adults. Nearly three-fourths live in Ohio, Pennsylvania, and Indiana. Other sizable communities are found in Iowa, Michigan, Missouri, New York, and Wisconsin.[12] With a loose network of some 1,400 congregations, Amish groups function without a national organization or periodic nationwide gatherings.

The Amish have enjoyed remarkable growth in the last half of the twentieth century. By the dawn of the twenty-first century, Old and New Order Amish groups had spread into more than 250 settlements in the United States with a total population exceeding 170,000.[13] As shown in figure 5.4, Old and New Order Amish church districts have increased almost sevenfold in the last five decades, from 200 districts in 1951, to more than 1,300 congregations by 2001.[14] In recent years, the Old and New Order Amish population has more than doubled every twenty years. In the nine-year period from 1991 to 2000, the Old and New Order population (members and children) in the United States soared from approximately 117,000 to more than 170,000.[15] This reflects an increase of 424 congregations for the nine-year period, about forty-seven new ones per year.

The Amish have grown for several reasons. First, they have large families, averaging about seven children per family. Second, they are able to persuade most of their young people to join and participate in the church. Across the nation, the retention rate is about 85 percent. In some settlements, it goes above 90 percent; in others, it dips below 70 percent. Third, visible symbols and restrictions on certain practices create cultural fences that help to mark

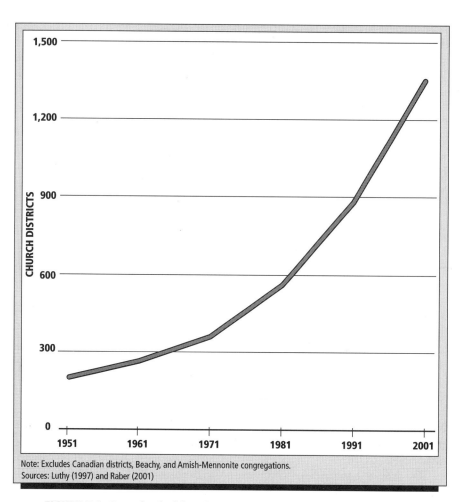

FIGURE 5.4 Growth of Old and New Order Amish Districts, 1951-2001

Note: Excludes Canadian districts, Beachy, and Amish-Mennonite congregations.
Sources: Luthy (1997) and Raber (2001)

off social borders and promote Amish identity. Finally, the Amish are willing to adapt, to make some cultural compromises with the larger society. This flexibility, at least in some settlements, has helped them to modernize and keep more of their youth in the church. In multiple ways, these factors have contributed to the growth and expansion of Amish society.

TWO BIG CHANGES

In the last quarter of the twentieth century, two major changes have transformed Amish life: private schools and the rapid rise of nonfarm work. These important changes will levy a major impact on Amish society for years to come. The massive consolidation of public schools and growing pressure to attend high school sparked clashes between Amish parents and government officials in the middle of the twentieth century. Confrontations in several states led to arrests and brief stints in jail. Finally, after many legal skirmishes, the U.S. Supreme Court in 1972 gave its blessing to the Amish eight-grade school system. The landmark case is known as *Wisconsin versus Yoder*. In the words of the high court, "There can be no assumption that today's majority is 'right' and the Amish and others are 'wrong.'" The justices concluded that, "A way of life that is odd or even erratic but interferes with no rights or interests of others is not to be condemned because it is different."[16]

Today the Amish operate about 1,200 private schools for some 32,000 Amish children.[17] Many of the schools are one-room buildings with twenty-five to thirty-five pupils and one teacher responsible for all eight grades. A few Amish children attend rural public schools in some states, but the vast majority go to private schools operated by a local board of parents.

Private schools play a critical role in the preservation of Amish culture. They reinforce Amish values and shield youth from contaminating ideas afloat in contemporary culture. Moreover, schools restrict friendships with non-Amish peers and impede the flow of Amish youth into higher education

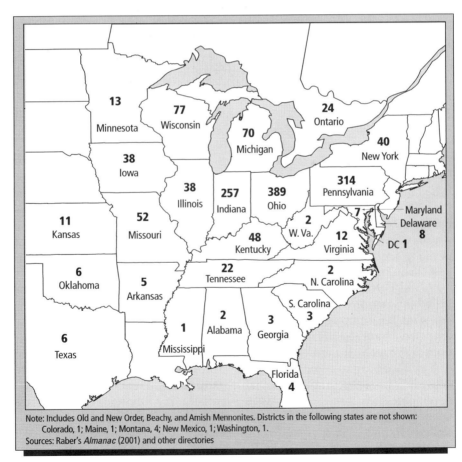

Note: Includes Old and New Order, Beachy, and Amish Mennonites. Districts in the following states are not shown: Colorado, 1; Maine, 1; Montana, 4; New Mexico, 1; Washington, 1.
Sources: Raber's *Almanac* (2001) and other directories

FIGURE 5.5 Distribution of Amish Congregations in North America

Many Amish men and women own and operate a variety of businesses and retail stores. Photo by Dennis Hughes

and professional life. Islands of provincialism, the schools promote practical skills that prepare their graduates for successful lives in Amish society.

Since 1975 another big change has been underway in Amish society. In many settlements, farmers have abandoned their plows for jobs in small shops and industries. In some settlements, Amish entrepreneurs have established hundreds of small businesses, some of which have annual sales topping $5 million. In other communities, Amish people work in industries operated by non-Amish in rural areas. Until the mid-twentieth century, the Amish were a rural farming people. Today they are still a rural people, but in many settlements less than half of them are farming. In some communities, the number of farming families even dips below 10 percent.

Good business opportunities and the rising costs of farming have propelled this major transformation of Amish life.[18] The shift away from farming is the most important and consequential change in Amish society in the past two centuries. It carries seeds of transformation that over the generations will touch all aspects of Amish culture: interaction with outsiders, use of English, access to technology, gender roles, child-rearing practices, leisure activities, lifestyles, and the social organization of community life. The development of three social classes—farmers, day laborers, and entrepreneurs—has already disturbed traditional patterns of equality in some Amish settlements. The occupational transformation is indeed a big change, one that will reshape the identity and texture of Amish life for generations to come.

Chapter 6

THE BRETHREN

> We cannot testify for our descendants—
> as their faith is, so shall be their outcome.
> —*Alexander Mack Sr., 1713*[1]

BRETHREN ORIGINS

Unlike Hutterites, Mennonites, and Amish, who descend directly from the sixteenth-century Anabaptists, the Brethren claim a mixed parentage of German Pietism and Anabaptism.[2] Founded in the German village of Schwarzenau, the Brethren began in 1708, about fifteen years after the Amish had formed. The Brethren rejected the established Lutheran, Reformed, and Catholic practices of their day and also the excessive mysticism and individualism of the Radical Pietists. Influenced by Mennonites whom they admired but considered spiritually lukewarm, they rebaptized each other in the Eder River. They grafted Anabaptist understandings of the church onto Pietist roots of spirituality, hoping to recreate the primitive faith of the early church.[3]

The Brethren World consists of seven affiliations with a thousand members or more, plus some small independent groups. The four largest bodies are the Church of the Brethren (137,000 members), the Fellowship of Grace Brethren Churches (34,000), the Brethren in Christ (20,000), and the Brethren Church (nearly 11,000). The adult membership of the Brethren World is nearly 212,000, with an estimated population of 293,000. The Brethren in Christ have ties to both the Mennonites and the Brethren. We have included them in the Brethren orbit because of their name as well as their historic ties to Pietism. Nevertheless, today they participate in the Mennonite Central Committee, the Mennonite World Conference, and other Mennonite organizations.[4]

Members carrying the Brethren name range across the spectrum from strict sectarians who use horse-and-carriage transportation to cosmopolitan professionals in urban centers. Only three small affiliations with a total of five congregations use horse-drawn transportation.[5] The proportion of Brethren dressing plain and following traditional practice is quite small. More than 90 percent of those under the Brethren banner have exchanged their plain dress for contemporary clothing.[6]

Known as German Baptist Brethren and often nicknamed Dunkers, the Brethren migrated to North America between 1719 and 1740. They spread south and west with the frontier, fanning outward across Pennsylvania, Maryland, and Virginia, on into the Carolinas and Kentucky, and westward

TABLE 6.1 Congregations, Membership, and Population of Brethren Groups

BRETHREN BODY	CONGREGATIONS		MEMBERSHIP		POPULATION	
	N	%	N	%	N	%
Church of the Brethren	1,071	59.1	137,037	64.7	185,000	63.1
Grace Brethren	307	16.9	34,467	16.3	46,530	15.9
Brethren in Christ	196	10.8	20,043	9.5	27,058	9.2
The Brethren Church	115	6.4	10,641	5.0	14,365	4.9
Old German Baptist Brethren	54	3.0	5,952	2.8	13,392	4.5
Other Brethren Groups	69	3.8	3,612	1.7	7,015	2.4
Total	1,812	100.0	211,752	100.0	293,360	100.0

Note: Grace Brethren totals include Conservative Grace Brethren churches. Church of the Brethren totals include nine congregations (282 members, or half of 563) with a dual affiliation with the Mennonite Church and twenty-two congregations (2,254 members) with a dual affiliation with various other denominations.

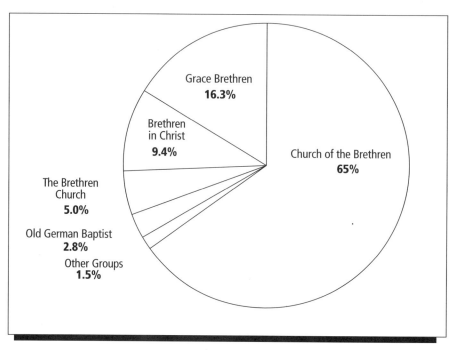

FIGURE 6.1 Adult Membership of Brethren Groups

into Illinois, Kansas, Missouri, the Dakotas, and even to the Pacific Coast. The Brethren in Christ emerged in the 1780s in western Lancaster County (Pa.) near the Susquehanna River. Initially known as River Brethren, many of the Brethren in Christ came from Mennonite backgrounds. They were influenced by the pietistic themes of the German Baptist Brethren and adopted some Brethren practices, including the Love Feast, immersion baptism, the wearing of beards, and the election of church leaders.

Between 1790 and 1880, the German Baptist Brethren grew from a small German-speaking sect of 1,500 members to a widely dispersed English-

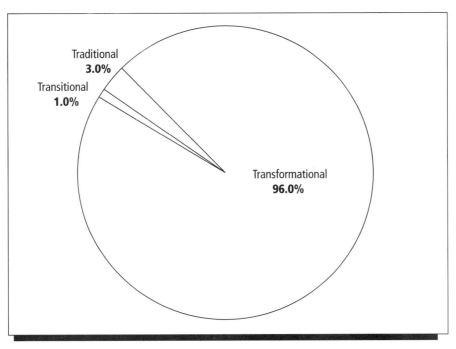

Traditional
3.0%

Transitional
1.0%

Transformational
96.0%

FIGURE 6.2 Brethren Membership by Type of Assimilation

speaking group of some 58,000 members in 500 congregations. The German Baptist Brethren often settled near Mennonites and Amish, especially in Pennsylvania, Virginia, Ohio, Indiana, and Kansas. Moreover, their revival-ist preaching and fervent evangelism enabled them to entice some adherents from both Mennonite and Amish folds. Mennonites and Brethren agreed on many issues, such as nonresistance, nonconformity, nonswearing of oaths, a plain lifestyle, and the accountability of church members to the local con-gregation.[7] However, the mode of baptism was a major point of contention that often evoked heated disputes. The Brethren baptized by trine immer-sion; the Amish and Mennonites by pouring or sprinkling.

During the 1860s and 1870s, the German Baptist Brethren were torn by controversies involving church discipline, plain dress, revivalism, higher education, and various departures from the "ancient order" of the Brethren. Between 1881 and 1883, these controversies among the German Baptist Brethren generated a three-way division that produced the Old German Baptist Brethren, the Brethren Church, and the Church of the Brethren.[8] In 1881, some 4,000 proponents of traditional ways formed the Old German Baptist Brethren Church. In 1883 some 5,000 so-called Progressives estab-lished the Brethren Church, today based in Ashland, Ohio, and often called the Ashland Brethren. In 1939 the Fellowship of Grace Brethren Churches in Winona Lake, Indiana, separated from the Brethren Church over issues of doctrinal interpretation prompted in part by American Fundamentalism, which attracted the Grace Brethren.

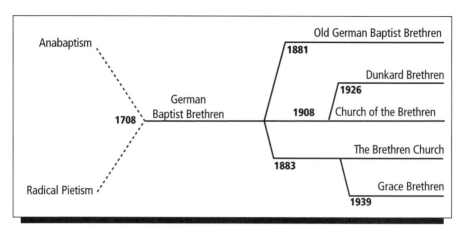

FIGURE 6.3 Formation of Brethren Groups

The large remaining group in 1883, known as the Conservatives, numbered about 60,000 and formed the main trunk of the German Baptist Brethren. In 1908, on the occasion of their two-hundredth anniversary, they changed their name to the Church of the Brethren. Today their headquarters are in Elgin, Illinois. A century after their three-way division, the major Brethren groups cooperated to produce a *Brethren Encyclopedia* (1983-84). Later they convened several Brethren World Assemblies that involved all of the major groups.

THE CHURCH OF THE BRETHREN

The largest denomination flowing from the baptisms in the Eder River in 1708 is the Church of the Brethren. Its 137,000 members are divided into twenty-three districts that cover thirty-nine states. Brethren tend to cluster most heavily in four states that have 69 percent of their membership: Pennsylvania, Virginia, Ohio, and Indiana. By 1770, the Brethren had begun holding a national Annual Meeting that was eventually called Annual Conference.[9]

Throughout the nineteenth century and into the middle of the twentieth century, Annual Conference decisions carried heavy moral authority across the church. They had binding authority much like the Ordnung in Amish life and the decisions of regional conferences in the Mennonite Church. In the last half of the twentieth century, the agenda of Annual Conference shifted more toward worship, fellowship, declarations on social issues, and decisions involving national programs and structure. However, the Annual Conference continues to play a dominant role in shaping the ethos and identity of the church. The General Board and the executive secretary of the denomination are responsible to the Annual Conference. *The Messenger* is the official monthly publication of the church.

The current turn-of-the-century theme for the Church of the Brethren is "Another Way of Living: Continuing the Work of Jesus—Simply, Peacefully,

Together." This phrase captures several key Brethren values: a Christocentric emphasis on discipleship, simplicity of life, peacemaking, and the church as community. Echoing some of the themes of Radical Pietism, the Brethren emphasize that they are a noncreedal church; indeed, they take some satisfaction in saying, "We have no creed except the New Testament." The Brethren have also stressed the importance of individual conscience on matters of personal and social morality.

Emphasizing their noncreedal nature, the ethos of the denomination accents integrity of relationships above proclamations of truth, process more than specific guidelines, praxis rather than doctrine, and seeking the mind of Christ rather than setting exact expectations. In the words of former general secretary, Donald Miller, "The greatest sin for Brethren is to stop talking with each other."[10] One leader noted, "A pastor will more likely be fired for a breach of community than for a weird belief."

The words of the unofficial Brethren churchwide anthem, "Move in Our Midst," captures many Brethren sentiments:

Move in our midst, thou Spirit of God. . . .
Walk with us through the storm and the calm. . . .
Teach us to love with heart, soul, and mind. . . .
Kindle our hearts to burn with thy flame. . . .
Spirit of God, thy love makes us strong. (Kenneth I. Morse)[11]

Brethren deacons prepare to bake unleavened bread for a congregational Love Feast. Photo by Daniel Rodriguez

According to one pastor, this communal ethos of the Brethren is sometimes better caught than taught and better felt than studied.

In recent years the Church of the Brethren has grappled with issues of creedalism, identity, decentralization, mission philosophy, and calling pastoral leadership. For some members and pastors, the noncreedal stance leaves things too flexible and fuzzy, and thus some want the church to be more explicit about its beliefs. Members have also debated mission philosophy.[12] Should the church initiate mission projects and try to establish Brethren churches in other countries? Or is it more appropriate to respond to requests for assistance from indigenous churches in various global settings? How does the church find adequate pastoral leadership, trained in a Brethren context, to provide congregational leadership for the future? This issue is also faced by many mainline denominations.

As shown in figure 6.4, membership in the Church of the Brethren has declined in the past four decades, from a high of 200,000 in 1960 to about 137,000 today. This has caused some concern and prompted a renewed interest in missions and church planting at home and abroad. The gentle, laid-back style of the Brethren, however, sometimes hinders church growth. "With our ethos, how do we evangelize?" asked one pastor. "We have more of a come, see, and feel approach, rather than a come, hear, and believe approach."

The Church of the Brethren tends to participate in ecumenical activities

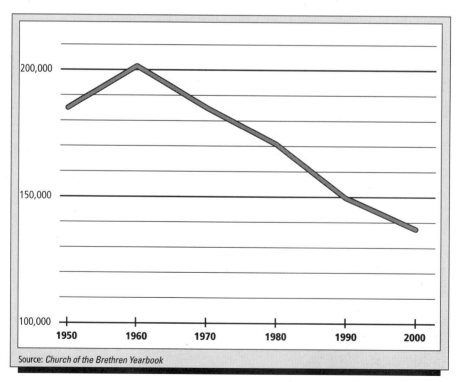

Source: *Church of the Brethren Yearbook*

FIGURE 6.4 Church of the Brethren Membership in the United States, 1950-2000

A Church of the Brethren pastor preaching at Sunday worship. Photo by Daniel Rodriguez

more than some of the other Brethren groups. The church, for example, joined the National Council of Churches in 1941 and the World Council of Churches in 1948. Brethren representatives have played active leadership roles in a variety of ecumenical efforts, at local and at regional levels.[13]

The Brethren have been active in a variety of service ministries, including Brethren Service reconstruction work in Europe after World War II and, in recent years, through many Brethren Voluntary Service projects at home and abroad. The Brethren Service Center in New Windsor, Maryland, coordinates many Brethren service efforts and activities. The On Earth Peace Assembly provides a vehicle for coordinating and fostering the peace witness of the Brethren. In addition, the Association of Brethren Caregivers supports an extensive network of deacons and other forms of caregiving in local congregations across the denomination.

A network of individuals and congregations formed the Brethren Revival Fellowship in 1959, to help retain some of the traditional views and practices of the church. The Brethren Revival Fellowship describes itself as "a concern movement within the Church of the Brethren, seeking to call the church to a firm stand for the authority of the Scriptures, and to an emphasis upon the teachings of the New Testament as historically understood by the Brethren."[14] This conservative-leaning fellowship operates inside the formal denominational structure, organizes various conferences, youth work camps, and voluntary service units. It publishes the *Brethren Revival Fellowship Witness*, which circulates to some 11,000 households. The continuing presence of BRF, as it is known, inside the larger church body is a testimony to the high regard Brethren have for unity.

THE BRETHREN CHURCH

The Brethren Church, headquartered in Ashland, Ohio, is the heir of the progressive group that separated from the German Baptist Brethren in 1883. Sometimes known as the Ashland Brethren, the Brethren Church has about 11,000 members in 115 congregations that are heavily concentrated in Indiana, Ohio, and Pennsylvania. The congregations are clustered in nine geographic districts that hold their own annual conferences in addition to the yearly meeting of the General Conference of the denomination.

While affirming basic Brethren understandings of faith, the Brethren Church reflects a conservative Protestant and evangelical stance and has a strong mission program. The Brethren Church sponsors but does not operate Ashland Theological Seminary and Ashland University. The Brethren church continues to baptize by trine immersion and observes a threefold Love Feast, including feetwashing, a common meal, and bread-and-cup communion. Affirming the classic Anabaptist theme of discipleship, the church declares, "Obedience to Christ is the center of Brethren life." This conviction, they note, has led to the practice of "nonconformity, nonresistance, and nonswearing." In a centennial statement, the Brethren Church reaffirmed its noncreedal stance with these words: "The Bible, and the Bible alone, is our all-sufficient creed and rule of practice."[15]

THE FELLOWSHIP OF GRACE BRETHREN CHURCHES

A division within the Brethren Church in 1939 split the membership into two groups. One became known as the Ashland Brethren, because of their support of Ashland College; the other was the Grace Brethren, supporters of Grace Theological Seminary, founded in 1937. The Grace Brethren emerged out of the Brethren Church after several years of debate over doctrinal issues triggered by fundamentalism as well as church polity.[16] Advocates of more fundamental understandings of faith formed the National Fellowship of Brethren Churches in 1940; in 1976 they were renamed the Fellowship of Grace Brethren Churches.

Today the Fellowship of Grace Brethren Churches numbers about 32,000 members in 260 congregations in the United States, with strong concentrations in Pennsylvania, Ohio, and California. They have a vigorous international mission program that claims some 1,100 congregations with 300,000 members abroad.

The Fellowship of Grace Brethren Churches describes itself as "churches that work together to love and honor Jesus Christ by seeking God, proclaiming the word of God, reaching the lost, planting churches, developing leaders, and nurturing relationships." The strong evangelical emphasis of the fellowship has helped to propel its growth in recent years and also made it attractive occasionally to Mennonites and members of other Brethren groups.[17]

In the early 1990s, about thirty congregations with less than 10 percent of the national membership formed the Conservative Grace Brethren Church Association. The conservative group gelled because of differences related to local church autonomy and trine immersion baptism. Counting about forty-five congregations, the Conservative Grace Brethren are located primarily in Ohio and Pennsylvania.

THE OLD GERMAN BAPTIST BRETHREN

A number of smaller groups and independent congregations also fill out the Brethren landscape. The largest of these is the Old German Baptist Brethren, who count some fifty congregations and nearly 6,000 members. This is the Old Order group that divided from the German Baptist Brethren in 1881 to preserve some of the older, traditional Brethren practices.[18]

The Old German Baptist Brethren set out to vindicate the "old paths" and the "ancient order" of the church. Rejecting evangelistic innovations and other adaptations, they sought to retain the simpler practices of the early nineteenth century. The Old Order Brethren have experienced a great deal of change since the 1880s, but through it all they have sustained remarkable unity. In fact, unity is a precondition for remaining *Brethren*, as they understand the term. Buttressing their order with a strong Annual Meeting and a close-knit fellowship, they have maintained ancient practices that other Brethren abandoned long ago.

Numbering about 4,000 when they formed in 1881, today the Old German Baptist Brethren count some 6,000 adult members in sixteen states from Pennsylvania to California. The largest concentrations are in Ohio, Indiana, California, and Virginia. Together, these four states account for 65 percent of their members. In the last half of the twentieth century, slow but steady growth has increased their number by over 50 percent.[19]

The Old Order German Baptist Brethren are organized into congregations called church districts, with clear geographic boundaries. Members must join the district where they live. Typically, each district has one meetinghouse, and its name refers to natural surroundings (Sugar Grove) or a water source used for baptizing (Cedar Creek, Beaver Dam, Spruce Run).

Worship is staggered among neighboring districts, typically every other Sunday. Off Sundays provide an opportunity to worship with kindred Brethren in a neighboring district. Visiting ministers are often invited to preach. After singing the final hymn, visiting Brethren spend the afternoon eating lunch and fellowshipping with members of the host congregation. Sundays become a dynamic gathering of the spiritual family, brothers and sisters uniting for a season of worship and fellowship.

The Old German Baptist Brethren continue to wear plain clothing, and most of the men wear the traditional Brethren beard. They own automobiles, use electricity, and are involved in business as well as agriculture. They have preserved many historic Brethren practices and rituals. Several small groups and independent congregations have broken off from the Old German Baptist Brethren. Two small groups use horse-drawn transportation: the Old Order German Baptists and the Old Brethren German Baptists.

THE DUNKARD BRETHREN

The Dunkard Brethren, with about 1,000 members, left the Church of the Brethren in 1926 because they felt the larger body was "drifting away from apostolic standards and settling back into the world." The conservatives were especially concerned that the parent body was replacing plain dress with popular styles, to serve and witness better in the world.[20] The Dunkard Brethren continue to emphasize the importance of plain dress in their own witness to the world. They describe themselves as "Bible believing, conservative, and family oriented." A number of independent congregations and small groups have broken off from the Dunkard Brethren.

In addition, we find in the Brethren orbit a number of other groups that use the Brethren name or observe Brethren practices. These are identified in the listing of groups in section C of the Resources.

THE BRETHREN IN CHRIST

This group emerged about 1780 in Eastern Pennsylvania and blended together features from both the Mennonite-Anabaptist tradition and the Brethren-Pietist lineage.[21] First known as River Brethren, many of the originators were from Mennonite backgrounds, but they were heavily influenced by contacts with the Brethren. From the Mennonites, they brought discipleship, nonresistance, nonconformity, and practices such as the holy kiss, nonswearing of oaths, and patterns of church discipline. From the Brethren, they borrowed trine immersion baptism, the Love Feast, wearing of the beard, the election of church officials, and the role of deacon visits to individual families for self-examination in preparation for the Love Feast.

In the early twentieth century, the Brethren in Christ were also influenced by the Wesleyan holiness movement. Today they claim a threefold lineage: Anabaptism, Pietism, and Wesleyanism.

Around 1862, the River Brethren changed their name to Brethren in Christ. Prior to the name change, two offshoot groups emerged in about

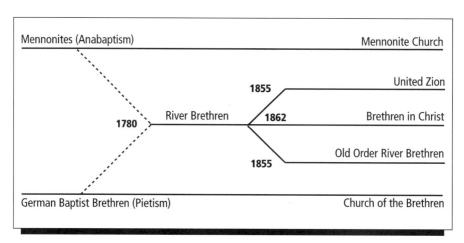

FIGURE 6.5 Formation of Brethren in Christ Groups in the United States

Brethren in Christ members converse at their Annual Conference. Photo by Ron Ross

1855 and continue today: the Old Order River Brethren and the United Zion Church.[22] The Old Order River Brethren drive automobiles, but members wear plain clothing and the men wear beards, which leads to easy confusion with the Amish. This group carries the Old Order torch within the Brethren in Christ heritage. The United Zion Churches have less than 1,000 members and are located in eastern Pennsylvania.

The Brethren in Christ are headquartered in Grantham, Pennsylvania, and today number about 20,000 members in 196 congregations. Their primary strongholds are in Pennsylvania, Ohio, Florida, and California. They also have congregations in Canada. Messiah College at Grantham, founded by the Brethren in Christ in 1909, continues to relate to the church with a covenant agreement. The official publication of the church is the *Visitor*. For many years, the Brethren in Christ have supported the service ministries of the Mennonite Central Committee and have participated in gatherings of the Mennonite World Conference.

The Brethren in Christ have embarked on a major church-planting effort to increase the number of "healthy congregations in partnership to impact the world for Jesus Christ" to 325 congregations by 2010. To shape their identity and mission, the denomination has developed ten core values.[23] These include experiencing God's love and grace, believing the Bible, worshiping God, following Jesus, belonging to the community of faith, witnessing to the world, serving compassionately, pursuing peace, living simply, and relying on God. In broad strokes, these values embody the essential beliefs of the Brethren in Christ.

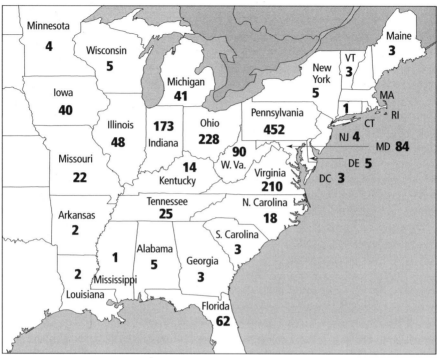

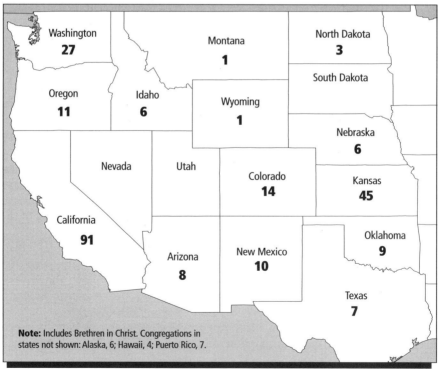

Minnesota 4

Wisconsin 5

Michigan 41

Maine 3

VT 3

New York 5

MA 1

RI

CT

Iowa 40

Illinois 48

Indiana 173

Ohio 228

Pennsylvania 452

NJ 4

MD 84

Missouri 22

Kentucky 14

W. Va. 90

Virginia 210

DE 5

DC 3

Arkansas 2

Tennessee 25

N. Carolina 18

S. Carolina 3

Louisiana 2

Mississippi 1

Alabama 5

Georgia 3

Florida 62

Washington 27

Montana 1

North Dakota 3

South Dakota

Oregon 11

Idaho 6

Wyoming 1

Nebraska 6

Nevada

Utah

Colorado 14

Kansas 45

California 91

Arizona 8

New Mexico 10

Oklahoma 9

Texas 7

Note: Includes Brethren in Christ. Congregations in states not shown: Alaska, 6; Hawaii, 4; Puerto Rico, 7.

FIGURE 6.6 Distribution of Brethren Congregations in the United States

The churches within the broader Brethren tribe blend together the legacies of both Anabaptism and Pietism. Those that are faithful to their Pietist heritage emphasize the importance of a loving spirit in personal and church relationships. This theme cultivates a corporate ethos where the spirit of truth takes precedence over the literal letter of doctrine and where the compassion of Jesus supersedes denominational dogma. Through their many and varied ministries, Brethren churches of every stripe seek to give a witness to the gospel, "For the glory of God and our neighbor's good."[24]

Chapter 7

THE HUTTERITES

Whoever follows Christ must give up
acquiring things and holding property.
—*Peter Riedemann, 1540*

HUTTERITE BRANCHES

The Hutterites are organized into three major groups, the Dariusleut, Lehrerleut, and Schmiedeleut.[1] All three groups have colonies in both the United States and Canada. About one-fourth of the Hutterites (119 colonies) live in the United States, primarily in South Dakota and Montana, and the remaining three-fourths (309 colonies) reside in Canada. The Hutterite population of adults and children in the United States numbers about 13,000. The Bruderhof Communities, a separate Anabaptist communal group that has had various relationships with the Hutterites, is also included in this chapter. The Bruderhof has six communities and a population of children and adults of some 2,000.[2]

The three branches of Hutterites—Schmiedeleut, Dariusleut, and Lehrerleut—share many common beliefs, but they have separate leaders and function as independent groups. Members of the three leuts (branches) rarely intermarry. Though there is much diversity within each group, the Lehrerleut tend to be the most traditional. The Schmiedeleut, on the other hand, are the most progressive in their use of technology and interaction with the outside world. Two affiliations within the Schmiedeleut emerged in the 1990s from a rather contentious division.

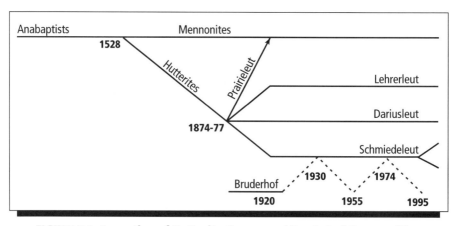

FIGURE 7.1 Formation of Hutterite Groups and Bruderhof Communities

The Hutterites are fast becoming diverse in their approach to community living, their use of technology, and their interaction with the outside world. There are many variations in dress and practice within and between the different leuts, making generalizations difficult and hazardous. For example, some colonies permit bicycles and others do not; some allow radios but most do not. One Hutterite described the differences this way: "The Lehrerleut are one kind of Hutterite, the Dariusleut another, the Schmiedeleut another—yet all three groups share a basic grounding and a raft of common traditions and influences." To an outsider, everything may look the same, but beneath the surface, "there is a great deal of variety and many different trends are underway, even among the more conservative colonies."[3] At the risk of sweeping important differences aside, we profile some of the more common patterns of Hutterite life.

In the early 1990s, a painful division within the Schmiedeleut resulted in two Schmiedeleut branches known as the Gibb and Oiler groups. The division reflected some trends that had begun years before. The more progressive Oiler faction at one time had been affiliated with the Bruderhof Communities. Today there are about sixty Schmiedeleut Oiler colonies; most are in Canada but ten are based in the United States. They are nicknamed Oilers because communal funds at one time were supposedly invested in oil. Their formal name is the Schmiedeleut Conference of the Hutterian Brethren.

Most of the Schmiedeleut colonies in the United States align themselves with the Gibb group, named for attorney Donald Gibb, who provided legal advice during the division. The Gibb group calls itself the Schmiedeleut Committee Group and has colonies in both the United States and Canada. This division within the Schmiedeleut has been difficult and complicated. Even within some colonies, members are divided. Some of the members of a Gibb colony, for example, may personally align themselves with the Oilers, and vise versa. Other members remain somewhat neutral despite the affiliation of their particular colony.

HUTTERITE LIFE

The oldest communal group in North America, the Hutterites have enjoyed remarkable growth in the twentieth century. In the United States and Canada, the three immigrant colonies of the 1870s have multiplied to

TABLE 7.1
Colonies, Membership, Population of Hutterites and Bruderhof Communities

HUTTERITE BODY	CONGREGATIONS		MEMBERSHIP		POPULATION	
	N	%	N	%	N	%
Schmiedeleut	67	53.6	3,685	52.0	8,291	53.0
Lehrerleut	33	26.4	1,485	21.0	3,341	21.4
Dariusleut	19	15.2	780	11.0	1,755	11.3
Bruderhof	6	4.8	1,140	16.0	2,236	14.3
TOTAL	125	100.0	7,090	100.0	15,623	100.0

Hutterite colonies use state-of-the-art equipment to farm thousands of acres.
Photo by Ivan Glick

nearly 430 colonies, with some ninety souls each. Anti-German sentiments inflamed by the patriotic fervor of World War I spurred Hutterite leaders to close their colonies in the United States and head for Canada in 1917. Within one year, fifteen colonies were established across the border. The rapid exodus to Canada in 1918 left only one surviving colony in South Dakota. Some years later, as the fires of patriotism waned, many of the old colony sites in South Dakota were repossessed by new colonies—giving the Hutterites a permanent base in both countries by midcentury.

Unlike other Anabaptist groups, the Hutterites live in colonies segregated from the larger society. Many colonies farm thousands of acres that seem to stretch forever beneath generous prairie skies. Colony buildings, clustered like a small village, are often invisible from major highways. Although outside consultants and suppliers visit on a regular basis, each colony is physically cloistered from the outside world. The business operations are linked to the economy of the region, but residential segregation insulates colonists from daily interaction with outsiders.

Nearby colonies often help each other with special projects that require extra labor, and they join for weddings and funerals. But the world of the local colony is *the* world of the typical Hutterite. In the words of one Hutterite, "We have our own little country." Without television and other mass media, life revolves around the cares of a hundred kindred souls.

Every fifteen to twenty years, depending on local conditions, colonies divide as they outgrow their facilities. The colony lives as an extended family, eating meals together in a common dining hall and sharing laundry facilities. Each family has an apartment with a coffee area, living room, bathroom, and bedrooms. Three or four apartments adjoin each other in long barrack-like houses encircling the dining facilities and church building in the hub of the colony. The typical family has five or six children. Youth attend school through the eighth grade and are usually baptized into the Hutterite faith between the ages of eighteen and twenty-five.

The Hutterites speak Hutterisch, originally a German dialect from southern Austria and northern Italy; in school they also learn English. They study an archaic form of High German typically used in their sermons. Their Hutterisch dialect is peppered with many words from the countries of their European sojourn.[4] The dialect enables them to converse directly, as it were, with their religious ancestors, who are much closer to them in spirit than their English neighbors, who speak the idiom of an unregenerate world. Language, thus, helps to mark the boundaries between sacred and secular, pious and profane.

Although Hutterites reject many worldly values, they have no scruples about tapping worldly technology to boost farm productivity. Colonies vary in their mix of agricultural enterprises. A typical colony might have 100 cows, 1,000 hogs, 50,000 turkeys, and farm some 5,000 to 10,000 acres of land. Colony-owned trucks and vans haul supplies, products, and people. Huge tractors pull a full array of modern equipment across vast stretches of colony land. Large trailer trucks haul grain and feed to nearby mills. In

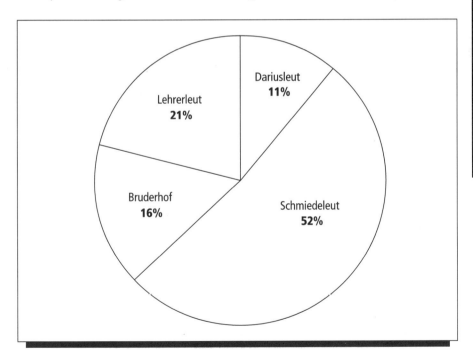

FIGURE 7.2 Adult Membership of Hutterite Colonies and Bruderhof Communities in the United States

recent years many colonies have established sizeable industries related to wood, metal, stainless steel, feed, and other manufacturing operations that sell products outside the colony. This trend toward nonagricultural industries will likely accelerate in the future.

Computers track management records and control equipment for farming and business operations.[5] Each colony also has large shops that specialize in woodworking, plumbing, electrical, and mechanical expertise to support the colony operations. New buildings are constructed, equipped, and repaired by colony members themselves. Most colony kitchens are fully automated, with electric ovens, mixers, and freezers. Although tradition dictates many religious and social norms, the Hutterites widely embrace modern technology for farming and household operations.

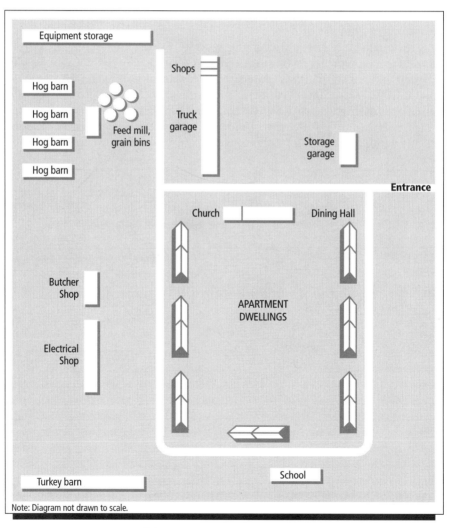

FIGURE 7.3 Spatial Arrangement of a Typical Hutterite Colony

COMMUNITY OF GOODS

Hutterite life balances on a tripod of socioreligious values: sharing goods in a community of faith, surrendering self-will for communal harmony, and separating from an evil world. The abolition of private property is the hallmark of Hutterite culture and distinguishes them from other Anabaptist groups. In Hutterite eyes, private property symbolizes greed and vanity and leads to many other expressions of evil. An early Hutterite writer even called private property a "murderous" and "noxious weed," and charged that greed, "one of the worst sins, . . . belongs together with fornication and all other impurity."[6]

Sharing material goods is seen as the highest and most obedient form of Christian love. In the words of a Hutterite writer, "Christ taught that the greatest commandment is to love God above everything else and your neighbor as yourself. In order to fulfill this highest command of love, we pattern our life according to the first apostolic church of Acts."[7] Living in community is motivated by the example of the early church as described in Acts (2:44-45): "All who believed were together and had all things in common; they would sell their possessions and goods and distribute the proceeds to all, as any had need."

Apart from a few personal things—clothes, knickknacks, dishes, books—individual Hutterites have no real property. Everyone works without pay. Some colonies provide a monthly allowance of $2 to $10 for personal effects, but others do not. Allowances are sometimes accumulated several months to buy a special treasure, such as a pair of binoculars. In some colonies, parents receive $20 per child to buy Christmas gifts for the children. About once a year, individuals receive an allotment of clothing from the colony manager. A family may have a few personal belongings and some furniture, but the larger household items are owned by the colony. At baptism, members relinquish any claim to colony property. Those who leave colony life may take only the clothes they are wearing and a few personal items when they make their exit to the larger world.

The colony, organized as a legal corporation, buys and sells products on the public market and with other colonies, often dealing with large quantities. The corporation pays taxes and owns title to the land and equipment. Colonies are somewhat self-sufficient, having their own gardens, orchards, poultry, and cattle, as well as shoemakers, tailors, and electricians. Nevertheless, they must purchase many supplies and much equipment from outside distributors. Bartering of furniture, toys, vegetables, clothing, and antiques sometimes occurs within colonies, between colonies, and between colonists and outsiders. Other colonies forbid bartering because it encourages personal gain and runs counter to traditional Hutterite teaching.

Community of goods, taught by the Hutterites long before Karl Marx was born, is not easy to preserve in a world that considers private property an inalienable human right. One Hutterite writer says, "Life in community is a daily battle" against selfishness and jealousy.[8] A Hutterite leader once noted that two obstacles block the path to Christian community: "self-will"

Two Hutterite boys in front of their colony home. Photo by Ivan Glick

and "worldly possessions." In many respects, Hutterites seek to convert self-will to sweet surrender and selfishness to joyful sharing.

As Andreas Ehrenpreis wrote in 1650, "All believers must be led to joyful submissiveness. It is in this submission that we break with the Devil and our self-will. . . . Nobody belongs to himself."[9] The call to surrender brings a yieldedness, a surrender of self for the welfare of the community. This surrender of self extends beyond a mystical purging of vanity; it must translate into a daily sharing of material goods. By blending together personal surrender and communal sharing, sinful humans are able to enter the ark (the boat) of the Lord.

SEPARATION FROM THE WORLD

The Hutterites experienced extensive persecution in Europe before they came to the United States in the 1870s. The large Hutterian history book, *The Chronicle*, lists 2,173 martyrs who "laid down their lives for the Master and the Church."[10] The stories of martyrdom, recorded in German, remain alive in Hutterite memory today. Anecdotes, sermons, and publications reiterate the stories of suffering that shape the Hutterian view of the world. The stinging persecution chiseled into the Hutterite mind a deep and lasting suspicion of the world.

The call to separation from the world is buttressed with religious language and biblical teaching. Hutterites note that "the world hated" Jesus (John 15:18) and that the Scriptures say "the whole world lies in wickedness" (cf. 1 John 5:19).[11] Suffering became the mark of true Christian discipleship, a sure sign that one is walking in the footsteps of the Savior.

Viewing the Hutterite colony as an ark in troubled waters is a prominent metaphor in Hutterite life. The image of the ark underscores the sharp lines of separation, for as one Hutterite preacher noted, "You are either in the ark or out of it."[12]

Hutterite conflicts with civil authorities in the twentieth century have flared up over land use, taxes, education, military service, and Social Security.[13] The discord is often fueled by the rapid growth of Hutterite colonies. When new colonies form, they frequently disturb the social life of rural communities. Several colonies in the same area, each with 8,000 acres of land, can dramatically impact land prices, school systems, and local consumer markets. Hence, Hutterites sometimes face protests from citizen groups and business organizations when they prepare to plant new colonies. In some cases, the antagonism has escalated into arson or vandalism.[14]

Government attempts to expand public education have also pricked Hutterite convictions. Believing that the education of their offspring is essential to preserving their way of life, Hutterites have refused to bus their children to consolidated schools filled with secular ideas, teachers, and peers.

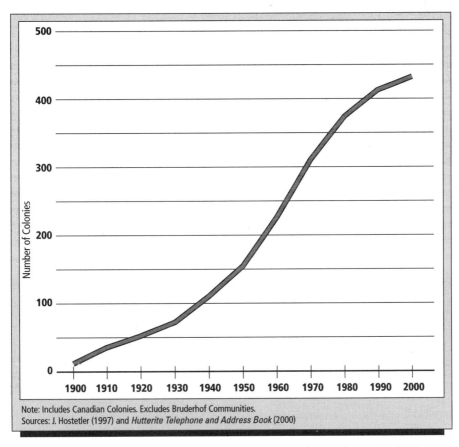

Note: Includes Canadian Colonies. Excludes Bruderhof Communities.
Sources: J. Hostetler (1997) and *Hutterite Telephone and Address Book* (2000)

FIGURE 7.4 Growth of Hutterite Colonies in North America: 1900-2000

The typical compromise places a small public school on each colony.[15] The public school system provides a non-Hutterite teacher and supervises the curriculum in a one-room school on colony facilities. It is a workable arrangement for both parties. Public officials can select teachers and monitor curriculum. The Hutterites are pleased because their children can remain on the colony and are not exposed to worldly influences. Moreover, colony elders can monitor the school and urge the teacher to respect Hutterite values. Hutterites also operate their own German school, which often meets in the same classroom for an hour or so each day. The German school imparts distinctive Hutterite values and beliefs to the young.

The Hutterites pay a "deemed income tax," estimated by dividing colony income by the number of adults, taking appropriate deductions, and then paying an average tax for each member. The colonies do not participate in Social Security, which they consider unnecessary for a group that cares for the welfare and retirement of its own members. However, like other citizens they do pay income, school, real estate, and sales taxes.[16]

The Hutterite strategy for separation is rather simple: establish colonies in isolated rural areas beyond the reach of urban vice. By controlling the use of vehicles and monitoring who enters and leaves the colony, Hutterites are able to regulate interaction with outsiders. A member traveling outside a colony is often accompanied by another member, providing a mobile system of social control. Non-Hutterites often visit colonies to conduct business, and some Hutterite leaders participate in agricultural organizations. Several colonies are involved in social service projects in their local communities. A colony in Minnesota, for example, sends volunteers to assist in a homeless

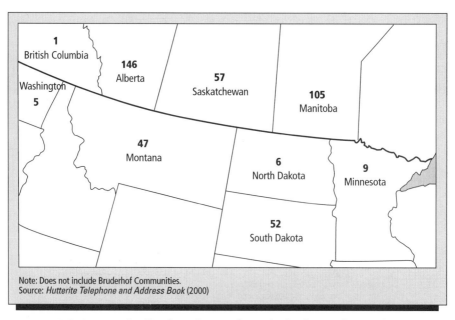

Note: Does not include Bruderhof Communities.
Source: *Hutterite Telephone and Address Book* (2000)

FIGURE 7.5 Distribution of Hutterite Colonies in North America

A Hutterite kindergarten teacher and her pupils. Photo by Jan Gleysteen

shelter. All things considered, however, contact with outsiders is limited.

Separation from the world is also maintained with taboos on television and other forms of mass media. "TV brings destruction," said a Hutterite teacher, "and Hollywood is the sewer pipe of the world." Despite the traditional taboos, some progressive colonies have televisions in their schools to watch educational videos and satellite broadcasts. Radios are also appearing in some colonies. Colonists may read farm magazines or newspapers, but the average member does not read *Time* or *Newsweek* on a regular basis. Worldly entertainment outside the colony is forbidden.

By regulating exposure to outside media, the colony limits contact with outsiders and filters contaminating influences, hoping to keep the ark secure and the world at bay. Easy access to ungodly values, Hutterites believe, would undermine their entire way of life. They do tap the services of outside professionals: veterinarians, medical doctors, dentists, lawyers, bankers, and accountants. Most babies, for example, are born in hospitals. Nevertheless, in all of these contacts, Hutterites are mindful that the ark of their salvation floats upon a sea of wickedness in which they could quickly drown.

BRUDERHOF COMMUNITIES

The Bruderhof Communities, formerly called The Society of Brothers, are a communal group that was inspired by the life and witness of the early Anabaptists, but it does not have direct ties to sixteenth-century Anabaptism. The Bruderhof Communities were inspired by the zeal of the original Hutterites, and over the years they have had various affiliations with Hutterite groups. The Bruderhof began in 1920 when German theologian Eberhard Arnold, his wife, Emmy, and a circle of fellow seekers left middle-class Berlin to found the first Bruderhof Community. After expulsion from Nazi Germany in 1937, members moved to England, next to Paraguay, and then to the United States in the 1950s. Today there are six Bruderhofs in the United States, two in England, and one in Australia. The adult membership in the United States is approaching 1,200.[17]

Arnold visited Hutterite colonies in the United States in 1930-31, and the two groups began to affiliate until the relationship dissolved in 1955. In 1974 their relationship with the Schmiedeleut branch of the Hutterites was restored, only to dissipate again in the mid 1990s. Unlike the traditional Hutterites whose primary source of growth comes from their own children, the Bruderhof Communities have attracted members from a variety of backgrounds, including some from the Church of the Brethren as well as Mennonite groups. They have received well-educated members with professional careers from both Anabaptist and non-Anabaptist backgrounds.

The Bruderhof is a twentieth-century attempt to practice radical Christianity in a communal context. Christ's spirit and teachings in the Sermon on the Mount and the practice of the early church recorded in Acts 2 and 4 form the foundation of Bruderhof life. Members have no private property but pool their money, possessions, and talents for the common good; in turn, the community provides and cares for each member. The community meets daily for meals, prayer, fellowship, singing, and decision making. The Bruderhof Communities have deliberately sought to reach beyond themselves in ministries of social justice that witness against capital punishment, abortion, and participation in war.

Unlike the traditional Hutterites, the Bruderhof Communities are not involved in large-scale farming. For over fifty years, a major portion of their income has come from manufacturing and selling sturdy toys and playground equipment for children. Community Playthings produces and distributes high-quality play equipment around the world. An additional source of income is Rifton Equipment, which produces and sells products for the care and development of people with disabilities and other special needs. Plough Publishing House, now at Farmington, Pennsylvania, is another mode of witness to the larger society. It publishes and sells books on radical discipleship and on social themes related to nonviolence, justice, family life, and living in Christian community.

RADICAL OBEDIENCE

These communal Anabaptist groups have undertaken a remarkable social experiment that, in the case of the Hutterites, has endured across the centuries. In their eyes, however, communalism is not an interesting social experiment but a sincere attempt to practice Christian teachings that point to eternal life. They believe their earthly efforts create in their colonies a foretaste of life eternal, what the Hutterites call "the vestibule of heaven." Outsiders may scoff at such notions and argue that, when measured by contemporary standards of happiness, colony life looks more like the anteroom of hell.

In traditional Hutterite colonies, the individual is permitted little self-expression through dress, music, art, and dance. The Bruderhof Communities, by contrast, welcome musical and artistic expression; yet they allow little room in communal life for critical thinking, sincere doubt, or ambiguity. Members are admonished to obey their elders. Private time and personal rights, so cherished in the larger culture, disappear in communal life. There is no private property, no personal bank account, no private meal, no personal phone to the outside world, little private space, and little personal time in colony life.

All the trappings of individualism—personal rights, belongings, and prerogatives—are stripped from the individual. No worries about career goals, vacation plans, or consumer fashions flourish here where the community cares for all. Choice, that symbol of freedom that tops contemporary virtues, is severely constrained in colony life.

The community reigns supreme over the individual in traditional Hutterite colonies. Male leaders assign occupational roles. The community determines work schedules, allots clothing, assigns apartments, allocates wine, sanctions marriages, requires attendance at church, shames deviants, and excommunicates the wayward. Based on its interpretation of Scripture and tradition, the community determines what is virtue and vice, what is sacred and profane, even in the realm of personal behavior. In this patriarchal society, "community" means that male leaders determine the rules and speak on behalf of heaven.

Hutterite colonies may not be heaven on earth, but they do raise interesting questions about contemporary life. The stable patterns of community life curtail the growing list of maladies so prevalent in postmodern societies: alienation, homelessness, drug addiction, divorce, domestic abuse, depression, and loneliness. Private property is abolished, but everyone is fed, clothed, and housed, with more than ample means. Children are disciplined, but they are very welcomed and loved. Private space is limited, but loneliness is rare in the midst of colony life. These communal Anabaptists have made radical commitments that have endured over the centuries, commitments that shake contemporary assumptions about the sources of happiness and human well-being.

Chapter 8

THE MENNONITES

> Those who are born of God . . . show mercy and love, . . .
> comfort the afflicted, assist the needy, clothe the naked, feed the hungry,
> and do not turn their face from the poor.
> —*Menno Simons, 1552*

MENNONITE BODIES

Mennonites are the largest and most complicated tribe in the Anabaptist World. Differences in polity, ethnicity, history, and convictions have produced some thirty different groups in the United States, making it difficult to piece the puzzle together in an easy fashion. Two different ethnic and cultural streams from Europe muddle the story as well. Many Mennonites have a Swiss-German lineage, and others come from Dutch-Russian stock. Sizeable segments of Asian, Latino, and African-American members add to the colorful ethnic mosaic. Mennonites in Los Angeles and Philadelphia, for example, worship in nearly a dozen languages.

In addition, Mennonites migrated to North America in several waves, beginning in 1683 and continuing into the mid-twentieth century. The different immigrant groups exude distinctive cultural, historical, and theological flavors. All these factors create a complicated but fascinating story.[1]

In general, the Mennonite landscape divides into three parts that largely follow the traditional, transitional, and transformational contours outlined in chapter 4. On the traditional end are the Old Order Mennonite groups that preserve and perpetuate many older Mennonite customs. At the other end of the spectrum are transformer Mennonites who have largely assimilated into American society in dress, technology, and lifestyle. In the middle of the road are numerous conservative Mennonite groups that drive cars and engage in mission activity but still wear plain clothing and embrace conservative standards of doctrine and practice. These conservative groups account for about one-fifth of the Mennonite membership in the United States.

Three major bodies constitute the transformational churches—the Mennonite Church (92,000), the General Conference Mennonite Church (27,000), and the Mennonite Brethren (23,000). The likely integration of the Mennonite Church and the General Conference Mennonite Church into the Mennonite Church USA in 2002 will create a new national body that may number nearly 120,000.[2] Over the past five years, integration has dominated the agenda of these two groups. If the proposed merger is completed, the largest Mennonite body will be the Mennonite Church USA, followed by the Mennonite Brethren.

Table 8.1 Congregations, Membership, and Population of Mennonite Groups

MENNONITE BODY	CONGREGATIONS		MEMBERSHIP		POPULATION	
	N	%	N	%	N	%
Mennonite Church[a]	871	40.3	92,157	39.8	124,412	34.5
General Conference Mennonite Church[b]	179	8.3	27,507	11.9	37,134	10.3
Mennonite Brethren	168	7.8	22,777	9.8	30,723	8.5
Church of God in Christ Mennonite	111	5.1	12,152	5.2	23,088	6.4
Apostolic Christian Church of America[c]	79	3.7	12,113	5.2	23,015	6.4
Conservative Mennonite Conference	97	4.5	9,649	4.2	18,333	5.1
Old Order Groffdale Conference (Horse)	42	1.9	7,096	3.1	15,966	4.4
Old Order Weaverland Conference (Car)	33	1.5	5,574	2.4	12,517	3.5
Evangelical Mennonite Church	31	1.4	5,307	2.3	7,164	2.0
Other Smaller Groups[d]	552	25.5	37,364	16.1	67,897	18.8
Totals	2,163	100.0	231,696	100.0	360,249	100.0

[a] Includes 140 congregations and 13,490 members in congregations (2/3 of total) with a dual affiliation with the General Conference and eleven congregations and 396 members with other dual affiliations.

[b] Includes seventy congregations and 6,745 members with a dual affiliation with the Mennonite Church.

[c] The Apostolic Christian Church of America is not historically or organizationally related to Mennonite groups but is similar in many ways to conservative Mennonite groups.

[d] Includes small Old Order groups, small conferences, independent groups and congregations.

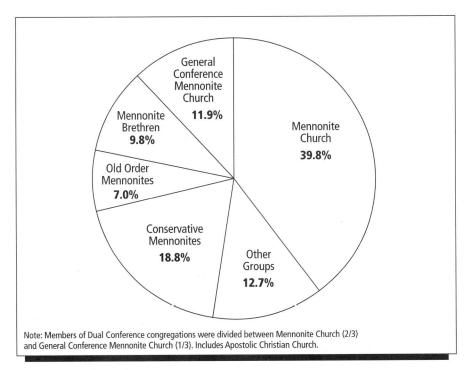

Note: Members of Dual Conference congregations were divided between Mennonite Church (2/3) and General Conference Mennonite Church (1/3). Includes Apostolic Christian Church.

FIGURE 8.1 Adult Membership of Mennonite Groups

As noted earlier, Mennonites began arriving in the Americas in 1683. Throughout the eighteenth century, Swiss and South-German Mennonites settled in Pennsylvania and soon became known as outstanding farmers. They gradually moved westward and southward with the frontier, settling in Maryland, Virginia, Ohio, Indiana, Illinois, and other states as well as in Upper Canada (now Ontario). Mennonites with Dutch-Russian roots came in later waves of immigration in the 1870s; they settled in the Great Plains, the far West, and Canada. After 1870 the Mennonite World became more diverse with the arrival of new immigrants and the emergence of Old Order groups in various parts of the country. Even greater division developed in the twentieth century as subgroups splintered off in various directions.[3]

SIMILAR GROUPS

Two groups—the Apostolic Christian Church of America and Charity Christian Fellowship—have been included with the Mennonite tribe, although they do not have direct organic ties to Mennonite groups. They consider themselves Anabaptist churches and are quite similar in many ways to some of the conservative Mennonite churches.

The Apostolic Christian Church of America began in the 1830s in Switzerland, under the leadership of Samuel Froehlich, who was influenced by the Anabaptists and their teaching. Members of the church came to Lewis County, New York, in 1847 and attracted Amish there as well as in other states. Sometimes nicknamed "the New Amish," the group was never directly related to the Mennonite Church. Yet their congregations share many Anabaptist principles and characteristics found in conservative Mennonite churches.

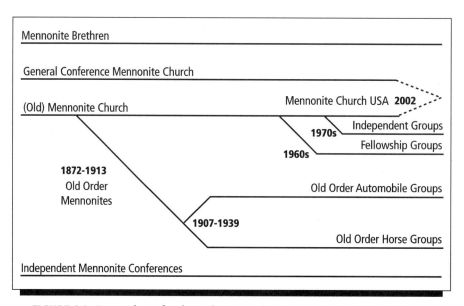

FIGURE 8.2 Formation of Selected Mennonite Groups in the United States

Mennonites from many backgrounds cooperate through Mennonite Disaster Service to aid victims of floods, tornadoes, and hurricanes. Photo by Sam Resendez

The Apostolic Church is largely rural and views higher education with extreme caution. Although there is not a prescribed dress code, members wear modest, plain clothing, and women wear a flowing prayer veiling. Baptism by immersion and a cappella singing is typical. Meetinghouses are fairly plain. Some seventy Apostolic congregations are scattered in twenty states, with a strong concentration in Illinois, Indiana, and Ohio. Apostolic Christian World Relief is the church's major mission agency. In some areas, congregations support projects sponsored by the Mennonite Central Committee and Mennonite Disaster Service.[4]

Charity Christian Fellowship also embraces many Anabaptist practices and bears similarities to some conservative Mennonite groups. Thus we have placed it under the Mennonite canopy. This network of churches formed in 1982 in eastern Pennsylvania. Coming from various plain Anabaptist groups, the fellowship resembles conservative Mennonite groups in many ways. Somewhat fundamentalist in doctrine and charismatic in expression, members practice foot washing, the holy kiss, and modest dress; the women wear a prayer covering. Congregations actively engage in evangelism and sometimes seek to win converts from other Anabaptist groups. Many families are deeply involved in home schooling. Many of their pastors have Amish and Mennonite surnames. Congregational names do not mention Mennonite or charity but often have names like "Victory," "Grace," "Remnant," "Harmony," and "Maranatha." The network name comes from a parent congregation, Charity Christian Fellowship, in eastern Pennsylvania.

OLD ORDER MENNONITES

As shown in figure 8.3, nearly 68 percent of Mennonites are found in transformational churches, 25 percent in transitional, and about 7 percent in Old Order groups. Most of the Old Orders emerged between 1872 and 1913.[5] These more traditional Mennonites reject higher education, restrict the use of technology, and practice a rural, separatist lifestyle. Old Order Mennonites can be sorted into two types: those who drive automobiles and those who do not. The two largest Old Order groups are the car-driving Weaverland Conference and the so-called Team Mennonites of the Groffdale Conference, who use horse-and-buggy transportation. Most of the Old Order groups have Swiss-German roots in the Mennonite Church.

After the Civil War, tradition-minded Mennonites began resisting certain innovations that were creeping into the Mennonite Church. Those who clung to traditional ways, the Old Ordnung, eventually were called Old Orders. The Old Order movement budded in the 1860s, near Elkhart, Indiana. A formal separation occurred in Indiana and Ohio in 1872 and spread to Ontario in 1889; to Lancaster, Pennsylvania, in 1893; and to the Harrisonburg, Virginia, area by 1901. Although never formally organized, the Old Order Movement was well entrenched by the turn of the century. What were the social forces and spiritual concerns that propelled this movement of renewal and resistance?

Mennonites with a more conservative bent protested the acceptance of Sunday school, evening services, revival meetings, the use of English in worship, the foreign missions movement, higher education, and other aspects of American culture that were beginning to influence Mennonite life. For Old Orders, the sources of spiritual renewal were found in a reaffirmation of older ways, not in innovative practices from the outside. More than mere reactionaries, they sought to renew the church by reclaiming and revitalizing the patterns of the past.

In all of these squabbles, tradition-minded Mennonites were not quarreling with basic Mennonite beliefs, nor simply resisting a tide of innovation that might sweep them into the mainstream. Instead, they were trying to preserve what they considered the core of Mennonite life. But beneath the rhetoric of public debate, there was a clash of different moral orders. Old Order sentiments ran against the progressive embrace of individualism, rationalization, and specialization that accompanied the rising tide of industrialization. Old Orders feared that all of these changes would eventually erode the spiritual and social foundations of their redemptive community.

Today the Groffdale Conference of Team Mennonites claims about 7,000 members in forty-two congregations in Pennsylvania and eight other states. Fairly rural and traditional, the Groffdale Mennonites speak Pennsylvania German, drive horse-drawn carriages, and use steel-wheeled tractors in their fields. In recent years, they have started a number of new settlements and expanded into Missouri, New York, and Wisconsin. Similar groups are found in Virginia as well as in Ontario.

The more progressive Old Order Weaverland Conference, based in

Pennsylvania, has some 5,500 members in thirty-four congregations in six states. For many years this group was known as the Black Bumper Mennonites because they required members to paint the chrome on their cars black. In the words of one member, "We wanted to have a separated car." Today ministers are still expected to have black bumpers, but the requirement has been relaxed for members; yet most of them drive dark-colored cars. The Weaverland Conference has adopted English in their worship services, but they do not have Sunday school. Their plain meetinghouses do not have pulpits but are equipped with electricity and sound systems. They use modern technology and many are involved in business. In some respects, they are similar to the Old German Baptist Brethren.

In addition to the sizeable Groffdale and Weaverland affiliations, about a dozen smaller Old Order groups fill the traditional enclaves of the Mennonite World. Some of these small splinter groups have fewer than fifty members. Combining all Old Order Mennonite groups yields some 17,000 members, who constitute about 7 percent of the total Mennonite membership.

CONSERVATIVE MENNONITE GROUPS

Some twenty different groups occupy the middle ground between Old Order communities and the transformational Mennonites.[6] These numerous and often-overlooked transitional groups constitute about 25 percent of the Mennonite community. Some of these conservative churches are organized into regional conference affiliations, others fellowship with similar congre-

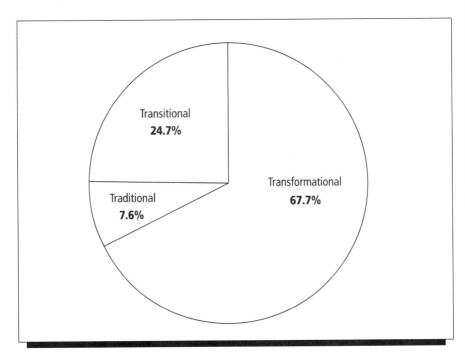

FIGURE 8.3 Distribution of Mennonite Membership by Type of Assimilation

gations, and still others are largely independent. No central structure holds the various groups together. However, several publishing operations and mission agencies serve many of the congregations that have conservative inclinations.[7]

The groups in this middle ground come primarily from three directions. Some come from Amish or Old Order Mennonite backgrounds. They have drifted from their Old Order moorings but not enough to float directly into more progressive Mennonite bodies. Other groups were part of larger transformational Mennonite groups, but assimilated more slowly, and for various reasons dropped their formal affiliation. Still other conservative Mennonite groups are rooted in older regional conferences that never joined the nationwide General Conference of the Mennonite Church when it organized in 1898.

These middle-of-the-road transitional groups are largely rural, but many of the members no longer farm. Although they dress plain, ordain lay ministers, and emphasize separation from the world, they have few restrictions on technology for agriculture or business purposes. Homes are equipped with telephones and electricity. Virtually all of the transitional Mennonite groups forbid television and a few have a taboo on radios and/or computers.

The conservative Mennonites are conservers. More rural in orientation than their more assimilated cousins, these transitional Mennonites are less likely to pursue higher education, practice professional occupations, participate in politics, and advocate for social justice. They embody the historic Mennonite standards of nonresistance and separation from the world and will excommunicate members who do not uphold conservative standards. These groups strongly detest divorce. They also oppose the ordination of women, which is acceptable among some transformational Mennonite groups.

A directory of conservative Mennonite groups describes their worldview: "In these days of moral decadence and spiritual apostasy, it is our desire to uphold the doctrines of the Scriptures as historically taught by the Mennonite Church."[8] The directory mentions seven specific practices: separation from the world, nonresistance, separation of church and state, permanence of marriage, the Christian women's veiling, moral purity, and leadership by men. Many of the conservative groups think that mainstream Mennonite groups have drifted away from historic Mennonite practices by abandoning plain dress, participating in politics, discarding the women's prayer veiling, permitting members to divorce and remarry, and ordaining women to ministry. These issues, along with a more conservative and rural lifestyle, set the transitional groups apart from the transformational congregations.

The two largest conservative Mennonite groups are the Church of God in Christ (Holdeman) Mennonites (12,000) and the Conservative Mennonite Conference (9,600), which formed in 1910 from Amish roots. This latter group operates the Rosedale Bible Institute in Ohio and sponsors a vigorous missions program. The Holdeman Mennonites originated in

1859 and have 111 congregations in thirty-three states. They practice shunning and advocate the doctrine of a one-true church.

Other conservative Mennonite groups and conferences emerged in the mid to late twentieth century as a reaction to progressive changes underway in the larger Mennonite Church. A number of so-called Fellowship Churches emerged in the 1950s and 1960s. The Eastern Per...sylvania Mennonite Church separated from the Lancaster Mennonite Conference in 1969. One researcher has identified five types of conservative Mennonite groups that embody various degrees of conservative thinking and practice.[9] Throughout the last quarter of the twentieth century, several small conferences and clusters of conservative Mennonite congregations formed. Many of these are briefly described in the group profiles in section C of the Resources.

THE MENNONITE CHURCH

The Mennonite Church is the largest (92,000) and most prominent of the transformational Mennonite groups. Earlier it was called the Old Mennonite Church. If both denominations agree, this body will merge with the General Conference Mennonite Church in 2002 to form a new national body—the Mennonite Church USA. The historical ethos of the Mennonite Church was largely shaped by Swiss-German immigrants of the eighteenth century. Today, however, the Mennonite Church is sprinkled with many strains of ethnicity, race, nationality, and language.

Organized into seventeen regional conferences, the Mennonite Church

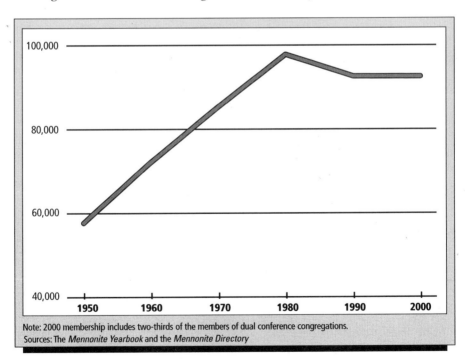

Note: 2000 membership includes two-thirds of the members of dual conference congregations.
Sources: The *Mennonite Yearbook* and the *Mennonite Directory*

FIGURE 8.4 Mennonite Church Membership in the United States, 1950-2000

A communion service at the West Union (Iowa) Mennonite congregation.
Photo by Wayne Gehman

formed as a national body in 1898 when some of the regional conferences began working together in a General Conference. The denomination meets every other year in a General Assembly that attracts leaders, congregational representatives, and members. It operates five national program boards for education, missions, publications, congregational ministries, and mutual aid.

For many years the *Gospel Herald* was the church's official publication. In February 1998, *The Mennonite* became the weekly publication for both the Mennonite Church and the General Conference Mennonite Church, in anticipation of their probable merger in 2002. The organizational structure of the church is in flux because the anticipated merger will combine many of the present administrative units into components of the new denomination, The Mennonite Church USA.

Diversity is rife across the Mennonite Church. Some congregations located in more rural areas embody a traditional outlook in doctrine, practice, and lifestyle. Other congregations in Chicago, Los Angeles, and New York as well as many suburban areas are quite cosmopolitan. Some follow informal patterns of worship, others are more formal, still others have a charismatic flavor. The ethnic mix is growing as well. White people of European ancestry still dominate the formal church structures, but growing numbers of Latinos, African-Americans, Asians, and others from diverse ethnic, social, and religious backgrounds participate in the life of the church. Recognized bodies within the Mennonite Church represent African-Americans, Hispanics, Hmong, Lao, Native Americans, and Vietnamese.

Many Mennonites have served in international mission or service programs with the Mennonite Central Committee or a mission board and bring to the life of the church a broad international perspective. Despite the departure of some congregations in the face of the merger, a wide spectrum of theological views remains afloat across the church.

THE GENERAL CONFERENCE MENNONITE CHURCH

The General Conference Mennonite Church began in 1860 in West Point, Iowa, when representatives from various Mennonite groups, interested in cooperation, formed a new body. Members of some of the congregations that later joined the General Conference were German-speaking immigrants who had come to the United States and Canada from Poland, Prussia, and Russia in the 1870s. Many of these new immigrants settled in the Midwest and central states, especially in Kansas. Compared with the Mennonite Church, the General Conference Mennonite Church had a stronger Dutch-Russian flavor, flourished more in the central states, and granted more autonomy to local congregations. The General Conference Mennonite Church had some strains of German and Swiss ethnicity as well, giving it a more multicultural flavor than the Mennonite Church.

The General Conference Mennonites never developed distinctive patterns of plain clothing like many regions of the Mennonite Church did in the early part of the twentieth century. In some regions of the country, the General Conference Church assimilated into American culture more quickly than the Mennonite Church did in the first half of the twentieth century. Yet in some communities, General Conference Mennonites spoke a German dialect or maintained a German worship service longer. Nevertheless, the Mennonite Church, at least before World War II, was generally more sepa-

This original adobe house in Kansas was built by Russian Mennonite immigrants in the 1870s. Photo by Jan Gleysteen

ratist in many of its long-established communities.

The General Conference Mennonite Church coordinates its churchwide work through commissions on home ministries, overseas ministries, and education. Meetings of its General Conference provide direction and authority for the work of the commissions. *The Mennonite,* which began publication in 1885, was the official periodical of the denomination until 1998, when the name was reused for a magazine representing the Mennonite Church as well. If the merger plans are adopted, the General Conference Mennonite Church's administrative structures and programs will merge with the Mennonite Church's to form the new Mennonite Church USA in 2002.

TRANSFORMATION AND MERGER

In the 1990s, discussions about the possible merger of the Mennonite Church and the General Conference Mennonite Church have sparked lively and animated debate across both bodies. After informal discussions for many years, a formal action to initiate the integration process was taken in 1995. The two denominations have somewhat different theological traditions and forms of polity. Historically, the Mennonite Church placed considerable authority in its regional conferences. On the other hand, the General Conference Mennonite Church has had a stronger congregational form of governance. This created some fears on both sides. Some Mennonite Church members worried that already-dwindling conference authority would actually vanish. General Conference Mennonite Church representatives feared that their congregations might lose some of their independence. What would membership in the new body mean?

The move toward integration built on a long history of cooperation between the two bodies that among other cooperative ventures included joint seminary education, calling pastors across denominational lines, co-publishing Sunday school materials, producing hymnals together, holding joint assemblies (in 1983, 1989, 1995, 1999), and more recently forming a single executive board, a new Constituency Leaders Council, and developing proposals for new program agencies and other united work. In sum, the integration process involved joining the ministries of the major bodies by creating new things, not merely patching together old ones, in a task of transformation. Thus delegates at Nashville in July 2001 will decide whether to merge their polity, after having already merged much of their ministry activities over many years.

Leaders faced a challenge in trying to merge program boards and educational institutions, all with their own traditions. Moreover, heated debates over the issue of homosexuality complicated the merger plans. A few Mennonite Church regional conferences had placed on probation or severed ties with congregations that had accepted noncelibate gay and lesbian members. This issue stretched the sensitivities of some congregations, regional conferences, and the denomination as a whole; it also fueled discussions about the meaning and implications of membership in the new Mennonite Church USA.

Several clusters of congregations in various parts of the country withdrew from the Mennonite Church to protest the merger and/or because they felt the new church would become too lenient on issues such as homosexuality and other matters of biblical interpretation. Other congregations were awaiting the outcome of the merger to decide their long-term affiliation.[10] Many of the dissenting congregations also felt that firm standards of biblical authority were dissolving in the larger body.

The organizational restructuring, the blending of two denominational cultures, and the debate over homosexuality stirred passions, making the years from 1998 through 2000 both interesting and tumultuous. Meanwhile, some congregations and conferences, eager for merger, began dual affiliations before the proposed denominational marriage. By the end of 2000, some 210 congregations with over 20,000 members had essentially blessed the merger by initiating dual affiliations. Resistance to integration was stronger in some of the older and traditional communities, whereas younger and smaller regional conferences often welcomed the merger.

THE MENNONITE BRETHREN

Some 10,000 Mennonite and Hutterite immigrants came to the United States in the 1870s and 1880s from Prussia and Russia. Russian Mennonite farmers, along with other Russian immigrants, brought a hardy and productive variety of red winter wheat with them to the prairie states. Despite the agricultural interests they shared, numerous historical, geographical, cultural, and theological differences hindered the new immigrants from easily blending with the earlier Amish and Mennonite immigrants of Swiss-German stock.

Some of the Prussian and Russian Mennonites joined the General Conference Mennonite Church, and others formed the Mennonite Brethren Church. Members of this latter group trace their roots back to renewal movements among Mennonites in Russia, beginning in 1860. Influenced by Pietism, the Mennonite Brethren emphasize a heartfelt devotion, and practice immersion baptism; hence, they have some theological affinities with Baptist groups, Brethren groups, and the Brethren in Christ.

In the 1880s and 1890s, Mennonite Brethren immigrants established about a dozen congregations in Kansas, Nebraska, and the Dakotas. Eventually the Mennonite Brethren moved westward to California, a stronghold of the denomination today, claiming more than a third (62) of their congregations. Many Mennonite Brethren also settled in Canada; by the end of the twentieth century, over half of their membership was north of the border.

Today the Mennonite Brethren have 168 congregations organized into five regional districts in the central and western areas of the United States. The Mennonite Brethren have not participated in the merger discussions leading to the proposed Mennonite Church USA, though they do participate in Mennonite Central Committee and support many other inter-Mennonite projects. They also have had occasional conversations with the Brethren in

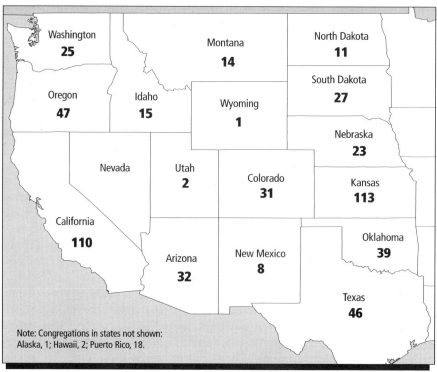

Note: Congregations in states not shown:
Alaska, 1; Hawaii, 2; Puerto Rico, 18.

FIGURE 8.5 Distribution of Mennonite Congregations in the United States

Christ, with whom they share many common theological threads: baptism by immersion, an emphasis on personal piety, and a strong evangelical orientation.

THE MENNONITE WORLD

Many cultural, regional, ethnic, and theological differences crisscross the American Mennonite landscape today. With some thirty distinct subgroups, it is hazardous to make generalizations about the Mennonite family. However, we can draw one conclusion without qualification: the big issue on the agenda of the transformational groups in recent years has been the proposed birth of the Mennonite Church USA. Endless discussions over new administrative alignments, organizational changes, polity issues, and membership—especially as it relates to homosexual members—have trumped all the other issues in the Mennonite mind, at least in the two largest bodies.

The animated debates about integration and homosexuality have rarely touched the conservative enclaves of Mennonite life, where talk of merger stirred little interest. But in the mainstream bodies, all eyes focused on Nashville, Tennessee, where the two partners would convene in July 2001 to make a decision about their marriage, which was slated to officially begin in February 2002.

In any event, by the turn of the twenty-first-century, the descendants of Menno could be found singing in Chinese, English, German, Spanish, and Vietnamese. Some were driving horse-drawn carriages on back roads while others drove their Corollas on metropolitan freeways. Some wore plain dress and others sported designer clothing. Some manufactured computer software and others prohibited the use of it. Nevertheless, in their congregations, varied cultural settings, and occupational pursuits, Mennonites sought to proclaim the kingdom of God in word and deed.

Chapter 9

EDUCATION, SERVICE, AND MISSION

> Restore in us the virtues of mercy, justice, truth, and peace
> So that . . . the kingdom of God may be manifest.
> —*Leonor de Méndez, Anabaptist leader in Guatemala City*[1]

THE WORLD OF INSTITUTIONS

Beyond the pale of congregations and denominational structures, a host of programs, projects, and organizations dot the landscape of the Anabaptist World. Some of these bodies are official agencies operated by a church, but many of them are privately administered. Lay members, acting without the formal endorsement of a denominational body, have frequently formed organizations—camps, schools, publishing companies, service agencies, or mission boards—to serve Anabaptist groups.

Of all four tribes, the Mennonites have been the most aggressive institution builders. Hutterite life revolves around their colonies, which meet virtually all of their social and economic needs. Thus there is little need for institution building beyond the orbit of the colony. The Amish, with their strong local and congregational commitments, have always been cautious about building large, national organizations. In recent years more informal committees and networks have emerged among the Amish, to provide aid for fire, storm, liability, and medical costs. However, apart from a National Steering Committee to coordinate legal and political issues with government officials, the Amish have not created bureaucratic structures.

The Brethren have built national agencies and organizations, but not on the scale of the Mennonites. In some cases, following their ecumenical spirit, the Brethren have initiated organizations but have then "given them away" to the larger Christian community. Heifer Project International, begun by members of the Church of the Brethren in 1942 to provide heifers for needy farmers abroad, exemplifies this pattern. Now an independent development agency and no longer operated by the Brethren, Heifer Project International provides animals and agricultural assistance around the globe.

The Mennonites, on the other hand, have been more aggressive at building, keeping, and growing their institutions. However, within the Mennonite world, there are differences. Mennonites of Swiss-German backgrounds have been some of the more active institution builders. Institution-building tendencies reflect a combination of theological, social, and ethnic impulses as well as a group's position in the larger social world. Building institutions is one means of constructing and perpetuating a group's religious and/or ethnic identity.

In other words, churches that are more comfortable with the larger culture will more likely use the institutions of the broader society than build their own. Moreover, the groups that were influenced by Pietism—Mennonite Brethren, Church of the Brethren, and Brethren in Christ—have also been less likely to build institutions. The propensity to build institutions arises at the intersection of, among other factors, ethnicity, theological views, and the extent of a group's assimilation into the larger culture.[2]

EDUCATION

Patterns of education vary considerably across the Anabaptist World by tribe and affiliation.[3] The Amish operate about 1,200 elementary schools for some 32,000 children.[4] Most of these are one- or two-room facilities. For the most part, teachers are Amish. Strictly speaking, these are private rather than parochial schools because a group of parents serve as trustees. In several states some Amish pupils attend rural public schools. Amish youth attended public schools until the mid-twentieth century, when the massive consolidation of public schools stirred protest and gave rise to hundreds of Amish schools. In 1972 the United States Supreme Court in the case of

TABLE 9.1
Colleges and Universities Affiliated with Brethren and Mennonite Groups

DENOMINATION	LOCATION	ENROLLMENT
Brethren Church		
Ashland University	Ashland, Ohio	1,950
Brethren in Christ		
Messiah College	Grantham, Pennsylvania	2,800
Church of the Brethren		
Bridgewater College	Bridgewater, Virginia	1,200
Elizabethtown College	Elizabethtown, Pennsylvania	1,630
Juniata College	Huntingdon, Pennsylvania	1,200
Manchester College	North Manchester, Indiana	1,130
McPherson College	McPherson, Kansas	400
University of La Verne	La Verne, California	1,350
Grace Brethren		
Grace College	Winona Lake, Indiana	840
General Conference Mennonite Church		
Bethel College	North Newton, Kansas	450
Bluffton College	Bluffton, Ohio	990
Mennonite Brethren		
Fresno Pacific University	Fresno, California	780
Tabor	Hillsboro, Kansas	510
Mennonite Church		
Eastern Mennonite University	Harrisonburg, Virginia	880
Goshen College	Goshen, Indiana	1,020
Hesston College	Hesston, Kansas	400

Note: No colleges or universities are affiliated with Amish or Hutterite bodies. Enrollment refers to approximate undergraduate (full-time-equivalent) students.

Wisconsin versus Yoder granted that Amish and Old Order Mennonite youth could leave school at the age of fourteen to work in apprentice programs at home. In the last quarter of the twentieth century, the rapid rise of private schools among the Amish has played an important role in preserving their identity and cultural distinctives.

Unlike the Amish and Mennonites, Brethren groups established virtually no elementary and secondary schools. The Dunkard Brethren and Old German Baptist Brethren have founded a few elementary schools, but even many of the Old German Baptist Brethren send their youth to public high schools. Six colleges and universities established by Church of the Brethren groups maintain various levels of affiliation with the church.[5] The student bodies of some of the colleges have more than 10 percent Brethren students, but others claim less than 5 percent.

In 1962 colleges associated with the Church of the Brethren organized Brethren Colleges Abroad, an international educational program. Brethren Colleges Abroad is based at Manchester College (Indiana) and serves numerous Anabaptist-related colleges as well as other colleges. It places students in a variety of international educational settings. The Brethren Church established Ashland University, but the institution is no longer closely affiliated with the church. In 1909 the Brethren in Christ started Messiah Missionary and Training School, which eventually became the four-year Messiah College, located near Harrisburg, Pennsylvania.

The Mennonites have been much more aggressive in establishing schools at all levels, but most of their elementary schools and high schools were begun by Mennonites with Swiss-German roots. Mennonite elementary and secondary schools grew rapidly after World War II in response to the consolidation of public schools and various changes in them.

The Old Order Mennonites have about 275 schools for some 8,000 pupils.[6] Many of these are one- or two-room facilities. In addition, various conservative Mennonite groups operate about 275 elementary and/or high schools. Some of these have several rooms and are often larger than the one-room schools. Transformational Mennonite groups operate about eighty-five elementary and/or high schools. Twenty-five of these provide high school education; some are sizeable operations with several hundred pupils.[7] Most of the schools serve both Mennonite and non-Mennonite students. Seven colleges and universities are affiliated with Mennonite bodies, as shown in Table 9.1. At these institutions of higher education, the organizational patterns of church affiliation vary, and the percentage of Mennonite students ranges from 15 percent to 65 percent.

Setting the Hutterites aside for a moment, an interesting pattern emerges among the other three tribes. The Amish have a broad network of elementary schools but no high schools or colleges. The Brethren established numerous colleges but few elementary or high schools. In the Mennonite World, educational institutions were established at all three levels, but elementary and high school initiatives have been driven primarily by parents associated with the Mennonite Church.

Bethel College (Kansas) is one of the many colleges established by Anabaptist groups. Photo courtesy Bethel College

Whether or not a group establishes schools at the elementary and high school level may reflect national trends as well as the extent of a group's assimilation. In the eastern states, mainstream Brethren groups had assimilated earlier in the twentieth century than many of the Mennonite groups. By 1940, many Brethren were already serving as teachers and principals in public schools and had little interest in forming private schools. In comparison, their Mennonite neighbors were more separated from society at that point and more ready to establish church-related schools.

At the postsecondary level, a variety of seminaries, Bible colleges, and Bible institutes serve Anabaptist constituents. Bethany Theological Seminary and Ashland Theological Seminary serve the Church of the Brethren and the Brethren Church, respectively. Grace Theological Seminary relates to the Fellowship of Grace Brethren churches. In the Mennonite orbit, Associated Mennonite Biblical Seminary (Indiana), Eastern Mennonite Seminary (Virginia), and Mennonite Brethren Biblical Seminary (California) are the major providers of theological training.

The Brethren in Christ do not operate a seminary. Hutterites, Amish, and most transitional Mennonite groups ordain lay ministers and do not encourage formal theological training. Many of the conservative Mennonite groups have short-term Bible schools and institutes to provide training for lay leaders.[8]

MISSION AND SERVICE AGENCIES

Anabaptists in the United States have organized a host of mission and service agencies. The bulk of these were started in the twentieth century. Although Brethren and Mennonite groups began international mission efforts in the last decades of the nineteenth century, mission activity accelerated rapidly after 1920. Patterns of mission and service vary enormously among the groups. The Hutterites are least likely to engage in mission and service projects beyond their colonies. Nevertheless, some members of progressive Schmiedeleut colonies serve in soup kitchens, homeless shelters, and similar projects in their communities.[9]

Traditional groups such as the Old Order Amish and Old Order Mennonites rarely engage in evangelism. But many of them do participate in service projects organized by the Mennonite Central Committee and Mennonite Disaster Service. More progressive Amish groups like the Beachy Amish and Amish Mennonite Churches have organized various mission and outreach programs. Many conservative Mennonite churches also are involved in missions. Various Amish Mennonite, Beachy Amish, and conservative Mennonite Churches have founded about 120 congregations in numerous countries: Australia, Belize, Costa Rica, Dominican Republic, El Salvador, Guatemala, Kenya, Mexico, Nigeria, Paraguay, and the Philippines, among others.[10]

Young people from the True Life Church of the Brethren, Dominican Republic, take their witness to an outlying town. Photo by David Radcliff

Amish Mennonite and conservative Mennonite churches support some of the larger mission and service agencies. Amish-Mennonite Aid, established in 1955, has eighty-three missionaries in four countries. The Mission Interests Committee, formed in 1952, has about thirty-five missionaries serving in northwest Ontario, Belgium, and Ireland. Christian Aid Ministries, an international relief program based in Berlin, Ohio, and Ephrata, Pennsylvania, distributes food, clothing, medicine, and literature in various countries, in the wake of war and natural disasters. Haiti Missions enjoys support from various Amish and conservative Mennonite groups. Christian Mission Charities of Indiana distributes material aid, literature, and Bibles especially in countries of Eastern Europe. Specific groups of Amish Mennonite and conservative Mennonite groups operate numerous smaller mission and service agencies.[11]

Virtually all of the transformational groups have active mission programs: the Mennonite Brethren, the General Conference Mennonite Church, and the Mennonite Church. These bodies have sent hundreds of representatives to serve in many countries around the world. The Mennonite Brethren have developed an innovative international mission agency, with representatives from several countries serving in various regions of the globe.

In addition, regional mission boards in Pennsylvania, Oregon, and Virginia are also active in domestic and international mission projects. The largest of these is Eastern Mennonite Missions, with some 360 representatives in thirty-nine countries. With an annual budget of about $7 million, this agency has established some twenty-one overseas conferences with a membership of about 215,000 members. Many of the Mennonite mission programs combine mission and service ministries in one way or another.

When it comes to service agencies in the Anabaptist World, the Mennonite Central Committee is the largest of them all. About twenty-two Anabaptist groups support the service ministries of the Mennonite Central Committee (MCC) that began in 1920. Based in Akron, Pennsylvania, this inter-Mennonite and Brethren in Christ agency typically has about 900 volunteers in some fifty countries around the world. With an annual budget of $70 million, the Mennonite Central Committee engages in refugee work, material aid, international development, and a variety of peace and justice concerns involving mediation, anti-racism, and women's concerns.

A surprisingly broad band of Amish, Mennonites, and Brethren in Christ participate in Disaster Relief Auctions by volunteering time and contributing funds. Mennonite Disaster Service, a major national agency supported by many Mennonite groups, responds to tornadoes, floods, hurricanes, and earthquakes in North and Central America.

Among Brethren groups, the Fellowship of Grace Brethren churches has been active in international mission efforts. Outside the United States, some 1,100 congregations with 300,000 members bear witness to the efforts of Grace Brethren evangelism.[12] The Brethren Church and the Brethren in Christ also have developed substantial mission efforts. Traditional and transitional Brethren groups such as the Old German Baptist Brethren, the Old

Order River Brethren, and the Dunkard Brethren have been less evangelistic and more likely to support relief and disaster projects.

In the late nineteenth century and early twentieth century, the Church of the Brethren mounted a vigorous foreign mission enterprise. The Global Mission Partnerships ministry of the Church of the Brethren coordinates a variety of mission and service programs, including Brethren Volunteer Service and overseas mission efforts in several countries. Rather than developing separate Brethren churches in overseas settings, the Church of the Brethren has typically supported ecumenical mission partnerships and the development of indigenous churches. For example, in Nigeria about 135,000 members of the EYN Church have a fraternal relationship with the Church of the Brethren.[13]

The Brethren Service Center in New Windsor, Maryland, coordinates a variety of service activities. These include disaster and relief auctions, Brethren Disaster Service, and many forms of material aid distributed through Church World Service and other ecumenical church agencies.

Extensive and far-reaching mission and service activities pulsate throughout Anabaptist communities. These groups have invested millions of dollars, thousands of volunteer hours, and hundreds of professional staff to give witness to the gospel of Jesus Christ and offer a cup of cold water in the name of Christ to refugees, victims, and other needy people around the globe.

SERVICE ORGANIZATIONS

A broad array of parachurch agencies has developed among the transformational groups as shown in table 9.2. These specialized agencies, typically not operated by an official church body, serve members as well as the general public. As shown in table 9.2, the Anabaptist World in the United States includes eighty-five camps and retreat centers. The bulk of these emerged after 1950. They are found primarily among transformational

TABLE 9.2
Service Organizations Related to Amish, Mennonite, and Brethren Groups

TYPE OF ORGANIZATION		N
Camps and Retreat Centers		86
Retirement Homes and Centers		105
Thrift Shops		42
Ten Thousand Villages Outlets		120
Health-Related Agencies		54
Health Organizations	8	
Child Welfare	6	
Disabilities	16	
Hospitals	9	
Mental Health Agencies	15	
Information/Interpretative Centers		13
Historical Libraries/Archives		50

Sources: *Mennonite Directory* (2000), *Church of the Brethren Yearbook* (2000), *Amish Mennonite Directory* (2000), and *Mennonite Church Information* (2000).

groups that have adopted suburban and urban lifestyles. These retreat centers support a variety of camping and outdoor programs for members and others.

Anabaptist groups have organized more than a hundred retirement centers. Although a few of these began in the early twentieth century, retirement centers have flourished in recent years as Anabaptists have moved from farm to suburb and city. Among the traditional Hutterites and Amish, as well as among many of the transitional groups, the elderly retire with children or extended family. Smaller families, nonfarm occupations, and geographic mobility have encouraged the rapid rise and expansion of retirement centers.

Both the Mennonite Central Committee and the Brethren Service Center support programs selling handcrafted goods produced by overseas artisans to encourage international development. Many Brethren congregations support SERRV, initially established by the Brethren, which distributes handcrafted products in the United States. Ten Thousand Villages, developed by the Mennonite Central Committee, has some 120 retail outlets across the United States. In addition, forty-two thrift or "reuzit" shops collect, repair, and sell used clothing and furniture to promote the stewardship of these items.

Some Mennonites pioneered in the development of mental health programs as a result of their experience working as conscientious objectors in hospitals during World War II. Today fifty-five health-related agencies across the Anabaptist landscape are involved in medical care, child welfare, mental health, and disability, to name but a few of the health-related activities. The Church of the Brethren has established a National Association of Brethren Caregivers that provides a variety of caregiving services through congregational deacons, chaplains, disability programs, and whole-person health ministries.

A variety of mutual aid programs span the four tribes. These range from spontaneous material aid in local congregations to formal insurance programs for auto, fire, life, and health. Dozens of regional and small denominational aid programs stretch across the Mennonite World. At the national level, Mennonite Mutual Aid and the Mutual Aid Association of the Church of the Brethren provide a variety of aid and insurance programs.

Numerous historical libraries, information centers, and interpretative programs have also flourished in recent years. Some of these are tied to colleges and others to denominational offices, but many of them depend on the efforts of volunteers. The Mennonites have been active in preserving historical materials, publishing historical studies, and interpreting their story to the larger public. The Amish and Hutterites have a keen interest in their history but have been hesitant to tell their story in a public fashion. In regions where Mennonite and Amish communities overlap, the Mennonites have often "interpreted" Amish life to tourists and other interested people. In the past two decades, the numerous projects undertaken by *The Brethren Encyclopedia* reflect a renewed commitment to historical studies among some Brethren groups.

PEACE AND JUSTICE PROGRAMS

The traditional and transitional Anabaptist groups typically emphasize a quiet nonresistance that rejects violence, participation in war, political involvements, and litigation. This approach stresses a willingness to suffer in the face of injustice. Such "defenselessness" was a trademark of many Anabaptist groups and continues to be the norm among the more traditional communities today.

Diverse understandings of peace and justice flourish among the transformational groups. For some Anabaptist bodies, an unapologetic commitment to active peacemaking is the signature of Anabaptist identity. Others worry that an overemphasis on peace and justice neglects spiritual issues and thwarts evangelistic efforts. Some of the groups that have been influenced by American Evangelicalism and Fundamentalism give little attention to peacemaking or at least see it as marginal to their theological identity.

Many Mennonite and Brethren bodies, however, give evidence of enduring commitments to various forms of peacemaking, sometimes involving political action. Both the Mennonites and the Brethren have a Washington Office to monitor national issues for member groups and to give an Anabaptist witness to federal programs on behalf of their officials and constituents. Peace and justice programs and academic majors have also been established at many Mennonite and Brethren colleges.

In the Church of the Brethren, a variety of programs reflect their historic commitments for peace and justice: a Global Women's Project, the On Earth Peace Assembly, the Brethren Peace Fellowship, and the Womaen's Caucus.[14] Many of the projects, global and domestic, of the Mennonite Central Committee involve peace and justice concerns. The Mennonite Church has a network of Peace Evangelists who seek to link peace with evangelism and promote a peacemaking lifestyle in many areas of life.

Mennonite Conciliation Service provides training and expertise in mediation and conflict transformation. Moreover, most of the Mennonite denominations have peace and justice commissions at national, regional, and/or local levels. Christian Peacemaker Teams is a cooperative effort of numerous Mennonite and Brethren groups to train peacemakers to engage in negotiations, nonviolent direct action, and human rights advocacy in international settings of conflict.

ANABAPTIST COOPERATION AND ECUMENICITY

Some Anabaptist bodies know little of each other, but others cooperate frequently on a variety of projects. Cooperation occurs within tribes as well as between them. Denominational history, theological identity, and degree of assimilation all play a role in encouraging or hindering cooperative ventures. In some regions Old Order Mennonites and Amish support the same private schools. A variety of publications, such as *Family Life, The Diary, The Blackboard Bulletin*, and *The Budget,* serve numerous Old Order groups. Because of their geographic location and commitment to colony life, the Hutterites have been less involved in cooperative ventures.

This broom maker in Bolivia is a micro-credit client of Mennonite Economic Development Associates (MEDA). With a small loan, she was able to hire employees and boost production fivefold to 250 brooms per week. MEDA Photo by Bob Kroeker

Amish groups assist each other through their National Steering Committee; some of them also support the relief and disaster projects of the Mennonite Central Committee and Mennonite Disaster Service. In many ways, Mennonite Central Committee is the grandparent of inter-Mennonite cooperation because in one way or another, about twenty-two groups participate under its umbrella. The collaborative efforts of the Mennonite Central Committee have also spawned more than a dozen other inter-Mennonite agencies.[15] Considerable informal cooperation also occurs among the many branches of conservative Mennonites who often read similar publications and support the same service and mission organizations.

The Mennonite Church and the Church of the Brethren cooperate on a variety of projects in addition to the Christian Peacemaker Teams mentioned above. In the 1970s, the Church of the Brethren and several Mennonite groups cooperated to produce the Foundation Series of Sunday school curriculum materials. In the 1990s, the Church of the Brethren, Brethren in Christ, General Conference Mennonite Church, and the Mennonite Church began producing Jubilee: God's Good News, a Sunday school curriculum series for children. In 1992 the joint publication of a hymnal by the Church of the Brethren, Mennonite Church, and General Conference Mennonite Church was a major cooperative landmark. *Hymnal: A Worship Book* has been widely adopted by Mennonite and Brethren Congregations.[16]

Mennonite and Brethren groups have frequently collaborated on peacemaking ventures, beginning as early as 1935, when the Historic Peace

Churches first convened. Mennonite and Brethren groups have supported a series of Believers Church Conferences as well as the current Believers Church Bible Commentary series. Individual members work together through the Mennonite and Brethren Marriage Encounter Program. Members of various Brethren and Mennonite groups also participate together in the Brethren-Mennonite Council for Lesbian and Gay Concerns.

Oftentimes cooperation between groups is easier when they are at a similar level of assimilation. For example, transformational Mennonites and Brethren may find it easier to cooperate with each other on some matters than with some of the Old Order groups within their own tribe. The patterns of cooperation often depend on the particular issue at hand. Cooperation on worship materials may be more difficult than partnerships related to historical projects or disaster service. In any event, a spirit of cooperation among numerous groups graces many of the education, mission, and service efforts of the Anabaptist witness both at home and abroad.

Chapter 10

ANABAPTIST WORLD
2000

Dare to become a global church.
—*Gilberto Flores, Hispanic Ministries Leader*[1]

THE GREAT TRANSFORMATION

The present turn-of-the-century texture of Anabaptist life in the United States reflects the social transformations that impacted the Anabaptist World in powerful ways throughout the twentieth century. Like other religious and ethnic communities, Anabaptist groups were profoundly changed by the social transformations in American society. By the end of the century, different responses to these changes by various Anabaptist communities produced a colorful fabric of Anabaptist diversity.

In 1900 many Anabaptist communities were quite sectarian, drawing sharp lines of distinction between themselves and the larger society. For the most part, they were rural churches ensconced in the social web of their local communities. The majority of families were farmers who saw little need for education. Patriarchy, separatism, and ruralism shaped the ethos of the Anabaptist World.

Certainly there were exceptions to these sweeping generalizations. Several groups had founded colleges and started mission endeavors by 1900, but the Anabaptist World of 1900 was largely white, Euro-centric, and rural. That is still the case for some Anabaptist communities in 2000, yet most of them have been profoundly changed by the social transformations of American society in the twentieth century. Even Old Order groups that at first glance appear to be dressed in eighteenth-century costumes have also been touched by the massive tide of social change.

The great transformation rippled across Anabaptist communities in several waves and along various dimensions. A few of the major waves can only be briefly noted here. Some Anabaptist groups accepted many changes in stride while others resisted them. Others resisted them initially and then eventually succumbed to the shifting social forces around them. A few of the Old Order communities successfully resisted new inventions such as the automobile, telephone, and television. Virtually all of the communities, some more than others, made discerning judgments about the changes, adapting some and rejecting others. In short, the twentieth century was a period of assimilation into the larger society for many Anabaptist communities, especially for the transformer groups.

The absorption of American ways involved both cultural values and social structures. There was an accelerated acculturation—a growing acceptance of core American values of individualism, progress, science, and civic responsibility. Many Anabaptist groups also became more involved in the social networks, organizations, and political structures of the larger society. Many began to think of themselves as American citizens rather than merely as members of religious groups outside the political mainstream. A Brethren minister actually became governor of Pennsylvania, for example, as early as 1914, much to the chagrin of many of his people.

For many Anabaptists, the great transformation meant climbing up the social ladder and stepping into the center of American culture. It was a story of rising social mobility and greater engagement in the cultural mainstream of American life. While all this is true, at the same time the traditional and some of the transitional Anabaptist communities staunchly resisted being swallowed up by the forces of progress. Many of the transformer groups also have rejected certain aspects of the broader cultural ethos such as violence, to name but one. Nevertheless, in occupation, education, lifestyle, and the use of technology, many members of transformer groups gradually adopted many mainstream values and practices. Some of the more salient dimensions of change are listed in table 10.1.

A variety of technological innovations that surfaced in American life in the early decades of the twentieth century stirred controversy in some Anabaptist communities; depending on the response, they either spurred assimilation or became symbols of resistance. Electricity, telephones, automobiles, and radios were some of the key inventions that accelerated assim-

TABLE 10.1 Dimensions of Transformation in Anabaptist Communities, 1900-2000

Technology	New forms of technology (car, airplane, television, Internet) changed community life and congregational patterns.
Occupations	A major shift from farm to factory, business, professional, and service roles.
Residence	Transition from rural areas to urban and suburban residence.
Mobility	Frequent change of residence and occupation; more travel.
Institutions	A proliferation of church-related organizations: mission boards, schools, publishing houses, retirement centers, and service agencies.
Education	The establishment of colleges and the acceptance of higher education.
Gender roles	New awareness and sensitivity to gender-bounded behavior in family and congregational life. The ordination of women, in some groups.
Pastoral training	The establishment of seminaries and professional theological training.
Ethnicity	New ethnic and racial groups involved in the life of churches.
Mission agencies	A rise of mission agencies with domestic and overseas programs.
Service agencies	The growth of service agencies addressing disasters, peace, social justice, refugee aid, and international development.
Family size	Shrinking extended families. More single people, divorces, and remarriages.
Tourism	The rise of tourism focused on traditional Anabaptist communities.
Political action	Growing involvement in political action, office holding, and voting.

Note: These changes have had the greatest impact among transformer groups. Some of the traditional and transitional groups have deliberately resisted them.

ilation or began to separate the more traditional Anabaptist communities from the broader society.

Institution-building initiatives—colleges, publishing houses, mission boards, service agencies, retirement centers, and camps—became a distinctive earmark of twentieth-century activity. These projects tended to drive a wedge between traditional groups and transformational ones, and they provided a new form of ethnic identity for the latter. In some groups, the establishment of colleges and later elementary and secondary schools was an important means of appropriating the Anabaptist tradition for the next generation. The transformer groups' involvement in institutions, especially in education, encouraged greater specialization in congregational life in the areas of pastoral leadership, music, and Christian education.

A massive occupational transformation caused many changes. After the Civil War, the broader society rapidly moved from an agricultural to an industrial society. However, many Anabaptist communities lagged behind, remaining agricultural for two or three generations longer. Some Anabaptists had left their plows before World War II, but for many of them the war disrupted rural life and opened new vistas through alternate service that led to higher education, new occupations, and urban residence. By the end of the twentieth century, the number of farmers in the transformer groups was low. Even within many of the traditional and transitional groups—though still rural based—the proportion of farmers had dropped below 50 percent.

The Civil Rights Movement of the 1960s and the Vietnam War protests stirred Anabaptist sensitivities for social justice and peacemaking. Involvement in both Civil Rights and Vietnam protests cultivated a growing commitment to activist forms of peacemaking and social justice, propelling some Anabaptists into the political arena in new ways. A renewed emphasis on radical Anabaptist discipleship led some into social justice ministries and activist forms of peacemaking.

Mission efforts at home and abroad were another important source of change in the life of local congregations. Mission personnel had to struggle with the interface of gospel-and-culture issues in ways that encouraged them to reflect and critique traditional practices. In the United States and overseas, new converts to the faith raised questions about the credibility of customs and traditions long taken for granted. The mission efforts increased the numbers, and also the diversity of Anabaptist communities. All these factors were catalysts of change among the transformer groups.

In the last quarter of the twentieth century, understandings of the role of women changed in many of the transformer congregations. Although patriarchal views of gender persisted among the traditional and transitional groups at the turn of the twenty-first century, some of the transformer groups were ordaining women as pastors. Women held major roles in many local congregations and in churchwide agencies. Nevertheless, the ordination of women remained a contentious issue within some of the transformer groups.

At the close of the twentieth century, global understandings of the church were emerging, prompted by economic globalization, growing overseas churches, Internet technology, and changing mission philosophies. For many groups, their mission efforts and congregational partners in other countries were creating a new understanding of the church as an international kingdom of God that transcended national boundaries.[2]

The social transformations of American society impacted different communities at different times and in different ways. The Church of the Brethren, for example, absorbed American cultural values more quickly than the Mennonite Church in the first half of the twentieth century. But after midcentury, the rate of assimilation increased in the Mennonite Church. By the end of the twentieth century, the two groups were quite similar in education, occupation, dress, lifestyle, and other indicators of acculturation. In the broader Anabaptist World, the technological transformation created a great divide between groups that were willing to go with the flow of progress and those resisting it, like the Old Orders. A digital divide emerged—a line between those who welcomed computers and modern media and those who resisted them. These contrasting responses added new streaks of diversity across the Anabaptist landscape.

GROWING DIVERSITY

In virtually every way the Anabaptist World in the United States has never been more diverse with regard to race, ethnicity, lifestyle, occupation, and wealth. The social transformations of the twentieth century created all forms of diversity in their wake. The social homogeneity of nineteenth-century Anabaptist communities evaporated, to the extent that it ever existed. To be sure, the Amish and Hutterites as well as traditional Brethren and Mennonite groups exhibit a monochrome culture that remains white and European. Nevertheless, many rainbow colors of race and ethnicity now grace many of the transformer groups.

Despite several hundred congregations whose language and culture have non-European roots, whites of European descent remain the dominant players in many churchwide boards and agencies. Indeed, in the mid-1990s, the Mennonite Central Committee began sponsoring an extensive project called Damascus Road to address racism in congregations and churchwide agencies. Nonetheless, people of various colors and ethnic roots were participating in new ways in the broader life of the church by the end of the twentieth century.

Discussions about homosexuality, which had surfaced in several churches during the last quarter of the century, came to the fore in the 1980s and 1990s, first in the Church of the Brethren and later in the Mennonite Church. The discussions rarely penetrated the enclaves of the traditional and transitional groups. Yet same-sex issues remained divisive and hotly contested among transformer groups at the beginning of the new century.

In terms of wealth and lifestyle, the Anabaptist World has never been more divided. The agricultural legacy developed values of hard work,

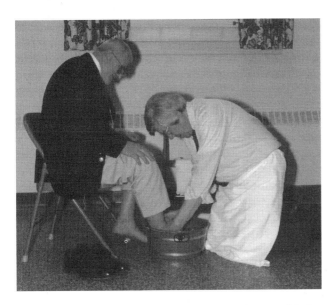

Feetwashing is a ritual of service in the Brethren Love Feast and in the communion service of many Mennonite congregations.
Photo by Daniel Rodriguez

integrity, and an entrepreneurial spirit that enabled many Anabaptists to do well in professional and business ventures in the last half of the twentieth century. The creation of wealth enabled an upward social mobility that produced an upper-middle class of Anabaptists. Others working as small farmers and day laborers in rural areas continued to have modest incomes that could only support a frugal lifestyle. Some congregations in urban areas also had members with modest incomes. Meanwhile, other members and congregations were serving in destitute areas ridden with poverty.

Patterns of congregational life display diversity as well. Some congregations meet in homes for worship; others have built and support large multifaceted facilities. Worship styles range from long somber services among the Old Order groups to charismatic praise services in others, from formal services to informal ones with worship bands and dramatic skits. The modes and means of worship reflect ancient customs as well as spontaneous creativity. Many different expressions of Anabaptist piety abound at the beginning of the twenty-first century. Some forms are quite traditional, communal, and somber. Others are loud, noisy, and expressive.

For some Anabaptists, piety consists of faithful adherence to tradition and custom. For others, true piety means mustering the courage to address social injustice. Still for others, outreach and evangelism are the marks of genuine faith. Those embracing a wholistic gospel contend that these are false choices because a genuine Christian faith entails all of them.

GROWTH

Membership in the Anabaptist World in the United States more than tripled during the twentieth century, rising from about 150,000 to nearly 540,000.[3] As noted earlier, groups can only grow by having and raising children in the faith or by attracting other converts. Several factors in the twentieth century dramatically changed the patterns of growth. The departure from farming reduced family size, reflecting the typical worldwide trends that accompany industrialization. In addition, the use of artificial means of birth control also shrank the size of families. In many transformer groups, a family of seven to eight children was typical in the 1920s and 1930s, but by the turn of the century many typical families had only two or three children.

The transformer groups with small families faced an additional growth-related challenge. Because of their assimilation into American society, many of their own children left the church for a multitude of reasons, many of which were noble. Consequently, transformer churches needed converts if they were to grow or even to maintain membership. In the course of the century, many of them developed strong mission and evangelism programs. Those with effective mission programs grew. The Grace Brethren, the Mennonite Brethren, and the Brethren in Christ exemplify groups that were able to grow through their evangelistic efforts.

Transformer churches that shied away from aggressive means of evangelism faced decline because of small families and the loss of some of their own children. The Church of the Brethren, for example, struggled with this dilemma in the last quarter of the twentieth century.

In general the growth trends reveal that most of the Old Order (traditional) communities are vigorous and growing because of large families and a strong retention rate. A few of the small sectarian groups are declining. Generally however, groups like the Old Order Amish are growing not

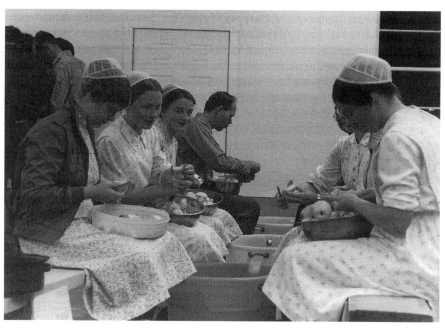

Young adults in a conservative Mennonite congregation cut apples for relief.
Photo by Kevin & Bethany Shank/Dogwood Ridge Photography

through evangelism but by biological reproduction and creating communities that attract their children. The rapid growth of the Amish—doubling every twenty years—is remarkable when compared with the slow growth of the transformers despite all their outreach efforts.

Many of the transitional groups also show small but stable growth. Despite some efforts at evangelism, the growth in these groups typically comes from their own children. The patterns of growth vary somewhat from group to group, especially among the transformer groups. Those with aggressive outreach programs show growth, and those with weak evangelistic efforts are, for the most part, in decline.

THE STRUGGLE FOR THE ANABAPTIST SOUL

The Anabaptist soul struggles with many choices, challenges, and challengers. Some members are attracted to fundamentalist approaches that clarify and define doctrines in ways that erase ambiguity and offer psychological security and certainty. Evangelical approaches that focus on soul saving to the exclusion of social justice and peacemaking also attract some members who assume that evangelism is the primary form of spiritual outreach. Charismatic appeals attract others who want a richer emotional experience and a greater sense of mystery.

The Anabaptist soul is also challenged by the cerebral types, the academics, who delight in analysis over action and favor reflection over emotion. Die-hard traditionalists, on the other hand, also challenge the legacy by arguing that true faith is found in faithful obedience to the dictates of tradition. At the other side of the Anabaptist camp, some individualists are willing to tolerate virtually anything because "everything is up to the individual," and the church, in their thinking, has no right to exercise moral discernment over individual behavior. Skeptics also challenge the tradition by suggesting that all is relative because the truth claims of a theological tradition, or the gospel for that matter, have lost their meaning and credibility in a postmodern world, where everything is up for grabs.

The realities of the broader religious marketplace also confront the heritage; some argue that congregations should comfort the afflicted rather than afflict the comfortable. Congregations, they claim, should address the real needs of real people and not try to perpetuate a particular theological tradition. Finally, freeloaders from within also threaten to dissolve the tradition because they tap and enjoy its benefits without committing time and resources to its renewal. All these forces in different ways confront and challenge the Anabaptist legacy and stretch it in many directions.

IDENTITY AND RENEWAL

At the end of the twentieth century, denominational loyalties and identities were in decline across America. Mobility, mass media, and a consumer mentality encouraged church shopping and a marketplace orientation to church involvement. Do tribal identities matter in a postmodern world? Must denominational identities be shed in a rapidly changing global society? Do theological labels hinder effective evangelism? Is a generic gospel the most effective and truthful reflection of the spirit of Christ?

In many ways, the gospel carries an inherent contradiction. On one hand, it lauds simple belief in Christ, love, compassion, and the fruits of the Spirit. Nevertheless, humans hunger for belonging, identity, social patterns, and habitual routines. Tribal and denominational identities provide important points of orientation beyond a generic-brand faith. The irony here is that even the supposedly generic-gospel churches, over time, develop their own patterns, customs, and identities. In short, *every* human appropriation of the gospel, under the surface, has its own set of human values, biases, interpretations, and perspectives.

Moreover, many believers have encountered the gospel and developed their religious convictions through the auspices of denominational agencies and organizations. Camps, schools, Sunday schools, publishing houses, and mission agencies are all vehicles of grace in one form or another, carrying and purveying the gospel story. Appeals to a generic "Jesus only" gospel are deceptively simple and often downright false because they are never neutral; they always bring a bias, albeit hidden, that shapes the reading of the gospel and the interpretation of Scripture.

Tribal traditions can easily become archaic customs that trap the human spirit, shirk social responsibility, and exclude others. Generic gospel approaches, however simple, soon falter over time without the benefit of stable tribal structures. Tribes, denominations, and theological traditions can certainly become stiff ethnic enclaves that foster exclusion and judgment. However, with rituals of renewal and self-criticism, a theological heritage can provide a vehicle for interpreting the gospel, a place to stand that provides perspective, identity, and belonging. And so it is with Anabaptism. It provides spiritual wisdom from the sages and saints that can be appropriated even in a postmodern setting. It is one of many places to stand among Christian traditions. But it *is* a place to stand, and a place to stand is a valuable resource among the shifting sands of relativism in a postmodern era.

Who are the real Anabaptists? Are they the traditionalists, who seek to practice their faith on the outskirts of society in quiet and peaceful pastures? Or are they the transformers, who seek to save souls, pursue the kingdom of peace, and confront injustice around the globe? Anabaptists articulate and practice their common commitments in many different ways.

The real Anabaptists, wherever they are found, are those who heed the call of Jesus to come, follow, and embrace the cross of expensive discipleship. The real Anabaptists are those who commit their time, energy, dollars, and love to the life and ministry of a local congregation. The real Anabaptists are those who proclaim the gospel of peace in word and deed throughout the world. The real Anabaptists are those who heed the voice of the Spirit, the authority of Scripture, and the admonition of their siblings in a gathered, visible community called the church.

How does a radical tradition—one that is historically rooted in the critique of religious custom—renew and revitalize itself? A believers church has

Brethren in Christ youth celebrate the completion of a service project.
Photo by Margie Hess

a shelf life of only one generation. Each generation anew must be invited to join the community of faith as adults. Thus the community and the theological tradition are always on trial, always dependent upon the free choice of each succeeding generation. Thus it should be, and must be, in the context of a believers church. But voluntary commitments carry the risk that the baton may be dropped and that the community of faith may falter and lose its appeal. Hence, the vitality and longevity of a believers church always depend on the renewing presence and work of the Holy Spirit.

One thing is certain in a postmodern setting: a tradition of faith will not automatically renew and replace itself. In stable rural settings of bygone days, many things could be taken for granted because they were tightly woven into the fabric of social life. But in a post-Christian and pluralistic society, nothing can be taken for granted. Everything is always up for grabs. In such a setting, the church must be intentional, creative, and assertive if the soul of Anabaptism is to flourish and thrive.

Part 2
Resources

METHODS AND
DATA SOURCES

SELECTION OF GROUPS

We have cast a fairly broad and inclusive net in selecting groups to be included in *Anabaptist World USA*. In general, we included groups that meet *one* of the following criteria: (1) direct historical connections to the sixteenth-century Anabaptist Movement, (2) continued use of an Amish, Brethren, Hutterite, or Mennonite identity in their official name, and/or (3) affirmation of an Anabaptist theological identity by leaders and a desire to be included.

We did not include one-time Anabaptist groups who have dropped their name or theological identity, even though they may have had historical connections. We have also not included groups that carry the Brethren name—Plymouth Brethren and Evangelical United Brethren—but which are not linked to the Schwarzenau Brethren of 1708.

The Missionary Church was not included even though it has historic ties with Amish and Mennonite bodies. The Missionary Church still participates in Mennonite Mutual Aid to a certain extent and maintains a few other Mennonite ties. Although the Missionary Church has retained some ties to its Anabaptist heritage, it does not explicitly affirm it nor carry the Mennonite name; hence, we did not include it.[1]

Missing also are Quaker groups, Moravians, Baptists, Disciples of Christ (Christian Church), Churches of Christ, and Church of God (Anderson). Some of these groups have participated in the ongoing series of Believers Church Conferences that began in 1967, and they do share some characteristics with churches in the Anabaptist family.[2]

We have not included the groups mentioned above because for the most part they did not meet at least one of the three criteria. There is ample historical evidence that early Baptist leaders in England and on the Continent were in conversation with Mennonite Anabaptists both in England and in Holland. For a discussion of these influences, see Durnbaugh (1985) and Estep (1996). Nevertheless, Baptists did not explicitly affirm an Anabaptist identity and generally did not embrace pacifism. Under the rubric of the believers church, Durnbaugh (1985) traces the connections between Anabaptists and some related bodies, including the Baptists, Quakers, Methodists, Disciples of Christ, and the Plymouth Brethren.

MEMBERSHIP ESTIMATES

We compiled the membership estimates from official denominational directories and listings as noted below, as well as from knowledgeable informants in some of the groups. Some of the Old Order groups track the number of families and households but do not keep a list of individual members. Among some of the small independent and Old Order groups, we had to rely on membership estimates provided by helpful leaders of the groups.

The Old Order Amish generally do not keep a list of individual members, but a listing of congregations is updated each year in Ben J. Raber's *Almanac,* published in Baltic, Ohio. We used Raber's *Almanac 2001* as well as helpful informants and regional directories to identify Amish congregations. Nevertheless, a few districts may be missing from our listing.

Estimating Old Order Amish membership is complicated and hazardous because the size of church districts varies somewhat by affiliation and region of the country. We know that in the Elkhart-Lagrange (Ind.) settlement, districts average about 60 members; and the Lancaster (Pa.) settlement has nearly 80 adults per district. These averages are based on actual enumerations of church districts in the Elkhart-Lagrange settlement, provided by Thomas Meyers of Goshen College, and from a sample of ten districts in the Lancaster settlement. Some outlying districts affiliated with Lancaster are smaller. Swartzentruber districts tend to be somewhat smaller than others. We have assigned an *estimated average* to each Old Order Amish Church district; the *actual* membership of a particular district may be more or less than our estimate for that district. However, the use of averages across the country generates reasonable estimates of state and national totals.

We used the following estimates of baptized members for various Old Order and New Order Amish groups: 75 for each district in the Lancaster settlement and related districts in Pennsylvania and other states; 60 for Delaware, Indiana, and Ohio districts; 50 for Swartzentruber districts; and 55 for *all* other Amish districts. Using these estimates, the Old Order and New Order Amish districts average 59.3 members across the country, and average 133 souls per district if the membership of 59.3 is multiplied by 1.25 to obtain the count for unbaptized children and youths. We have used actual membership numbers for the Beachy Amish and Amish Mennonite groups whenever possible.

POPULATION ESTIMATES

We estimated total population numbers for adults and children in all groups. From several studies, we know that the number of unbaptized children and youth in Old Order groups exceeds the number of baptized members. Hence, in traditional groups, we have conservatively multiplied the number of adult members by 1.25, yielding 125 unbaptized souls (56% of total population) for every 100 baptized members (44% of total); thus for every 100 members, we count a combined total population of 225 children and adults. Most of the transitional groups also have large families but somewhat smaller ones than the Old Orders. For every 100 members in transitional groups, we multiplied by 0.9 yielding ninety children for 100 members.

Among transformational groups, family size is much smaller, more people remain single, and the age of baptism is typically lower. All of these factors substantially reduce the number of unbaptized youth. We estimated 35 unbaptized youth for every 100 members (0.35 x 100), yielding a total population of 135 per transformational group. These assumptions shape our population estimates throughout the book. Once again, we must underscore the fact that all of our membership and population figures are *estimates*. We think they are reasonable projections based on our best sources, but nonetheless they are estimates. Many of the formal sources and directories from which we have gathered membership data are listed below.

CHANGES AND UPDATES

We hope to periodically update the Directory of Congregations in *Anabaptist World USA,* and so we welcome corrections, deletions, additions, and changes. Changes can be sent by e-mail to Kraybill4@aol.com or mailed to Donald B. Kraybill, Messiah College, One College Avenue, Grantham, PA 17027. We welcome all updates and suggestions in order to improve the accuracy of the Directory.

PUBLISHED SOURCES OF MEMBERSHIP ESTIMATES

1. *Amish Mennonite Directory 2000*
2. *Brethren Church Directory 2000*
3. *Church of the Brethren Yearbook 2000*
4. *Dunkard Brethren Directory 2000*
5. *Hutterite Telephone and Address Directory 2000*
6. *Mennonite Church Information 2000*
7. *Mennonite Directory 2000*
8. *New Order Amish Directory 1999*
9. *Ohio Amish Directory, Holmes County and Vicinity 2000*
10. *Old German Baptist Brethren, Directory of Officials 2000*
11. *Old Order Weaverland Conference (Mennonite) Directory 2000*
12. *Raber's Almanac 2001*

Membership numbers for the following groups were provided by official offices or representatives: Apostolic Christian Church of America, Brethren in Christ, Conservative Grace Brethren, Fellowship of Grace Brethren Churches, Bruderhof Communities, Hutterite Colonies. Membership estimates for many of the smaller groups were provided by leaders and informants in those groups.

LISTING OF
GROUPS BY TRIBE

Tribe	Assimilation	Congregations	Members	Population
AMISH				
Amish Mennonite	Transitional	13	1,222	2,322
Amish Mennonite Unaffiliated*	Transitional	16	737	1,400
Beachy Amish	Transitional	103	7,365	13,993
New Order Amish	Traditional	60	3,495	7,864
New Order Amish Fellowship	Traditional	10	466	1,049
Old Order Amish	Traditional	1,159	69,578	156,551
Old Order Amish Andy Weaver**	Traditional	NA	NA	NA
Old Order Amish Byler*	Traditional	NA	NA	NA
Old Order Amish Nebraska	Traditional	14	775	1,744
Old Order Amish Renno**	Traditional	NA	NA	NA
Old Order Amish Swartzentruber	Traditional	64	3,156	7,101
Old Order Amish Swiss Groups**	Traditional	NA	NA	NA
Old Order Amish Troyer**	Traditional	NA	NA	NA
BRETHREN				
Bible Brethren*	Transitional	1	15	30
Brethren Church, The	Transformational	115	10,641	14,365
Brethren Community Fellowship*	Transitional	1	75	143
Brethren Fellowship*	Transitional	1	35	63
Brethren in Christ, The	Transformational	196	20,043	27,058
Brethren Revival Fellowship***	NA	NA	NA	NA
Church of the Brethren	Transformational	1,071	137,037	185,000
Church of the Brethren: Dual Affiliated	Transformational	22	2,254	3,043
Church of the Brethren/Mennonite: Dual Affiliated*	Transformational	9	563	760
Conservative Baptist Brethren*	Transitional	2	130	247

* These entries are independent congregations or small affiliations that have not been classified as a "group" because they do not have at least 250 members and two affiliated congregations. A total of sixty-three "groups" were identified.
** Four Old Order Amish groups (Andy Weaver, Renno, Swiss, and Troyer) were large enough to be considered a group, but the districts and members were not identified in the Directory of Congregations in part 3. Members of these four groups are counted with the Old Order Amish districts and membership.
*** These entries are identified for information purposes but did not have official member congregations at the end of 2000.
NA = Not Applicable or Not Available

Brethren	Assimilation	Congregations	Members	Population
Conservative Brethren*	Transitional	2	80	152
Conservative German Baptist Brethren*	Transitional	1	15	29
Conservative Grace Brethren	Transformational	46	2,421	3,268
Dunkard Brethren	Transitional	26	1,048	1,991
German Baptist Brethren*	Transitional	2	110	200
German Seventh-Day Baptists*	Traditional	2	73	139
Grace Brethren Churches, Fellowship of	Transformational	261	32,046	43,262
Independent Brethren*	Transitional	5	219	416
Old Brethren	Traditional	5	250	551
Old Brethren German Baptists*	Traditional	1	50	113
Old German Baptist Brethren	Traditional	54	5,965	13,421
Old Order German Baptists*	Traditional	3	125	281
Old Order River Brethren	Traditional	5	328	738
United Zion	Transformational	11	783	1,488
HUTTERITE				
Bruderhof Communities	Transitional	6	1,140	2,236
Dariusleut Hutterite	Traditional	19	780	1,755
Lehrerleut Hutterite	Traditional	33	1,485	3,341
Schmiedeleut Hutterite	Traditional	67	3,685	8,291
MENNONITE				
Association of Evangelical Mennonite Congregations***	NA	NA	NA	NA
Apostolic Christian Church of America	Transitional	79	12,113	23,015
Bethel Mennonite Fellowship	Transitional	10	452	835
Caribbean Mennonite Conference*	Transitional	5	198	376
Charity Christian Fellowship	Transitional	24	1,467	2,787
Church of God in Christ Mennonite	Transitional	111	12,152	22,805
Conservative Mennonite Conference	Transitional	97	9,649	18,238
Conservative Mennonite Conference/ Mennonite Church: Dual Conference*	Transformational	3	352	652
Conservative Mennonite Unaffiliated*	Transitional	10	807	1,533
Cornerstone Mennonite Churches	Transformational	3	1,451	1,959
Cumberland Valley Mennonite Church	Transitional	6	406	771
Eastern Pennsylvania Mennonite Church	Transitional	50	3,470	6,593
Evangelical Mennonite Brethren	Transformational	4	455	614
Evangelical Mennonite Church	Transformational	31	5,307	7,164
Evangelical Mennonite Mission Conference*	Transformational	1	216	292
General Conference Mennonite Church	Transformational	179	27,507	37,134
Good News Mennonite Fellowship	Transformational	16	467	887
Hope Mennonite Fellowship	Transitional	4	309	587
Hopewell Mennonite District	Transformational	10	1,022	1,315
Independent Mennonite Congregations*	Transformational	52	4,887	6,597
Keystone Mennonite Fellowship	Transitional	17	950	1,805
Kleine Gemeinde*	Transitional	1	70	133
Manhattan Mennonite Church*	Transformational	1	80	108
Mennonite Biblical Alliance	Transitional	18	1,001	1,902
Mennonite Brethren	Transformational	168	22,777	30,723

Mennonite	Assimilation	Congregations	Members	Population
Mennonite Christian Fellowship	Transitional	23	1,294	2,459
Mennonite Church	Transformational	871	92,157	124,412
Mennonite Church/General Conference Dual Conference*	Transformational	210	20,235	27,317
Mennonite Church Dual Affiliated*	Transformational	2	114	154
Mennonite Church USA***	NA	NA	NA	NA
Mennonite Evangelical Churches	Transformational	3	250	336
Mennonite Unaffiliated Congregations*	Transitional	77	3,814	7,171
Mid-Atlantic Mennonite Fellowship	Transitional	16	1,299	2,468
Mid-West Mennonite Fellowship	Transitional	27	1,335	2,537
Nationwide Mennonite Fellowship Churches	Transitional	47	2,175	4,133
Ohio Wisler Mennonite Churches	Transitional	5	421	800
Old Colony Mennonite*	Traditional	1	407	916
Old Order Mennonite Groffdale Conference	Traditional	42	7,096	15,966
Old Order Mennonite John Martin Congregations*	Traditional	3	77	173
Old Order Mennonite Noah Hoover Congregations*	Traditional	3	219	493
Old Order Mennonite Reidenbach Group(s)	Traditional	10	361	812
Old Order Mennonite Stauffer Groups	Traditional	10	1,149	2,585
Old Order Mennonite Unaffiliated*	Traditional	11	465	1,046
Old Order Mennonite Virginia Conference	Traditional	3	426	959
Old Order Mennonite Weaverland Conference	Traditional	34	5,574	12,500
Old Order Mennonite Wenger/Weaver	Traditional	3	308	693
Old Order Mennonite Wisler Conference	Traditional	7	780	1,755
Old Order Orthodox Mennonite*	Traditional	2	27	61
Pilgrim Mennonite Conference	Transitional	15	965	1,833
Reformed Mennonite Church	Transitional	9	278	626
Reinlaender Mennonite Church	Traditional	2	465	1,046
South Atlantic Mennonite Conference*	Transitional	4	194	369
Southeastern Mennonite Conference	Transitional	15	687	1,305
United Mennonite*	Transitional	2	17	34
Washington-Franklin Mennonite Conference	Transitional	13	1,296	2,462
Western Conservative Mennonite Fellowship	Transitional	10	612	1,140
York-Adams Mennonite Churches	Transitional	5	266	505

Section C

PROFILES OF
GROUPS BY TRIBE

AMISH
Amish Mennonite

This cluster of thirteen Amish Mennonite congregations is scattered across five states, with concentrations in Arkansas, Illinois, and Missouri. Many of them trace their roots to the "sleeping preacher" congregations that left progressive Amish Mennonite churches in the early 1900s. Hostetler and Kauffman family names are prominent. Similar to the Beachy Amish in some respects, members are permitted to own automobiles. Some congregations, but not all, speak the Pennsylvania German dialect.

Overview   Transitional. Congregations, 13. Members, 1,222. Pop. (population), 2,322.

States   AR, 3 (congregations); CO, 1; IL, 3; MO, 5; WI, 1.

Contact   Rt. 1, PO Box 350-A, Buffalo, MO 65622; ☎ 417-345-2895.

Amish Mennonite Unaffiliated[*]

This is a cluster of congregations that considers themselves unaffiliated Amish Mennonites but do not have a formal name other than Amish Mennonite. Many of these congregations maintain fellowship together but do not have a formal organization. Included in this category are the Unaffiliated Amish Mennonite Churches of Tennessee and Kentucky. They dress plainly, speak the Pennsylvania German dialect, but drive automobiles. Members of some congregations come from Beachy Amish, Conservative Mennonite, and Wisler Mennonite backgrounds. Included in this category is a small Old Order Amish Mennonite horse-and-buggy group in Clark, Ohio.

---

[*] These entries are independent congregations or small affiliations that have not been classified as a "group" because they do not have at least 250 members and two affiliated congregations. A total of sixty-three "groups" were identified.

[**] Four Old Order Amish groups (Andy Weaver, Renno, Swiss, and Troyer) were large enough to be considered a group, but the districts and members were not identified in the Directory of Congregations in part 3. Members of these four groups are counted with the Old Order Amish districts and membership.

[***] These entries are identified for information purposes but did not have official member congregations at the end of 2000.

NA = Not Applicable or Not Available

Note: Throughout the book the Commonwealth of Puerto Rico is classified as a state.

Overview   Transitional. Congregations, 16. Members, 737. Pop., 1,400.
States   DC, 1; FL, 1; IN, 1; KY, 2; NM, 1; OH, 1; PA, 2; TN, 6;
           TX, 1.
Contact   NA (not available or not applicable).

Beachy Amish

The Beachy Amish emerged in the 1920s in Somerset and Lancaster Counties of Pennsylvania, under the leadership of Bishop Moses Beachy. Most of the members came from Old Order Amish backgrounds. Today the Beachy Amish have 103 congregations in twenty-two states. They do not have an annual conference but do hold periodic meetings of ordained officials. More progressive than other Amish groups, members drive cars, have electricity in their homes, and support an aggressive evangelistic program. Members wear plain dress, and men wear trimmed beards. There are several subaffiliations within the Beachy Amish churches.

Overview   Transitional. Congregations, 103. Members, 7,365. Pop.,
           13,993.
States   AL, 2; AR, 2; FL, 2; GA, 3; IA, 2; IL, 4; IN, 14; KS, 3; KY, 8;
           MD, 1; ME, 1; MI, 1; MN, 1; MO, 2; NY, 3; OH, 20; OK, 1;
           PA, 15; SC, 3; TN, 5; TX, 2; VA, 8.
Contact   NA.

New Order Amish

The New Order Amish emerged in 1966 in Holmes County, Ohio. Today sixty New Order congregations are scattered in thirteen states, but the majority (34) of them are found in Ohio. There are two circles of affiliation within the New Order orbit. Some districts permit electricity in the homes and tractors in the fields, but others do not. Most New Order congregations have Sunday school, youth Bible study meetings, and emphasize greater individual expression of religious experience than the Old Order Amish.

Overview   Traditional. Congregations, 60. Members, 3,495. Pop., 7,864.
States   FL, 1; IL, 2; IN, 2; KS, 2; KY, 5; MD, 1; MI, 1; MT, 1; NC, 2;
           NY, 1; OH, 34; PA, 6; WI, 2.
Contact   NA.

New Order Amish Fellowship

This group separated from the New Order Amish of Holmes County in 1986. The Fellowship does not always use the name Amish. According to their leaders, they place less emphasis on rules and regulations and more emphasis on heartfelt experience. The Fellowship churches are less traditional than the other New Order groups in the Holmes County area. They permit tractors in the fields and electricity in the homes. The congregations are primarily in Ohio.

Overview   Traditional. Congregations, 10. Members, 466. Pop., 1,049.
State   Primarily OH.
Contact   NA.

Old Order Amish

The Old Order Amish form the main trunk of the Amish groups in the United States. The label *Old Order* emerged in the 1860s-1880s, as progressive congregations became Amish Mennonite. Those keeping the *alte Ordnung* eventually became known as the Old Order Amish. Various sub-affiliations have emerged under the Old Order canopy; however, most of the districts consider themselves simply Amish or Old Order Amish. Combining all the Old Order subgroups yields a total of 1,237 Old Order districts and a combined Old Order Amish membership of 73,609. The Old Order Amish are scattered in twenty-one states, mostly east of the Mississippi, but about 70 percent of the congregations and members are in Ohio, Pennsylvania, and Indiana. These numbers do not include the twenty-four Amish districts in Canada.

Overview   Traditional. Congregations, 1,237. Members, 73,609. Pop.,
            165,620. (These totals include the Nebraska and
            Swartzentruber subgroups, also identified separately below.)
States   DE, 8 (districts); IA, 35; IL, 29; IN, 239; KS, 6; KY, 30; MD, 5;
            MI, 66; MN, 6; MO, 44; MT, 3; NY, 32; OH, 290; OK, 5;
            PA, 277; TN, 3; TX, 3; VA, 4; WA, 1; WI, 71; WV, 2.
Contact   NA.

Old Order Amish Andy Weaver**

Under the leadership of Bishop Andy Weaver, this group formed in Holmes County, Ohio, in 1952. The network of more than thirty congregations, primarily in Ohio, practices a fairly strict form of shunning and maintains fellowship with districts holding similar views and living in other settlements. They have more restrictions on technology than many Ohio Old Order groups. In the Directory, the Andy Weaver church districts are considered Old Order Amish and are not separately identified.

Overview   Traditional.
States   Primarily OH.
Contact   NA.

Old Order Amish Byler*

The Byler Amish formed in 1849 in Mifflin County, Pennsylvania. They are distinguished by their yellow-top buggies. They have three congregations in Mifflin County and are also affiliated with districts near New Wilmington, Pennsylvania. In the Directory, their church districts are considered Old Order Amish and are not separately identified.

Overview   Traditional.
State   PA.
Contact   NA.

Old Order Amish Nebraska

One of the most conservative groups, the Nebraska Amish organized in Mifflin County, Pennsylvania, in 1881 through the assistance of a bishop who was living in Nebraska at the time. Conservative in lifestyle and their use of technology, they are noted for their white-top buggies. There are several subaffiliations within the Nebraska group.

Overview   Traditional. Congregations, 14. Members, 775. Pop., 1,744.
States   OH, 1; PA, 13.
Contact   NA.

Old Order Amish Renno**

The Renno group formed in 1863 in Mifflin County, Pennsylvania. They are sometimes called the "One Suspender" group because the Ordnung limits men to wearing one suspender. The dozen or so districts in this network are located primarily in Pennsylvania. In the Directory, they are considered Old Order Amish districts and are not separately identified.

Overview   Traditional.
Contact   NA.

Old Order Amish Swartzentruber

One of the more conservative groups, the Swartzentrubers formed in 1913 in Holmes County, Ohio. Now their sixty-four congregations are scattered in twelve states with over half (33) in Ohio.

Overview   Traditional. Congregations, 64. Members, 3,156. Pop., 7,101.
States   IA, 1; IN, 1; KY, 3; MI, 2; MN, 6; MO, 1; MS, 1; NY, 4;
            OH, 33; PA, 1; TN, 8; WI, 3.
Contact   NA.

Old Order Amish Swiss Groups**

More than fifty Old Order Amish districts have a distinctive Swiss ethnic flavor. Located primarily in Adams and Allen Counties, Indiana, they came directly to the midwest from Switzerland and neighboring areas of France in the 1850s. In addition to Indiana, they have settlements in Michigan, Missouri, Ohio, and Pennsylvania. There are several subgroups within the Swiss communities. In the Directory, the Swiss districts are considered Old Order Amish and are not separately identified.

Overview   Traditional.
Contact   NA.

Old Order Amish Troyer**

In many ways the Troyer group is similar to their parent group, the Swartzentrubers. The Troyer group originated in about 1931 in Holmes County, Ohio. Today the Troyer group has congregations in Ohio, New York, Pennsylvania, Michigan, and Ontario. In the Directory, the Troyer districts are considered Old Order Amish and are not separately identified.

Overview   Traditional.
Contact   NA.

BRETHREN
Bible Brethren*
These Brethren have one congregation that uses two meetinghouses in Abbottstown and Carlisle, Pennsylvania. They broke off from the Church of Brethren in 1948.

Overview   Transitional. Congregation, 1. Members, 15. Pop., 30.
State   PA, 1.
Contact   NA.

Brethren Church, The
The Brethren Church formed in 1883 by branching off from the German Baptist Brethren (later, Church of the Brethren). It was known as the "progressive" wing at the time of the division. Today the Brethren Church headquarters are in Ashland, Ohio. Sometimes they are referred to as the "Ashland Brethren." The group's 115 congregations are found in eighteen states, but 78 percent of the members live in Ohio, Indiana, and Pennsylvania.

Overview   Transformational. Congregations, 115. Members, 10,641. Pop., 14,365.
States   AZ, 3; CA, 3; DC, 1; DE, 1; FL, 4; IL, 3; IN, 34; KS, 3; KY, 2; MD, 4; MI, 1; NE, 1; NJ, 1; OH, 22; PA, 18; VA, 8; WV, 5; WY, 1.
Contact   524 College Ave., Ashland, OH 44805; ☎ 419-289-1708; E-mail: brethren@brethrenchurch.org; Website: www.brethrenchurch.org.

Brethren Community Fellowship*
This congregation in Modesto, California, separated from the Old German Baptist Brethren in the early 1990s.

Overview   Transitional. Congregation, 1. Members, 75. Pop., 143.
State   CA, 1.
Contact   NA.

Brethren Fellowship*
These independent Brethren have one congregation in Ephrata, Pennsylvania. The congregation left the Dunkard Brethren in the early 1990s and upholds more conservative standards than the parent group.

Overview   Transitional. Congregation, 1. Members, 35. Pop., 63.
State   PA, 1.
Contact   NA.

Brethren in Christ, The
The Brethren in Christ emerged around 1780 in eastern Pennsylvania. They blended Anabaptist-Mennonite influences with the Pietist strains of the German Baptist Brethren. The Brethren in Christ have congregations in twenty states, with Pennsylvania, Florida, Ohio, and California dominating.

About 51 percent of the members live in Pennsylvania. The Brethren in Christ also have congregations in Canada. The Brethren in Christ support the Mennonite Central Committee and participate in the Mennonite World Conference.

Overview   Transformational. Congregations, 196. Members, 20,043. Pop., 27,058.

States   CA, 15; FL, 17; GA, 1; IA, 1; IL, 1; IN, 4; KS, 4; KY, 5; MD, 4; MI, 6; NM, 2; NY, 2; OH, 15; OK, 3; OR, 3; PA, 99; TN, 4; VA, 8; WI, 1; WV, 1.

Contact   431 Grantham Rd., Grantham, PA 17027; ☎ 717-697-2634; E-mail: bic@messiah.edu; Website: www.bic-church.org.

Brethren Revival Fellowship***

This network of congregations in the Church of the Brethren holds membership in the parent body, and their congregations are included in the Church of the Brethren membership. The network formed in 1959 to advocate for more traditional Brethren standards of doctrine and practice. The Fellowship operates inside the denominational structure. It holds workshops and conferences, organizes youth work camps and voluntary service units, and publishes a newsletter.

Contact   Brethren Revival Fellowship, PO Box 543, Ephrata, PA 17522; ☎ 717-626-5079; Website: www.brfwitness.org.

Church of the Brethren

The Church of the Brethren, the largest of the Brethren bodies, traces its roots to the German Baptist Brethren beginning at Swarzenau, Germany, in 1708. At its bicentennial in 1908, the body changed its name to the Church of the Brethren. Congregations are found in thirty-nine states, with about 70 percent of the members living in Pennsylvania (41,951), Virginia (24,811), Ohio (15,027), and Indiana (11,909). The membership numbers reported here include congregations affiliated with other denominations and half the membership of congregations that hold a dual affiliation with the Mennonite Church.

Overview   Transformational. Congregations, 1,071. Members, 137,037. Pop., 185,000.

States   AL, 5; AR, 2; AZ, 4; CA, 28; CO, 10; DC, 2; DE, 3; FL, 16; IA, 27; ID, 6; IL, 44; IN, 98; KS, 30; KY, 4; LA, 2; MD, 62; ME, 3; MI, 25; MN, 4; MO, 19; MT, 1; NC, 17; ND, 3; NE, 4; NJ, 1; NM, 2; NY, 2; OH, 103; OK, 6; OR, 4; PA, 237; PR, 7; SC, 1; TN, 19; TX, 5; VA, 172; VT, 1; WA, 12; WI, 2; WV, 78 (includes dual affiliations).

Contact   1451 Dundee Ave., Elgin, IL 60120; ☎ 847-742-5100; E-mail: brethren.org; Website: www.brethren.org.; unofficial Website: www.cob-net.org.

Church of the Brethren: Dual Affiliated*

Twenty-two congregations have an affiliation with the Church of the Brethren and other denominations such as the American Baptists, the United Church of Christ, the Christian Disciples, The Brethren Church, the Southern Baptists, and the United Methodists. The membership of Church of the Brethren congregations with dual affiliations is included with the total membership of the Church of the Brethren listed above.

Overview   Transformational. Congregations, 22. Members, 2,254.
            Pop., 3,043.
States   CA, 1; CO, 1; IA, 5; IL, 1; MD, 1; MI, 2; MT, 1; PA, 3;
            VA, 2; WA, 4; WV, 1.
Contact   NA.

Church of the Brethren/Mennonite: Dual Affiliated*

Nine Church of the Brethren congregations have dual affiliations with their own denomination and the Mennonite Church. The membership of these congregations is equally divided between the membership count of the Mennonite Church and of the Church of the Brethren.

Overview   Transformational. Congregations, 9. Members, 563. Pop., 760.
States   AR, 1; IL, 1; IN, 1; MD, 1; MI, 2; MO, 1; PA, 1; WV, 1.
Contact   NA.

Conservative Baptist Brethren*

The Conservative Baptist Brethren have two congregations in Pennsylvania, one in Lititz and one in Frystown (near Bethel). This group separated from the Dunkard Brethren in 1986 and is more conservative than the parent body.

Overview   Transitional. Congregations, 2. Members, 130. Pop., 247.
State   PA, 2.
Contact   NA.

Conservative Brethren*

These two unrelated, independent congregations call themselves Conservative Brethren. The one in Millbach, Pennsylvania, came from the Conservative Baptist Brethren in 1990. The one in Palmyra, Virginia, originated from the Church of the Brethren in 1955.

Overview   Transitional. Congregations, 2. Members, 80. Pop., 152.
States   PA, 1; VA, 1.
Contact   NA.

Conservative German Baptist Brethren*

Located in New Freedom, Pennsylvania, these Brethren withdrew from the Dunkard Brethren in 1931 in order to revive some of the Old Brethren traditions such as beards for ordained leaders.

Overview   Transitional. Congregation, 1. Members, 15. Pop., 29.
State   PA, 1.
Contact   NA.

Profiles of Groups by Tribe

Conservative Grace Brethren

The Conservative Grace Brethren separated from the Fellowship of Grace Brethren Churches in 1989-91. This conservative branch formed over issues related to congregational autonomy, trine immersion baptism, women in ministry, and other matters of biblical interpretation. The Conservative Grace Brethren congregations are found in fourteen states, with the highest concentration (16) in Ohio.

Overview   Transformational. Congregations, 46. Members, 2,421.
            Pop., 3,268.
States   CO, 1; FL, 1; IA, 2; IN, 5; MD, 1; MI, 5; NY, 1; OH, 16;
            OR, 1; PA, 9; TN, 1; VT, 1; WA, 1; WV, 1.
Contact   13839 N. Liberty Rd., Mount Vernon, OH 43050.
            ☎ 740-392-4253.

Dunkard Brethren

The Dunkard Brethren emerged in 1926 in response to changes in the Church of the Brethren. Members continue to wear plain dress and uphold other traditional practices of the Church of the Brethren. The group's primary concentration is in Pennsylvania, but congregations are found in thirteen other states as well.

Overview   Transitional. Congregations, 26. Members, 1,048. Pop., 1,991.
States   CA, 2; CO, 1; IA, 1; IN, 2; KS, 1; MD, 2; MI, 1; MO, 1;
            NM, 2; OH, 3; OR, 1; PA, 7; VA, 1; WV, 1.
Contact   Website: www.geocities.com/heartland/pointe/8024/main.html.

German Baptist Brethren*

The two congregations (in Missouri and Wisconsin) in this affiliation separated from the Old German Baptist Brethren in 1997.

Overview   Transitional. Congregations, 2. Members, 110. Pop., 200.
States   MO, 1; WI, 1.
Contact   NA.

German Seventh-Day Baptists*

These two small congregations trace their roots to the Ephrata Cloister, an eighteenth-century celibate community in northern Lancaster County, Pennsylvania, whose leader, Conrad Beissel, had been affiliated with the German Baptist Brethren. This small cluster of Brethren is no longer celibate and has two congregations, Snow Hill and Salemville, Pennsylvania.

Overview   Traditional. Congregations, 2. Members, 73. Pop., 139.
State   PA, 2.
Contact   780 Golden Rule Rd., New Enterprise, PA 16664.
            ☎ 814-793-9476.

Grace Brethren Churches, Fellowship of

The Grace Brethren Churches emerged in 1940 from a division within the Ashland-based Brethren Church. Today the Fellowship has 261 congregations in twenty-nine states, with the largest clusters in Pennsylvania (50), Ohio (49), and California (36). The Fellowship supports aggressive evangelistic efforts by local congregations.

Overview   Transformational. Congregations, 261. Members, 32,046. Pop., 43,262.

States   AK, 6; AZ, 1; CA, 36; CO, 2; CT, 1; DE, 1; FL, 22; GA, 1; HI, 4; IA, 8; IN, 18; KS, 2; KY, 3; MD, 10; MI, 2; NC, 1; NE, 1; NJ, 1; NM, 4; OH, 49; OR, 1; PA, 50; SC, 2; TN, 1; TX, 2; VA, 16; VT, 1; WA, 12; WV, 3;

Contact   PO Box 386, Winona Lake, IN 46590; ☎ 803-648-7078; Website: www.fgbc.org.

Independent Brethren*

Independent Brethren is the name used by two congregations (Blue Rock and Marsh Creek). Three other congregations do not carry the independent name but are unaffiliated Brethren congregations. The one in New Jersey withdrew from the Brethren Church in 2000. The congregations in Pennsylvania were formerly affiliated with the Church of the Brethren.

Overview   Transitional. Congregations, 5. Members, 219. Pop., 416.

States   NJ, 1; PA, 4.

Contact   NA.

Old Brethren

This group emerged as a conservative branch from the Old German Baptist Brethren in 1913. The Old Brethren were more plain and conservative than the main group, but today they are similar in many respects to the Old German Baptist Brethren. Like the parent group, they drive cars, dress plain, and have meetinghouses. Their congregations tally two in Indiana, one in Ohio, and two in California. They have organized their own private schools.

Overview   Traditional. Congregations, 5. Members, 250. Pop., 551.

States   CA, 2; IN, 2; OH, 1.

Contact   NA.

Old Brethren German Baptists*

The one congregation of this Indiana affiliation formed in 1939 as a conservative branch from the Old Brethren. It is the most traditional of the Old Order Brethren groups. Members use horse-drawn transportation and do not use tractors or electricity.

Overview   Traditional. Congregation, 1. Members, 50. Pop., 113.

State   IN, 1.

Contact   NA.

Old German Baptist Brethren

This group formed in 1881 during the three-way division of the German Baptist Brethren. An Old Order group, it seeks to preserve many traditional practices of the German Baptist Brethren. This is the largest of the traditional Brethren groups. The Old German Baptist Brethren have congregations in sixteen states, with the largest number in Ohio (16) and Indiana (9).

Overview   Traditional. Congregations, 54. Members, 5,965. Pop., 13,421.
States   CA, 4; FL, 2; GA, 1; IN, 9; KS, 5; MD, 1; MI, 1; MO, 1;
            MS, 1; OH, 16; OR, 1; PA, 4; VA, 4; WA, 2; WI, 1; WV, 1.
Contact   PO Box 791, Greenville, OH 45331.

Old Order German Baptists*

This community of three congregations in west-central Ohio separated from the Old German Baptist Brethren in 1921. They travel by horse and carriage but do use tractors for fieldwork. They do not permit electric power or telephones.

Overview   Traditional. Congregations, 3. Members, 125. Pop., 281.
State   OH, 3.
Contact   NA.

Old Order River Brethren

The Old Order River Brethren trace their roots to an 1855 division among the River Brethren in eastern Pennsylvania who, a few years later, became known as the Brethren in Christ. Thus the Old Order River Brethren are the traditional strand of the Brethren in Christ. The members of this group wear plain clothing and hold their worship services in homes as well as in a school and in community centers. One congregation occasionally uses a meetinghouse. Although they drive cars, they are sometimes mistaken for Amish because of their similar dress and long flowing beards. There are three subaffiliations, including a small one of about fifteen members that uses horse-drawn transportation.

Overview   Traditional. Congregations, 5. Members, 328. Pop., 738.
States   IA, 1; PA, 4.
Contact   NA.

United Zion

Originally called United Zion's Children, this group emerged from a division among the River Brethren (now Brethren in Christ) in 1855. Led by Matthias Brinser, the group constructed a meetinghouse before such facilities were sanctioned by the River Brethren. United Zion members dress modestly, and some of the women wear prayer coverings. All eleven of their congregations are located in Pennsylvania.

Overview   Transformational. Congregations, 11. Members, 783.
            Pop., 1,488.
State   PA, 11.
Contact   NA.

HUTTERITES
Bruderhof Communities

Formerly called the Society of Brothers, this group has nine Bruderhofs, four in New York, two in Pennsylvania, as well as three overseas. The adult membership in the United States exceeds 1,100. The Bruderhof began in Germany in 1920, migrated to England, then to Paraguay, and eventually to the United States in the 1950s. It has had various associations with Hutterite groups at different times.

Overview   Transitional. Congregations, 6. Members, 1,140. Pop., 2,236.
States   NY, 4; PA, 2.
Contact   Woodcrest Bruderhof, PO Box 903, Rte. 213, Rifton, NY
            12471; ☎ 845-658-8351; Website: www.Bruderhof.org.

Dariusleut Hutterites

One of three Hutterite branches, the Dariusleut formed in Russia in 1860 under the leadership of Darius Walter. The Darisuleut group is the moderate branch of the three Hutterite groups and has about 135 colonies in North America; nineteen are in the United States, mostly in Montana.

Overview   Traditional. Congregations, 19. Members, 780. Pop., 1,755.
States   MT, 14; WA, 5.
Contact   NA.

Lehrerleut Hutterites

This is the most conservative of the Hutterite groups. The Lehrerleut formed in about 1877, after they had migrated from Russia to the United States under the leadership of Jacob Wipf, a teacher. Today they have 122 colonies in North America, with thirty-three of them in Montana.

Overview   Traditional. Congregations, 33. Members, 1,485. Pop., 3,341.
State   MT, 33.
Contact   NA.

Schmiedeleut Hutterites

One of the three Hutterite branches, the Schmiedeleut, formed in 1859 in Russia, when Michael Waldner reinstituted community of goods. Today the Schmiedeleut are the most progressive Hutterite branch. They have about 170 colonies in North America, including sixty-seven in the United States, mostly in South Dakota. In the 1990s two subgroups, called Gibbs and Oilers, formed within the Schmiedeleut colonies. About ten of the colonies in the United States are aligned with the Oilers; the remainder are Gibb colonies.

Overview   Traditional. Congregations, 67. Members, 3,685. Pop., 8,291.
States   MN, 9; ND, 6; SD, 52.
Contact   NA.

Profiles of Groups by Tribe

157

MENNONITES
Association of Evangelical Mennonite Congregations***

An Evangelical Anabaptist Fellowship formed in 1992 to promote conservative and evangelical views in Mennonite and Brethren circles. Not a formally organized group of congregations, the Fellowship consisted of a network of individuals and pastors who circulated a newsletter and held seminars and workshops. In the fall of 2000, the EAF held a meeting at Paradise, Pennsylvania, to lay plans to organize an Association of Evangelical Mennonite Congregations as an alternative affiliation to the proposed Mennonite Church USA. The mission of the Association is to draw congregations together around a common commitment to Anabaptist distinctives, within a framework of orthodox, evangelical doctrine.

Contact   120 Maple Ave., Harleysville, PA 19438; ☎ 215-256-6200;
           Website: www.aemc2000.org.

Apostolic Christian Church of America

This group began in the 1830s in Switzerland under the leadership of Samuel Froehlich, who was influenced by the Anabaptists and their teaching. The Apostolic Church came to Lewis County, New York, in 1847 and attracted Amish there, as well as in other states. Sometimes nicknamed "the New Amish," the group was never directly related to a Mennonite body, but its congregations share many Anabaptist principles and characteristics with conservative Mennonite churches. They sometimes support projects sponsored by the Mennonite Central Committee and Mennonite Disaster Service. Their congregations are scattered in twenty states, with a strong concentration in Illinois, Indiana, and Ohio.

Overview   Transitional. Congregations, 79. Members, 12,113.
           Pop., 23,015.
States   AL, 1; AZ, 3; CA, 2; CO, 1; CT, 1; DC, 1; FL, 3; GA, 1; IA, 8;
           IL, 19; IN, 11; KS, 6; MN, 3; MO, 4; NY, 1; OH, 9; OR, 2;
           PA, 1; TN, 1; TX, 1.
Contact   805 West Cruger Rd., PO Box 52, Eureka, IL 61530;
           Website: www.apostolicchristian.org.

Bethel Mennonite Fellowship

This cluster of churches withdrew from the Conservative Mennonite Fellowship (which later disbanded) in 1983. Supportive of several mission efforts, these congregations have a Bethel Bible School in Seymour, Missouri. They promote conservative Mennonite practices and do not use radios. Their congregations are in six states with concentrations in Indiana and Missouri.

Overview   Transitional. Congregations, 10. Members, 452. Pop., 835.
States   AR, 1; IN, 3; MD, 1; MI, 1; MO, 3; OK, 1.
Contact   4230 Highway 17, Summerville, MO 65571; ☎ 417-932-5286.

Caribbean Mennonite Conference*

These Puerto Rican congregations separated from the Puerto Rican Conference of the Mennonite Church in the 1970s. They are more conservative in doctrine and dress than the Mennonite Church Conference.

Overview   Transitional. Congregations, 5. Members, 198. Pop., 376.
State   PR, 5.
Contact   NA.

Charity Christian Fellowship

This network of churches formed in 1982 in eastern Pennsylvania. Coming from various plain Anabaptist groups, members and congregations resemble conservative Mennonite groups in many ways. Rather fundamentalist in doctrine and charismatic in expression, they practice foot washing and the holy kiss. They wear modest dress, and women wear the prayer covering. They support an aggressive program of evangelism and win converts from other Anabaptist groups and from outside groups. Their twenty-four congregations are found in fifteen states, with the strongest concentrations in Ohio and Pennsylvania.

Overview   Transitional. Congregations, 24. Members, 1,467. Pop., 2,787.
States   CO, 1; GA, 1; IA, 1; ID, 1; IN, 1; MI, 1; NC, 2; NY, 2; OH, 4; OK, 1; PA, 4; TN, 2; TX, 1; WA, 1; WI, 1.
Contact   NA.

Church of God in Christ Mennonite

Also known as the Holdeman Mennonites, this group formed in 1859 under the leadership of John Holdeman. Similar in some ways to other conservative Mennonite groups, the Holdeman Church teaches the doctrine of a one-true church and also practices shunning. Men wear abbreviated beards, and women wear black scarves or bonnets. The 111 congregations in the United States are scattered in thirty-three states, with the heaviest concentration (23) in Kansas. There are also Holdeman congregations in Canada.

Overview   Transitional. Congregations, 111. Members, 12,152. Pop., 22,805.
States   AL, 2; AR, 2; AZ, 6; CA, 4; CO, 2; FL, 2; GA, 3; IA, 3; ID, 6; IL, 1; IN, 1; KS, 23; KY, 2; LA, 2; ME, 1; MI, 3; MN, 1; MO, 5; MS, 6; NC, 1; ND, 1; NE, 3; NM, 1; NY, 2; OH, 2; OK, 4; OR, 1; PA, 4; SD, 2; TN, 2; TX, 8; WA, 2; WI, 3.
Contact   420 N. Wedel Ave., Moundridge, KS 67107.

Conservative Mennonite Conference

Organized in 1910 at Pigeon, Michigan, this group was first known as the Conservative Amish Mennonite Conference, but dropped the *Amish* name in 1954. Many of the early members came from Amish Mennonite backgrounds but could not endorse the more centralized structures emerging in the Mennonite Church. Today the Conservative Mennonite Conference is an autonomous body, having fraternal relations with numerous Mennonite bodies and organizations. They emphasize the authority of the Scriptures and nonconformity to the world. Plain dress is worn by many members in rural areas but often not by members in more urban congregations. Their denominational headquarters and their Rosedale Bible Institute are located in Rosedale, Ohio. Congregations are scattered in twenty states, with the largest concentration in Ohio (23).

Overview   Transitional. Congregations, 97 Members, 9,649 Pop., 18,238.

States   AZ, 5; DE, 5; FL, 8; GA, 1; IA, 5; IL, 2; IN, 10; KS, 2; KY, 7; MD, 2; MI, 10; MN, 2; NM, 2; NY, 3; OH, 23; OK, 1; PA, 4; SC, 1; TX, 2; VA, 2.

Contact   9910 Milford Center Rd., Irwin, OH 43029; ☎ 740-857-1234; E-mail: email-cmcrosedale@juno.com; Website: www.cmcrosedale.org.

Conservative Mennonite Conference/Mennonite Church: Dual Conference*

These congregations are affiliated with both the Conservative Mennonite Conference and the Mennonite Church.

Overview   Transformational. Congregations, 3. Members, 352. Pop., 652.

States   AR, 1; NY, 2.

Contact   NA.

Conservative Mennonite Unaffiliated*

This cluster of congregations is not affiliated with the Conservative Mennonite Conference, yet many members come from that background. They tend to be more rural and conservative than the congregations in the category of Mennonite Unaffiliated. Five of their ten congregations are in Ohio and the remainder in four other states.

Overview   Transitional. Congregations, 10. Members, 807. Pop., 1,533.

States   CO, 1; IN, 2; OH, 5; OK, 1; WI, 1.

Contact   NA.

Cornerstone Mennonite Churches

This group of churches formed in the early 1990s largely from the Virginia Mennonite Conference. Leaders emphasize a fundamental and evangelical interpretation of the Scriptures; they support a strong program of outreach and the Cornerstone Bible Institute. They have used a cell group approach to church growth and evangelism. The Cornerstone network of churches is based in Virginia's Shenandoah Valley.

Overview   Transformational. Congregations, 3. Members, 1,451. Pop., 1,959.

State   VA, 3.

Contact   PO Box 1366, Harrisonburg, VA 22801; ☎ 540-432-2355; E-mail: ccmikeg@aol.com; Website: www.cornerstonenet.org.

Cumberland Valley Mennonite Church

This independent conference formed in 1971 in south-central Pennsylvania. The member congregations were a conservative cluster in the former Washington and Franklin County Mennonite Conference. Emphasizing conservative doctrine, dress, and practice, this conference has three congregations in Pennsylvania and three in Maryland.

Overview   Transitional. Congregations, 6. Members, 406. Pop., 771.
States   MD, 3; PA, 3.
Contact   6734 White Church Rd., Shippensburg, PA 17257;
            ☎ 717-532-2473.

Eastern Pennsylvania Mennonite Church

This group took root in 1969 in the Lancaster, Pennsylvania, area when five conservative bishops and some forty other ordained leaders withdrew from the Lancaster Mennonite Conference over issues related to dress, television, and other cultural changes. The Eastern Pennsylvania Mennonite Church developed a more conservative discipline and continues to uphold traditional Mennonite standards of doctrine, dress, and practice. Today the Eastern Pennsylvania Mennonite Church has congregations in thirteen states; the bulk of them (32) are in Pennsylvania.

Overview   Transitional. Congregations, 50. Members, 3,470. Pop., 6,593.
States   DE, 2; FL, 1; GA, 1; IL, 3; MA, 1; MD, 2; MO, 2; NJ, 1;
            NY, 2; PA, 32; TX, 1; VT, 1; WI, 1.
Contact   Rt. 1, PO Box 140, Womelsdorf, PA 19567; ☎ 610-589-4374.

Evangelical Mennonite Brethren

These congregations are a remnant group of a larger church known as the Evangelical Mennonite Brethren that in 1987 changed its name to Fellowship of Evangelical Bible Churches (not included in this book). The Evangelical Mennonite Brethren trace their roots to Russian Mennonites who migrated to Nebraska and Minnesota in the 1870s. Today their four congregations are each located in a different state.

Overview   Transformational. Congregations, 4. Members, 455. Pop., 614.
States   KS, 1; MN, 1; MT, 1; SD, 1.
Contact   NA.

Evangelical Mennonite Church

Formed in 1865 from an Amish background, this group was known for many years as the Egly Amish because their leader was Henry Egly. By 1908 their name was changed to the Defenseless Mennonite Church; in 1948 they became the Evangelical Mennonite Church. Strongly shaped by modern Evangelicalism, many of their congregations have a weak Mennonite identity. In the summer of 2000, their delegate body voted on a proposal to delete *Mennonite* from their name; it lost by a 3 percent vote margin. With headquarters in Fort Wayne, Indiana, congregations are in five states, and about one-third of them are in Illinois.

Overview   Transformational. Congregations, 31. Members, 5,307.
Pop., 7,164.

States   IL, 12; IN, 7; KS, 3; MI, 3; OH, 6.

Contact   NA.

Evangelical Mennonite Mission Conference*

This congregation in Seminole, Texas, is an outreach of the Evangelical Mennonite Mission Conference based in Winnipeg, Manitoba, Canada.

Overview   Transformational. Congregation, 1. Members, 216. Pop., 292.

State   TX, 1.

Contact   NA.

General Conference Mennonite Church

The General Conference Mennonite Church formed in 1860 at West Point, Iowa, when representatives from various Mennonite bodies, seeking union, organized a new conference. As the conference grew, its membership included older immigrants of German stock as well as many new immigrant congregations of Dutch-Russian backgrounds. General Conference Mennonite Church congregations are found in both the United States and Canada. The General Conference is the major partner with the Mennonite Church in forming the proposed Mennonite Church USA. Congregations in the United States are located in fourteen states, with the largest concentrations in Kansas, Pennsylvania, Oklahoma, and Illinois. The count of congregations and members includes *one-third* of the 210 congregations and the 20,235 members that have a dual affiliation with the General Conference Mennonite Church and the Mennonite Church.

Overview   Transformational. Congregations, 179. Members, 27,507.
Pop., 37,134.

States   CO, 3; GA, 1; IA, 1; IL, 10; IN, 8; KS, 34; MI, 1; MO, 1;
NE, 2; OH, 7; OK, 14; PA, 25; TX, 1; VA, 1 (the state location of Dual Conference congregations appears under the entry for MC/GC: Dual Conference).

Contact   722 Main St., PO Box 347, Newton KS 67114;
☎ 316-283-5100; E-mail: doriss@gcmc.org.

Good News Mennonite Fellowship

The Good News Fellowship has sixteen congregations. Thirteen are in Alabama, with the remainder in the Panhandle of Florida. This group, which formed in 2000, came largely from congregations that had been affiliated with the Lancaster Mennonite Conference. This Fellowship formed because of geographical proximity, concerns about joining the proposed Mennonite Church USA, more conservative views on women in ministry, and other issues.

Overview   Transformational. Congregations, 16. Members, 467.
Pop., 887.

States   AL, 13; FL, 3.

Contact   NA.

Hope Mennonite Fellowship

This group formed in 1981 when a bishop withdrew from the Eastern Pennsylvania Mennonite Church. Today the group has four congregations, all in Pennsylvania.

Overview   Transitional. Congregations, 4. Members, 309. Pop., 587.
State   PA, 4.
Contact   137 Chapel Rd., Newmanstown, PA 17073; ☎ 717-949-3983.

Hopewell Mennonite District

This network of congregations in eastern Pennsylvania had been part of the Atlantic Coast Conference of the Mennonite Church. During 2000 they were in the process of forming their own autonomous body, with the proposed name of Apostolic Fellowship of the Radical Church Network. The Apostolic Fellowship did not plan to affiliate with the new Mennonite Church USA. They have a charismatic emphasis and a strong church planting effort.

Overview   Transformational. Congregations, 10. Members, 1,022.
            Pop., 1,315.
States   NJ, 1; PA, 9.
Contact   1675 Hopewell Rd., Elverson, PA 19520. ☎ 610-286-6308.

Independent Mennonite Congregations*

Some fifty-three congregations in twenty states consider themselves "Independent" congregations. These are not an organized body. Many support non-Mennonite evangelical mission programs. West of the Mississippi, many of these congregations had formerly been a part of the General Conference Mennonite Church but have cut formal ties with that body. Influenced by Fundamentalism, they supported institutions such as Grace Bible College (now University) in Omaha, Nebraska. Members of congregations in this grouping do not wear plain clothing and in this respect are unlike many members of Mennonite Unaffiliated congregations.

Overview   Transformational. Congregations, 53. Members, 4,887.
            Pop., 6,597.
States   AL, 1; AZ, 4; GA, 1; ID, 1; IN, 9; KS, 5; KY, 1; MI, 1; MN, 1;
          MO, 1; MS, 1; ND, 1; NJ, 1; OH, 1; OK, 1; OR, 7; PA, 10;
          SD, 3; VT, 1; WA, 2.
Contact   NA.

Keystone Mennonite Fellowship

The network of congregations in this independent conference emerged in 1985 in the Lancaster, Pennsylvania, area because some ordained leaders wanted to preserve more conservative standards than the Lancaster Mennonite Conference, which was affiliated with the Mennonite Church. At first the Fellowship functioned within the Lancaster Conference, but eventually it formed a separate affiliation in 1999. The group encourages plain dress, discourages television, and takes a more traditional stand on many Mennonite

Profiles of Groups by Tribe

163

doctrines and practices. All of the seventeen Keystone congregations are in eastern Pennsylvania except for one in Maryland and one in South Dakota.

Overview   Transitional. Congregations, 17. Members, 950. Pop., 1,805.
States   MD, 1; PA, 15; SD, 1.
Contact   2105 Old Lancaster Pike, Reinholds, PA 17569;
            ☎ 610-775-4059.

Kleine Gemeinde*

With a German name meaning "Little Church," this congregation traces its historical roots to Mexico, Canada, and Russia. This particular congregation migrated from Mexico to Boley, Oklahoma, in the 1970s. One of the more conservative Mennonite groups, they operate their own school in their church building.

Overview   Transitional. Congregation, 1. Members, 70. Pop., 133.
State   OK, 1.
Contact   NA.

Manhattan Mennonite Church*

This congregation in Kansas has a triple affiliation with the Mennonite Church, the General Conference Mennonite Church, and the Mennonite Brethren. Many members are involved with Kansas State University.

Overview   Transformational. Congregation, 1. Members, 80. Pop., 108.
State   KS, 1.
Contact   NA.

Mennonite Biblical Alliance

The congregations in this alliance formed in the spring of 2000, largely from the Conservative Mennonite Conference, over concerns about the declining use of the women's prayer covering, women in ministry, and the interpretation of Scripture. Their eighteen congregations are scattered over nine states.

Overview   Transitional. Congregations, 18. Members, 1,001. Pop., 1,902.
States   IN, 4; MD, 1; MS, 1; NC, 2; NY, 1; OH, 4; PA, 1; SC, 1;
            VA, 3.
Contact   NA.

Mennonite Brethren

The Mennonite Brethren emerged among Russian Mennonites in the 1860s and migrated to the United States and Canada in the late nineteenth century. Today the Mennonite Brethren congregations are located in both Canada and the States, with more than sixty in California alone. The Mennonite Brethren, one of the three major mainstream Mennonite groups, have not been involved in the formation of the proposed Mennonite Church USA. Maintaining a strong evangelical orientation, they support many Mennonite Central Committee projects as well as other inter-Mennonite activities. Most of the congregations are located west of the Mississippi River.

Overview Transformational. Congregations, 168. Members, 22,777.
     Pop., 30,723.

States AR, 2; AZ, 3; CA, 62; CO, 4; IL, 1; KS, 16; MN, 4; MO, 1;
     MT, 2; NC, 6; ND, 3; NE, 6; NY, 1; OK, 13; OR, 10; SD, 9;
     TX, 11; UT, 1; WA, 11.

Contact NA.

Mennonite Christian Fellowship

This group emerged from the Beachy Amish Church in the late 1950s but adopted their present name in the 1990s to assume a more Mennonite identity. Many members come from an Amish background. The Fellowship urges converts from Old Order communities to testify to a born-again faith experience. Today the Fellowship churches are typically more conservative than the Beachy Amish. Their twenty-three congregations are scattered in nine different states, with six in Missouri and six in Pennsylvania.

Overview Transitional. Congregations, 23. Members, 1,294. Pop., 2,459.

States CA, 1; KY, 2; MD, 1; MO, 6; NY, 1; OH, 1; PA, 6; TN, 4;
     WV, 1.

Contact NA.

Mennonite Church

This is the major Mennonite body anticipating merging with the General Conference Mennonite Church to form the proposed Mennonite Church USA in 2002. Unlike the Brethren, who formed a national body in the 1700s, the Mennonite Church did not organize a national General Conference until 1898. Some of the regional conferences joined the national body later, and others remained independent until 1971, when the Mennonite Church was reorganized. The Mennonite Church has seventeen regional conferences and congregations in forty-one states. Nearly 400 of its congregations are in Pennsylvania, Ohio, and Virginia, with 273 in Pennsylvania alone. The count of congregations and members includes *two-thirds* of the 210 congregations and 20,235 members who have a dual affiliation with the General Conference Mennonite Church.

Overview Transformational. Congregations, 871. Members, 92,157.
     Pop., 124,412.

States AK, 1; AL, 1; AR, 2; CO, 12; CT, 3; DC, 3; DE, 2; FL, 25;
     GA, 3; HI, 2; IL, 31; IN, 55; KS, 10; KY, 3; LA, 4; MA, 3;
     MD, 17; ME, 1; MI, 28; MN, 2; MO, 9; MS, 7; MT, 3;
     NC, 10; ND, 2; NJ, 11; NM, 1; NY, 34; OH, 69; OK, 2;
     PA, 273; PR, 10; SC, 2; TN, 4; TX, 9; VA, 54; VT, 2; WI, 3;
     WV, 7 (the state location of Dual Conference congregations
     appears under the enrty for MC/GC: Dual Conference).

Contact 421 S. 2nd St., Ste. 600, Elkhart, IN 46516; ☎ 219-294-7131;
     E-mail: mcgb@juno.com.

Mennonite Church/General Conference: Dual Conference*

About 210 congregations have had a dual affiliation with the Mennonite Church and the General Conference Mennonite Church prior to the proposed formation of the Mennonite Church USA in 2002. These congregations do not have their own organization but have simply maintained a dual affiliation with the two major bodies. They in essence began forming the Mennonite Church USA at the grassroots and regional level before the proposal for a nationwide merger. By the end of 2000, three new integrated regional conferences had formed: Pacific Northwest, Pacific Southwest, and Central Plains. Thirty-eight congregations are in California, and eighteen in Oregon. Of the 210 congregations and 20,235 members with dual affiliation, we have allocated one-third to the General Conference Mennonite Church and two-thirds to the Mennonite Church. Using this formula, the Dual Conference congregations and members were included in the totals for the Mennonite Church and the General Conference Mennonite Church but are also repeated here.

Overview   Transformational. Congregations, 210. Members, 20,235. Pop., 27,317.

States   AZ, 9; CA, 38; CO, 5; FL, 2; IA, 22; ID, 5; IL, 12; IN, 6; KS, 9; KY, 1; MA, 1; MD, 2; MI, 3; MN, 12; MO, 1; MT, 6; NC, 2; ND, 2; NE, 11; NM, 2; NY, 3; OH, 7; OR, 18; PA, 4; SD, 11; TX, 7; WA, 7; WI, 2.

Contact   NA.

Mennonite Church Dual Affiliated*

Two congregations have an affiliation with the Mennonite Church as well as with other denominations—the American Baptists (Arizona) and Elim Fellowship (New York).

Overview   Transformational. Congregations, 2. Members, 114. Pop., 154.

States   AZ, 1; NY, 1.

Contact   NA.

Mennonite Church USA***

This is the new Mennonite body that will likely be formed by the merger of the General Conference Mennonite Church and the Mennonite Church in 2002. Integration discussions have been underway for many years.

Mennonite Evangelical Churches

This group of three congregations originated in Canada and until recently were known as the Evangelical Mennonite Conference. They have congregations in Paris and Seminole, Texas, and also a congregation and a school in Kansas.

Overview   Transformational. Congregations, 3. Members, 250. Pop., 336.

States   KS, 1; TX, 2.

Contact   NA.

Mennonite Unaffiliated Congregations*

Seventy-seven congregations have dropped their formal affiliation with larger Mennonite bodies because of differences over doctrine, biblical interpretation, or practice. Eleven of these are located in Pennsylvania; the remainder are distributed over twenty-four other states. Many of these came from Mennonite Church backgrounds. Members of the Mennonite Unaffiliated congregations wear plain clothing but are typically *less* traditional than the Conservative Mennonite Unaffiliated churches. On the other hand, the Mennonite Unaffiliated congregations are *more* plain than the Independent Mennonite Churches, which tend to be more transformational and have more roots in the General Conference Mennonite Church.

Overview   Transitional. Congregations, 77. Members, 3,814. Pop., 7,171.
States   AR, 2; CA, 1; FL, 3; GA, 5; IA, 2; ID, 1; IL, 3; IN, 7; MD, 1; MI, 5; MN, 3; MO, 1; MS, 3; MT, 2; ND, 2; NE, 1; OH, 6; OR, 2; PA, 11; PR, 1; SC, 4; VA, 5; WA, 1; WI, 4; WV, 1.
Contact   NA.

Mid-Atlantic Mennonite Fellowship

This group formed in the Lancaster, Pennsylvania, area in 1978. Some of their congregations and members came from the Eastern Pennsylvania Mennonite Church, some from the Lancaster Mennonite Conference, and others from the Old Order Weaverland Conference. On a number of practices, such as the use of radios, the Mid-Atlantic Fellowship is less conservative than the Eastern Pennsylvania Mennonite Church. All but one of the sixteen congregations in this Fellowship are located in Pennsylvania.

Overview   Transitional. Congregations, 16. Members, 1,299. Pop., 2,468.
States   NY, 1. PA, 15.
Contact   784 Orchard Rd., Manheim, PA 17545; ☎ 717-664-4658.

Mid-West Mennonite Fellowship

Numerous conservative Mennonite churches of various backgrounds formed the Mid-West Fellowship in 1977 and opened a Maranatha Mennonite Bible School in Lansing, Michigan, in 1978. Mission outreach tends to be initiated by individual congregations rather than by the Fellowship as a whole. Some of the congregations of this Fellowship are located in Canada. In the United States, there are twenty-seven congregations, with concentrations in Ohio, Michigan, and Indiana.

Overview   Transitional. Congregations, 27. Members, 1,335. Pop., 2,537.
States   AZ, 1; IN, 5; KS, 1; MI, 5; MN, 2; MO, 1; OH, 8; PA, 1; WI, 3.
Contact   13550 W. Peninsula Rd., Hayward, WI 54843; ☎ 715-634-2553.

Nationwide Mennonite Fellowship Churches

A sizeable number of congregations from several different backgrounds began affiliating in the late 1950s and early 1960s. Lifestyle changes in some of the larger Mennonite bodies prompted the formation of the so-called Fellowship churches. Today about forty-seven congregations spread over nineteen states are part of this network.

Overview   Transitional. Congregations, 47. Members, 2,175. Pop., 4,133.

States   CA, 2; CO, 1; DE, 1; IA, 1; IN, 1; KY, 4; MA, 1; MD, 1; MI, 1; MO, 1; NC, 3; NM, 2; NY, 2; OH, 5; PA, 10; UT, 1; VA, 2; WI, 7; WY, 1.

Contact   18 Rd. 5577, Farmington, NM 87401; ☎ 505-632-3269.

Ohio Wisler Mennonite Churches

This group formed in 1973 when several churches that were part of the car-driving Old Order Wisler Mennonite Conference in Ohio and Indiana began to affiliate as the Ohio Wisler Mennonite Churches. Moving in a more progressive Mennonite direction, they adopted Sunday schools and more aggressive forms of outreach. All five of the present congregations are located in Ohio.

Overview   Transitional. Congregations, 5. Members, 421. Pop., 800.

State   OH, 5.

Contact   4215 W. Garfield Rd., Coumbiana, Ohio 44408; ☎ 330-482-4222.

Old Colony Mennonite*

This congregation traces its roots to the Old Colony Mennonites of Mexico and Canada. In 1977 it established a congregation at Seminole in western Texas. It was the first and the largest of four Mennonite groups to settle in the Seminole area. Some of their constituents are migrant laborers from Mexico, who follow the seasonal harvests.

Overview   Traditional. Congregation, 1. Members, 407. Pop., 916.

State   TX, 1.

Contact   NA.

Old Order Mennonite Groffdale Conference

This sizeable group of horse-and-buggy-driving Mennonites traces its roots to the 1893 Old Order division in Lancaster, Pennsylvania. Some years later, in 1927, the Old Order community in Lancaster divided over automobile use. The Groffdale Conference was the more conservative branch that became known as the Team Mennonites because they continued using a team (horse and carriage) for transportation. In recent years they have expanded into eight other states, including New York, Missouri, and Wisconsin. However, twenty of their forty-two congregations remain in Pennsylvania.

Overview   Traditional. Congregations, 42. Members, 7,096. Pop., 15,966.

States   IA, 2; IN, 4; KY, 2; MI, 1; MO, 3; NY, 4; OH, 2; PA, 20; WI, 4.

Contact   NA.

Old Order Mennonite John Martin Congregations*

These horse-and-buggy-driving Mennonites left the Old Order Groffdale Conference in 1993, when the Groffdale Conference allowed ministers to have telephones and household electricity (which other members already had). There are three congregations, one each in Pennsylvania, Kentucky, and Missouri.

Overview   Traditional. Congregations, 3. Members, 77. Pop., 173.
States   KY, 1; MO, 1; PA, 1.
Contact   NA.

Old Order Mennonite Noah Hoover Congregations*

These Mennonites formed an affiliation in 1963 but trace their roots to the Stauffer Mennonite division of 1845 and its subsequent subgroups. Members from a variety of backgrounds have been attracted to this group, led by minister Noah Hoover, because restrictions on technology are coupled with personal spirituality and high moral standards for youth. Internal combustion engines are not permitted. In an unusual departure from Mennonite practice, the men wear beards. The group, with three congregations, began in Snyder County, Pennsylvania, but then resettled to Kentucky (1978) and Missouri (1993).

Overview   Traditional. Congregations, 3. Members, 219. Pop., 493.
States   KY, 2; MO, 1.
Contact   NA.

Old Order Mennonite Reidenbach Group(s)

In 1942 the Reidenbach Mennonites withdrew from the Old Order Groffdale Conference because they felt participation in Civilian Public Service (CPS) camps would compromise their stance on separation from the world. They are also known as the "35ers" because about thirty-five people were involved in the original division. Now they are divided into some ten subgroups identified by the names of the various leaders. They have extremely conservative restrictions on technology: no tractors, telephones, electricity, or rubber on carriage wheels. Eight of their ten congregations are located in Pennsylvania, and one each in Missouri and Kentucky.

Overview   Traditional. Congregations, 10. Members, 361. Pop., 812.
States   KY, 1; MO, 1; PA, 8.
Contact   NA.

Old Order Mennonite Stauffer Group(s)

The Stauffer Mennonites are an Old Order group that broke off from the Lancaster Mennonite Conference in 1845, before the larger national Old Order movement of the 1880s. Sometimes called the Pike Mennonites, this is a horse-and-buggy group that does not use electricity or use tractors for fieldwork. Five of their ten congregations are located in Pennsylvania; the others are scattered in five other states.

Overview   Traditional. Congregations, 10. Members, 1,149. Pop., 2,585.

States   IL, 1; KY, 1; MD, 1; MO, 1; OH, 1; PA, 5.
Contact   NA.

Old Order Mennonite Unaffiliated*

These horse-and-buggy-driving Mennonites are fairly exclusive and conservative. They emerged from several different backgrounds and have some interaction with each other, but not formal intergroup fellowship. There are eleven congregations in four states: Pennsylvania, Tennessee, Maine, and Kentucky. They include a Martin Weaver group, a Brubaker group, a "Pike"-Weaver group, and an Aaron Martin group. Many of the members came from Old Order Stauffer groups.

Overview   Traditional. Congregations, 11. Members, 465. Pop., 1,046.
States   KY, 2; ME, 1; PA, 4; TN, 4.
Contact   NA.

Old Order Mennonite Virginia Conference

Part of the nationwide Old Order Movement, this group separated from the Virginia Mennonite Conference in 1901. They are similar to the Old Order Groffdale Conference, but they do not speak Pennsylvania German. Also in contrast to the Groffdale Conference, they do have pulpits in their meetinghouses and rubber tires on their tractors.

Overview   Traditional. Congregations, 3. Members, 426. Pop., 959.
State   VA, 3.
Contact   NA.

Old Order Mennonite Weaverland Conference

This group traces its roots to the Old Order division of 1893 in Pennsylvania, when Bishop Jonas Martin and his followers withdrew from the Lancaster Mennonite Conference. The Old Order community in Lancaster separated into two branches in 1927, when the Weaverland Conference accepted automobiles and the Groffdale Conference continued using horse-drawn carriages. For many years, members of the Weaverland Conference were known as "Black Bumpers" because members were required to paint any chrome on their cars black. This practice still continues for ministers, but not for members, who typically have dark-colored cars. The Weaverland Conference no longer uses the Pennsylvania German dialect in their services, but older members speak it. Reflecting Old Order ways, they do not have Sunday school, revival meetings, or organized mission/evangelism programs. They do use electricity, telephones, and modern farm machinery. Twenty-three of their thirty-four congregations are in Pennsylvania.

Overview   Traditional. Congregations, 34. Members, 5,574. Pop., 12,500.
States   IA, 1; MO, 4; NY, 3; PA, 23; VA, 1; WI, 2.
Contact   NA.

Old Order Mennonite Wenger/Weaver

These horse-and-buggy congregations, similar to the Old Order Groffdale Conference, maintain close contact with one another. They permit the use of pneumatic tires on buggies, tractors, and farm machinery. The Wenger congregations are located in Virginia, and the one Weaver congregation is in Indiana.

Overview   Traditional. Congregations, 3. Members, 308. Pop., 693.
States   IN, 1; VA, 2.
Contact   NA.

Old Order Mennonite Wisler Conference

Tracing its roots to a 1907 division of Old Order Mennonites in Ohio and Indiana, this automobile-driving group is similar to the Old Order Mennonite Weaverland Conference. The name Wisler comes from an early Old Order Mennonite leader, Jacob Wisler. They are commonly known as the Ohio-Indiana Wisler conference.

Overview   Traditional. Congregations, 7. Members, 780. Pop., 1,755.
States   IN, 3; MI, 1; MN, 1; OH, 2.
Contact   NA.

Old Order Orthodox Mennonite*

These Mennonites have one congregation in Kentucky and a small house church under way in Pennsylvania. They are affiliated with an Old Order Orthodox Mennonite group in Gorrie, Ontario.

Overview   Traditional. Congregations, 2. Members, 27. Pop., 61.
States   KY, 1; PA, 1.
Contact   NA.

Pilgrim Mennonite Conference

Ten of this group's fifteen congregations are located in Pennsylvania, the state where it began in 1991. The Pilgrim Conference was formed by members who withdrew from the Eastern Pennsylvania Mennonite Church because they differed on ideas about church leadership and wanted more flexible practices. Similar in many respects to the mother body, the Pilgrim Conference has an active prison ministry, holds tent-meeting revivals, and operates numerous schools, including the Pilgrim Mennonite Bible School.

Overview   Transitional. Congregations, 15. Members, 965. Pop., 1,833.
States   FL, 1; GA, 1; MS, 1; NY, 1; OH, 1; PA, 10.
Contact   40 Ketterman Hill Rd., Richland, PA 17087; ☎ 717-933-5667.

Reformed Mennonite Church

One of the first subgroups to form in the United States, the Reformed Mennonites separated from the Lancaster Mennonite Conference in 1812. The group wanted to restore some traditional practices of the Mennonite Church as well as establish new ones; members were sometimes known as New Mennonites. They wear plain patterns of dress but own automobiles.

Profiles of Groups by Tribe

171

With some 2,000 members around 1900, the Reformed Mennonites have experienced a steady decline in the twentieth century, to fewer than 300 members today.

Overview   Transitional. Congregations, 9. Members, 278. Pop., 626.
States   IL, 1; MI, 1; OH, 3; PA, 3; TN, 1.
Contact   NA.

Reinlaender Mennonite Church

This group with Russian roots migrated to Seminole, Texas, simultaneously from both Mexico and Canada in 1977. They live a more simple and spartan lifestyle than their nearby Old Colony Mennonite neighbors.

Overview   Traditional. Congregations, 2. Members, 465. Pop., 1,046.
States   KS, 1; TX, 1.
Contact   NA.

South Atlantic Mennonite Conference*

This small conference formed out of the southeastern Mennonite Conference primarily because of the geographical proximity of the congregations. Three of their four congregations are in Georgia.

Overview   Transitional. Congregations, 4. Members, 194. Pop., 369.
States   GA, 3; SC, 1.
Contact   Rt. 1, PO Box 149F, Olar, SC 29843; ☎ 803-368-3029.

Southeastern Mennonite Conference

This body withdrew from the Virginia Conference of the Mennonite Church in 1971 in order to maintain more conservative dress requirements. Many of the staff members of Christian Light Publications are affiliated with the Southeastern Conference congregations. The conference has two congregations in Puerto Rico.

Overview   Transitional. Congregations, 15. Members, 687. Pop., 1,305.
States   PR, 2; VA, 10; WV, 3.
Contact   631 Mountain Rd., Front Royal, VA 22630; ☎ 540-635-0375.

United Mennonite*

These two small house churches have separated from the Reformed Mennonite Church.

Overview   Transitional. Congregations, 2. Members, 17. Pop., 34.
State   PA, 2.
Contact   NA.

Washington-Franklin Mennonite Conference

This independent conference traces its roots to the Washington (Co., Md.) and Franklin (Co., Pa.) Mennonite Conference, which formed in south-central Pennsylvania and northern Maryland around 1790. The bulk of the congregations are in the Hagerstown, Maryland, area. It is one of the more traditional independent Mennonite conferences.

Overview   Transitional. Congregations, 13. Members, 1,296. Pop., 2,462.

States   KY, 2; MD, 9; PA, 2.

Contact   885 Shields Rd., St. Thomas, PA 17252; ☎ 717-369-2540.

Western Conservative Mennonite Fellowship

With seven of its congregations in Oregon, this conservative leaning group was once known as the "Bible Mennonites." They formed in 1973 and attracted congregations from several different backgrounds.

Overview   Transitional. Congregations, 10. Members, 612. Pop., 1,140.

States   CO, 1; ID, 1; OR, 7; WA, 1.

Contact   35340 S. E. Porter, Estacada, OR 97023; ☎ 503-630-7405.

York-Adams Mennonite Churches

Known officially as the Conservative Mennonite Churches of York and Adams Counties, Pennsylvania, this small conference of churches separated from the Lancaster Mennonite Conference in 1975 because they wanted to uphold more traditional practices. In many ways they are similar to the Eastern Pennsylvania Mennonite Church.

Overview   Transitional. Congregations, 5. Members, 266. Pop., 505.

State   PA, 5.

Contact   410 Hershey Heights Rd., Hanover, PA 17331;
☎ 717-630-2441.

Profiles of Groups by Tribe

173

LISTING OF DUAL AFFILIATED CONGREGATIONS

Church of the Brethren/Others	Congs.	Members
Church of the Brethren/Mennonite	8	552
Church of the Brethren/Brethren Church	2	88
Church of the Brethren/American Baptist	8	1,167
Church of the Brethren/United Church of Christ	7	604
Church of the Brethren/Christian Church (Disciples)	2	262
Church of the Brethren/United Methodist	2	70
Church of the Brethren/Southern Baptist	1	44
Mennonite Church/General Conference		
Central Plains Conference	65	8,962
Pacific Northwest Conference	30	2,760
Pacific Southwest Conference	47	3,174
Other Congregations	68	5,365
TOTAL Mennonite Church/General Conference: Dual Conference	210	20,261
Mennonite Church/Others		
Mennonite Church/Conservative Mennonite Conference	3	351
Mennonite Church/Mennonite Brethren	1	8
Mennonite Church/American Baptist	1	5
Mennonite Church/Elim Fellowship	1	109
Mennonite Brethren/General Conference/Mennonite Church	1	80

Section E

LISTING OF REGIONAL DISTRICTS AND CONFERENCES

Brethren in Christ	Membership
Allegheeny	3,912
Atlantic	5,939
Central	1,441
Midwest	696
Pacific	1,577
Southeast	2,476
Susquehanna	3,969
Church of the Brethren	
Atlantic Northeast	15,830
Atlantic Southeast	2,075
Idaho	708
Illinois-Wisconsin	5,057
Indiana, Northern	6,550
Indiana, South/Central	5,489
Michigan	1,368
Mid-Atlantic	10,177
Missouri-Arkansas	884
Northern Plains	3,023
Ohio, Northern	6,361
Ohio, Southern	9,043
Oregon-Washington	1,430
Pacific Southwest	3,359
Pennsylvania, Middle	9,235
Pennsylvania, Southern	7,953
Pennsylvania, Western	10,191
Shenandoah	14,698
Southeastern	2,759
Southern Plains	886
Virlina	11,460
Western Plains	3,963
West Marva	5,805
General Conference Mennonite Church	
Central	8,595
Eastern	4,615
Northern	4,221

Pacific Northwest*	2,828
Pacific Southwest*	2,913
Western	12,281
Mennonite Brethren	
Central	2,447
Latin America (South Texas)	295
North Carolina	209
Pacific	12,338
Southern	6,783
Mennonite Church	
Allegheny	3,579
Atlantic Coast	6,092
Central Plains*	8,045
Franconia	7,278
Franklin	1,375
Gulf States	676
Illinois	4,449
Indiana-Michigan	11,859
Lancaster	19,617
New York	1,267
North Central	482
Ohio	11,102
Puerto Rico	472
Rocky Mountain	1,577
South Central	4,400
Southeast	2,268
Virginia	8,761
Mennonite Independent Conferences	
Bethel Fellowship	452
Caribbean Mennonite Conference	198
Cumberland Valley	406
Eastern Pennsylvania Mennonite Church	3,470
Good News Mennonite Fellowship	467
Hope Mennonite Fellowship	309
Keystone Mennonite Fellowship	950
Mid-Atlantic Mennonite Fellowship	1,299
Mid-West Mennonite Fellowship	1,335
Nationwide Mennonite Fellowship Churches	2,175
Ohio Wisler Mennonite Churches	421
Pilgrim Mennonite Conference	965
South Atlantic Mennonite Conference	194
Southeastern Mennonite Conference	687
Washington-Franklin Mennonite Conference	1,296
Western Conservative Mennonite Fellowship	612

* An integrated MC/GC conference/district.

STATE
SUMMARIES

Due to rounding, percentages for these summaries do not always total 100 percent. Abbreviations appear in some entries:

Conf.	Conference
Cong/s.	Congregation(s), district(s), or colony(ies)
Consrv.	Conservative
DA	Dual Affiliated
DC	Dual Conference
Mems.	Members (baptized membership)
O. O.	Old Order
Pop.	Population (members, children, and other participants)

ALABAMA

The Anabaptist membership in Alabama consists of 74 percent Mennonite, 22 percent Brethren, and 4 percent Amish. There are a total of 25 Anabaptist congregations in Alabama. Over half the congregations are affiliated with the Good News Mennonite Fellowship.

	Cong.	Mems.	Mems. %	Pop.	Pop. %
Amish					
Beachy Amish	2	52	100	99	100
Brethren					
Church of the Brethren	5	262	100	354	100
Mennonite					
Apostolic Christian Church of America	1	45	5	86	5
Church of God in Christ Mennonite	2	316	36	600	37
Good News Mennonite Fellowship	13	414	47	787	49
Independent Mennonite Congregations	1	60	7	81	5
Mennonite Church	1	45	5	61	4
Subtotals	18	880	100	1,615	100
Totals					
Amish	2	52	4	99	5
Brethren	5	262	22	354	17
Mennonite	18	880	74	1,615	78
Statewide Totals	25	1,194	100	2,068	100

ALASKA

The Anabaptist membership in the state of Alaska consists of 99 percent Brethren and 1 percent Mennonite. Six of the seven congregations are affiliated with the Fellowship of Grace Brethren Churches.

	Cong.	Mems.	Mems. %	Pop.	Pop. %
Brethren					
Grace Brethren Churches	6	1,308	100	1,766	100
Mennonite					
Mennonite Church	1	18	100	24	100
Totals					
Brethren	6	1,308	99	1,766	99
Mennonite	1	18	1	24	1
Statewide Totals	7	1,326	100	1,790	100

ARIZONA

The state of Arizona's Anabaptist membership is 79 percent Mennonite and 21 percent Brethren. The Church of the Brethren represents 64 percent of the total members in the Brethren tribe, while the Mennonite Church/General Conference: Dual Conference congregations represent 58 percent of the membership in the Mennonite tribe. Arizona has a total of 40 Anabaptist congregations.

	Cong.	Mems.	Mems. %	Pop.	Pop. %
Brethren					
Brethren Church	3	145	32	196	32
Church of the Brethren	4	296	64	400	64
Grace Brethren Churches	1	18	4	24	4
Subtotals	8	459	100	620	100
Mennonite					
Apostolic Christian Church of America	3	220	13	418	16
Church of God in Christ Mennonite	6	187	11	355	14
Consrv. Mennonite Conf.	5	163	10	310	12
Independent Mennonite Congregations	4	29	2	39	2
Mennonite Brethren	3	67	4	90	3
Mennonite Church/General Conf.: DC	9	976	58	1,318	51
Mennonite Church: DA	1	5	0.3	7	0.3
Mid-West Mennonite Fellowship	1	34	2	65	2
Subtotals	32	1,681	100	2,602	100
Totals					
Brethren	8	459	21	620	19
Mennonite	32	1,681	79	2,602	81
Statewide Totals	40	2,140	100	3,222	100

ARKANSAS

With a total of 17 congregations, the Anabaptist membership in the state of Arkansas consists of 60 percent Mennonite, 35 percent Amish, and 5 percent Brethren. The Church of God in Christ Mennonite represents 53 percent of the total membership in the Mennonite tribe. There are five Amish congregations, three of which are Amish Mennonite.

	Cong.	Mems.	Mems. %	Pop.	Pop. %
Amish					
Amish Mennonite	3	228	77	433	77
Beachy Amish	2	67	23	127	23
Subtotals	5	295	100	560	100

	Cong.	Mems.	Mems. %	Pop.	Pop. %
Brethren					
Church of the Brethren	1	17	40	23	40
Church of the Brethren/Mennonite: DA	1	26	60	35	60
Subtotals	2	43	100	58	100
Mennonite					
Bethel Mennonite Fellowship	1	42	8	80	9
Church of God in Christ Mennonite	2	273	53	519	58
Consrv. Mennonite Conf./Mennonite Church: DA	1	31	6	42	5
Mennonite Brethren	2	71	14	96	11
Mennonite Church	2	54	10	73	8
Mennonite Unaffiliated Congregations	2	46	9	87	10
Subtotals	10	517	100	897	100
Totals					
Amish	5	295	35	560	37
Brethren	2	43	5	58	4
Mennonite	10	517	60	897	59
Statewide Totals	17	855	100	1,515	100

CALIFORNIA

The state of California has a total of 201 Anabaptist congregations. Fifty-five percent of the total congregations are affiliated with the Mennonites, and 45 percent of the congregations with the Brethren. The Mennonite Brethren represent 75 percent of the total membership in the Mennonite tribe. Fellowship of Grace Brethren Churches represent 48 percent of the Brethren membership.

	Cong.	Mems.	Mems. %	Pop.	Pop. %
Brethren					
Brethren Church	3	112	1	151	1
Brethren Community Fellowship	1	75	1	143	1
Brethren in Christ	15	1,444	14	1,949	13
Church of the Brethren	27	2,929	28	3,954	27
Church of the Brethren: DA	1	62	1	84	1
Dunkard Brethren	2	91	1	173	1
Grace Brethren Churches	36	4,970	48	6,710	46
Old Brethren	2	85	1	191	1
Old German Baptist Brethren	4	599	6	1,348	9
Subtotals	91	10,367	100	14,703	100
Mennonite					
Apostolic Christian Church of America	2	78	1	148	1
Church of God in Christ Mennonite	4	799	6	1,518	9
Mennonite Brethren	62	9,366	75	12,644	73
Mennonite Christian Fellowship	1	21	0.2	40	0.2
Mennonite Church/General Conf.: DC	38	2,198	18	2,967	17
Mennonite Unaffiliated Congregations	1	15	0.1	29	0.2
Nationwide Mennonite Fellowship Churches	2	49	0.4	93	1
Subtotals	110	12,526	100	17,439	100
Totals					
Brethren	91	10,367	45	14,703	46
Mennonite	110	12,526	55	17,439	54
Statewide Totals	201	22,893	100	32,142	100

COLORADO

The Anabaptist membership in the state of Colorado consists of 73 percent Mennonite, 26 percent Brethren, and 1 percent Amish. In Colorado there is one Amish Mennonite congregation but no Old Order Amish. In the Brethren tribe, the Church of the Brethren has the most congregations (10); the Mennonite Church (with 12) is the largest Mennonite group.

	Cong.	Mems.	Mems. %	Pop.	Pop. %
Amish					
Amish Mennonite	1	30	100	57	100
Brethren					
Church of the Brethren	9	504	58	680	57
Church of the Brethren: DA	1	113	13	153	13
Consrv. Grace Brethren	1	23	3	31	3
Dunkard Brethren	1	50	6	95	8
Grace Brethren Churches	2	173	20	234	20
Subtotals	14	863	100	1,193	100
Mennonite					
Apostolic Christian Church of America	1	35	1	67	2
Charity Christian Fellowship	1	49	2	93	3
Church of God in Christ Mennonite	2	136	6	258	8
Consrv. Mennonite Unaffiliated	1	36	2	68	2
General Conf. Mennonite Church	3	106	4	143	4
Mennonite Brethren	4	512	21	691	20
Mennonite Church	12	1,079	45	1,457	43
Mennonite Church/General Conf.: DC	5	358	15	483	14
Nationwide Mennonite Fellowship Churches	1	40	2	76	2
Western Consrv. Mennonite Fellowship	1	41	2	55	2
Subtotals	31	2,392	100	3,391	100
Totals					
Amish	1	30	1	57	1
Brethren	14	863	26	1,193	26
Mennonite	31	2,392	73	3,391	73
Statewide Totals	46	3,285	100	4,641	100

CONNECTICUT

The state of Connecticut has five Anabaptist congregations consisting of one Brethren congregation and four Mennonite congregations. The congregations affiliated with the Mennonites represent 96 percent of the total Anabaptist membership in the state.

	Cong.	Mems.	Mems. %	Pop.	Pop. %
Brethren					
Grace Brethren Churches	1	21	100	28	100
Mennonite					
Apostolic Christian Church of America	1	338	61	642	68
Mennonite Church	3	219	39	296	32
Subtotals	4	557	100	938	100
Totals					
Brethren	1	21	4	28	3
Mennonite	4	557	96	938	97
Statewide Totals	5	578	100	966	100

DELAWARE

The Anabaptist membership in the state of Delaware is 53 percent Mennonite, 28 percent Amish, and 19 percent Brethren. There are eight Old Order Amish congregations in the state. The Conservative Mennonite Conference represents 65 percent of the total Mennonite membership. There are 23 congregations in the state of Delaware.

	Cong.	Mems.	Mems. %	Pop.	Pop. %
Amish					
O. O. Amish	8	480	100	1,080	100%
Brethren					
Brethren Church	1	24	8	32	8
Church of the Brethren	3	260	82	351	82
Grace Brethren Churches	1	32	10	43	10
Subtotals	5	316	100	426	100
Mennonite					
Consrv. Mennonite Conf.	5	593	65	1,127	68
Eastern Pennsylvania Mennonite Church	2	139	15	264	16
Mennonite Church	2	154	17	208	13
Nationwide Mennonite Fellowship Churches	1	25	3	48	3
Subtotals	10	911	100	1,647	100
Totals					
Amish	8	480	28	1,080	34
Brethren	5	316	19	426	14
Mennonite	10	911	53	1,647	52
Statewide Totals	23	1,707	100	3,153	100

DISTRICT OF COLUMBIA

The District of Columbia claims Amish, Brethren, and Mennonites. Mennonites represent 52 percent of the Anabaptist membership, the Brethren 45 percent, and the Amish 3 percent. All the Amish members are part of one unaffiliated Amish Mennonite congregation. The District of Columbia has a total of eight Anabaptist congregations.

	Cong.	Mems.	Mems. %	Pop.	Pop. %
Amish					
Amish Mennonite Unaffiliated	1	18	100	34	100
Brethren					
Brethren Church	1	93	34	126	34
Church of the Brethren	2	178	66	240	66
Subtotals	3	271	100	366	100
Mennonite					
Apostolic Christian Church of America	1	10	3	19	4
Mennonite Church	3	299	97	404	96
Subtotals	4	309	100	423	100
Totals					
Amish	1	18	3	34	4
Brethren	3	271	45	366	44
Mennonite	4	309	52	423	51
Statewide Totals	8	598	100	823	100

State Summaries

FLORIDA

The state of Florida hosts Amish, Brethren, and Mennonites. The Anabaptist membership in the state consists of 52 percent Brethren, 45 percent Mennonite, and 3 percent Amish. Sixty-five percent of Mennonites are affiliated with the Mennonite Church. Thirty-eight percent of the Brethren tribe are affiliated with the Church of the Brethren. There are a total of 114 Anabaptist congregations in the state.

	Cong.	Mems.	Mems. %	Pop.	Pop. %
Amish					
Amish Mennonite Unaffiliated	1	24	10	46	10
Beachy Amish	2	171	72	325	69
New Order Amish	1	44	18	99	21
Subtotals	4	239	100	470	100
Brethren					
Brethren Church	4	291	6	393	6
Brethren in Christ	17	1,604	35	2,165	35
Church of the Brethren	16	1,730	38	2,336	37
Consrv. Grace Brethren	1	10	0.2	14	0.2
Grace Brethren Churches	22	945	21	1,276	20
Old German Baptist Brethren	2	29	1	65	1
Subtotals	62	4,609	100	6,249	100
Mennonite					
Apostolic Christian Church of America	3	134	3	255	4
Church of God in Christ Mennonite	2	202	5	384	6
Consrv. Mennonite Conf.	8	763	19	1,450	24
Eastern Pennsylvania Mennonite Church	1	20	1	38	1
Good News Mennonite Fellowship	3	53	1	101	2
Mennonite Church	25	2,579	65	3,482	58
Mennonite Church/General Conf.: DC	2	56	1	76	1
Mennonite Unaffiliated Congregations	3	137	3	185	3
Pilgrim Mennonite Conf.	1	24	1	46	1
Subtotals	48	3,968	100	6,015	100
Totals					
Amish	4	239	3	470	4
Brethren	62	4,609	52	6,249	49
Mennonite	48	3,968	45	6,017	47
Statewide Totals	114	8,816	100	12,736	100

GEORGIA

The Anabaptist membership in the state of Georgia consists of 66 percent Mennonite, 21 percent Amish, and 13 percent Brethren. In Georgia, there are three Beachy Amish congregations but no Old Order Amish group. Of the 27 congregations in Georgia, 21 are Mennonite.

	Cong.	Mems.	Mems. %	Pop.	Pop. %
Amish					
Beachy Amish	3	315	100	599	100
Brethren					
Brethren in Christ	1	23	12	31	10
Grace Brethren Churches	1	135	68	182	59
Old German Baptist Brethren	1	42	21	95	31
Subtotals	3	200	100	308	100

	Cong.	Mems.	Mems. %	Pop.	Pop. %
Mennonite					
Apostolic Christian Church of America	1	12	1	23	1
Charity Christian Fellowship	1	33	3	63	4
Church of God in Christ Mennonite	3	335	33	517	31
Consrv. Mennonite Conf.	1	38	4	72	4
Eastern Pennsylvania Mennonite Church	1	38	4	72	4
General Conf. Mennonite Church	1	19	2	26	2
Independent Mennonite Cong.	1	45	4	61	4
Mennonite Church	3	128	13	173	10
Mennonite Unaffiliated Congs.	5	202	20	384	23
Pilgrim Mennonite Conf.	1	48	5	91	5
South Atlantic Mennonite Conf.	3	112	11	213	13
Subtotals	21	1,010	100	1,695	100
Totals					
Amish	3	315	21	599	23
Brethren	3	200	13	308	12
Mennonite	21	1,010	66	1,695	65
Statewide Totals	27	1,525	100	2,602	100

HAWAII

There are a total of six Anabaptist congregations in the state; two congregations are Mennonite and four are Grace Brethren.

	Cong.	Mems.	Mems. %	Pop.	Pop. %
Brethren					
Grace Brethren Churches	4	240	100	324	100
Mennonite					
Mennonite Church	2	78	100	105	100
Totals					
Brethren	4	240	75	324	76
Mennonite	2	78	25	105	24
Statewide Totals	6	318	100	429	100

IDAHO

The state of Idaho has twenty-one Anabaptist congregations; fifteen are Mennonite and six are Brethren. All of the Brethren congregations are affiliated with the Church of the Brethren. The Church of God in Christ Mennonite represents 49 percent of the Mennonite membership.

	Cong.	Mems.	Mems. %	Pop.	Pop. %
Brethren					
Church of the Brethren	6	700	100	945	100
Mennonite					
Charity Christian Fellowship	1	27	2	51	2
Church of God in Christ Mennonite	6	643	49	1,222	56
Independent Mennonite Congregations	1	20	2	27	1
Mennonite Church/General Conf.: DC	5	505	39	682	31
Mennonite Unaffiliated Congregations	1	75	6	143	7
Western Consrv. Mennonite Fellowship	1	33	3	63	3
Subtotals	15	1,303	100	2,188	100

Totals	Cong.	Mems.	Mems. %	Pop.	Pop. %
Brethren	6	700	35	945	30
Mennonite	15	1,303	65	2,188	70
Statewide Totals	21	2,003	100	3,133	100

ILLINOIS

The Anabaptist membership in the state of Illinois is 66 percent Mennonite, 24 percent Brethren, and 10 percent Amish. In the Mennonite tribe, the Apostolic Christian Church of America represents 37 percent of the total membership; the Church of the Brethren claims 88 percent of the Brethren membership. In all, Illinois has 182 Anabaptist congregations.

	Cong.	Mems.	Mems. %	Pop.	Pop. %
Amish					
Amish Mennonite	3	265	12	504	10
Beachy Amish	4	296	13	562	12
New Order Amish	2	86	4	194	4
O. O. Amish	29	1,595	71	3,589	74
Subtotals	38	2,242	100	4,849	100
Brethren					
Brethren Church	3	408	8	551	8
Brethren in Christ	1	62	1	84	1
Church of the Brethren	42	4,665	88	6,298	88
Church of the Brethren/Mennonite: DA	1	150	3	203	3
Church of the Brethren: DA	1	26	0.5	35	0.5
Subtotals	48	5,311	100	7,171	100
Mennonite					
Apostolic Christian Church of America	19	5,393	37	10,247	44
Church of God in Christ Mennonite	1	24	0.2	46	0.2
Consrv. Mennonite Conf.	2	268	2	509	2
Eastern Pennsylvania Mennonite Church	3	235	2	447	2
Evangelical Mennonite Church	12	2,034	14	2,746	12
General Conf. Mennonite Church	10	1,487	10	2,007	9
Mennonite Brethren	1	11	0.1	15	0.1
Mennonite Church	31	4,239	29	5,723	25
Mennonite Church/General Conf.: DC	12	733	5	990	4
Mennonite Unaffiliated Congs.	3	150	1	285	1
O. O. Mennonite Stauffer Group	1	29	0.2	65	0.3
Reformed Mennonite Church	1	43	0.3	97	0.4
Subtotals	96	14,646	100	23,177	100
Totals					
Amish	38	2,242	10	4,849	14
Brethren	48	5,311	24	7,171	20
Mennonite	96	14,646	66	23,177	66
Statewide Totals	182	22,199	100	35,197	100

INDIANA

The Amish represent 28 percent of Indiana's Anabaptist membership with 257 congregations. The Old Order Amish have 92 percent of the Amish membership. Of the statewide Anabaptist membership, Mennonites with 35 percent and Brethren groups with 36 percent are nearly the same size. The Church of the Brethren has 96 congregations with 59 percent of the Brethren membership. The Mennonite Church has 55 congregations representing 49 percent of the Mennonite membership.

	Cong.	Mems.	Mems. %	Pop.	Pop. %
Amish					
Amish Mennonite Unaffiliated	1	34	2	65	2
Beachy Amish	14	990	6	1,881	5
New Order Amish	2	130	1	293	1
O. O. Amish	239	14,415	92	32,434	93
O. O. Amish Swartzentruber	1	50	0.3	113	0.3
Subtotals	257	15,619	100	34,786	100
Brethren					
Brethren Church	34	3,773	19	5,094	18
Brethren in Christ	4	231	1	312	1
Church of the Brethren	96	11,899	59	16,064	56
Church of the Brethren/Mennonite: DA	1	10	0.05	14	0.05
Consrv. Grace Brethren	5	361	2	487	2
Dunkard Brethren	2	80	0.4	152	1
Grace Brethren Churches	18	2,135	11	2,882	10
Old Brethren	2	130	1	293	1
Old Brethren German Baptist	1	50	0.2	113	0.4
Old German Baptist Brethren	9	1,464	7	3,294	11
Subtotals	172	20,133	100	28,705	100
Mennonite					
Apostolic Christian Church of America	11	2,254	11	4,283	14
Bethel Mennonite Fellowship	3	70	0.4	133	0.4
Charity Christian Fellowship	1	78	0.4	148	0.5
Church of God in Christ Mennonite	1	52	0.3	99	0.3
Consrv. Mennonite Conf.	10	1,261	6	2,396	8
Consrv. Mennonite Unaffiliated	2	146	1	277	1
Evangelical Mennonite Church	7	1,259	6	1,700	6
General Conf. Mennonite Church	8	2,231	11	3,012	10
Independent Mennonite Congregations	9	687	4	927	3
Mennonite Biblical Alliance	4	242	1	460	2
Mennonite Church	55	9,588	49	12,944	43
Mennonite Church/General Conf.: DC	6	332	2	448	2
Mennonite Unaffiliated Congregations	7	346	2	657	2
Mid-West Mennonite Fellowship	5	305	2	580	2
Nationwide Mennonite Fellowship Churches	1	25	0.1	48	0.2
O. O. Mennonite Groffdale Conf.	4	286	1	644	2
O. O. Mennonite Wenger/Weaver Group	1	35	0.2	79	0.3
O. O. Mennonite Wisler Conf.	3	420	2	945	3
Subtotals	138	19,617	100	29,780	100
Totals					
Amish	257	15,619	28	34,786	37
Brethren	172	20,133	36	28,705	31
Mennonite	138	19,617	35	29,780	32
Statewide Totals	567	55,369	100	93,271	100

IOWA

In the state of Iowa, the Anabaptist membership is 48 percent Mennonite, 32 percent Brethren, and 20 percent Amish. The Old Order Amish represent 92 percent of the Amish membership; the Church of the

Brethren claims 63 percent of the Brethren tribe. The Mennonite Church/General Conference: Dual Conference congregations represent 65 percent of the Mennonite membership. Iowa has 124 congregations.

	Cong.	Mems.	Mems. %	Pop.	Pop. %
Amish					
Beachy Amish	2	174	8	331	7
O. O. Amish	35	1,925	90	4,331	91
O. O. Amish Swartzentruber	1	50	2	113	2
Subtotals	38	2,149	100	4,775	100
Brethren					
Brethren in Christ	1	29	1	39	1
Church of the Brethren	22	2,175	63	2,936	62
Church of the Brethren: DA	5	424	12	572	12
Consrv. Grace Brethren	2	60	2	81	2
Dunkard Brethren	1	80	2	152	3
Grace Brethren Churches	8	677	19	914	19
O. O. River Brethren	1	33	1	74	2
Subtotals	40	3,478	100	4,768	100
Mennonite					
Apostolic Christian Church of America	8	915	18	1,739	21
Charity Christian Fellowship	1	24	0.5	46	1
Church of God in Christ Mennonite	3	162	3	308	4
Consrv. Mennonite Conf.	5	477	9	906	11
General Conf. Mennonite Church	1	8	0.2	11	0.1
Mennonite Church/General Conf.: DC	22	3,370	65	4,550	56
Mennonite Unaffiliated Congregations	2	34	1	65	1
Nationwide Mennonite Fellowship Churches	1	63	1	120	1
O. O. Mennonite Groffdale Conf.	2	120	2	270	3
O. O. Mennonite Weaverland Conf.	1	44	1	99	1
Subtotals	46	5,217	100	8,114	100
Totals					
Amish	38	2,149	20	4,775	27
Brethren	40	3,478	32	4,768	27
Mennonite	46	5,217	48	8,114	46
Statewide Totals	124	10,844	100	17,657	100

KANSAS

In the state of Kansas, Mennonites have 82 percent of the total Anabaptist membership. The Brethren are next with 16 percent, and the Amish represent 3 percent of the total membership. The General Conference Mennonite Church has 34 congregations representing 42 percent of the Mennonite membership. There are six Old Order Amish congregations in the total of 169 Anabaptist congregations.

	Cong.	Mems.	Mems. %	Pop.	Pop. %
Amish					
Beachy Amish	3	320	42	608	38
New Order Amish	2	110	14	248	15
O. O. Amish	6	330	43	743	46
Subtotals	11	760	100	1,599	100

	Cong.	Mems.	Mems. %	Pop.	Pop. %
Brethren					
Brethren Church	3	99	2	134	2
Brethren in Christ	4	339	8	458	8
Church of the Brethren	30	2,943	73	3,973	67
Dunkard Brethren	1	78	2	148	2
Grace Brethren Churches	2	104	3	140	2
Old German Baptist Brethren	5	481	12	1082	18
Subtotals	45	4,044	100	5,935	100
Mennonite					
Apostolic Christian Church of America	6	498	2	946	3
Church of God in Christ Mennonite	23	3,628	17	6,893	22
Consrv. Mennonite Conf.	2	201	1	382	1
Evangelical Mennonite Brethren	1	140	1	189	1
Evangelical Mennonite Church	3	421	2	568	2
General Conf. Mennonite Church	34	8,920	42	12,042	39
Independent Mennonite Congs.	5	981	5	1,324	4
Manhattan Mennonite Church: GC/MB/MC	1	80	0.4	108	0.3
Mennonite Brethren	16	3,670	17	4,955	16
Mennonite Church	10	1,568	7	2,117	7
Mennonite Church/General Conf.: DC	9	922	4	1,245	4
Mennonite Evangelical Churches	1	33	0.2	45	0.1
Mid-West Mennonite Fellowship	1	27	0.1	51	0.2
Reinlaender Mennonite Church	1	78	0.4	176	1
Subtotals	113	21,167	100	31,041	100
Totals					
Amish	11	760	3	1,599	4
Brethren	45	4,044	16	5,935	15
Mennonite	113	21,167	82	31,041	80
Statewide Totals	169	25,971	100	38,575	100

KENTUCKY

Kentucky has 94 Anabaptist congregations, of which 48 are Amish. The Anabaptist membership is 56 percent Amish, 31 percent Mennonite, and 13 percent Brethren. There are 30 Old Order Amish congregations in Kentucky, representing 62 percent of the Amish membership, plus three Old Order Amish Swartzentruber districts.

	Cong.	Mems.	Mems. %	Pop.	Pop. %
Amish					
Amish Mennonite Unaffiliated	2	133	5	253	4
Beachy Amish	8	493	18	937	16
New Order Amish	5	276	10	621	10
O. O. Amish	30	1,730	62	3,893	64
O. O. Amish Swartzentruber	3	150	5	338	6
Subtotals	48	2,782	100	6,040	100
Brethren					
Brethren Church	2	59	9	80	9
Brethren in Christ	5	232	36	313	36
Church of the Brethren	4	262	41	354	41
Grace Brethren Churches	3	87	14	117	14
Subtotals	14	640	100	864	100

	Cong.	Mems.	Mems. %	Pop.	Pop. %
Mennonite					
Church of God in Christ Mennonite	2	195	13	371	12
Consrv. Mennonite Conf.	7	220	14	418	13
Independent Mennonite Cong.	1	12	1	16	1
Mennonite Christian Fellowship	2	127	8	241	8
Mennonite Church	3	61	4	82	3
Mennonite Church/General Conf.: DC	1	16	1	22	1
Nationwide Mennonite Fellowship Churches	4	210	14	399	13
O. O. Mennonite Groffdale Conf.	2	210	14	473	15
O. O. Mennonite John Martin Congs.	1	24	2	54	2
O. O. Mennonite Noah Hoover Congs.	2	190	12	428	14
O. O. Mennonite Reidenbach Group	1	32	2	72	2
O. O. Mennonite Stauffer Group	1	37	2	83	3
O. O. Mennonite Unaffiliated	2	129	8	290	9
O. O. Orthodox Mennonite	1	21	1	47	2
Washington-Franklin Mennonite Conf.	2	54	4	103	3
Subtotals	32	1,538	100	3,099	100
Totals					
Amish	48	2,782	56	6040	60
Brethren	14	640	13	864	9
Mennonite	32	1,538	31	3,099	31
Statewide Totals	94	4,960	100	10,003	100

LOUISIANA

In Louisiana there are two Brethren congregations and six Mennonite congregations. The Mennonite Church claims 53 percent of the total Mennonite membership; the Church of the Brethren is the only Brethren group.

	Cong.	Mems.	Mems. %	Pop.	Pop. %
Brethren					
Church of the Brethren	2	171	100	231	100
Mennonite					
Church of God in Christ Mennonite	2	298	47	402	47
Mennonite Church	4	333	53	450	53
Subtotals	6	631	100	852	100
Totals					
Brethren	2	171	21	231	21
Mennonite	6	631	79	852	79
Statewide Totals	8	802	100	1083	100

MAINE

The state of Maine claims Amish, Brethren, and Mennonite groups and has a total of seven Anabaptist congregations.

	Cong.	Mems.	Mems. %	Pop.	Pop. %
Amish					
Beachy Amish	1	12	100	23	100
Brethren					
Church of the Brethren	3	92	100	124	100

	Cong.	Mems.	Mems. %	Pop.	Pop. %
Mennonite					
Church of God in Christ Mennonite	1	3	6	6	7
Mennonite Church	1	29	57	39	45
O. O. Mennonite Unaffiliated	1	19	37	43	49
Subtotals	3	51	100	88	100
Totals					
Amish	1	12	8	23	10
Brethren	3	92	59	124	53
Mennonite	3	51	33	88	37
Statewide Totals	7	155	100	235	100

MARYLAND

The Anabaptist membership in the state of Maryland consists of 77 percent Brethren, 20 percent Mennonite, and 3 percent Amish. There are nine Washington-Franklin Mennonite Conference congregations, representing 32 percent of the Mennonite membership. The Church of the Brethren has 60 congregations, representing 71 percent of the Brethren membership. Maryland has a total of 133 Anabaptist congregations.

	Cong.	Mems.	Mems. %	Pop.	Pop. %
Amish					
Beachy Amish	1	55	11	105	9
New Order Amish	1	179	35	403	36
O. O. Amish	5	275	54	619	55
Subtotals	7	509	100	1127	100
Brethren					
Brethren Church	4	593	5	801	5
Brethren in Christ	4	252	2	340	2
Church of the Brethren	60	8,768	71	11,837	71
Church of the Brethren/Mennonite: DA	1	31	0.3	42	0.3
Church of the Brethren: DA	1	86	1	116	1
Consrv. Grace Brethren	1	20	0.2	27	0.2
Dunkard Brethren	2	44	0.4	84	1
Grace Brethren Churches	10	2,521	20	3,403	20
Old German Baptist Brethren	1	7	0.1	16	0.1
Subtotals	84	12,322	100	16,666	100
Mennonite					
Bethel Mennonite Fellowship	1	34	1	65	1
Consrv. Mennonite Conf.	2	350	11	665	12
Cumberland Valley Mennonite Church	3	160	5	304	5
Eastern Pennsylvania Mennonite Church	2	106	3	201	4
Keystone Mennonite Fellowship	1	12	0.4	23	0.4
Mennonite Biblical Alliance	1	44	1	84	1
Mennonite Christian Fellowship	1	54	2	103	2
Mennonite Church	17	893	27	1,206	21
Mennonite Church/General Conf.: DC	2	240	7	324	6
Mennonite Unaffiliated Congregations	1	90	3	171	3
Nationwide Mennonite Fellowship Churches	1	55	2	105	2
O. O. Mennonite Stauffer Group	1	170	5	383	7
Washington-Franklin Mennonite Conf.	9	1,055	32	2,005	36
Subtotals	42	3,263	100	5,639	100

	Cong.	Mems.	Mems. %	Pop.	Pop. %
Totals					
Amish	7	509	3	1,127	5
Brethren	84	12,322	77	16,666	71
Mennonite	42	3,263	20	5,639	24
Statewide Totals	133	16,094	100	23,432	100

MASSACHUSETTS

The state of Massachusetts has a total of six Anabaptist congregations; all of them are Mennonite. The Mennonite Church represents 71 percent of the membership in the Mennonite tribe. A Mennonite Church/General Conference: Dual Conference congregation holds 17 percent of the Mennonite membership.

	Cong.	Mems.	Mems. %	Pop.	Pop. %
Mennonite					
Eastern Pennsylvania Mennonite Church	1	28	9	53	12
Mennonite Church	3	220	71	297	67
Mennonite Church/General Conf.: DC	1	52	17	70	16
Nationwide Mennonite Fellowship Churches	1	11	4	21	5
Subtotals	6	311	100	441	100
Totals					
Mennonite	6	311	100	441	100
Statewide Totals	6	311	100	441	100

MICHIGAN

The Anabaptist membership in the state of Michigan consists of 40 percent Mennonite, 38 percent Amish, and 21 percent Brethren. Sixty-six Old Order Amish congregations hold 95 percent of the Amish membership. The Church of the Brethren is the largest Brethren group, with 57 percent of the Brethren membership. The Mennonite Church has 28 congregations with 46 percent of the Mennonite members.

	Cong.	Mems.	Mems. %	Pop.	Pop. %
Amish					
Beachy Amish	1	51	1	97	1
New Order Amish	1	45	1	101	1
O. O. Amish	66	3,630	95	8,168	95
O. O. Amish Swartzentruber	2	100	3	225	3
Subtotals	70	3,826	100	8,591	100
Brethren					
Brethren Church	1	4	0.2	5	0.2
Brethren in Christ	6	245	11	331	11
Church of the Brethren	21	1,212	57	1,636	56
Church of the Brethren/Mennonite: DA	2	73	3	99	3
Church of the Brethren: DA	2	159	7	215	7
Consrv. Grace Brethren	5	236	11	319	11
Dunkard Brethren	1	51	2	97	3
Grace Brethren Churches	2	114	5	154	5
Old German Baptist Brethren	1	37	2	83	3
Subtotals	41	2,131	100	2,939	100

	Cong.	Mems.	Mems. %	Pop.	Pop. %
Mennonite					
Bethel Mennonite Fellowship	1	43	1	58	1
Charity Christian Fellowship	1	52	1	99	2
Church of God in Christ Mennonite	3	365	9	694	11
Consrv. Mennonite Conf.	10	717	18	1,362	21
Evangelical Mennonite Church	3	231	6	312	5
General Conf. Mennonite Church	1	100	2	135	2
Independent Mennonite Cong.	1	60	1	81	1
Mennonite Church	28	1,831	46	2,472	39
Mennonite Church/General Conf.: DC	3	93	2	126	2
Mennonite Unaffiliated Congs.	5	253	6	481	8
Mid-West Mennonite Fellowship	5	78	2	148	2
Nationwide Mennonite Fellowship Churches	1	31	1	59	1
O. O. Mennonite Groffdale Conf.	1	27	1	61	1
O. O. Mennonite Wisler Conf.	1	108	3	243	4
Reformed Mennonite Church	1	30	1	68	1
Subtotals	65	4,019	100	6,399	100
Totals					
Amish	70	3,826	38	8,591	48
Brethren	41	2,131	21	2,939	16
Mennonite	65	4,019	40	6,399	36
Statewide Totals	176	9,976	100	17,929	100

MINNESOTA

Minnesota has 60 Anabaptist congregations, of which 34 are Mennonite. There are nine Hutterite colonies in Minnesota, representing 13 percent of the Anabaptist membership. The 13 Amish congregations include six Old Order Amish Swartzentruber districts.

	Cong.	Mems.	Mems. %	Pop.	Pop. %
Amish					
Beachy Amish	1	82	12	156	10
O. O. Amish	6	330	46	743	47
O. O. Amish Swartzentruber	6	300	42	675	43
Subtotals	13	712	100	1,574	100
Brethren					
Church of the Brethren	4	242	100	327	100
Hutterite					
Schmiedeleut Hutterite	9	495	100	1,114	100
Mennonite					
Apostolic Christian Church of America	3	402	16	764	20
Church of God in Christ Mennonite	1	41	2	78	2
Consrv. Mennonite Conf.	2	30	1	57	2
Evangelical Mennonite Brethren	1	180	7	243	6
Independent Mennonite Cong.	1	190	8	257	7
Mennonite Brethren	6	500	20	675	18
Mennonite Church	4	90	3	96	3
Mennonite Church/General Conf.: DC	12	940	37	1,269	34
Mennonite Unaffiliated Congs.	3	87	3	165	4
Mid-West Mennonite Fellowship	2	45	2	86	2
O. O. Mennonite Wisler Conf.	1	24	1	54	1
Subtotals	36	2,529	100	3,744	100

Totals	Cong.	Mems.	Mems. %	Pop.	Pop. %
Amish	13	712	18	1,574	23
Brethren	4	242	6	327	5
Hutterite	9	495	13	1,114	16
Mennonite	34	2,510	63	3,744	55
Statewide Totals	62	3,978	100	6,759	100

MISSISSIPPI

The state of Mississippi has 21 Anabaptist congregations; 19 are Mennonite. There is one Old Order Amish Swartzentruber and one Old German Baptist congregation. The Church of God in Christ Mennonite has 57 percent of the total Mennonite membership.

	Cong.	Mems.	Mems. %	Pop.	Pop. %
Amish					
O. O. Amish Swartzentruber	1	40	100	90	100
Brethren					
Old German Baptist Brethren	1	9	100	20	100
Mennonite					
Church of God in Christ Mennonite	6	907	57	1,723	61
Independent Mennonite Cong.	1	18	1	24	1
Mennonite Biblical Alliance	1	54	3	103	4
Mennonite Church	7	361	23	487	17
Mennonite Unaffiliated Congs.	3	215	13	409	14
Pilgrim Mennonite Conf.	1	43	3	82	3
Subtotals	19	1,598	100	2,828	100
Totals					
Amish	1	40	2	90	3
Brethren	1	9	1	20	1
Mennonite	19	1,598	97	2,828	96
Statewide Totals	21	1,647	100	2,938	100

MISSOURI

The Anabaptist membership in the state of Missouri is 49 percent Mennonite, 39 percent Amish, and 12 percent Brethren. The Old Order Amish represent 79 percent of the membership in the Amish tribe; the Church of the Brethren has 86 percent of the Brethren membership. Missouri has a total of 121 Anabaptist congregations.

	Cong.	Mems.	Mems. %	Pop.	Pop. %
Amish					
Amish Mennonite	5	610	20	1159	17
Beachy Amish	2	32	1	61	1
O. O. Amish	44	2,420	79	5,445	81
O. O. Amish Swartzentruber	1	16	1	36	1
Subtotals	52	3,078	100	6,701	100
Brethren					
Church of the Brethren	18	802	86	1,083	80
Church of the Brethren/Mennonite: DA	1	11	1	15	1
Dunkard Brethren	1	22	2	42	3
German Baptist Brethren	1	40	4	90	7

	Cong.	Mems.	Mems. %	Pop.	Pop. %
Old German Baptist Brethren	1	54	6	122	9
Subtotals	22	929	100	1,352	100
Mennonite					
Apostolic Christian Church of America	4	213	6	405	6
Bethel Mennonite Fellowship	3	247	7	469	7
Church of God in Christ Mennonite	5	529	14	1,005	14
Eastern Pennsylvania Mennonite Church	2	98	3	186	3
General Conf. Mennonite Church	1	213	6	288	4
Independent Mennonite Cong.	1	32	1	43	1
Mennonite Brethren	1	17	0.4	23	0.4
Mennonite Christian Fellowship	6	362	10	688	10
Mennonite Church	9	654	17	883	12
Mennonite Church/General Conf.: DC	1	64	2	86	1
Mennonite Unaffiliated Cong.	1	30	1	57	1
Mid-West Mennonite Fellowship	1	15	0.4	29	0.4
Nationwide Mennonite Fellowship Churches	1	61	2	116	2
O. O. Mennonite Groffdale Conf.	3	480	13	1,080	15
O. O. Mennonite John Martin Group	1	40	1	90	1
O. O. Mennonite Noah Hoover Group	1	29	1	65	1
O. O. Mennonite Reidenbach Group	1	36	1	81	1
O. O. Mennonite Stauffer Group	1	114	3	257	4
O. O. Mennonite Weaverland Conf.	4	558	15	1,256	18
Subtotals	47	3,792	100	7,107	100
Totals					
Amish	52	3,078	39	6,701	44
Brethren	22	929	12	1,352	9
Mennonite	47	3,792	49	7,107	47
Statewide Totals	121	7,799	100	15,160	100

MONTANA

The Anabaptist membership in the state of Montana consists of 70 percent Hutterite, 24 percent Mennonite, 5 percent Amish, and 1 percent Brethren. There are a total of 47 Hutterite colonies; 33 are Lehrerleut and 14 are Dariusleut. Montana has a total of 66 Anabaptist congregations.

	Cong.	Mems.	Mems. %	Pop.	Pop. %
Amish					
New Order Amish	1	18	12	41	12
O. O. Amish	3	130	88	293	88
Subtotals	4	148	100	334	100
Brethren					
Church of the Brethren: DA	1	30	100	41	100
Hutterite					
Dariusleut Hutterite	14	630	30	1,418	30
Lehrerleut Hutterite	33	1,485	70	3,341	70
Subtotals	47	2,115	100	4,759	100
Mennonite					
Evangelical Mennonite Brethren	1	85	12	115	12
Mennonite Brethren	2	150	21	203	21
Mennonite Church	3	172	24	232	24
Mennonite Church/General Conf.: DC	6	265	37	358	37
Mennonite Unaffiliated Congs.	2	37	5	70	7
Subtotals	14	709	100	978	100

Totals	Cong.	Mems.	Mems. %	Pop.	Pop. %
Amish	4	148	5	334	5
Brethren	1	30	1	41	1
Hutterite	47	2,115	70	4,759	78
Mennonite	14	709	24	978	16
Statewide Totals	66	3,002	100	6,112	100

NEBRASKA

Nebraska has a total of 29 Anabaptist congregations; 23 are Mennonite and six are Brethren. The Mennonite Church/General Conference: Dual Conference congregations represent 68 percent of the Mennonite membership; the Church of the Brethren claims 77 percent of the Brethren membership.

	Cong.	Mems.	Mems. %	Pop.	Pop. %
Brethren					
Brethren Church	1	69	15	93	15
Church of the Brethren	4	365	77	493	77
Grace Brethren Churches	1	40	8	54	8
Subtotals	6	474	100	640	100
Mennonite					
Church of God in Christ Mennonite	3	212	6	403	8
General Conf. Mennonite Church	2	396	11	535	11
Mennonite Brethren	6	498	14	672	13
Mennonite Church/General Conf.: DC	11	2,474	68	3,340	66
Mennonite Unaffiliated Cong.	1	56	2	106	2
Subtotals	23	3,636	100	5,056	100
Totals					
Brethren	6	474	12	640	11
Mennonite	23	3,636	88	5,056	89
Statewide Totals	29	4,110	100	5,696	100

NEW JERSEY

The Anabaptist membership in the state of New Jersey is divided between 73 percent Mennonite and 27 percent Brethren. Eleven congregations affiliate with the Mennonite Church, representing 86 percent of the total Mennonite membership. There are a total of 17 Anabaptist congregations in the state.

	Cong.	Mems.	Mems. %	Pop.	Pop. %
Brethren					
Brethren Church	1	8	4	11	3
Church of the Brethren	1	124	58	167	53
Grace Brethren Churches	1	32	15	43	14
Independent Brethren	1	51	24	97	30
Subtotals	4	215	100	318	100
Mennonite					
Eastern Pennsylvania Mennonite Church	1	38	6	72	9
Independent Mennonite Cong.	1	48	8	65	8
Mennonite Church	11	509	86	687	83
Subtotals	13	595	100	824	100

	Cong.	Mems.	Mems. %	Pop.	Pop. %
Totals					
Brethren	4	215	27	318	28
Mennonite	13	595	73	824	72
Statewide Totals	17	810	100	1,142	100

NEW MEXICO

The state of New Mexico, home of Amish, Brethren, and Mennonites, has a total of 19 Anabaptist congregations; ten are affiliated with the Brethren. There is one Amish Mennonite Unaffiliated congregation in the state. Nationwide Mennonite Fellowship Churches represent 34 percent of the total membership in the Mennonite tribe.

	Cong.	Mems.	Mems. %	Pop.	Pop. %
Amish					
Amish Mennonite Unaffiliated	1	14	100	27	100
Brethren					
Brethren in Christ	2	87	20	117	19
Church of the Brethren	2	111	25	150	24
Dunkard Brethren	2	33	7	63	10
Grace Brethren Churches	4	213	48	288	47
Subtotals	10	444	100	618	100
Mennonite					
Church of God in Christ Mennonite	1	10	3	19	4
Consrv. Mennonite Conf.	2	90	29	171	32
Mennonite Church	1	43	14	58	11
Mennonite Church/General Conf.: DC	2	60	19	81	15
Nationwide Mennonite Fellowship Churches	2	105	34	200	38
Subtotals	8	308	100	529	100
Totals					
Amish	1	14	2	27	2
Brethren	10	444	58	618	53
Mennonite	8	308	40	529	45
Statewide Totals	19	766	100	1,174	100

NEW YORK

The Anabaptist membership in the state of New York is 61 percent Mennonite, 26 percent Amish, 9 percent Hutterite, and 5 percent Brethren. There are four Bruderhof Communities in New York, 32 Old Order Amish congregations, and four Old Order Amish Swartzentruber districts. The Mennonite Church claims 38 percent of the membership in the Mennonite tribe. With 790 members, the Old Order Mennonite Groffdale Conference has 16 percent of the Mennonite total; the Conservative Mennonite Conference, with 684 members, has 14 percent of the Mennonite total. New York has a total of 113 Anabaptist congregations.

	Cong.	Mems.	Mems. %	Pop.	Pop. %
Amish					
Beachy Amish	3	128	6	243	5
New Order Amish	1	42	2	95	2

State Summaries

195

	Cong.	Mems.	Mems. %	Pop.	Pop. %
O. O. Amish	32	1760	83	3,960	83
O. O. Amish Swartzentruber	4	200	9	450	9
Subtotals	40	2,130	100	4,748	100
Brethren					
Brethren in Christ	2	64	16	86	16
Church of the Brethren	2	302	75	408	75
Consrv. Grace Brethren	1	38	9	51	9
Subtotals	5	404	100	545	100
Hutterite					
Bruderhof Communities	4	730	100	1,457	100
Mennonite					
Apostolic Christian Church of America	1	55	1	105	1
Charity Christian Fellowship	2	121	2	230	3
Church of God in Christ Mennonite	2	29	1	55	1
Consrv. Mennonite Conf.	3	684	14	1,300	15
Consrv. Mennonite Conf./ Mennonite Church: DA	2	321	6	610	7
Eastern Pennsylvania Mennonite Church	2	129	3	245	3
Mennonite Biblical Alliance	1	35	1	67	1
Mennonite Brethren	1	16	0.3	22	0.2
Mennonite Christian Fellowship	1	85	2	162	2
Mennonite Church	34	1,923	38	2,596	30
Mennonite Church/General Conf.: DC	3	196	4	265	3
Mennonite Church: DA	1	109	2	147	2
Mid-Atlantic Mennonite Fellowship	1	26	1	49	1
Nationwide Mennonite Fellowship Churches	2	70	1	133	2
O. O. Mennonite Groffdale Conf.	4	790	16	1,778	20
O. O. Mennonite Weaverland Conf.	3	417	8	938	11
Pilgrim Mennonite Conf.	1	32	1	61	1
Subtotals	64	5,038	100	8,763	100
Totals					
Amish	40	2,130	26	4,748	31
Brethren	5	404	5	545	4
Hutterite	4	730	9	1,457	9
Mennonite	64	5,038	61	8,763	56
Statewide Totals	113	8,302	100	15,513	100

NORTH CAROLINA

The state of North Carolina has 46 Anabaptist congregations, and 26 are Mennonite. The Anabaptist membership in North Carolina is 57 percent Brethren, 39 percent Mennonite, and 3 percent New Order Amish. There is one Grace Brethren congregation. The Church of the Brethren represents 96 percent of the Brethren membership.

	Cong.	Mems.	Mems. %	Pop.	Pop. %
Amish					
New Order Amish	2	106	100	239	100
Brethren					
Church of the Brethren	17	1,662	96	2,244	96
Grace Brethren Churches	1	76	4	103	4
Subtotals	18	1,738	100	2,347	100

	Cong.	Mems.	Mems. %	Pop.	Pop. %
Mennonite					
Charity Christian Fellowship	2	98	8	186	10
Church of God in Christ Mennonite	1	98	8	186	10
Mennonite Biblical Alliance	2	73	6	139	8
Mennonite Brethren	6	209	18	282	15
Mennonite Church	10	443	37	598	33
Mennonite Church/General Conf.: DC	2	105	9	142	8
Nationwide Mennonite Fellowship Churches	3	159	13	302	16
Subtotals	26	1,185	100	1,835	100
Totals					
Amish	2	106	3	239	5
Brethren	18	1,738	57	2,347	53
Mennonite	26	1,185	39	1,835	42
Statewide Totals	46	3,029	100	4,421	100

NORTH DAKOTA

The Anabaptist membership in the state of North Dakota consists of 54 percent Mennonite, 32 percent Hutterite, and 15 percent Brethren. There are six Schmiedeleut Hutterite colonies among a statewide total of 20 Anabaptist congregations.

	Cong.	Mems.	Mems. %	Pop.	Pop. %
Brethren					
Church of the Brethren	3	150	100	203	100
Hutterite					
Schmiedeleut Hutterite	6	330	100	743	100
Mennonite					
Church of God in Christ Mennonite	1	98	18	186	23
Independent Mennonite Cong.	1	85	15	115	14
Mennonite Brethren	3	202	37	273	33
Mennonite Church	2	86	16	116	14
Mennonite Church/General Conf.: DC	2	53	10	72	9
Mennonite Unaffiliated Congs.	2	29	5	55	7
Subtotals	11	553	100	817	100
Totals					
Brethren	3	150	15	203	12
Hutterite	6	330	32	743	42
Mennonite	11	553	54	817	46
Statewide Totals	20	1,033	100	1,763	100

OHIO

Ohio has a total of 788 Anabaptist congregations. Some 290 Old Order Amish congregations represent 75 percent of the Amish membership, alongside 34 New Order Amish districts and 33 Old Order Amish Swartzentruber ones. The Church of the Brethren has 103 congregations that represent 49 percent of the Brethren membership. The Mennonite Church has 69 congregations representing 45 percent of the statewide Mennonite tribe.

	Cong.	Mems.	Mems. %	Pop.	Pop. %
Amish					
Amish Mennonite Unaffiliated	1	8	0.03	15	0.03
Beachy Amish	20	1,442	6	2,740	5
New Order Amish	34	2,030	9	4,568	9
New Order Amish Fellowship	10	466	2	1,049	2
O. O. Amish	290	17,370	75	39,082	76
O. O. Amish Nebraska	1	60	0.3	135	0.3
O. O. Amish Swartzentruber	<u>33</u>	<u>1,650</u>	<u>7</u>	<u>3,713</u>	<u>7</u>
Subtotals	389	23,026	100	51,302	100
Brethren					
Brethren Church	22	2,632	8	3,553	8
Brethren in Christ	15	870	3	1,175	3
Church of the Brethren	103	15,027	49	20,286	46
Consrv. Grace Brethren	16	978	3	1,320	3
Dunkard Brethren	3	181	1	344	1
Grace Brethren Churches	49	9,263	30	12,505	29
Old Brethren	1	30	0.1	68	0.2
Old German Baptist Brethren	16	1,875	6	4,219	10
O. O. German Baptists	<u>3</u>	<u>125</u>	<u>0.4</u>	<u>281</u>	<u>0.6</u>
Subtotals	228	30,981	100	43,751	100
Mennonite					
Apostolic Christian Church of America	9	1,327	6	2,521	7
Charity Christian Fellowship	4	289	1	549	2
Church of God in Christ Mennonite	2	284	1	540	2
Consrv. Mennonite Conf.	23	2,904	13	5,518	15
Consrv. Mennonite Unaffiliated	5	565	2	1,074	3
Evangelical Mennonite Church	6	1,362	6	1,839	5
General Conf. Mennonite Church	7	1,865	8	2,518	7
Independent Mennonite Cong.	1	490	2	662	2
Mennonite Biblical Alliance	4	359	2	682	2
Mennonite Christian Fellowship	1	83	0.4	158	0.4
Mennonite Church	69	10,207	45	13,779	39
Mennonite Church/General Conf.: DC	7	801	3	1,081	3
Mennonite Unaffiliated Congs.	6	364	2	692	2
Mid-West Mennonite Fellowship	8	599	3	1,138	3
Nationwide Mennonite Fellowship Churches	5	201	1	382	1
Ohio Wisler Mennonite Churches	5	421	2	800	2
O. O. Mennonite Groffdale Conf.	2	340	1	765	2
O. O. Mennonite Stauffer Group	1	89	0.4	200	1
O. O. Mennonite Wisler Conf.	2	228	1	513	1
Pilgrim Mennonite Conf.	1	61	0.3	116	0.3
Reformed Mennonite Church	<u>3</u>	<u>70</u>	<u>0.3</u>	<u>158</u>	<u>0.4</u>
Subtotals	171	22,909	100	35,685	100
Totals					
Amish	389	23,026	30	51,302	39
Brethren	228	30,981	40	43,751	33
Mennonite	<u>171</u>	<u>22,909</u>	<u>30</u>	<u>35,685</u>	<u>27</u>
Statewide Totals	788	76,916	100	130,738	100

OKLAHOMA

The Anabaptist membership in the state of Oklahoma breaks down to 82 percent Mennonite, 12 percent Brethren, and 6 percent Amish in a total of 54 congregations. There are 13 Mennonite Brethren congregations, representing 54 percent of the Mennonite membership. Oklahoma has five Old Order Amish congregations and one Beachy Amish congregation.

	Cong.	Mems.	Mems. %	Pop.	Pop. %
Amish					
Beachy Amish	1	46	14	87	12
O. O. Amish	5	275	86	619	88
Subtotals	6	321	100	706	100
Brethren					
Brethren in Christ	3	241	37	325	37
Church of the Brethren	6	412	63	556	63
Subtotals	9	653	100	881	100
Mennonite					
Bethel Mennonite Fellowship	1	16	0.4	30	0.5
Charity Christian Fellowship	1	6	0.1	11	0.2
Church of God in Christ Mennonite	4	449	10	853	13
Consrv. Mennonite Conf.	1	139	3	264	4
Consrv. Mennonite Unaffiliated	1	21	0.5	40	1
General Conf. Mennonite Church	14	1,108	24	1496	23
Independent Mennonite Cong.	1	24	1	32	0.5
Kleine Gemeinde	1	70	2	133	2
Mennonite Brethren	13	2,465	54	3,328	51
Mennonite Church	2	236	5	319	5
Subtotals	39	4,534	100	6,506	100
Totals					
Amish	6	321	6	706	9
Brethren	9	653	12	881	11
Mennonite	39	4,534	82	6,506	80
Statewide Totals	54	5,508	100	8,093	100

OREGON

The state of Oregon has a total of 58 Anabaptist congregations. Mennonites represents 92 percent of the membership in Oregon, and Brethren groups claim 8 percent. The Mennonite Church/General Conference: Dual Conference congregations represent 32 percent of the total membership in the Mennonite tribe.

	Cong.	Mems.	Mems. %	Pop.	Pop. %
Brethren					
Brethren in Christ	3	133	27	180	26
Church of the Brethren	4	260	52	351	50
Consrv. Grace Brethren	1	12	2	16	2
Dunkard Brethren	1	7	1	13	2
Grace Brethren Churches	1	60	12	81	12
Old German Baptist Brethren	1	25	5	56	8
Subtotals	11	497	100	697	100
Mennonite					
Apostolic Christian Church of America	2	135	3	257	3
Church of God in Christ Mennonite	1	109	2	207	3
Independent Mennonite Congs.	7	1179	22	1,592	20
Mennonite Brethren	10	1574	29	2,125	27
Mennonite Church/General Conf.: DC	18	1749	32	2,361	30
Mennonite Unaffiliated Congs.	2	145	3	276	4

	Cong.	Mems.	Mems. %	Pop.	Pop. %
Western Consrv. Mennonite Fellowship	7	502	9	954	12
Subtotals	47	5,393	100	7,772	100
Totals					
Brethren	11	497	8	697	8
Mennonite	47	5,393	92	7,772	92
Statewide Totals	58	5,890	100	8,469	100

PENNSYLVANIA

The state of Pennsylvania has Amish, Brethren, Hutterite, and Mennonite congregations. There are 277 Old Order Amish districts in the state, representing 87 percent of the Amish membership. Alongside those are 13 Old Order Amish Nebraska congregations and 15 Beachy Amish ones. The Mennonite Church with 273 congregations claims 55 percent of the total Mennonite membership in the state. Pennsylvania has seven Old Order Mennonite affiliations, including the Old Order Groffdale and Weaverland Conferences with 43 congregations that claim about 15 percent of the Mennonite membership in the state. The Church of the Brethren has 233 congregations and thus 63 percent of the Brethren membership in the state. The Brethren in Christ have 99 congregations, and the Grace Brethren have 50. Pennsylvania has 1,284 Anabaptist congregations, more than any other state.

	Cong.	Mems.	Mems. %	Pop.	Pop. %
Amish					
Amish Mennonite Unaffiliated	2	240	1	456	1
Beachy Amish	15	1,466	7	2,785	6
New Order Amish	6	310	1	698	1
O. O. Amish	277	18,755	87	42,199	88
O. O. Amish Nebraska	13	715	3	1,609	3
O. O. Amish Swartzentruber	1	50	0.2	113	0.2
Subtotals	314	21,536	100	47,860	100
Brethren					
Bible Brethren	2	35	0.1	79	0.1
Brethren Church	18	1,236	2	1,669	2
Brethren Fellowship	1	35	0.1	67	0.1
Brethren in Christ	99	13,404	20	18,095	20
Church of the Brethren	233	41,951	63	56,634	62
Church of the Brethren/Mennonite: DA	1	161	0.2	217	0.2
Church of the Brethren: DA	3	715	1	965	1
Consrv. Baptist Brethren	2	130	0.2	247	0.3
Consrv. Brethren	1	40	0.1	76	0.1
Consrv. German Baptist Brethren	1	15	0.02	29	0.03
Consrv. Grace Brethren	9	537	1	725	1
Dunkard Brethren	7	309	0.5	587	1
German Seventh-Day Baptist	2	73	0.1	139	0.2
Grace Brethren Churches	50	5,980	9	8,073	9
Independent Brethren	4	168	0.3	319	0.4
Old German Baptist Brethren	4	501	1	1,127	1
O. O. River Brethren	4	295	0.4	664	1
United Zion	11	783	1	1,488	2
Subtotals	452	66,368	100	91,200	100

	Cong.	Mems.	Mems. %	Pop.	Pop. %
Hutterite					
Bruderhof Communities	2	410	100	779	100
Mennonite					
Apostolic Christian Church of America	1	33	0.1	63	0.1
Charity Christian Fellowship	4	420	1	798	1
Church of God in Christ Mennonite	4	387	1	735	1
Consrv. Mennonite Conf.	4	557	1	1,058	1
Cumberland Valley Mennonite Church	3	246	0.4	467	1
Eastern Pennsylvania Mennonite Church	32	2,506	4	4,761	5
General Conf. Mennonite Church	25	4,243	7	5,728	6
Hope Mennonite Fellowship	4	309	1	587	0.6
Hopewell Mennonite District	9	974	2	1,315	1
Independent Mennonite Congs.	10	315	1	425	0.5
Keystone Mennonite Fellowship	15	930	2	1,767	2
Mennonite Biblical Alliance	1	44	0.1	84	0.1
Mennonite Christian Fellowship	6	270	0.5	513	1
Mennonite Church	273	31,883	55	43,042	46
Mennonite Church/General Conf.: DC	4	998	2	1,347	1
Mennonite Unaffiliated Congs.	11	843	1	1,602	2
Mid-Atlantic Mennonite Fellowship	15	1,273	2	2,419	3
Mid-West Mennonite Fellowship	1	85	0.1	162	0.2
Nationwide Mennonite Fellowship Churches	10	505	1	960	1
O. O. Mennonite Groffdale Conf.	20	4,380	8	9,855	11
O. O. Mennonite John Martin Group	1	13	0.02	29	0.03
O. O. Mennonite Reidenbach Group	8	293	1	659	1
O. O. Mennonite Stauffer Group	5	710	1	1,598	2
O. O. Mennonite Unaffiliated	4	178	0.3	401	0.4
O. O. Mennonite Weaverland Conf.	23	4,347	7	9,781	11
O. O. Orthodox Mennonite	1	6	0.01	14	0.01
Pilgrim Mennonite Conf.	10	757	1	1,438	2
Reformed Mennonite Church	5	144	0.2	324	0.3
Washington-Franklin Mennonite Conf.	2	187	0.3	355	0.4
York-Adams Mennonite Churches	5	266	0.5	505	1
Subtotals	516	58,102	100	92,792	100
Totals					
Amish	314	21,536	15	47,860	21
Brethren	452	66,368	45	91,200	39
Hutterite	2	410	0.3	779	0.3
Mennonite	516	58,102	40	92,792	40
Statewide Totals	1,284	146,416	100	232,631	100

PUERTO RICO

Puerto Rico's Anabaptist membership consists of 68 percent Mennonites and 32 percent Brethren. The Mennonite Church has ten congregations representing 66 percent of the Mennonite membership. Puerto Rico has a total of 25 Anabaptist congregations.

	Cong.	Mems.	Mems. %	Pop.	Pop. %
Brethren					
Church of the Brethren	7	328	100	443	100
Mennonite					
Caribbean Mennonite Conf.	5	198	28	376	35
Mennonite Church	10	462	66	624	58

	Cong.	Mems.	Mems. %	Pop.	Pop. %
Mennonite Unaffiliated Cong.	1	30	4	57	5
Southeastern Mennonite Conf.	2	5	1	10	1
Subtotals	18	695	100	1,067	100
Totals					
Brethren	7	328	32	443	29
Mennonite	18	695	68	1,067	71
Commonwealth Totals	25	1,023	100	1,510	100

SOUTH CAROLINA

The state of South Carolina has 15 Anabaptist congregations, three of which are Beachy Amish. South Carolina's Anabaptist membership is 52 percent Mennonite, 24 percent Brethren, and 23 percent Amish. Mennonite Unaffiliated Congregations represent 56 percent of the Mennonite membership.

	Cong.	Mems.	Mems. %	Pop.	Pop. %
Amish					
Beachy Amish	3	216	100	410	100
Brethren					
Church of the Brethren	1	53	24	72	24
Grace Brethren Churches	2	171	76	231	76
Subtotals	3	224	100	303	100
Mennonite					
Consrv. Mennonite Conf.	1	12	2	23	3
Mennonite Biblical Alliance	1	62	13	118	13
Mennonite Church	2	58	12	78	9
Mennonite Unaffiliated Congs.	4	267	56	507	58
South Atlantic Mennonite Conf.	1	82	17	156	18
Subtotals	9	481	100	882	100
Totals					
Amish	3	216	23	410	26
Brethren	3	224	24	303	19
Mennonite	9	481	52	882	55
Statewide Totals	15	921	100	1,595	100

SOUTH DAKOTA

The Anabaptist membership in the state of South Dakota is 56 percent Mennonite and 44 percent Hutterite. There are 52 Schmiedeleut Hutterite colonies. South Dakota has a total of 79 Anabaptist congregations.

	Cong.	Mems.	Mems. %	Pop.	Pop. %
Hutterite					
Schmiedeleut Hutterite	52	2,860	100	6,435	100%
Mennonite					
Church of God in Christ Mennonite	2	156	4	296	6
Evangelical Mennonite Brethren	1	50	1	68	1
Independent Mennonite Congs.	3	515	14	695	14
Keystone Mennonite Fellowship	1	8	0.2	15	0.3
Mennonite Brethren	9	1,105	30	1,492	30
Mennonite Church/General Conf.: DC	11	1,790	49	2,417	48
Subtotals	27	3,624	100	4,983	100

	Cong.	Mems.	Mems. %	Pop.	Pop. %
Totals					
Hutterite	52	2,860	44	6,435	56
Mennonite	27	3,624	56	4,983	44
Statewide Totals	79	6,484	100	11,418	100

TENNESSEE

The state of Tennessee claims 65 Anabaptist congregations. Eight Old Order Amish Swartzentruber districts represent 37 percent of the Amish membership. The Church of the Brethren holds 77 percent of the membership in the Brethren tribe; the Mennonite Christian Fellowship claims 30 percent of the Mennonite membership.

	Cong.	Mems.	Mems. %	Pop.	Pop. %
Amish					
Amish Mennonite Unaffiliated	6	213	20	405	18
Beachy Amish	5	301	28	572	25
O. O. Amish	3	165	15	371	17
O. O. Amish Swartzentruber	8	400	37	900	40
Subtotals	22	1,079	100	2,248	100
Brethren					
Brethren in Christ	4	253	17	342	17
Church of the Brethren	19	1,168	77	1,577	77
Consrv. Grace Brethren	1	66	4	89	4
Grace Brethren Churches	1	24	2	32	2
Subtotals	25	1,511	100	2,040	100
Mennonite					
Apostolic Christian Church of America	1	9	1	17	1
Charity Christian Fellowship	2	122	16	232	17
Church of God in Christ Mennonite	2	110	15	209	15
Mennonite Christian Fellowship	4	223	30	424	30
Mennonite Church	4	142	19	192	14
O. O. Mennonite Unaffiliated	4	139	18	313	22
Reformed Mennonite Church	1	8	1	18	1
Subtotals	18	753	100	1,405	100
Totals					
Amish	22	1,079	32	2,248	39
Brethren	25	1,511	45	2,040	36
Mennonite	18	753	23	1,405	25
Statewide Totals	65	3,343	100	5,693	100

TEXAS

The Anabaptist membership in the state of Texas consists of 87 percent Mennonite, 9 percent Brethren, and 5 percent Amish. The Church of God in Christ Mennonite group has eight congregations that hold 20 percent of the Mennonite membership. Ten percent of the Mennonite membership is in 11 Mennonite Brethren congregations, and 16 percent is in nine Mennonite Church congregations. There are six Amish congregations in the state; two are Beachy Amish. Texas has fifty-nine Anabaptist congregations.

State Summaries

203

	Cong.	Mems.	Mems. %	Pop.	Pop. %
Amish					
Amish Mennonite Unaffiliated	1	53	30	101	30
Beachy Amish	2	101	58	192	57
O. O. Amish	3	20	11	45	13
Subtotals	6	174	100	338	100
Brethren					
Church of the Brethren	5	225	70	304	70
Grace Brethren Churches	2	98	30	132	30
Subtotals	7	323	100	436	100
Mennonite					
Apostolic Christian Church of America	1	7	0.2	13	0.2
Charity Christian Fellowship	1	27	1	51	1
Church of God in Christ Mennonite	8	654	20	1,243	22
Consrv. Mennonite Conf.	2	108	3	205	4
Eastern Pennsylvania Mennonite Church	1	54	2	103	2
Evangelical Mennonite Mission Conf.	1	216	7	292	5
General Conf. Mennonite Church	1	35	1	47	1
Mennonite Brethren	11	309	10	417	8
Mennonite Church	9	514	16	694	12
Mennonite Church/General Conf.: DC	7	304	9	410	7
Mennonite Evangelical Churches	2	216	7	292	5
Old Colony Mennonite	1	407	13	916	16
Reinlaender Mennonite Church	1	387	12	871	16
Subtotals	46	3,238	100	5,554	100
Totals					
Amish	6	174	5	338	5
Brethren	7	323	9	436	7
Mennonite	46	3,238	87	5,554	88
Statewide Totals	59	3,735	100	6,328	100

UTAH

The state of Utah has two Anabaptist congregations: one is affiliated with the Mennonite Brethren and the other with the Nationwide Mennonite Fellowship Churches.

	Cong.	Mems.	Mems. %	Pop.	Pop. %
Mennonite					
Mennonite Brethren	1	23	53	31	45
Nationwide Mennonite Fellowship Churches	1	20	47	38	55
Subtotals	2	43	100	69	100
Totals					
Mennonite	2	43	100	69	100
Statewide Totals	2	43	100	69	100

VERMONT

Vermont claims seven Anabaptist congregations; four are Mennonite and three are Brethren.

	Cong.	Mems.	Mems. %	Pop.	Pop. %
Brethren					
Church of the Brethren	1	52	38	70	38
Consrv. Grace Brethren	1	40	29	54	29

	Cong.	Mems.	Mems. %	Pop.	Pop. %
Grace Brethren Churches	1	44	32	59	32
Subtotals	3	136	100	183	100
Mennonite					
Eastern Pennsylvania Mennonite Church	1	25	13	48	18
Independent Mennonite Cong.	1	81	43	109	40
Mennonite Church	2	84	44	113	42
Subtotals	4	190	100	270	100
Totals					
Brethren	3	136	42	183	41
Mennonite	4	190	58	270	59
Statewide Totals	7	326	100	453	100

VIRGINIA

The Anabaptist membership in the state of Virginia consists of 72 percent Brethren, 26 percent Mennonite, and 2 percent Amish. The Church of the Brethren claims 88 percent of the Brethren membership. The Mennonite Church represents 66 percent of the membership in the Mennonite tribe. Virginia has 308 Anabaptist congregations.

	Cong.	Mems.	Mems. %	Pop.	Pop. %
Amish					
Beachy Amish	8	555	79	1,055	76
O. O. Amish	4	149	21	335	24
Subtotals	12	704	100	1,390	100
Brethren					
Brethren Church	8	791	3	1,068	3
Brethren in Christ	8	381	1	514	1
Church of the Brethren	170	24,811	88	33,495	87
Church of the Brethren: DA	2	162	1	219	1
Consrv. Brethren	1	40	0.1	76	0.2
Dunkard Brethren	1	10	0.04	19	0.05
Grace Brethren Churches	16	1,472	5	1,987	5
Old German Baptist Brethren	4	548	2	1,233	3
Subtotals	210	28,215	100	38,611	100
Mennonite					
Consrv. Mennonite Conf.	2	74	1	141	1
Cornerstone Mennonite Churches	3	1,451	14	1,959	13
General Conf. Mennonite Church	1	31	0.3	42	0.3
Mennonite Biblical Alliance	3	88	1	167	1
Mennonite Church	54	6,714	66	9,064	60
Mennonite Unaffiliated Congs.	5	237	2	450	3
Nationwide Mennonite Fellowship Churches	2	148	1	281	2
O. O. Mennonite Virginia Conf.	3	426	4	959	6
O. O. Mennonite Weaverland Conf.	1	136	1	306	2
O. O. Mennonite Wenger/Weaver Group	2	273	3	614	4
Southeastern Mennonite Conf.	10	600	6	1,140	8
Subtotals	86	10,178	100	15,123	100
Totals					
Amish	12	704	2	1,390	3
Brethren	210	28,215	72	38,611	70
Mennonite	86	10,178	26	15,123	27
Statewide Totals	308	39,097	100	55,124	100

WASHINGTON

The Anabaptist membership in the state of Washington is 54 percent Mennonite, 43 percent Brethren, 3 percent Hutterite, and 1 percent Amish. Washington has five Dariusleut Hutterite colonies and one Old Order Amish congregation. The Mennonite Brethren represent 73 percent of the Mennonite membership. The Fellowship of Grace Brethren Churches claims 38 percent of the Brethren membership. Washington has a total of 58 Anabaptist congregations.

	Cong.	Mems.	Mems. %	Pop.	Pop. %
Amish					
O. O. Amish	1	27	100	61	100
Brethren					
Church of the Brethren	8	700	32	945	30
Church of the Brethren: DA	4	470	21	635	20
Consrv. Grace Brethren	1	18	1	24	1
Grace Brethren Churches	12	840	38	1,134	36
Old German Baptist Brethren	2	192	9	432	14
Subtotals	27	2,220	100	3,170	100
Hutterite					
Dariusleut Hutterite	5	150	100	338	100
Mennonite					
Charity Christian Fellowship	1	30	1	57	1
Church of God in Christ Mennonite	2	106	4	201	5
Independent Mennonite Congs.	2	64	2	86	2
Mennonite Brethren	11	2,012	73	2,716	71
Mennonite Church/General Conf.: DC	7	502	18	678	18
Mennonite Unaffiliated Cong.	1	11	0.4	21	1
Western Consrv. Mennonite Fellowship	1	36	1	68	2
Subtotals	25	2,761	100	3,827	100
Totals					
Amish	1	27	1	61	1
Brethren	27	2,220	43	3,170	43
Hutterite	5	150	3	338	5
Mennonite	25	2,761	54	3,827	52
Statewide Totals	58	5,158	100	7,396	100

WEST VIRGINIA

Brethren groups claim 95 percent of the Anabaptist membership in the state of West Virginia. The Church of the Brethren has 76 congregations with 90 percent of the Brethren membership. The Mennonite Church has seven congregations representing 52 percent of the Mennonite tally. West Virginia has a total of 104 Anabaptist congregations.

	Cong.	Mems.	Mems. %	Pop.	Pop. %
Amish					
O. O. Amish	2	32	100	72	100
Brethren					
Brethren Church	5	228	3	308	3
Brethren in Christ	1	102	1	138	1
Church of the Brethren	76	6,605	90	8,917	89
Church of the Brethren/Mennonite: DA	1	101	1	136	1

	Cong.	Mems.	Mems. %	Pop.	Pop. %
Church of the Brethren: DA	1	7	0.1	9	0.1
Consrv. Grace Brethren	1	22	0.3	30	0.3
Dunkard Brethren	1	12	0.2	23	0.2
Grace Brethren Churches	3	253	3	342	3
Old German Baptist Brethren	1	34	0.5	77	1
Subtotals	90	7,364	100	9,980	100
Mennonite					
Mennonite Christian Fellowship	1	69	19	131	22
Mennonite Church	7	193	52	261	44
Mennonite Unaffiliated Cong.	1	26	7	49	8
Southeastern Mennonite Conf.	3	82	22	156	26
Subtotals	12	370	100	597	100
Totals					
Amish	2	32	0.4	72	1
Brethren	90	7,364	95	9,980	94
Mennonite	12	370	5	597	6
Statewide Totals	104	7,766	100	10,649	100

WISCONSIN

The state of Wisconsin's Anabaptist membership shows 66 percent Amish, 30 percent Mennonite, and 4 percent Brethren. Wisconsin has 71 Old Order Amish congregations representing 92 percent of the membership in the Amish tribe. The Old Order Mennonite Groffdale Conference has four congregations with 24 percent of the Mennonite membership. Wisconsin has a total of 113 Anabaptist congregations.

	Cong.	Mems.	Mems. %	Pop.	Pop. %
Amish					
Amish Mennonite	1	89	2	169	2
New Order Amish	2	119	3	268	3
O. O. Amish	71	3,905	92	8,786	92
O. O. Amish Swartzentruber	3	150	4	338	4
Subtotals	77	4,263	100	9,561	100
Brethren					
Brethren in Christ	1	47	19	63	14
Church of the Brethren	2	78	31	105	23
German Baptist Brethren	1	70	28	158	35
Old German Baptist Brethren	1	55	22	124	28
Subtotals	5	250	100	450	100
Mennonite					
Charity Christian Fellowship	1	91	5	173	5
Church of God in Christ Mennonite	3	355	18	675	18
Consrv. Mennonite Unaffiliated	1	39	2	74	2
Eastern Pennsylvania Mennonite Church	1	54	3	103	3
Mennonite Church	3	101	5	136	5
Mennonite Church/General Conf.: DC	2	83	4	112	4
Mennonite Unaffiliated Congs.	4	89	5	169	5
Mid-West Mennonite Fellowship	3	147	8	279	8
Nationwide Mennonite Fellowship Churches	7	363	19	690	19
O. O. Mennonite Groffdale Conf.	4	463	24	1,042	24
O. O. Mennonite Weaverland Conf.	2	166	9	374	9
Subtotals	31	1,951	100	3,827	100

State Summaries

207

	Cong.	Mems.	Mems. %	Pop.	Pop. %
Totals					
Amish	77	4,263	66	9,561	69
Brethren	5	250	4	450	3
Mennonite	31	1,951	30	3,827	28
Statewide Totals	113	6,464	100	13,838	100

WYOMING

The state of Wyoming has two Anabaptist congregations. One is affiliated with The Brethren Church and the other with the Nationwide Mennonite Fellowship Churches.

	Cong.	Mems.	Mems. %	Pop.	Pop. %
Brethren					
Brethren Church	1	76	100	103	100
Mennonite					
Nationwide Mennonite Fellowship Churches	1	34	100	65	100
Totals					
Brethren	1	76	69	103	61
Mennonite	1	34	31	65	39
Statewide Totals	2	110	100	168	100

RESOURCES ON
ANABAPTIST GROUPS

ANABAPTIST HISTORY (SIXTEENTH-CENTURY) RESOURCES
(Full citations appear in Section I.)

Literature
Anabaptist History and Theology, Arnold Snyder (1995)
Becoming Anabaptist, J. Denny Weaver (1987)
Believers Church, The, Donald F. Durnbaugh (1985)
Classics of the Radical Reformation, vols. 1-9 (1973-99)
Radical Reformation, The, George Williams (2000)
Martyrs Mirror, Braght (1950)
Mennonite Encyclopedia, The, vols. 1-5 (1955-59, 1990)

Historical Libraries
Mennonite Historical Library, Bluffton (Ohio) College
Mennonite Historical Library, Goshen (Ind.) College
Mennonite Library and Archives, Bethel College, N. Newton, Kan.
Menno Simons Historical Library, Eastern Mennonite University,
    Harrisonburg, Va.

Publications
The Mennonite Quarterly Review, Goshen (Ind.) College

AMISH RESOURCES
Literature
Amish Enterprise: From Plows to Profits, Kraybill and Nolt (1995)
Amish Society, John A. Hostetler (1993)
A History of the Amish, Steven M. Nolt (1992b)
Riddle of Amish Culture, The, Donald B. Kraybill (2001)
Why Do They Dress That Way? Stephen Scott (1986)

Historical Libraries
Heritage Historical Library, Alymer, Ontario
Illinois Mennonite Historical and Genealogical Society, Metamora, Ill.
Lancaster Mennonite Historical Library, Lancaster, Pa.
Ohio Amish Library, Millersburg, Ohio
Pequea Bruderschaft Library, Gordonville, Pa.

Publications
The Budget, Sugarcreek, Ohio
The Diary, Gordonville, Pa.
Die Botschaft, Lancaster, Pa.
Family Life, Aylmer, Ontario

Information Centers
Illinois Amish Interpretive Center, Arcola, Ill.
The Lancaster Mennonite Information Center, Lancaster, Pa.
Menno-Hof, Shipshewana, Ind.
Mennonite Information Center, Berlin, Ohio

BRETHREN RESOURCES
Literature
Brethren Encyclopedia, The, vols. 1-3 (1983-84)
Brethren Society, Carl F. Bowman (1995)
Fruit of the Vine, Donald Durnbaugh (1997)
Quest for Piety and Obedience, Carlton Wittlinger (1978)
Understanding Pietism, Dale Brown (1996)

Historical Libraries
Church of the Brethren Historical Library/Archives, Elgin, Ill.
Brethren in Christ Historical Library/Archives, Messiah College,
    Grantham, Pa.
Brethren Historical Library/Archives, Bridgewater (Va.) College
Brethren Room, Elizabethtown (Pa.) College
Brethren Historical Library/Archives, Juniata College, Huntingdon, Pa.

Publications
Brethren in Christ History and Life, Grantham, Pa.
The Brethren Evangelist (Brethren Church), Ashland, Ohio
Brethren Life and Thought (Church of the Brethren), Elizabethtown, Pa.
The Messenger (Church of the Brethren) Elgin, Ill.
Old Order Notes, Greenville, Ohio
The Vindicator (Old German Baptist Brethren), Covington, Ohio
The Visitor (Brethren in Christ), Nappanee, Ind.

Information Centers
The Young Center for Anabaptist and Pietist Studies, Elizabethtown (Pa.)
    College
The Sider Institute for Anabaptist, Pietist, and Wesleyan Studies, Messiah
    College, Grantham, Pa.

Websites
www.brethren.org
www.cob-net.org
www.bic-church.org

HUTTERITE RESOURCES
Literature
Hutterite Beginnings, Werner Packull (1995)
Hutterite Society, John A. Hostetler (1997)
Chronicle of the Hutterian Brethren, vols. 1-2 (1987, 1998)

Historical Libraries
Mennonite Historical Library, Goshen (Ind.) College
Archives of the Mennonite Church, Goshen (Ind.) College

Publications
The Plough (Bruderhof), Farmington, Pa.

Websites
www.hutterianbrethren.com
www.bruderhof.org

MENNONITE RESOURCES
Literature
Confession of Faith in a Mennonite Perspective (1995)
An Introduction to Old Order and Conservative Mennonite Groups,
    Stephen Scott (1995)
The Mennonite Encyclopedia, vols. 1-5 (1955-59, 1990)
The Mennonite Experience in America, vols. 1-4 (1985-96)
Through Fire and Water, Harry Loewen and Steve Nolt (1996)

Historical Libraries
Archives of the Mennonite Church, Goshen (Ind.) College
Center for Mennonite Brethren Studies, Fresno (Calif.) Pacific University
Lancaster Mennonite Historical Society, Lancaster, Pa.
Menno Simons Historical Library and Archives, Eastern Mennonite
    University, Harrisonburg, Va.
Mennonite Brethren Center, Tabor College, Hillsboro, Kan.
The Mennonite Historical Library, Goshen (Ind.) College
The Mennonite Library and Archives, Bethel College, N. Newton, Kan.
Muddy Creek Farm Library, Denver, Pa.

Publications
The Mennonite, Scottdale, Pa.
Mennonite Life, (on-line) www.Bethelks.edu/mennonitelife/
The Mennonite Quarterly Review, Goshen (Ind.) College
Mennonite Weekly Review, Newton, Kan.

Information Centers
Illinois Mennonite Heritage Center, Metamora, Ill.
Mennonite Information Center, Lancaster, Pa.

Kauffman Museum, N. Newton, Kan.
Mennonite Information Center, Berlin, Ohio
Mennonite Heritage Center, Harleysville, Pa.

Websites
www-personal.umich.edu//~bpl/mennocon.html
www.menno.net
www.thirdway.com/menno/mnmain.shtml

Section H

NOTES

1. Anabaptist Beginnings

1. Braght (1950:481-3, 546-7).

2. For readable introductions to the origins of the Anabaptist Movement, see Dyck (1993), Klaassen (2001), Loewen and Nolt (1996), Snyder (1995), and Weaver (1987). *The Mennonite Encyclopedia* (1956) covers a wide range of topics related to Anabaptist, Amish, Hutterite, and Mennonite beginnings. Snyder's (1995) work provides a recent overview of Anabaptist history and theology.

3. The classic account of Christian martyrdom and suffering from New Testament times through Anabaptist persecutions was compiled by Braght (1950) in 1660 in the *Martyrs Mirror*. An overview of Anabaptist suffering and persecution is provided by Dyck (1985; 1993:110-3) as well as Oyer and Kreider (1990). Reproductions of the graphic images of suffering drawn by the Dutch artist Jan Luyken, from *Martyrs Mirror,* are in *Drama* (1975).

4. See Snyder (1995) for an elaboration of these themes. Arnold Snyder's (1999) booklet, *From Anabaptist Seed*, provides a concise summary of the historical core of Anabaptist identity, with helpful discussion questions. Other summaries of key themes emerging from the Anabaptist Movement are in Durnbaugh (1985) and Littell (1964, 1967).

5. For a discussion of the historical setting and the significance of the Schleitheim Confession of Faith, more properly called the Brotherly Union of a Number of Children of God Concerning Seven Articles, see J. H. Yoder (1973:34-43).

6. Harold S. Bender (1944) proposed these three themes in his classic essay on *The Anabaptist Vision*. Roth (1995) has compiled a more recent collection of essays on the Anabaptist Vision.

7. Klaassen (2001) makes this argument in *Anabaptism: Neither Catholic nor Protestant*, and Paul Lederach (1980) calls Mennonite understandings of faith *A Third Way.*

8. Though many Anabaptist groups in the early years encouraged voluntary sharing of possessions to meet needs within the church, the *Stäbler* Movement, later called Hutterite, laid the foundation for the mandated sharing of goods. Packull (1995) has written an excellent history of the early formation of the Hutterites. Hostetler (1997) provides an account of their European origins as well as their migration and growth in North America. The two-volume *Chronicle* (1987, 1998) of Hutterite history, written by members and beginning in the sixteenth century, provides an intimate and detailed account of Hutterite history from an in-group perspective.

9. Riedemann's *Confession of Faith* was recently retranslated by Friesen (1999).

10. Gross (1998) describes Hutterite life and history during the Peter Walpot era, 1565-78, part of their so-called "golden years" of 1565 through 1592.

11. The story of the *Prairieleut* has recently been told by Janzen (1999).

12. Snyder (1995) and Weaver (1987) provide overviews and introductions to source materials on the early Anabaptists as well as Mennonites. *The Mennonite Encyclopedia* (vols. 1-5) is an excellent source of information; *The Complete Writings of Menno Simons* (1956) are also available. Recent scholarship often appears in *The Mennonite Quarterly Review.*

13. Hüppi (2000) provides a detailed description of Ammann. Helpful discussions of the identity and background of Jakob Ammann can be found in Baecher (2000), Furner (2000), and Hüppi (2000). The evidence provided by these scholars suggests that Jakob Ammann, a tailor by trade, converted to Anabaptism in 1679. He was probably 49 years old in 1693.

14. Numerous letters exchanged in the controversy have survived. Roth (1993) has newly translated them, providing an excellent overview of issues surrounding the division.

15. Steven M. Nolt (1992b) has written the best overall history of the Amish, including their European origins, North American migration, settlement patterns, and expansion in the United States.

16. Various nicknames for the Brethren have often referred to their form of immersion bap-

tism and reflect the German word *tunken* meaning "to dunk" or "immerse." Before the twentieth century, they were often called *Dunkers* in the United States. Durnbaugh (1997) has written the most recent history of the Brethren and compiled a collection of key sources related to their European origins (1958). Other important resources for understanding Brethren history include the works of Bowman (1995) and Stoffer (1989). Eberly (1991) has edited the complete writings of Alexander Mack Sr. *The Brethren Encyclopedia* (1983) offers an excellent source of information on all the Brethren groups.

17. This was the language used by Brethren founder, Alexander Mack Sr., when describing the Mennonites (Eberly, 1991:37).

18. Durnbaugh (1985) has written an excellent overview of the major radical groups that emerged as believers churches in the context of the Protestant Reformation. Herald Press is publishing a Believers Church Bible Commentary series, sponsored by six Anabaptist groups: the Brethren Church, the Brethren in Christ, the Church of the Brethren, the General Conference Mennonite Church, the Mennonite Brethren Church, and the Mennonite Church.

2. Contemporary Communities

1. Miller makes this observation in a short essay on "The Future of the Mennonite Church in Philadelphia," in Gingerich and Stoltzfus (2000:73).

2. It is somewhat difficult to identify distinctive Amish groups. In addition to an "Old Order" category including numerous unnamed subaffiliations, we have identified districts of Swartzentruber and Nebraska affiliations. We have counted the Renno, Byler, Troyer, and Andy Weaver affiliations each as a group, but we do not identify their specific districts in the Directory of Congregations (part 3). In addition, we have reckoned the Swiss districts a group even though they in fact are an ethnic-national category consisting of several affiliations. In any event, eleven is surely an undercount of the number of Amish groups.

3. These numbers are hypothetical because the merger will not take place until 2002, and some Mennonite congregations and conferences may choose not to join the proposed Mennonite Church USA, which could diminish its potential membership.

3. Common Convictions

1. We must be clear: we are not suggesting that these themes adequately reflect the complexity and diversity of sixteenth-century Anabaptism. Not all the early Anabaptists embraced these marks of Anabaptist identity, nor do all Anabaptist groups today endorse them; nevertheless, in our judgment they do circumscribe the essential core of Anabaptist faith and life as it has evolved over the generations. Bender (1944), Durnbaugh (1985), Littell (1964, 1967), and Snyder (1995, 1999) have identified some of the summary themes emerging from the Anabaptist Movement of the sixteenth century. The nine themes we discuss are an amalgamation of sixteenth-century points of distinction, practices that have crystalized over the generations, our own understandings of Anabaptist life today, and our aspirations for it.

2. Loewen (1985:34-5).

3. Since 1967, a dozen Believers Church Conferences have been convened to explore a variety of issues and practices from a believers church perspective. Durnbaugh (1998:217-227) describes the history, topics, and publications flowing from these conferences, often involving representatives from a variety of denominational backgrounds influenced by "free church" and "believers church" perspectives emerging from the Radical Reformation of the sixteenth century. A listing of the conferences and their subsequent publications can also be found in Stoffer (1997). Some of the publications related to the conferences include Brackney (1998), Eller (1990), Littell (1967), Stoffer (1997), and Strege (1986).

4. Many interpreters of the Anabaptist Movement have called it "noncreedal." For examples, see Littell (1964) and Durnbaugh (1985).

5. The text for this hymn appears on page 437 of *Hymnal: A Worship Book* (1992).

6. See chapter 4 of Brensinger (2000) for a discussion of this core value.

7. See Snyder (1999:18) for a more complete version of this catechism attributed to Balthasar Hubmaier.

8. Littell (1964) has shown how the restitution of the true church was a key concept and belief of the early Anabaptists. Bowman (1995:26-7) describes how the German Baptist Brethren viewed themselves as "primitive Christians" involved in restoring the apostolic church.

9. For a series of essays on the Lord's Supper in the believers church tradition, see Stoffer (1997).

10. Stayer (1990) provides conclusive evidence that many of the early Anabaptist communi-

ties practiced voluntary community of goods. For a collection of recent essays on mutual aid, see Swartley and Kraybill (1997).

11. In recent studies, Bush (1998) and Driedger and Kraybill (1994) trace the shift of Mennonite nonresistance from a quietist mode to an activist form of peacemaking in the twentieth century.

12. For a discussion of these issues among the Brethren in Christ, see a helpful article by Weaver-Zercher (1999).

13. These are the figures for the Brethren Disaster Auction held each year near Lebanon, Pennsylvania.

14. It is difficult for us to make a reliable estimate of worldwide membership because of the complexity of tracking church membership in some countries and the ambiguity about denominational identity in many international settings. Mennonites claim more than 600,000 members outside North America. The Fellowship of Grace Brethren churches count 300,000 overseas members. Adding the international members of many other Anabaptist denominations means that an estimate of a million is probably quite conservative. Many of the indigenous churches vary considerably on the extent of their denominational and Anabaptist identity.

15. There are subtle differences between Anabaptist and Reformed theological traditions on the meaning of the lordship of Christ. The Reformed theological tradition affirms the lordship of Christ especially as it relates to broader cultural issues and the development of organizations that contribute to civic well-being. The Anabaptist understanding of the lordship of Christ, at least in the last half of the twentieth century, has promoted a more counterculture social ethic, a critique of nationalism, and an accent on the international nature of the kingdom of God rising above national loyalties. The pacifist commitments of many Anabaptist groups have driven a cultural critique of nationalism and also a critique of the myth of redemptive violence. In sum, the meaning of the lordship of Christ in Anabaptist circles has generally called for a social critique of the broader culture rather than a transformation of it.

16. For an interesting discussion of Anabaptist views on boundaries and borders, see the article by Urry (1999).

17. For a fascinating essay on Mennonite controversies over the flag, consult Weaver-Zercher (1996).

4. Division and Diversity

1. Sociologist Fred Kniss (1997) studied 208 conflicts in several subgroups affiliated with the Mennonite Church from 1870 to 1985.

2. Alderfer (1999) for example, suggests that the Brethren in Christ are more tolerant of differences because of their "Brethren mind-set." The existence of the Brethren Revival Fellowship within the Church of the Brethren is an example of a division that did not occur. The Brethren Revival Fellowship continues to function as a network of conservative-leaning individuals and congregations within the Church of the Brethren.

3. Two helpful sources that discuss examples of union and merger in Mennonite life are John Thiesen's (1993) essay "Mennonites Are Forever Splitting, Aren't They?" and a March 1993 issue of *Mennonite Life* (vol. 48) that explored stories of Mennonite mergers.

4. Milton Gordon developed in depth this classical distinction in sociology (1997).

5. Any attempt to sort groups into social boxes creates problems. First, the boundaries between the boxes are never fixed or firm. Second, many groups straddle the boundaries; a group may be mostly in box C, yet partially in box B. Third, every group has its own share of diversity; with some members in one category and others in another. Fourth, different groups in the same box may be moving in different directions.

6. Most Old Order Amish and Old Order Mennonites speak Pennsylvania German (popularly called "Dutch" because in this case the word *Dutch* imitates the word *Deutsch,* meaning "German"), originating in the Palatinate of Germany. A few Amish and Mennonite communities that emigrated more directly from Switzerland can speak Swiss-German (Schweizer-Deutsch). Hutterites speak an evolved version of a nearly extinct German dialect called Tyrolean, from southern Austria and northern Italy. Many Mennonites whose ancestors came chiefly from the low-lying Netherlands can speak Low German (Plautdietsch, often called Plattdeutsch), a Dutch-German dialect.

7. The Eastern Pennsylvania Mennonite Church made radios a test of membership several years after the church had formed its own identity. In recent years, leaders also have tended to discourage high school education.

8. Some forms of plain dress are still worn by members of certain transformational groups. Typically, women carry the heaviest burden of wearing plain clothing.

9. There are, of course, many other indicators of assimilation, such as language, marriage, education, political involvement, and so on. For some Mennonite groups, prescribed patterns of plain dress were never used to symbolize separation from the world.

10. In some ways, the theological stance of Anabaptist transformer churches parallels the Reformed theological tradition's interest in transforming culture. Yet in other ways, Anabaptist transformers have a more countercultural bent that stands apart from and critiques the dominant cultural system. For a recent and excellent book that develops an Anabaptist theology of culture, see Friesen (2000).

11. For a longer discussion of the escalator as a metaphor of upward mobility within Anabaptist communities, see Driedger (1977) and Kraybill and Olshan (1994:72-4).

12. The October 2000 issue of *The Mennonite Quarterly Review* 74/4 has a dozen essays by "sympathetic Anabaptists" who describe how Anabaptist perspectives have shaped their life and theology—also published in *Engaging Anabaptism* (Herald Press, 2001). The essayists include such sympathizers as Hauerwas, Nancey Murphy, Glenn Stassen, Richard J. Mouw, and Rodney Clapp. The recent book by Kreider and Murray (2000) tells the story of Christians from many traditions in the United Kingdom who have embraced Anabaptism.

5. The Amish

1. For a fascinating discussion of the Amish in the American imagination, see the recent work of David Weaver-Zercher (2001). For a general history of the Amish, see Nolt (1992b) as well as chapters 2-3 of Hostetler (1993).

2. Kline and Beachy (1998:15).

3. Paton Yoder (1991) and P. Yoder and Estes (1999) chronicle issues that provoked controversy in the Amish communities in the last half of the nineteenth century and the subsequent formation of the Old Order groups. For discussions of the emergence of Old Order identities, see also chapters 8-9 of Nolt (1992b), chapter 8 of Schlabach (1988), and the work of Beulah Stauffer Hostetler (1992:5-25).

4. Nolt (1992b:221-2) and Luthy (1998:19-22) provide helpful introductions to the Swartzentruber Amish. Luthy (1998) also briefly discusses the origins of the Troyer group.

5. Kline and Beachy (1998) provide a historical account of New Order beginnings as well as a description of their current beliefs and practices. In 1999, Abana Books, Millersburg, Ohio, published a *New Order Amish Directory*.

6. Elmer S. Yoder (1987) wrote a history of the Beachy Amish.

7. The subaffiliations have not been identified for this project.

8. An *Amish Mennonite Directory* covering some 4,000 households and 137 congregations was published in 2000 by Abana Books. This directory includes many congregations affiliated with the Beachy Amish, as well as small independent congregations, and others that affiliate with like-minded congregations. Amish Mennonite Publications, Minerva, Ohio, is an agency that produces literature to serve many of these congregations.

9. In a few settlements, such as Kalona, Iowa, and Kokomo, Indiana, the Old Order Amish are permitted to use tractors in their fields. The vast majority of Old Order Amish settlements prohibit the use of tractors for fieldwork, but some of them allow tractors at the barns to operate high-power equipment.

10. There are a few exceptions in some communities and affiliations to these broad generalizations, but for the most part they apply to the bulk of Old Order Amish communities in North America. For example, one Old Order Amish congregation in Somerset County, Pennsylvania, has a meetinghouse, but this is a rare exception.

11. In chapter 12 of Kraybill and Olshan (1994), Mark Olshan describes the history and work of The National Amish Steering Committee.

12. Luthy (1992, 1994, 1997) has compiled a listing of all the Amish settlements in North America by state and province. His enumerations include the founding date of each settlement and its number of congregations.

13. These estimates are based on a nationwide assumption of 133 persons per district. The number of members per district varies somewhat from settlement to settlement. See section A in Resources for a discussion of the estimates used for various Amish groups and settlements in this study. The number of districts in 1991 comes from Luthy (1992). The number of districts in 2000 is from Raber (2001) as well as informants. These numbers include New Order and Old Order districts but not Beachy Amish or Amish Mennonite groups.

14. The 2001 estimate of 1,350 districts for the United States alone, includes 1,235 Old Order and 70 New Order districts in 2000, plus an *estimated* increase of 45 five new districts for 2001, yielding a grand total of 1,350 districts. Relying on Luthy's historical data and following

his ten-year increments beginning in 1951, we have used the five-decade period of 1951-2000 rather than the 1950-2000 period.

15. These estimates exclude Canada. They include United States Old Order and New Order districts and the following calculations: for 1991 we count 881 districts x 133 = 117,173; for 2000 we count 1,305 districts x 133 = 173,565. The estimate of 133 souls per district is based on the 2000 estimates used in this book.

16. Keim (1975) offers the full text of the Supreme Court's decision as well as several essays discussing the case.

17. These figures are reported in the January 2001 of the *The Blackboard Bulletin*'s "School Directory for 2000-2001" (7-24). Meyers (1993) and Huntington (1994) provide historical overviews of the rise of Amish schools and the various conflicts with the state. Hostetler and Huntington (1992) describe the cultural ethos and curriculum of Amish schools.

18. Kraybill and Nolt (1995) tell the story of this transformation in a study of the rise of Amish businesses in the Lancaster, Pennsylvania, settlement.

6. The Brethren

1. Eberly (1991:40).

2. A helpful introduction to Pietism is available in a concise overview by Dale W. Brown (1996), published by Evangel Press. Brown is a Church of the Brethren theologian, and Evangel Press is a Brethren in Christ publisher.

3. Background information on the emergence of the Schwarzenau Brethren, their migration, and their development in America appears in the following: Bowman (1995), Durnbaugh (1984, 1986, 1992, 1997), Stoffer (1989), and Willoughby (1999).

4. The Brethren in Christ, the third largest Brethren group, performed the Anabaptist-Pietist grafting process on American soil and therefore do not trace their roots directly to Schwarzenau. Because many of the early Brethren in Christ were formerly Mennonites, one could argue that they belong to the Mennonite tribe; nonetheless, their Pietist emphasis and their early associations with the German Baptist Brethren argue for the Brethren tribe.

5. The three affiliations are the Old Brethren German Baptists, with one congregation in Indiana; the Old Order German Baptists, with three congregations in Ohio; and a small subgroup of the River Brethren, in eastern Pennsylvania.

6. This estimate may be high because the large Church of the Brethren, which was coded in the transformational category, includes some congregations with members who wear plain clothing and who may more appropriately fit with the transitional groups.

7. Interestingly, Mennonites and Brethren disagree on how to spell *footwashing*. In the Brethren literature, it is usually spelled *feetwashing*, but among Mennonites it is typically *foot washing*.

8. Technically speaking, in the 1880s the large group of Conservatives were the main body of the German Baptist Brethren; in 1908 they assumed the name Church of the Brethren.

9. The first "Great Assembly" was likely held as early as 1742, but it is not clear how frequently the meetings were held. In any event, by the 1770s the large gatherings had become an Annual Meeting.

10. This quote is cited by Ralph Detrick (1990:59). I am grateful to Detrick for his help in clarifying and summarizing the ethos of the Church of the Brethren. For additional reading on this topic, see Detrick (1990:59-74).

11. Written by Brethren songwriter, Kenneth I. Morse, "Move in Our Midst" is found on page 418 of *Hymnal: A Worship Book* (1992).

12. The 1989 Annual Conference endorsed a revised statement on "Mission Theology and Guidelines," available from Brethren Press.

13. Before 1950 the National Council of Churches was called the Federal Council of Churches.

14. This description of their mission appears on their Internet Website. We have not identified BRF congregations in the Directory because they continue to maintain their membership in the Church of the Brethren. More information about the BRF can be found on their Website: www.brfwitness.org.

15. The quotes in this paragraph are posted on the denominational Website, including the Centennial Statement accepted by the 1983 General Conference of the Brethren Church; see the Website: www.brethrenchurch.org. The Website also posts an overview of the history and doctrine of the church.

16. *The Brethren Encyclopedia* (1:484-8) and Clouse (1988) describe the historical development of the Fellowship of Grace Brethren Churches.

Notes

217

17. These key phrases with an elaboration and the scriptural background of each appear on the Grace Brethren Website: www.fgbc.org.

18. For an introduction to the Old German Baptist Brethren, see chapter 5 in *On the Backroad to Heaven*, by Kraybill and Bowman (2001). Other introductory sources include Benedict (1992) and Miller (1973). A periodic journal *Old Order Notes*, edited by Fred Benedict, provides many helpful articles related to the Old German Baptist Brethren as well as other Old Order groups.

19. Membership in 1950 was less than 4,000; by the year 2000, it had exceeded 6,000. Several separations from the Old German Baptist Brethren church during the twentieth century slightly reduced their membership. Existing groups that separated from the Old German Baptist Brethren include the following: Old Brethren (organized in 1913), Old Order German Baptist Church (organized in 1921), Old Brethren German Baptist Church (organized in 1939), Brethren Community Fellowship (formed in the early 1990s), and the German Baptist Brethren (emerged in 1997).

20. The quotations in this paragraph have come from a Dunkard Brethren Website: www.geocities.com/heartland/pointe/8024/main.html.

21. For a history of the Brethren in Christ, see the work of Wittlinger (1978). Durnbaugh (1993) discusses the relationship between the Brethren in Christ (River Brethren) and the Church of the Brethren (German Baptist Brethren) in 1780, at the inception of the River Brethren. For a series of recent essays on Brethren in Christ heritage, see Sider (1999).

22. Scott (1978) and Wittlinger (1978) both discuss the origin and separation of these groups from the River Brethren in about 1855.

23. A book of essays, *Focusing Our Faith,* edited by Terry L. Brensinger (2000), elaborates on the Brethren in Christ core values.

24. This phrase was used by the early Brethren printer, Christopher Sauer Jr.

7. The Hutterites

1. Some sections in this chapter are adapted from chapter 2 on "The Hutterites" in Kraybill and Bowman (2001).

2. Two other communal groups not discussed in this chapter are Reba Place Fellowship (Evanston, Ill.) and Plow Creek Community (Tiskilwa, Ill.), Anabaptist communities that are affiliated with the Mennonite Church.

3. Personal correspondence to Donald B. Kraybill from Robert Rhodes dated 13 September 1999. Rhodes is a first-generation Hutterite who joined a Schmiedeleut colony in Minnesota.

4. The Hutterisch German dialect has roots in Austria and northern Italy, specifically Carinthian and Tyrolean, but also Russian elements and increasingly some English. An archaic form of High German is used in most sermons and taught in the German schools of the colonies, but this is quite different from modern German. Elements of Hutterisch also enter into many sermons.

5. The use of computers varies considerably. In more progressive colonies, computers are used for business and personal purposes. Some colonies have Web pages. One colony in Manitoba has a site that describes the Hutterian Church: www.hutterianbrethren.com. Some colonies also use satellite-linked weather and market news sources.

6. Ehrenpreis (1978:62, 35-6).

7. Waldner (1990:5).

8. Waldner (1990:3).

9. Ehrenpreis (1978) introduces these ideas in a long epistle he wrote in 1650 on "Brotherly Community—The Highest Command of Love." The quote comes from Ehrenpreis (1978:64-5).

10. *The Chronicle of the Hutterian Brethren,* vol. 1 (1987).

11. Hofer (1973:34-5) cites 1 John 5:19 and other biblical passages that underscore separation from the world.

12. John A. Hostetler (1997:153).

13. See William Janzen (1990) for an excellent study of Hutterite church-state relations.

14. An arsonist ignited a fire on 8 March 1998 at a new colony (Camrose) near Shelby, Montana, that caused some $100,000 in damage. This was the third act of vandalism aimed at new property bought by the Hutterites. Authorities suspect it was set by outsiders resentful of the Hutterite expansion.

15. In a few cases, some colonies have established their own private schools. A few colonies have sent their own members to college for teacher training so they can teach in colony schools.

16. In one colony in the United States, the corporate income is divided equally among all fam-

ilies, and individual taxes are paid accordingly, with returns filed for each family. They pay corporate and property taxes, just like any other corporation or farm. The steward and a hired accountant file all the tax forms for the individual families.

17. Introductions to Bruderhof life and history can be found in books by Baum (1998), Eberhard Arnold (1997), Emmy Arnold (1999), and Oved (1996).

8. The Mennonites

1. Redekop (1989) and Kauffman and Driedger (1991) have written sociological introductions and analyses of Mennonite society. The later work reports the survey results about a host of beliefs and practices from 3,500 respondents in five different Mennonite groups.

2. The projected 120,000 includes the current Mennonite Church membership of 92,145, and the General Conference Mennonite Church membership of 27,507. These numbers include the 20,000 members in 210 congregations that already have a dual affiliation. Some congregations may choose not to join the new integrated body; those decisions could lower the eventual membership of the Mennonite Church USA.

3. An excellent introduction to the history of the Mennonites in North America appears in the four-volume work *Mennonite Experience in America,* authored by Juhnke (1989), MacMaster (1985), Schlabach (1988), and Toews (1996).

4. See Klopfenstein (1984) for a history of the group. Nolt (1992b:115-7) discusses their relationship with the Amish. Several break-off groups from the Apostolic Christian Church of America have not been included in this study because they display fewer Anabaptist traits.

5. The first groups formed in Indiana and Ohio in 1872; the last one in York County, Pennsylvania, in 1913. Scott (1996) provides an excellent introduction to the many varieties of Old Order and conservative Mennonite groups living in the United Sates and Canada. Hoover, Miller, and Freeman (1978) offer a good overview of Old Order Mennonite history from an Old Order Mennonite perspective. The best historical introduction to the Old Order Mennonites and Amish in nineteenth-century America is chapter 8 on "Keeping the Old Order," in Schlabach (1988:201-229). Hoover (1982) compiled an excellent collection of primary source materials on Old Order views at the time of their formation. In an insightful essay, Beulah Stauffer Hostetler (1992) compares the emergence of several Old Order groups between 1850 and 1900. The most prolific Old Order Mennonite writer is Isaac Horst, a Canadian. Horst (2000) has recently published a collection of his essays.

6. The best introduction to these groups can be found in chapters 6 and 8 of Stephen Scott's (1996) book, *Old Order and Conservative Mennonite Groups.*

7. Christian Light Publications (PO Box 1212, Harrisonburg, VA 22803-1212) is a major publisher that supplies many of the conservative Mennonite Churches.

8. The conservative Mennonite churches are described this way in the publisher's note to *Mennonite Church Information 2000,* which includes many of these churches.

9. Stephen Scott (1996:162-3) identifies five types: (1) Ultra Conservative, (2) Intermediate Conservative, (3) Moderate Conservative, (4) Fundamental Conservative, and (5) Theological Conservative.

10. The Association of Evangelical Mennonite Congregations (AEMC) and the Hopewell District churches provide two examples of groups that were in the process of forming independent affiliations at the end of the year 2000.

The AEMC's mission is briefly described in the group profiles in section C. About 100 representatives from thirty congregations, interested in an alternative to the new Mennonite Church USA, attended an open meeting on September 30, 2000, at the Paradise Mennonite Church in Pennsylvania. The AEMC planned to formally accept congregations into the Association during the year 2001.

The Hopewell District churches, which had functioned within the Atlantic Coast Conference of the Mennonite Church in eastern Pennsylvania, were also in the midst of forming an independent body at the end of 2000. The proposed name of the new group was the Apostolic Fellowship of the Radical Church Network. Sharing some similar concerns with the Association of Evangelical Mennonite Congregations, the proposed Apostolic Fellowship had a more charismatic flavor. The proposed network did not plan to affiliate with the new Mennonite Church USA. The Apostolic Fellowship emphasized evangelism, biblical absolutes, local church (rather than denominational) training and credentialing for pastors, as well as a charismatic philosophy of ministry.

9. Education, Service, and Mission

1. *Courier* (the quarterly publication of Mennonite World Conference) 15/4 (2000): 16.

2. In an excellent article, Steve Nolt (1998) compares the institution-building activities of the Mennonite Church and the Church of the Brethren in the area of mutual aid. Nolt shows that although both groups made theological affirmations about mutual aid, the Mennonite Church more actively established mutual aid organizations in the mid-twentieth century. Such institution-building activity is a way of reconstructing ethnic identity and resisting structural assimilation into the larger society. Additional investigation of this fascinating question awaits future study.

3. The major sources for our estimates of the number of schools are the following: *Amish Mennonite Directory* (2000), *The Blackboard Bulletin* (Jan. 2001), *Mennonite Church Information* (2000), *New Order Amish Directory* (1999), *Mennonite Directory* (2000), and the *Church of the Brethren Yearbook* (2000).

4. *The Blackboard Bulletin* (Jan. 2001) reports these numbers for 2000-01.

5. Other colleges were established by the Brethren around the turn of the twentieth century but eventually closed or merged with other institutions. The present-day colleges and universities function largely as independent entities and maintain different patterns of relationship with the respective church agencies in their area.

6. *The Blackboard Bulletin* (Jan. 2001:22).

7. The largest high schools are Lancaster Mennonite (810), Christopher Dock (400), Central Christian (347), Eastern Mennonite (307), and Bethany Christian (234).

8. Eight Bible schools and institutes are listed in *Mennonite Church Information* (2000), a directory of the more conservative Mennonite Churches.

9. In an exception to the Hutterite pattern, the Bruderhof Communities have a variety of social justice and outreach ministries.

10. This estimate of overseas congregations comes from *Mennonite Church Information* (2000) and the *Amish Mennonite Directory* (2000).

11. A description of many of these service and mission programs is provided in the *Amish Mennonite Directory* (2000).

12. Grace Brethren officials provided this estimate in the fall of 2000.

13. These are the estimated numbers provided by the Global Mission Partnerships of the Church of the Brethren. The full name of the EYN Church is Ekkesiyar Yan'uwa a Nigeria.

14. The unusual spelling of the Womaen's Caucus, established in 1973, uses an *a* for each woman and an *e* for all women.

15. Redekop (1995) tells this story and identifies the various groups.

16. One of the issues that emerged in the production of the hymnal involved discussions about the inclusion of historic Christian creeds in a section of worship resources. The earlier *Mennonite Hymnal* included both the Apostles' Creed and the Nicene Creed. Reflecting their noncreedal tradition, Church of the Brethren representatives preferred not to include any creeds. In a compromise solution, the new hymnal printed the Apostles' Creed without naming it and did not include the Nicene Creed.

10. Anabaptist World 2000

1. Quoted in an article by John A. Lapp (2001:111).

2. In a helpful overview of the Mennonite world in 2000, John A. Lapp (2001:99-120) among many other observations noted that Anabaptist identity in the twenty-first century will be increasingly defined by the new majority of Anabaptists living in Africa, Asia, and Latin America.

3. Precise membership numbers are not available for 1900. However, based on several sources, 150,000 seems a reasonable estimate. The 1890 United States Census provided the closest turn-of-the-century count of religious groups, but these estimates are likely undercounted. Bowman (1995:96, 113) provides estimates for Brethren groups, and Juhnke (1989:54) discusses Mennonite and Amish membership for 1900. The estimate of 150,000 assumes about 80,000 Brethren (German Baptist Brethren, Old German Baptist Brethren, and Brethren Church), 60,000 members of various Mennonite and Amish groups, 4,000 Brethren in Christ, and 6,000 Hutterites and other small groups. These estimates come from the sources noted above as well as from various yearbooks and the assistance of several archivists.

Section A. Methods and Data Sources

1. For a discussion of the historical connections, see *The Mennonite Encyclopedia* (3:710-1). We are grateful to Steven Nolt for helping to clarify the historical development of the Missionary Church with the following information. The Missionary Church is the product of a 1969 merger of the United Missionary Church (UMC) and the Missionary Church

Association (MCA). The UMC was much larger than the MCA. Both were of Anabaptist origin, though somewhat different. The United Missionary Church grew out of (Old) Mennonite and Brethren in Christ roots in Indiana, Pennsylvania, Ontario, and Ohio. Until 1947 the group was known as the Mennonite Brethren in Christ (MBIC) and considered a part of the Mennonite family of denominations. In 1947 the group adopted the UMC name and started its own college (Bethel College, Mishawaka, Ind.). In the 1950s it withdrew from active MCC participation. In eastern Pennsylvania MBIC did not join the UMC but formed the Bible Fellowship Church. The MCA—the other, much-smaller member in the 1969 merger—stemmed from the Egly Amish (today's Evangelical Mennonite Church) in the Fort Wayne area. In general, the MCA was less "Mennonite" in its orientation than the UMC.

2. Several of these denominations have a restorationist heritage—an interest in restoring elements of the early apostolic church in harmony with the spirit of the church in the book of Acts. Littell's (1964) study documents how this vision of the church motivated many sixteenth-century Anabaptists. For a series of essays on this theme of restitution in various churches, see also the special March 1976 issue of the *Journal of American Academy of Religion* (vol. 44).

Section I

SELECTED REFERENCES

The following entries include sources the authors cited in the author-date system in the Notes plus other select works and periodicals related to the various groups.

Alderfer, Owen H.
1999   "The Brethren Mind-Set: The Way of the Brethren." In *Reflections on a Heritage*. Ed. E. Morris Sider. Grantham, Pa.: The Brethren in Christ Historical Society.
Amish Mennonite Directory
2000   Millersburg, Ohio: Abana Books.
Arnold, Eberhard
1997   *God's Revolution: Justice, Community, and the Coming Kingdom*. Farmington, Pa.: Plough Publishing House.
Arnold, Emmy
1999   *A Joyful Pilgrimage: My Life in Community*. Farmington, Pa.: Plough Publishing House.
Baecher, Robert
2000   "Research Note: The 'Patriarche' of Sainte-Marie-aux-Mines." *The Mennonite Quarterly Review* 74:145-58.
Baum, Marcus
1998   *Against the Wind: Eberhard Arnold and the Bruderhof*. Farmington, Pa.: Plough Publishing House.
Bender, Harold S.
1944   *The Anabaptist Vision* (pamphlet, 44 pp.). Scottdale, Pa.: Herald Press.
1957   "The Anabaptist Vision." In *The Recovery of the Anabaptist Vision*. Ed. Guy F. Hershberger. Scottdale, Pa.: Herald Press.
Benedict, Fred W.
1967   "A Brief Account of the Origin and a Description of the Brethren Love Feast." Pendleton, Ind.: Old Brotherhood Publishers.
1992   "The Old Order Brethren in Transition." In *Brethren in Transition*. Ed. Emmert F. Bittinger. Camden, Maine: Penobscot Press.
Blackboard Bulletin, The
1957-   Monthly periodical for Old Order Amish teachers. Aylmer, Ont.: Pathway Publishers.
Bowman, Carl F.
1995   *Brethren Society: The Cultural Transformation of a Peculiar People*. Baltimore: The Johns Hopkins Univ. Press.
Brackney, William H., ed.
1998   *The Believers Church: A Voluntary Church*. Kitchener, Ont.: Pandora Press; and Scottdale, Pa.: Herald Press.
Braght, Thieleman J. van, compiler
1950   *The Bloody Theater* or *Martyrs Mirror of the Defenseless Christians*. Scottdale, Pa.: Herald Press. Original in Dutch at Dordrecht, 1660.

Brensinger, Terry L., ed.
2000   *Focusing Our Faith: Brethren in Christ Core Values.* Nappanee, Ind.: Evangel Publishing House.
Brethren Encyclopedia, The
1983-84 Vols. 1-3. Philadelphia and Oak Brook, Ill.: Brethren Encyclopedia.
Brothers Unite
1988   Ed., trans., the Hutterite Brethren. Ulster Park, N.Y.: Plough Publishing House.
Brown, Dale W.
1996   *Understanding Pietism.* 2d ed. Nappanee, Ind.: Evangel Publishing House.
Budget, The
1890-   Sugarcreek, Ohio. Weekly newspaper for Amish and Mennonite communities.
Bush, Perry
1998   *Two Kingdoms, Two Loyalties: Mennonite Pacifism in Modern America.* Baltimore: Johns Hopkins Univ. Press.
Chronicle of the Hutterian Brethren, The
1987   Vol. 1. Trans., ed. the Hutterian Brethren. Rifton, N.Y.: Plough Publishing House.
1998   Vol. 2. Trans., ed. the Hutterian Brethren. Ste. Agathe, Manitoba: Crystal Spring Colony.
Church of the Brethren Yearbook
2000   Elgin, Ill.: Brethren Press.
Classics of the Radical Reformation
1973-99 Nine-volume series offers translations and commentary on sixteenth-century Anabaptist writers and leaders. Scottdale, Pa.: Herald Press.
Clouse, Robert G.
1988   "Brethren and Modernity: Change and Development in the Progressive Grace Church." *Brethren Life and Thought* 33:205-17.
Confession of Faith of the Mennonites: Church Forms and Guidelines of the Weaverland Conference
1996   Weaverland Conference: Lancaster, Pa.
Confession of Faith in a Mennonite Perspective
1995   Scottdale, Pa.: Herald Press.
Cronk, Sandra L.
1981   "Gelassenheit: The Rites of the Redemptive Process in Old Order Amish and Old Order Mennonite Communities." *The Mennonite Quarterly Review* 55:544.
Detrick, Ralph L.
1990   "Multi-Ethnic Congregations: The Theological Challenge." Doctor of Ministry thesis. Bethany Theological Seminary, Oak Brook, Ill. (later, Richmond, Ind.).
Directory of the Groffdale Conference Mennonite Churches
1997   3d ed. Kutztown, Pa.: Laura N. Shirk.
Directory of the Lancaster County Amish
1996   Vols. 1-2. Gordonville, Pa.: Pequea Publishers.
Directory of the Weaverland Conference Mennonite Churches
2000   Womelsdorf, Pa.: Ruth Ann Wise.
Drama of the Martyrs, The
1975   Lancaster Pa.: Mennonite Historical Associates.
Driedger, Leo
1977   "The Anabaptist Identification Ladder: Plain Urban Continuity in Diversity." *The Mennonite Quarterly Review* 51:278-91.

Driedger, Leo, and Donald B. Kraybill
    1994   *Mennonite Peacemaking: From Quietism to Activism.* Scottdale, Pa.: Herald Press.

Durnbaugh, Donald F.
    1958   *European Origins of the Brethren.* Elgin, Ill.: The Brethren Press.
    1984   *Meet the Brethren.* Elgin, Ill.: Brethren Press for the Brethren Encyclopedia.
    1985   *The Believer's Church: The History and Character of Radical Protestantism.* Scottdale, Pa.: Herald Press.
    1986   *Church of the Brethren: Yesterday and Today.* Elgin, Ill.: Brethren Press.
    1992   *Brethren Beginnings: The Origin of the Church of the Brethren in Early Eighteenth Century Europe.* Philadelphia: Brethren Encyclopedia.
    1993   "Nineteenth-Century Dunker Views of the River Brethren." *The Mennonite Quarterly Review* 67: 133-51.
    1997   *Fruit of the Vine.* Elgin, Ill.: The Brethren Press.
    1998   "Afterword: The Believers Church Conferences." In *The Believers Church: A Voluntary Church,* Ed. William H. Brackney. Kitchener, Ont: Pandora Press; and Scottdale, Pa.: Herald Press.

Dyck, Cornelius J.
    1985   "The Suffering Church in Anabaptism." *The Mennonite Quarterly Review* 59:5-23.
    1993   *An Introduction to Mennonite History: A Popular History of the Anabaptists and the Mennonites.* 3d ed. Scottdale, Pa.: Herald Press.

Eberly, William R., ed.
    1991   *The Complete Writings of Alexander Mack.* Winona Lake, Ill.: BMH Books.

Ehrenpreis, Andreas, and Claus Felbinger
    1978   *Brotherly Community: The Highest Command of Love.* Rifton, N.Y.: Plough Publishing House.

Eller, David B., ed.
    1990   *Servants of the Word: Ministry in the Believers Church.* Elgin, Ill.: Brethren Press.

Estep, William R.
    1996   *The Anabaptist Story: An Introduction to Sixteenth-Century Anabaptism.* 3d ed. Grand Rapids: Eerdmans Publishing Co.

Family Life
    1968-   Monthly periodical for Old Order Amish and Mennonite communities. Aylmer, Ont.: Pathway Publishers.

Friedmann, Robert
    1961   *Hutterite Studies.* Goshen, Ind.: Mennonite Historical Society.

Friesen, Duane K.
    2000   *Artists, Citizens, Philosophers Seeking the Peace of the City: An Anabaptist Theology of Culture.* Scottdale, Pa.: Herald Press.

Friesen, John J., trans., ed.
    1999   *Peter Riedemann's Hutterite Confession of Faith.* Scottdale, Pa.: Herald Press.

Furner, Mark
    2000   "Research Note: On the Trail of Jacob Ammann." *The Mennonite Quarterly Review* 74:326-8.

Gingerich, Jeff, and Miriam Stoltzfus
    2000   *All God's Children: Philadelphia Mennonites of Lancaster Conference, 1899-1999.* Leola, Pa. Imperial Graphics.

Gordon, Milton M.
1997   *Assimilation in American Life: The Role of Race, Religion and National Origins*. X ed. Toronto: Oxford Univ. Press. (original, 1964).
Gross, Leonard
1998   *The Golden Years of the Hutterites*. Rev. ed. Kitchener, Ont.: Pandora Press; and Scottdale, Pa.: Herald Press.
Harrison, Wes
1997   *Andreas Ehrenpreis and Hutterite Faith and Practice*. Kitchener, Ont.: Pandora Press; and Scottdale, Pa.: Herald Press.
Hershberger, Guy F., ed.
1957   *The Recovery of the Anabaptist Vision*. Scottdale, Pa.: Herald Press.
Hofer, John
1988   *The History of the Hutterites*. Rev. ed. Altona, Man.: D. W. Friesen & Sons.
Hofer, Peter
1973   *The Hutterian Brethren and Their Beliefs*. Starbuck, Man.: The Hutterian Brethren Manitoba.
Hofer, Samuel
1991   *Born Hutterite*. Saskatoon, Sask.: Hofer Publishing.
1998   *The Hutterites: Lives and Images of a Communal People*. Saskatoon, Sask.: Hofer Publishers.
Hoover, Amos B., compiler
1982   *The Jonas Martin Era (1875-1925)*. Denver, Pa.: Muddy Creek Farm Library.
Hoover, Amos, David L. Miller, and Leonard Freeman
1978   "The Old Order Mennonites." In *Mennonite World Handbook*, 374-81. Carol Stream, Ill.: Mennonite World Conference.
Horst, Isaac R.
2000   *A Separate People: An Insider's View of Old Order Mennonite Customs and Traditions*. Scottdale, Pa: Herald Press.
Hostetler, Beulah Stauffer
1992   "The Formation of the Old Orders." *The Mennonite Quarterly Review* 66:5-25.
Hostetler, John A.
1993   *Amish Society*. 4th ed. Baltimore: Johns Hopkins Univ. Press.
1997   *Hutterite Society*. 2d ed. Baltimore: Johns Hopkins Univ. Press.
Hostetler, John A., and Gertrude E. Huntington
1992   *Amish Children: Education in the Family, School, and Community*. 2d ed. Fort Worth, Tex.: Harcourt Brace Jovanovich.
1996   *The Hutterites in North America*. 3d ed. Philadelphia: Holt, Rinehart, and Winston.
Hostetter, C. Nelson
1997   *Anabaptist-Mennonites Nationwide USA*. Morgantown, Pa.: Masthof Press.
Huntington, Gertrude E.
1994   "Persistence and Change in Amish Education." In *The Amish Struggle with Modernity*. Ed. Donald B. Kraybill and Marc A. Olshan. Hanover, N.H.: Univ. Press of New England.
Hüppi, John
2000   "Research Note: Identifying Jacob Ammann." *The Mennonite Quarterly Review* 74:329-339.
Hymnal: A Worship Book
1992   Prepared by Churches in the Believers Church Tradition. Jointly published: Elgin, Ill.: Brethren Press; Newton, Kan.: Faith & Life Press; and Scottdale, Pa.: Mennonite Publishing House.

Igou, Brad, compiler
    1999   *The Amish in Their Own Words: Amish Writings from 25 Years of Family Life Magazine.* Scottdale, Pa.: Herald Press.

Janzen, Rod A.
    1999   *The Prairie People: Forgotten Anabaptists.* Hanover, N.H.: Univ. Press of New England.

Janzen, William
    1990   *Limits on Liberty.* Toronto: Univ. of Toronto Press.

Juhnke, James C.
    1989   *Vision, Doctrine, War: Mennonite Identity and Organization in America, 1890-1930.* Vol. 3 of *The Mennonite Experience in America.* Scottdale, Pa.: Herald Press.

Kauffman, J. Howard, and Leo Driedger
    1991   *The Mennonite Mosaic: Identity and Modernization.* Scottdale, Pa.: Herald Press.

Keim, Albert N.
    1975   *Compulsory Education and the Amish: The Right Not to Be Modern.* Boston: Beacon Press.

Klaassen, Walter
    2001   *Anabaptism: Neither Protestant nor Catholic.* 3d ed. Kitchener, Ont.: Pandora Press; Scottdale, Pa.; Herald Press.
    1981   Ed. *Anabaptism in Outline: Selected Primary Sources.* Scottdale, Pa.: Herald Press.
    1991   "Gelassenheit and Creation." *The Conrad Grebel Review* 7:23-35.

Kline, Edward A., and Monroe L. Beachy
    1998   "History and Dynamics of the New Order Amish of Holmes County, Ohio." *Old Order Notes,* no. 18, fall-winter, 7-20.

Klopfenstein, Perry A.
    1984   *Marching to Zion: A History of the Apostolic Christian Church of America, 1847-1982.* Fort Scott, Kan.: Sekan Printing Co.

Kniss, Fred
    1997   *Disquiet in the Land: Cultural Conflict in American Mennonite Communities.* New Brunswick, N.J.: Rutgers Univ. Press.

Kraybill, Donald B.
    1990   *The Upside Down Kingdom.* 2nd ed. Scottdale, Pa.: Herald Press.
    1993   Ed. *The Amish and the State.* Baltimore: Johns Hopkins Univ. Press.
    1998   *The Puzzles of Amish Life.* Rev. ed. Intercourse, Pa: Good Books.
    2001   *The Riddle of Amish Culture.* 2nd ed. Baltimore: Johns Hopkins Univ. Press.

Kraybill, Donald B., and Carl F. Bowman
    2001   *On the Backroad to Heaven: Old Order Hutterites, Mennonites, Amish, and Brethren.* Baltimore: Johns Hopkins Univ. Press.

Kraybill, Donald B., and Steven M. Nolt
    1995   *Amish Enterprise: From Plows to Profits.* Baltimore: Johns Hopkins Univ. Press.

Kraybill, Donald B., and Marc A. Olshan, eds.
    1994   *The Amish Struggle with Modernity.* Hanover, N.H.: Univ. Press of New England.

Kreider, Alan, and Stuart Murray
    2000   *Coming Home: Stories of Anabaptists in Britain and Ireland.* Kitchener, Ont.: Pandora Press; and Scottdale, Pa.: Herald Press.

Lapp, John A.
    2001   "Mennonites in the Year 2000." *The Mennonite Quarterly Review* 75:99-120.

Lederach, Paul
    1980   *A Third Way.* Scottdale, Pa.: Herald Press.

Littell, Franklin H.
1964   *The Origins of Sectarian Protestantism.* N.Y.: Macmillan Co.
1967   "The Concerns of the Believers Church." In *The Chicago Theological Seminary Register* 58/2:12-8.
1970   "The Contribution of the Free Churches." In *The Chicago Theological Seminary Register* 60/6:47-57.

Loewen, Harry, and Steven M. Nolt
1996   *Through Fire and Water: An Overview of Mennonite History.* Scottdale, Pa.: Herald Press.

Loewen, Howard John
1985   *One Lord, One Church, One Hope, and One God: Mennonite Confessions of Faith.* Elkhart, Ind.: Institute of Mennonite Studies.

Luthy, David
1992   "Amish Settlements Across America: 1991." *Family Life* 25 (Apr.): 19-24.
1994   "Amish Migration Patterns: 1972-1992." In *The Amish Struggle with Modernity.* Eds. Donald B. Kraybill and Marc A. Olshan. Hanover, N.H.: Univ. Press of New England.
1997   "Amish Settlements Across America: 1996." *Family Life* 30 (May): 20-24.
1998   "The Origin and Growth of the Swartzentruber Amish." *Family Life* 30 (Aug.-Sept.): 19-22.
2000   *Why Some Amish Communities Fail: Extinct Settlements, 1961-1999.* Aylmer, Ont.: Pathway Publishers.

MacMaster, Richard K.
1985   *Land, Piety, Peoplehood: The Establishment of Mennonite Communities in America, 1683-1790.* Vol. 1 of *The Mennonite Experience in America.* Scottdale, Pa.: Herald Press.

Menno Simons
1956   *The Complete Writings of Menno Simons (1496-1561).* Ed. J. C. Wenger. Scottdale, Pa.: Herald Press.

Mennonite Church Information
2000   Harrisonburg, Va.: Christian Light Publications, Inc.

Mennonite Directory
2000-01 Vols. 2-3. Scottdale Pa.: Herald Press.

Mennonite Encyclopedia, The: A Comprehensive Reference Work on the Anabaptist-Mennonite Movement
1955-59 Vols. 1-4. Hillsboro, Kan.: Mennonite Brethren Publishing House; Newton, Kan.: Mennonite Publication Office; Scottdale, Pa.: Mennonite Publishing House.
1990   Vol. 5, Scottdale, Pa.: Herald Press.

Meyers, Thomas J.
1993   "Education and Schooling." In *The Amish and the State.* Ed. Donald B. Kraybill. Baltimore: Johns Hopkins Univ. Press.

Miller, Marcus
1973   *Roots by the River. The History, Doctrine, and Practice of the Old German Baptist Brethren in Miami County, Ohio.* Piqua, Ohio: Hammer Graphics, Inc.

New Order Amish Directory
1999   Millersburg, Ohio: Abana Books.

Nolt, Steven M.
1992a   "The Mennonite Eclipse." *Festival Quarterly* 19 (summer): 8-12.
1992b   *A History of the Amish.* Intercourse, Pa.: Good Books.
1998   "Formal Mutual Aid Structures Among American Mennonites and Brethren: Assimilation and Reconstructed Ethnicity." *Journal of American Ethnic History* 17:71-86.

Ohio Amish Directory, Holmes County and Vicinity
    2000   Walnut Creek: Carlisle Press.
Oved, Yaacov
    1996   *The Witness of the Brothers: A History of the Bruderhof.* New
           Brunswick, N.J.: Transaction Publishers.
Oyer, John, and Robert S. Kreider
    1990   *Mirror of the Martyrs.* Intercourse, Pa.: Good Books.
Packull, Werner O.
    1995   *Hutterite Beginnings: Communitarian Experiments During the
           Reformation.* Baltimore: Johns Hopkins Univ. Press.
Raber, Ben J., compiler
    1970-   *The New American Almanac.* Published yearly by Ben J. Raber, Baltic,
           Ohio. Gordonville, Pa.: Gordonville Print Shop. The almanac in
           German, *Die Neue Amerikanische Kalender*, begins in 1930.
Redekop, Calvin W.
    1989   *Mennonite Society.* Baltimore: Johns Hopkins Univ. Press.
    1995   "The Organizational Children of MCC." *Mennonite Historical
           Bulletin* 56 (Jan.): 71-86.
    1998   *Leaving Anabaptism: From Evangelical Mennonite Brethren to
           Fellowship of Evangelical Bible Churches.* Telford, Pa.: Pandora Press;
           and Scottdale, Pa.: Herald Press.
Roth, John D.
    1993   Trans., ed. *Letters of the Amish Division: A Sourcebook.* Goshen, Ind.:
           Mennonite Historical Society.
    1995   Ed. *Refocusing a Vision: Shaping Anabaptist Character in the 21st
           Century.* Goshen, Ind.: Mennonite Historical Society.
Schlabach, Theron F.
    1988   *Peace, Faith, Nation: Mennonites and Amish in Nineteenth-Century
           America.* Vol. 2 of *The Mennonite Experience in America.* Scottdale,
           Pa.: Herald Press.
"School Directory: 2000-2001"
    2001   In *The Blackboard Bulletin* (Jan.): 7-24
Scott, Stephen
    1978   "The Old Order River Brethren Church." In *Pennsylvania Mennonite
           Heritage* 1/3:13-22.
    1981   *Plain Buggies: Amish, Mennonite, and Brethren Horse-Drawn
           Transportation.* Intercourse, Pa.: Good Books.
    1986   *Why Do They Dress That Way?* Intercourse, Pa.: Good Books.
    1988   *The Amish Wedding and Other Special Occasions of the Old Order
           Communities.* Intercourse, Pa.: Good Books.
    1996   *An Introduction to Old Order and Conservative Mennonite Groups.*
           Intercourse, Pa.: Good Books.
Sider, E. Morris, ed.
    1999   *Reflections on a Heritage: Defining the Brethren in Christ.* Grantham,
           Pa.: The Brethren in Christ Historical Society.
Snyder, C. Arnold
    1995   *Anabaptist History and Theology: An Introduction.* Kitchener, Ont.:
           Pandora Press; and Scottdale, Pa.: Herald Press.
    1999   *From Anabaptist Seed.* Kitchener, Ont.: Pandora Press; and Scottdale,
           Pa.: Herald Press.
Stayer, James M.
    1990   *The German Peasants' War and Anabaptist Community of Goods.*
           Montreal: McGill-Queen's Univ. Press.
Stoffer, Dale
    1989   *Background and Development of Brethren Doctrines, 1650-1987.*
           Philadelphia: Brethren Encyclopedia.

1997   Ed. *The Lord's Supper: Believers Church Perspectives.* Scottdale, Pa.: Herald Press.

Stoltzfus, Louise
1994   *Amish Women: Lives and Stories.* Intercourse, Pa.: Good Books.
1998   *Traces of Wisdom: Amish Women and the Pursuit of Life's Simple Treasures.* N.Y.: Hyperion.

Strege, Merle D., ed.
1986   *Baptism and Church: A Believers Church Vision.* Grand Rapids, Mich.: Saqamore Books.

Swartley, Willard, and Donald B. Kraybill, eds.
1997   *Building Communities of Compassion: Mennonite Mutual Aid in Theory and Practice.* Scottdale: Herald Press.

Thiesen, John D.
1993   "Mennonites Are Forever Splitting, Aren't They?" *Gospel Herald,* Jan. 26, 1-3.

Toews, Paul
1996   *Mennonites in American Society, 1930-1970: Modernity and the Persistence of Religious Community.* Vol. 4 of *The Mennonite Experience in America.* Scottdale, Pa.: Herald Press.

Urry, James
1999   "Of Borders and Boundaries: Reflections on Mennonite Unity and Separation in the Modern World." *The Mennonite Quarterly Review* 73: 503-524.

Waldner, Tony
1990   *History of Forest River Community.* Fordville, N.D.: Forest River Community.

Weaver, J. Denny
1987   *Becoming Anabaptist: The Origin and Significance of Sixteenth-Century Anabaptism.* Scottdale, Pa.: Herald Press.

Weaver-Zercher, David
1996   "Between Two Kingdoms: Virginia Mennonites and the American Flag." *The Mennonite Quarterly Review* 70:165-90.
1999   "Open (to) Arms: The Status of the Peace Position in the Brethren in Christ Church." *Brethren in Christ Life* 22 (Jan.): 90-115.
2001   *The Amish in the American Imagination.* Baltimore: Johns Hopkins Univ. Press.

Weiler, Lloyd M.
1993   "An Introduction to Old Order Mennonite Origins in Lancaster County, Pennsylvania: 1893-1993." *Pennsylvania Mennonite Heritage* 16 (Oct.): 2-13.
1995   "Historical Overview of Weaverland Conference Origins." In *Directory of the Weaverland Conference Mennonite Churches.* 3d ed. Womelsdrof, Pa.: Ruth Ann Wise.

Williams, George Huntston
2000   *The Radical Reformation.* 3d ed. Philadelphia: Thomas Jefferson Univ. Press. (paperback reprint of 1992 hardback).

Willoughby, William G.
1999   *The Beliefs of the Early Brethren, 1706-1735.* Philadelphia: Brethren Encyclopedia.

Wittlinger, Carlton O.
1978   *Quest for Piety and Obedience: The Story of the Brethren in Christ.* Nappanee, Ind.: Evangel Press.

Yoder, Elmer S.
1987   *The Beachy Amish Mennonite Fellowship Churches.* Hartville, Ohio: Diakonia Ministries.

Yoder, John Howard
    1973   Trans., ed. *The Legacy of Michael Sattler.* Scottdale, Pa.: Herald Press.
    1994   *The Politics of Jesus.* 2d ed. Grand Rapids: Eerdmans.
Yoder, Paton
    1991   *Tradition and Transition: Amish Mennonites and Old Order Amish, 1800-1900.* Scottdale, Pa.: Herald Press.
Yoder, Paton, and Steven R. Estes
    1999   *Proceedings of the Amish Ministers' Meetings 1862-1878.* Goshen, Ind.: The Mennonite Historical Society.

Part 3
Directory of Congregations

DIRECTORY OF
CONGREGATIONS

INTRODUCTION

The Directory of Congregations lists the specific congregations of the Anabaptist groups in the United States that were identified in previous sections of the book. The listing contains the congregations and their affiliations as of December 31, 2000. The membership information is based on a variety of sources described in part 2, section A. Membership numbers, however, should always be viewed as estimates.

Among the Amish the membership estimates for specific church districts are *averages* for large groups, as explained in part 2, section A. Thus the membership *estimate* for specific Amish congregation in the directory may be different from the *actual* membership of the congregation (church district). To make the directory as accurate as possible as of December 31, 2000, about twenty Amish districts were added to the directory after the text was finalized. These additional districts are not included in the statistical summaries that appear earlier in the book.

About two dozen small new congregations have been included in the directory even though no members are listed. These fledgling congregations hold worship services, and some are in the process of accepting members into their fellowship.

The Directory of Congregations may not be used for commercial purposes or copied in any manner without the express written permission of the publisher.

The following abbreviations have been used throughout the directory:

Conf	Conference
Consrv	Conservative
DA	Dual Affiliated
DC	Dual Conference
Grace Brethren Churches	Fellowship of Grace Brethren Churches
O. O.	Old Order

KEY

STATE
TRIBE
Affiliation

Congregation Name	Town	Members

ALABAMA

AMISH

Beachy Amish

Emmanuel	Harstelle	31
Orrville	Orrville	21

BRETHREN

Church of the Brethren

Cedar Creek	Citronelle	115
Community	Oneonta	22
Easley	Cleveland	51
Fruitdale	Fruitdale	59
Sun Valley	Birmingham	15

MENNONITE

Apostolic Christian Church of America

Athens	Athens	45

Church of God in Christ Mennonite

Cedar Crest	Faunsdale	173
Southern Star	Emelle	143

Good News Mennonite Fellowship

Arise Ministries	Birmingham	4
Bethel	Brewton	25
Calvary	Brewton	41
Christian Fellowship	Atmore	102
Church at the Eastern Gate	Birmingham	4
Faith Chapel	Cleveland	49
Freedom in Christ	Mobile	6
Living Stones	Atmore	25
Mobile	Mobile	22
New Creation	Birmingham	12
New Vision	Birmingham	4
Southside	Birmingham	85
Straight Mountain	Springville	35

Independent Mennonite Congregation

Gospel Light	Atmore	60

Mennonite Church

Poarch Community	Atmore	45

ALASKA

BRETHREN

Grace Brethren Churches

Fellowship of Anchorage	Anchorage	310
Eagle River	Eagle River	99
Grace Community	Anchorage	635
Greatland	Anchorage	79
Kenai	Kenai	63
Peninsula	Soldonta	122

MENNONITE

Mennonite Church

Prince of Peace	Anchorage	18

ARIZONA

BRETHREN

Brethren Church, The

First	Tucson	79
Iglesia De Los Hermanos	Tucson	10
Northwest Community	Tucson	56

Church of the Brethren

Community	Mesa	44
First	Phoenix	100
Glendale	Glendale	103
Tucson	Tucson	49

Grace Brethren Churches

East Valley	Gilbert	18

MENNONITE

Apostolic Christian Church of America

Phoenix	Phoenix	183
Prescott	Prescott	17
Tucson	Tucson	20

Church of God in Christ Mennonite

Desert View	Yuma	38
Greasewood	Greasewood	4
Jeddito	Keams Canyon	3
Klagetoh/Wide Ruins	Chambers	6
Mountain View	Willcox	56
Sun Valley	El Mirage	80

Consrv Mennonite Conf

Cross Roads	Phoenix	19
Dios Con Nosotros	Phoenix	33
Grace	Phoenix	66
Paradise Valley	Phoenix	42
Southwest Navajo	Phoenix	3

Independent Mennonite Congregations

Gospel	Hotevilla	5
Oraibi	Kykotsmovi	10
Upper Room	Chinle	4
Waterless Mountain	Blue Gap	10

Mennonite Brethren

Copper Hills	Glendale	24
Desert Valley	Sun City	33
Spirit in the Desert	Phoenix	10

Mennonite Church/General Conf: DC

Black Mountain	Chinle	13
Emmanuel	Surprise	36
First	Phoenix	52
Good Shepherd	Phoenix	53
Koinonia	Chandler	82
Prescott	Prescott	30
Shalom	Tucson	47
Sunnyside	Phoenix	304
Trinity	Glendale	359

Mennonite Church: DA

Bacavi	Bacavi	5

Mid-West Mennonite Fellowship

Berean	Wickenburg	34

ARKANSAS

AMISH

Amish Mennonite

Bethel	Berryville	70
Mineral Springs	Nashville	105
Mount Zion	Mena	53

Beachy Amish

Hillcrest	Harrison	26
Shady Lawn	Mountain View	41

O. O. Amish

Lincoln	Lincoln	15

BRETHREN

Church of the Brethren

New Hope	Wynne	17

Church of the Brethren/Mennonite: DA

Brethren/Mennonite	Rogers	26

MENNONITE

Bethel Mennonite Fellowship

Strawberry	Strawberry	42

Church of God in Christ Mennonite

Gentry	Gentry	168
Three Rivers	Dumas	105

Consrv Mennonite Conf/Mennonite Church: DA

First	El Dorado	31

Mennonite Brethren

Grace Bible	Siloam Springs	19
Martin Box	Marshall	52

Mennonite Church

Bethel Springs	Mountain View	15
Calico Rock	Calico Rock	39

Mennonite Unaffiliated Congregations

Happy Hollow	Mountain View	15
West Richwoods	Mountain View	31

CALIFORNIA

BRETHREN

Brethren Church, The

Carson Oaks Community	Stockton	26
Northgate Community	Manteca	56
Rock Springs Community	Carlsbad	30

Brethren Community Fellowship

Modesto	Modesto	75

Brethren in Christ

Alta Loma	Alta Loma	266
Aqua Viva	Riverside	75
Community	Moreno Valley	93
Cristo La Roca	Upland	50
Etiwanda	Etiwanda	75
Fuente de Vida	Pomona	14
Gateway Community	Chino	183
Getsemani	Valinda	70
Lord's House	Alta Loma	35
New Community	Pomona	89
Ontario	Ontario	60
Riverside	Riverside	40
Upland	Upland	315
Walnut Valley	Walnut	51
Waukena	Waukena	28

Church of the Brethren

Bakersfield	Bakersfield	95
Bella Vista	Los Angeles	66
Central Evangelical	Los Angeles	52
Community	Fresno	497
Community	Paradise	41
Cornerstone	Reedley	96
Empire	Empire	98
Fellowship in Christ	Fremont	26
Glendale	Glendale	86
Glendora	Glendora	63
Hermanos Unidos en Cristo	Los Angeles	29
Imperial Heights	Los Angeles	49
La Verne	La Verne	522
Laton	Laton	37
Lindsay Community	Lindsay	70
Live Oak	Live Oak	95
Modesto	Modesto	296
North County	San Marcos	51
Panorama City	Panorama City	16
Pasadena	Pasadena	64
Pomona	Pomona	150
Principe de Paz	Santa Ana	46

San Diego	San Diego	150
San Francisco	San Francisco	50
South Bay	Redondo Beach	73
Valley View	Whittier	50
Waterford	Waterford	61

Church of the Brethren: DA

Prince of Peace	Sacramento	62

Dunkard Brethren

Pleasant Home	Modesto	83
Winterhaven	Beaumont	8

Grace Brethren Churches

Bellflower	Bellflower	230
Bible	Hemet	24
Cherry Valley	Beaumont	93
Chico	Chico	46
Community	Auburn	175
Community	Long Beach	81
Community	Whittier	339
Creek Park Community	La Mirada	93
Fellowship	Alta Loma	40
Grace Cambodia	Long Beach	138
Grace Community	Rialto	33
Grace Community	Riverside	132
Grace Community	Yucca Valley	21
Grace-Long Beach	Long Beach	1228
Iglesia Christiana	Lakewood	45
Iglesia Evangelica de los Hermanos	Long Beach	37
La Loma	Modesto	167
La Verne	La Verne	218
Los Altos	Long Beach	196
Maranatha	Santa Ana	42
Moorpark	Moorpark	60
Mountainside Community	San Bernardino	75
New Hope Community	Menifee Valley	27
Norwalk	Norwalk	94
Orange	Orange	94
Ripon	Ripon	223
River City	Sacramento	70
San Diego	San Diego	14
Santa Maria	Santa Maria	56
Santa Paula	Santa Paula	27
Seal Beach	Seal Beach	320
Simi Valley	Simi Valley	335
South Bay	San Jose	17
South Pasadena	South Pasadena	53
Tracy	Tracy	46
Whittier	Whittier	81

Old Brethren

Salida	Salida	55
Sonora	Sonora	30

Old German Baptist Brethren

Modesto	Modesto	277
Sierra Pines	Twain Harte	40
Tuolomne	Tuolomne	218
West Modesto	Modesto	64

MENNONITE

Apostolic Christian Church of America

Altadena	Altadena	49
San Diego	San Diego	29

Church of God in Christ Mennonite

Glenn	Glenn	239
Livingston	Livingston	278

Mission	Anaheim	2
Winton	Winton	280

Mennonite Brethren

Aposento Alta	Bakersfield	30
Bethany	Fresno	426
Blossom Valley	San Jose	721
Butler Avenue	Fresno	380
Cho Dai Church	Los Angeles	50
City Terrace	Los Angeles	56
College	Clovis	154
Companerismo Cristiano	Shafter	32
Country	Orland	52
Cristo es la Respuesta	Arleta	11
Dinuba	Dinuba	549
El Buen Pastor	Orange Cove	29
El Buen Pastor	San Fernando	30
El Camino	Santa Clara	52
El Faro	Reedley	86
El Shaddai Christian	Hayward	25
Encuentro con Jesus Cristo	Los Angeles	30
Ethiopian Christian	San Jose	97
Fig Garden	Fresno	65
First Ukranian	Sacramento	250
Fuente de Vida	Parlier	61
Grace Chinese	Upland	35
Greenhaven	Sacramento	97
Heritage	Bakersfield	283
Hermanos Menonitas	Fresno	20
Holy Light Korean	Clovis	20
Iglesia de Comunidad	Raisin City	35
Iglesia de Restauracion	Pacoima	100
Iglesia Los Hechos	San Jose	46
Iglesia Sinai	Sun Valley	40
India Community	Santa Clara	20
Japanese Bible	Bonita	10
Joong Ang Korean	Cypress	530
Journey	La Mirada	40
Kingsburg	Kingsburg	209
Korean Agape	Los Angeles	50
Korean Peace	Glendale	10
Laurelglen	Bakersfield	796
Lincoln Glen	San Jose	250
Living Hope	Downey	40
Madera Avenue	Madera	111
Mountain	Coarsegold	24
Mountain View	Clovis	100
New Life	Union City	25
North Fresno	Fresno	331
North Fresno Japanese	Fresno	10
Northwest	Bakersfield	25
Nueva Jerusalen	Long Beach	10
Reedley	Reedley	1200
Rosedale	Bakersfield	170
Russian Baptist	Castro Valley	79
Sanger	Sanger	15
Shafter	Shafter	303
Shalom Korean	Glendale	20
Shoreline	Capitola	46
Slavic Brethren	Fresno	125
Templo Calvario	Dinuba	22
Templo de Oracion	Traver	40
Templo La Paz	Orosi	47
Vida Nueva	Bakersfield	29

Vinewood	Lodi	285
Visalia	Visalia	532

Mennonite Christian Fellowship

Sierra Valley	Beckwourth	21

Mennonite Church/General Conf: DC

Amor Viviente	Fresno	40
Bethel	Santa Fe Springs	102
Calvary	Inglewood	68
Casa de Oracion	San Diego	15
Chinese	San Francisco	65
Community	Fresno	105
Cristo la Roca	Ontario	25
Cupertino	Cupertino	15
Evangelica Bethel	North Hollywood	154
Faith	Downey	20
Faith Chapel	Los Angeles	0
Family	Los Angeles	152
Fellowship	San Diego	22
First	Paso Robles	116
First	Reedley	329
First	San Francisco	49
First	Upland	48
Fuente de Vida	Upland	30
Hmong Community	Fresno	46
House of the Lord	La Puente	65
Iglesia Primera	Reedley	40
Indonesian Anugrah	Sierra Madre	79
Indonesian Bethel	Chino	45
Indonesian Christian	El Monte	25
Indonesian Hosana	Chino	64
Indonesian Imanuel	Downey	58
Indonesian Maranatha	Reseda	70
Indonesian Zion	Fullerton	25
International Christian	Orange	25
Maranatha Ethiopian	San Diego	20
Miracle of Faith	Los Angeles	30
Monte Sinai	South Gate	43
Mountain View	Upland	48
Pasadena	Pasadena	90
Peace Fellowship	Claremont	27
Prince of Peace	Los Angeles	10
Royal Dominion	Los Angeles	0
Trinity Taiwanese	Anaheim Hills	33

Mennonite Unaffiliated Congregation

Southern California	Lebec	15

Nationwide Mennonite Fellowship Churches

Alturas	Alturas	26
North Coast	Fortuna	23

COLORADO

AMISH

Amish Mennonite

Mountain View	Hotchkiss	30

BRETHREN

Church of the Brethren

Bethel	Arriba	19
Fellowship	Boulder	4
Fellowship	Pueblo	9
Haxtun	Haxtun	74
Northern Colorado	Windsor	66
Prince of Peace	Littleton	169
Rocky Ford	Rocky Ford	39
Spirit of Joy	Denver	14
Wiley	Wiley	110

Church of the Brethren: DA

Koinonia	Grand Junction	113

Consrv Grace Brethren

Denver	Denver	23

Dunkard Brethren

McClave	McClave	50

Grace Brethren Churches

Arvada	Arvada	96
Colorado Springs	Colorado Springs	77

MENNONITE

Apostolic Christian Church of America

Denver	Denver	35

Charity Christian Fellowship

Hope	Loveland	49

Church of God in Christ Mennonite

High Valley	Center	74
Mesa View	Montrose	62

Consrv Mennonite Unaffiliated

Sangre de Cristo	Westcliffe	36

General Conf Mennonite Church

Arvada	Arvada	28
Boulder	Boulder	62
New Friedensburg	Vona	16

Mennonite Brethren

Bellevue Acres	Littleton	118
Ethiopian Evangelical	Denver	300
Garden Park	Denver	64
Korean Mustard Seed	Denver	30

Mennonite Church

Beth El	Colorado Springs	163
East Holbrook	Cheraw	66
Emmanuel	La Junta	146
First	Colorado Springs	43
First	Denver	256
Glennon Heights	Lakewood	113
Glenwood	Glenwood Springs	49
Greeley	Greeley	80
La Jara	La Jara	7
Pueblo	Pueblo	50
Rocky Ford	Rocky Ford	90
Walsenburg	Walsenburg	16

Mennonite Church/General Conf: DC

Fort Collins	Fort Collins	32
Hmong	Arvada	45
Julesburg	Julesburg	67
Mountain Community	Palmer Lake	103
Peace	Aurora	111

Nationwide Mennonite Fellowship Churches

Grand Valley	Loma	40

Western Consrv Mennonite Fellowship

Sunny View	Montrose	41

CONNECTICUT

BRETHREN

Grace Brethren Churches

Colonial Chapel	Hartford	21

MENNONITE

Apostolic Christian Church of America

Rockville	Rockville	338

Mennonite Church

Abundant Life	Waterbury	50
Bible Fellowship	New Haven	80
Gospel Light	Bridgeport	89

DELAWARE

AMISH

O. O. Amish

East	Dover	60
Lower North	Dover	60
Middle North	Dover	60
Middle South	Hartly	60
South	Dover	60
Southeast	Wyoming	60
Upper North	Dover	60
West	Hartly	60

BRETHREN

Brethren Church, The

Mount Olivet	Georgetown	24

Church of the Brethren

Bethany	Farmington	100
Fellowship	Dover	31
Wilmington	Wilmington	129

Grace Brethren Churches

Newark	Newark	32

MENNONITE

Consrv Mennonite Conf

Cannon	Bridgeville	191
Central	Dover	121
Greenwood	Greenwood	184
Laws	Greenwood	70
Maranatha	Dover	27

Eastern Pennsylvania Mennonite Church

Highland	Bear	64
Kenton	Kenton	75

Mennonite Church

Centro Evangelistico	Wilmington	24
Tressler	Greenwood	130

Nationwide Mennonite Fellowship Churches

Pine Shore	Delmar	25

DISTRICT OF COLUMBIA

AMISH

Amish Mennonite Unaffiliated

Fellowship Haven	Washington DC	18

BRETHREN

Brethren Church, The

Southeast Christian Fellowship	Washington DC	93

Church of the Brethren

Celebration House Church	Washington DC	8
Washington City	Washington DC	170

MENNONITE

Apostolic Christian Church of America

Washington DC	Washington DC	10

Mennonite Church

Conquest Fellowship	Washington DC	36
Peabody Street	Washington DC	23
Washington Community	Washington DC	240

FLORIDA

AMISH

Amish Mennonite Unaffiliated

Grace	Sarasota	24

Beachy Amish

Pleasantview	Dade City	18
Sunnyside	Sarasota	153

Directory of Congregations

237

New Order Amish Fellowship

Pinecraft	Sarasota	44

BRETHREN

Brethren Church, The

Bloomingdale	Valrico	40
Bradenton	Bradenton	80
First	Sarasota	151
Iglesia de los Hermanos	Sarasota	20

Brethren in Christ

Aposanto de la Gracia	Pembroke Pines	28
Bethel	Kendall	218
Community Bible	Sarasota	82
Cristo Rey	Miami	40
Cristo Vive	Hialeah	475
Ebenezer	Hialeah	229
Esmima	Miami	53
Hialeah East	Hialeah	21
Maranatha	Hialeah	120
Monte Calvario	Miami	25
Mount Zion	Miami	64
Nueva Jerusalem	Hialeah	66
Palabra de Vida	Miami	41
Refugio de Amor	Miami	40
Refugio Eterno	West Palm Beach	25
Salem	Winter Park	35
Semilla de Fe	Miami	42

Church of the Brethren

Arcadia	Arcadia	22
Christ the Servant	Cape Coral	129
Clay County	Middleburg	139
Community	Orlando	95
Eglise des Freres Haitiens	Miami	172
First	Miami	33
First	Saint Petersburg	119
First	Winter Park	70
Good Samaritan	Brandon	69
Good Shepherd	Bradenton	323
J. H. Moore Memorial	Sebring	322
Jacksonville	Jacksonville	37
Lorida	Lorida	98
New Covenant	Gotha	38
North Fort Myers	North Fort Myers	34
Venice	Venice	30

Consrv Grace Brethren

Basinger Christian	Lake Placid	10

Grace Brethren Churches

Bradenton	Bradenton	47
Brooksville	Brooksville	45
Calvary	Deltona	51
Dr. Phillip's Community	Orlando	23
Eglise Evangelique de la Grace	Fort Lauderdale	0
Fort Myers	Fort Myers	35
Grace Bible	Gainesville	5
Grace Community	Fort Lauderdale	100
Grace Community	Ormond Beach	39
Gulfview	Port Richey	122
Iglesia Comunal	Tampa	16
Lakeland	Lakeland	46
Land O'Lakes	Land O'Lakes	0
Maitland	Maitland	61
North Port	North Port	28
Ocala	Ocala	34

Okeechobee	Okeechobee	92
Palm Harbor	Palm Harbor	55
Saint Petersburg	Saint Petersburg	86
Sebring	Sebring	19
Shoreline Community	Naples	0
Suntree	Melbourne	41

Old German Baptist Brethren

Homestead	Homestead	10
Pine Grove	Lakeland	19

MENNONITE

Apostolic Christian Church of America

Fort Lauderdale	Fort Lauderdale	57
North Fort Myers	North Fort Myers	20
Sarasota	Sarasota	57

Church of God in Christ Mennonite

Gospel Center	Sarasota	8
Walnut Hill	Walnut Hill	194

Consrv Mennonite Conf

Abundant Life	Sarasota	66
Berean	Tallahassee	61
Bethel	Blountstown	102
Bethel	Sarasota	261
Friendship	Sarasota	29
Palm Grove	Sarasota	183
Southmost	Florida City	12
Trinity	Tavares	49

Eastern Pennsylvania Mennonite Church

Peace River	Arcadia	20

Good News Mennonite Fellowship

Byrneville	Century	13
Cobbtown	Jay	30
Crestview	Crestview	10

Mennonite Church

Amor Viviente	Fort Lauderdale	30
Amor Viviente	Miami	200
Arca de Salvacion	Fort Myers	40
Ashton	Sarasota	158
Assemble de Grace	Immokolee	10
Bahia Vista	Sarasota	584
Bay Shore	Sarasota	516
Cape Christian	Cape Coral	253
College Hill	Tampa	76
Emmanuel	Gainesville	36
Good Shepherd	Miami	21
Homestead	Homestead	90
Iglesia Ebenezer	Apopka	100
New Beginnings	Saint Petersburg	30
Newtown Gospel	Sarasota	30
North Tampa	Tampa	26
Nouveau Testament	Miami	20
Oak Terrace	Blountstown	18
Peace	North Port	46
Peoples Chapel	Immokolee	14
Pine Creek	Arcadia	31
Seguidores de Cristo	Sarasota	27
Tabernacle of Bethlehem	Opa-Locka	89
Unity Pentacostal	Miami	95
Worship Center	Laurel	39

Mennonite Church/General Conf: DC

Encuentro de Renovacion	Boca Raton	16
Encuentro de Renovacion	Miami	40

Mennonite Unaffiliated Congregations

Red Oak	Blountstown	42
Sarasota	Sarasota	70

Tourist	Sarasota	25

Pilgrim Mennonite Conf

Pensacola	Pensacola	24

GEORGIA

AMISH

Beachy Amish

Clearview	Montezuma	104
Lake Grace	Jesup	47
Montezuma	Montezuma	164

BRETHREN

Brethren in Christ

Grace	Lawrenceville	23

Grace Brethren Churches

Greater Atlanta	Marietta	135

Old German Baptist Brethren

Blue Ridge	Cleveland	42

MENNONITE

Apostolic Christian Church of America

Atlanta	Atlanta	12

Charity Christian Fellowship

Emmanuel	Dublin	33

Church of God in Christ Mennonite

Harmony Springs	Avera	82
North Georgia	Bowersville	35
Stapleton	Pinecrest	218

Consrv Mennonite Conf

Faith	Cuthbert	38

Eastern Pennsylvania Mennonite Church

Metter	Metter	38

General Conf Mennonite Church

Atlanta	Atlanta	19

Independent Mennonite Congregation

Amor Viviente	Atlanta	45

Mennonite Church

Americus	Americus	30
Berea	Atlanta	68
Cell-ebration	Decatur	30

Mennonite Unaffiliated Congregations

Colquitt	Colquitt	8
Glad Tidings	Bartow	24
Gospel Light	Montezuma	80
Hartwell	Hartwell	44
Meigs	Meigs	46

Pilgrim Mennonite Conf

Dublin	Dublin	48

South Atlantic Mennonite Conf

Burkeland	Waynesboro	45
Hephzibah	Hephzibah	59
Lighthouse	Hillsboro	8

HAWAII

BRETHREN

Grace Brethren Churches

Ke Ola Hou	Ewa Beach	10
Shepherd's of Kauai	Kalaleo	0
Waimalu	Aiea	130
Waipio	Mililani	100

MENNONITE

Mennonite Church

New Life	Honolulu	48
Vietnamese	Honolulu	30

IDAHO

AMISH

O. O. Amish

Bonners Ferry	Bonners Ferry	60

BRETHREN

Church of the Brethren

Boise Valley	Meridian	48
Bowmont	Nampa	57
Fruitland	Fruitland	170
Mountain View	Boise	148
Nampa	Nampa	259
Twin Falls	Twin Falls	18

MENNONITE

Charity Christian Fellowship

Jubilee	Grangeville	27

Church of God in Christ Mennonite

Buhl	Buhl	125
Canyon	Hazelton	35
Grand View	Grand View	44
Mountain View	Bonners Ferry	284
Treasure Valley	New Plymouth	51
Valley View	Filer	104

Independent Mennonite Congregation

Indian Cove	Hammett	20

Mennonite Church/General Conf: DC

Emmaus	Meridian	20
Filer	Filer	83
First	Aberdeen	241
First	Nampa	101
Hyde Park	Boise	60

Mennonite Unaffiliated Congregation

Kootenai Valley	Naples	75

Western Consrv Mennonite Fellowship

Cataldo	Cataldo	33

ILLINOIS

AMISH

Amish Mennonite

Fairfield	Tampico	155
Mount Herman	Shelbyville	35
North Linn	Roanoke	75

Beachy Amish

Carrier Mills	Carrier Mills	38
Pleasant View	Arcola	135
Siloam Springs	Clayton	82
Trinity	Arthur	41

New Order Amish

Crawford	Flat Rock	34
Shawnee	Ava	52

O. O. Amish

Arcola	Arcola	55
Ava	Ava	55
Bagdad	Arcola	55
Belle Rive	Belle Rive	55
Bourbon	Tuscola	55
Cadwell	Arthur	55
Cooks Mill	Humboldt	55
East	Macomb	55
East Chesterville	Arcola	55
East Prairie	Arthur	55
Jonathan Creek	Sullivan	55
Lake Fork	Arthur	55
Macomb	Macomb	55

Martinsburg	Pleasant Hill	55
Mount Vernon	Mount Vernon	55
North Bourbon	Tuscola	55
North Cadwell	Arthur	55
North Cook Mills	Arcola	55
North County Line	Arthur	55
North Fairbanks	Arthur	55
North Prairie	Arthur	55
Northeast Fairbanks	Arthur	55
Opdyke	Opdyke	55
Pittsfield	Pittsfield	55
South Bourbon	Arcola	55
South County Line	Arthur	55
Southeast Fairbanks	Arthur	55
Southwest Fairbanks	Arthur	55
Sullivan	Sullivan	55
Tri-County	Arthur	55
Vienna	Vienna	55
West	Plymouth	55
West Chesterville	Arthur	55
West Prairie	Arcola	55

BRETHREN

Brethren Church, The

Cerro Gordo	Cerro Gordo	69
Lanark	Lanark	222
Milledgeville	Milledgeville	117

Brethren in Christ

Morrison	Morrison	62

Church of the Brethren

Allison Prairie	Pinkstaff	70
Astoria	Astoria	239
Boulder Hill	Montgomery	122
Canton	Canton	76
Cerro Gordo	Cerro Gordo	135
Champaign	Champaign	62
Charismatic Christian Center	Chicago	45
Cherry Grove	Lanark	57
Decatur	Decatur	41
Dixon	Dixon	320
Douglas Park	Chicago	27
Faith	Batavia	47
First	Chicago	105
First	Rockford	92
Franklin Grove	Franklin Grove	88
Freeport	Freeport	100
Girard	Girard	92
Highland Avenue	Elgin	416
Hurricane Creek	Smithboro	14
Kaskaskia	Saint Elmo	84
La Nueva Evangelica	Summit	41
La Place	La Place	106
Lanark	Lanark	254
Lena	Lena	38
Liberty	Liberty	50
Martin Creek	Fairfield	29
Milledgeville	Milledgeville	141
Mount Morris	Mount Morris	368
Naperville	Naperville	217
Oak Grove	Metamora	42
Oakley Brick	Oakley	95
Panther Creek	Roanoke	12
Peoria	Peoria	160
Polo	Polo	248
Romine	Salem	28
Springfield	Springfield	101
Virden	Virden	160
Walnut Grove	Parkersburg	29
West Branch	Mount Morris	29
Woodland	Astoria	41
Yellow Creek	Pearl City	37
York Center	Lombard	207

Church of the Brethren/Mennonite: DA

Reba Place	Evanston	150

Church of the Brethren: DA

La Motte Prairie	Palestine	26

MENNONITE

Apostolic Christian Church of America

Belvidere	Belvidere	28
Bloomington	Bloomington	256
Bradford	Bradford	138
Champaign	Champaign	67
Chicago	Chicago	102
Cissna Park	Cissna Park	239
Congerville	Congerville	195
Elgin	Elgin	195
Eureka	Eureka	385
Fairbury	Fairbury	329
Forrest	Forrest	318
Goodfield	Goodfield	347
Gridley	Gridley	340
Morton	Morton	554
Peoria	Peoria	614
Princeville	Princeville	337
Roanoke	Roanoke	448
Tremont	Tremont	339
Washington	Washington	162

Church of God in Christ Mennonite

Prairie	Arthur	24

Consrv Mennonite Conf

North Vine	Arthur	117
Sunnyside	Arthur	151

Eastern Pennsylvania Mennonite Church

Ewing	Ewing	79
Mount Pleasant	Anna	68
Orchardville	Keenes	88

Evangelical Mennonite Church

Bible	Eureka	92
Calvary Memorial	Palos Hills	38
Congerville	Congerville	334
Dewey	Dewey	89
Grace	Morton	571
Great Oaks	Metamora	70
Groveland	Groveland	72
Heartland	Normal	15
High Point	Worth	10
Northwoods	Peoria	520
Oak Grove	East Peoria	62
Salem	Gridley	161

General Conf Mennonite Church

Bethel	Pekin	42
Boynton	Hopedale	72
Calvary	Washington	402
Carlock	Carlock	106
Communidad de Fe	Chicago	40
First	Chicago	138
Flanagan	Flanagan	69
Grace Community	Chicago	341

Meadows	Meadows	145
North Danvers	Danvers	132
Mennonite Brethren		
Lakeview	Chicago	11
Mennonite Church		
Amor, Esperanza y Fe	Chicago	30
Arthur	Arthur	229
Bethel	Chicago	33
Cazenovia	Cazenovia	79
Centro Cristiano Vida Abundante	Cicero	600
Dillon	Tremont	51
East Bend	Fisher	303
East Peoria	East Peoria	89
Englewood	Chicago	51
Ethiopian Evangelical	Chicago	53
First	Morton	242
First Norwood	Peoria	42
Freeport	Freeport	152
Hopedale	Hopedale	326
Iglesia Gethsemani	Chicago	23
Iglesia Peniel	Summit Argo	64
Lombard	Lombard	197
Maple Lawn	Eureka	6
Metamora	Metamora	229
People for Reconciliation	Kanakee	20
Pleasant Hill	East Peoria	28
Reba Place	Rogers Park	63
Rehoboth	Saint Anne	39
Roanoke	Roanoke	372
Science Ridge	Sterling	148
Sonido de Alabanza	Cicero	300
Templo Alabanza	Moline	54
Trinity	Morton	164
Trinity New Life	Henry	79
Waldo	Flanagan	96
Willow Springs	Tiskilwa	77
Mennonite Church/General Conf: DC		
Christ Community	Schaumburg	52
Church at Normal	Normal	254
Community	Markham	55
Evanston	Evanston	20
First	Champaign-Urbana	118
Joy Fellowship	Peoria	45
Living Love	Peoria	8
North Suburban	Mundelein	24
Oak Park	Oak Park	45
Peoria North	Peoria	34
Plow Creek	Tiskilwa	25
United	Peoria	53
Mennonite Unaffiliated Congregations		
Linn	Roanoke	84
Shalom	Freeport	8
Sunnyside	Wayne City	58
O. O. Mennonite Stauffer Group		
Stauffer	Vandalia	29
Reformed Mennonite Church		
Sterling	Sterling	43

INDIANA
AMISH
Amish Mennonite Unaffiliated

Fairview	Nappanee	34

Beachy Amish		
Believers	Worthington	45
Berea	Bremen	74
Bethany	Kokomo	102
Clay Street	Bourbon	47
Fair Haven	Goshen	130
Fellowship	Berne	32
Fellowship Haven	Woodburn	25
Hebron	Lagrange	56
Maple Lawn	Nappanee	39
Mount Olive	Montgomery	140
Ridgeview	New Haven	28
Rosewood	Shipshewana	76
Southhaven	Millersburg	24
Woodlawn	Goshen	172
New Order Amish		
Liberty	Liberty	65
Salem	Salem	65
Worthington	Worthington	65
O. O. Amish		
Bellmore	Bellmore	75
Bloomfield	Lagrange	60
Blue Creek	Monroe	60
Cedar Road	Bremen	60
Clay	Lagrange	60
Clearspring 12	Lagrange	60
Clearspring 12-1	Lagrange	60
Clinton North Middleburg	Goshen	60
Clinton Prairie	Goshen	60
Clinton Union	Goshen	60
Community Center	Etna Green	60
Community Center North	Etna Green	60
East	Berne	60
East	Montgomery	60
East	Rushville	60
East A	Vevay	60
East B	Vevay	60
East Bloomfield	Lagrange	60
East Bremen	Bremen	60
East Clearspring	Lagrange	60
East Clinton	Goshen	60
East Emma	Topeka	60
East Fork	Shipshewana	60
East Honeyville	Topeka	60
East Jefferson	Geneva	60
East Johnson	Lagrange	60
East Millersburg	Millersburg	60
East Millwood	Nappanee	60
East Noble	Ligonier	60
East Shipshewana	Shipshewana	60
East Shipshewana West	Shipshewana	60
East Spencerville I	Spencerville	60
East Spencerville II	Spencerville	60
East Wabash	Geneva	60
East Washington	Salem	60
East Yoder Corner	Lagrange	60
Economy	Economy	60
Eden	Topeka	60
Eden 4	Topeka	60
Fish Lake	Goshen	60
Flat Rock	Milroy	60
Forks	Middlebury	60
Hagerstown	Hagerstown	75
Hastings	Milford	60

Name	Location	No.
Hawpatch	Lagrange	60
Hepton	Nappanee	60
Honeyville	Topeka	60
Howe	Howe	60
Jay County	Portland	60
Judson	Rockville	75
Lagrange	Lagrange	60
Lagrange 2	Lagrange	60
Locke	Nappanee	60
Locke Annex	Nappanee	60
Loogootee	Loogootee	60
Marshall	Marshall	75
Middle Barrens 53	Middlebury	60
Middle Barrens 54	Middlebury	60
Middle Clinton 55	Middlebury	60
Middle Clinton 67	Middlebury	60
Middle East	Berne	60
Middle East	Loogootee	60
Middle East Center	Montgomery	60
Middle Forks	Goshen	60
Middle Honeyville	Millersburg	60
Middle North	Odon	60
Middle Northwest	Montgomery	60
Middle Shipshewana 44	Shipshewana	60
Middle Shipshewana 45	Shipshewana	60
Middle South	Montgomery	60
Middle Topeka	Topeka	60
Middle West	Grabill	60
Middle West Honeyville	Millersburg	60
Middleburg	Goshen	60
Middlebury	Middlebury	60
Milford	Milford	60
Millersburg	Millersburg	60
Milroy Middle	Milroy	60
Montgomery	Montgomery	60
Nappanee	Nappanee	60
NonRaber A	Paoli	60
NonRaber B	Paoli	60
North	Kokomo	60
North	Monroe	60
North	Nappanee	60
North Barrens	Middlebury	60
North Beech Road	Nappanee	60
North Bogard	Odon	60
North Clinton	Middlebury	60
North Forks	Middlebury	60
North Hepton	Bremen	60
North Honeyville	Topeka	60
North Jefferson	Geneva	60
North Middle	Berne	60
North Middle Shipshewana	Shipshewana	60
North Millersburg	Millersburg	60
North Millwood	Nappanee	60
North Prairie	Berne	60
North Salem	Monroe	60
North Southwest	New Haven	60
North Wabash	Geneva	60
North Wauka	Ligonier	60
North Wolcottville	Wolcottville	60
North Wolcottville II	Wolcottville	60
North Yoder Corner	Shipshewana	60
Northeast	Grabill	60
Northeast	Loogootee	60
Northeast	Monroe	60
Northeast	New Haven	60
Northeast	Odon	60
Northeast Barrens	Shipshewana	60
Northeast Berne	Berne	60
Northeast Clearspring	Topeka	60
Northeast Clinton	Middlebury	60
Northeast Clinton 68	Middlebury	60
Northeast Emma	Topeka	60
Northeast II	Grabill	60
Northeast II	Odon	60
Northeast Monroe	Monroe	60
Northeast Salem	Monroe	60
Northeast Shipshewana	Shipshewana	60
Northeast Topeka	Topeka	60
Northeast Yoder Corner	Topeka	60
Northside District 50	Shipshewana	60
Northside District 50-1	Shipshewana	60
Northwest	Grabill	60
Northwest	Monroe	60
Northwest	Nappanee	60
Northwest	Odon	60
Northwest	Salem	60
Northwest Barrens	Middlebury	60
Northwest Barrens -70	Middlebury	60
Northwest Barrens -70-1	Middlebury	60
Northwest Berne	Berne	60
Northwest Berne II	Berne	60
Northwest Clinton	Middlebury	60
Northwest Forks	Middlebury	60
Northwest Honeyville	Shipshewana	60
Northwest II	Grabill	60
Northwest Lagrange	Lagrange	60
Plato	Lagrange	60
Pleasant	Bryant	60
Prairie Creek	Odon	60
Rochester	Rochester	60
Salem	Monroe	60
Scott	Shipshewana	60
Seybert North	Shipshewana	60
Seybert South	Shipshewana	60
Shady Acres East	Montgomery	60
Shady Acres West	Montgomery	60
Ship Lake	Shipshewana	60
Ship Lake North	Shipshewana	60
Shipshewana (42)	Shipshewana	60
Shipshewana 44-1	Shipshewana	60
South	Geneva	60
South	Kokomo	60
South	Lagrange	60
South	Millersburg	60
South Flatrock	Greensburg	60
South Forks	Middlebury	60
South Hepton	Bremen	60
South Honeyville	Topeka	60
South Howe	Howe	60
South Jefferson	Geneva	60
South Middle	Berne	60
South Middle Barrens	Middlebury	60
South Middle Forks	Middlebury	60
South Middle Shipshewana	Shipshewana	60
South Middle Shipshewana 41	Shipshewana	60

South Milford	Milford	60
South Milwood	Bourbon	60
South Nappanee	Nappanee	60
South Prairie	Berne	60
South Ship 41-2	Shipshewana	60
South Wabash Valley	Geneva	60
South Whitley	South Whitley	60
Southeast	Emma	60
Southeast	Geneva	60
Southeast	Lagrange	60
Southeast	Loogootee	60
Southeast	Milford	60
Southeast	New Haven	60
Southeast Barrens	Shipshewana	60
Southeast Clearspring	Topeka	60
Southeast District II	Geneva	60
Southeast District III	Geneva	60
Southeast Forks	Millersburg	60
Southeast Lagrange	Lagrange	60
Southeast Monroe	Monroe	60
Southeast Spencerville	Spencerville	60
Southeast Yoder Corner	Topeka	60
Southwest	Bryant	60
Southwest	Geneva	60
Southwest	Goshen	60
Southwest	Lagrange	60
Southwest	Montgomery	60
Southwest	Nappanee	60
Southwest	New Haven	60
Southwest Clinton	Goshen	60
Southwest Honeyville	Millersburg	60
Southwest Honeyville East	Millersburg	60
Southwest Lagrange	Lagrange	60
Southwest Yoder Corner	Topeka	60
Southwest Yoder Corner 1	Topeka	60
Steuben East	Hamilton	60
Stueben West	Hamilton	60
Taylor West Lagrange	Lagrange	60
Topeka 30	Topeka	60
Topeka 30-1	Topeka	60
Tri-County	Nappanee	60
Union Center	New Paris	60
Union Center East	New Paris	60
Union Center West	Nappanee	60
Vallonia	Vallonia	60
Wabash Valley	Geneva	60
Weldy	Nappanee	60
West	Geneva	60
West	Howe	60
West	Montgomery	60
West Barrens	Middlebury	60
West Beech	Bremen	60
West Berne	Berne	60
West Blue Creek	Berne	60
West Borkholder	Bremen	60
West Burlington	Bremen	60
West Clearspring	Topeka	60
West Clinton	Goshen	60
West Forks	Middlebury	60
West Honeyville	Goshen	60
West Howe	Howe	60
West Lagrange	Lagrange	60
West Marshall	Nappanee	60
West Middle Clinton	Goshen	60

West Nappanee	Nappanee	60
West Noble	Topeka	60
West Shipshewana	Shipshewana	60
West Spencerville	Spencerville	60
West Topeka	Topeka	60
West Union Center	Nappanee	60
West Wabash	Geneva	60
Wolcottville	Wolcottville	60
Yoder Corner	Shipshewana	60

O. O. Amish Swartzentruber

Orleans	Orleans	50
Paoli	Paoli	50

BRETHREN

Brethren Church, The

Ardmore First	South Bend	74
Brighton Chapel	Howe	145
Burlington First	Burlington	70
Center Chapel	Peru	37
College Corner	Wabash	94
Community	Mishawaka	49
Corinth	Twelve Mile	139
Cornerstone	Muncie	98
County Line	Lakeville	79
Dutchtown	Warsaw	45
Eagle's Nest	Peru	0
Elkhart First	Elkhart	153
Flora First	Flora	115
Goshen First	Goshen	271
Huntington First	Huntington	53
Jefferson	Goshen	329
Loree	Bunker Hill	102
Meadow Crest	Fort Wayne	56
Mexico First	Mexico	38
Milford First	Milford	145
Muncie First	Muncie	96
Nappanee First	Nappanee	269
New Paris First	New Paris	42
North Manchester First	North Manchester	307
Oakeville	Oakeville	99
Peru First	Peru	40
Roann First	Roann	64
Roanoke First	Roanoke	61
South Bend First	South Bend	143
Teegarden First	Plymouth	14
Tiosa	Rochester	50
Wabash First	Wabash	24
Warsaw First	Warsaw	111
Winding Waters	Elkhart	361

Brethren in Christ

Christian Union	Garrett	45
Mount Zion	Marengo	26
Nappanee	Nappanee	111
Union Grove	New Paris	49

Church of the Brethren

Agape	Fort Wayne	143
Akron	Akron	60
Anderson	Anderson	230
Andrews	Andrews	23
Antioch	Muncie	15
Arcadia	Arcadia	88
Baugo	Wakarusa	101
Beacon Heights	Fort Wayne	331
Beech Grove	Pendleton	132
Bethany	New Paris	144

Bethel Center	Hartford City	35
Blissville	Plymouth	245
Blue River	Columbia City	210
Bremen	Bremen	161
Buck Creek	Mooreland	45
Buffalo	Buffalo	53
Burnettsville	Burnettsville	48
Camp Creek	Etna Green	123
Cedar Creek	Garrett	97
Cedar Lake	Auburn	122
Christ, Our Shepherd	Indianapolis	93
Columbia City	Columbia City	70
Crest Manor	South Bend	100
Eel River	Silver Lake	94
Elkhart City	Elkhart	211
Elkhart Valley	Elkhart	132
English Prairie	Howe	52
Four Mile	Liberty	33
Goshen City	Goshen	313
Guernsey	Monticello	39
Hickory Grove	Dunkirk	50
Huntington	Huntington	118
Kokomo	Kokomo	198
La Porte	La Porte	76
Lafayette	Lafayette	50
Liberty Mills	Liberty Mills	136
Lincolnshire	Fort Wayne	179
Little Pine	Goshen	50
Living Faith	Flora	279
Locust Grove	Newcastle	70
Logansport	Logansport	95
Loon Creek	Huntington	42
Lower Deer Creek	Camden	46
Manchester	North Manchester	748
Manos de Cristo	South Bend	4
Maple Grove	New Paris	165
Marion	Marion	51
Markle	Markle	49
Mexico	Mexico	439
Michigan City	Michigan City	43
Middlebury	Middlebury	258
Mount Pleasant	Bourbon	69
Nappanee	Nappanee	201
Nettle Creek	Hagerstown	124
New Hope	Seymour	23
New Paris	New Paris	166
New Salem	Milford	81
North Liberty	North Liberty	131
North Webster	North Webster	84
North Winona	Warsaw	112
Northview	Indianapolis	80
Osceola	Osceola	155
Peru	Peru	130
Pine Creek	North Liberty	151
Pipe Creek	Peru	78
Pleasant Chapel	Ashley	95
Pleasant Dale	Decatur	306
Pleasant Valley	Middlebury	33
Plymouth	Plymouth	235
Portland	Portland	35
Prince of Peace	South Bend	119
Prymont	Delphi	129
Richmond	Richmond	37
Roann	Roann	249

Rock Run	Goshen	113
Rossville	Rossville	177
Salamonie	Salamonie	183
South Creek	Pierceton	35
South Creek	South Whitley	35
Syracuse	Syracuse	116
Turkey Creek	Nappanee	69
Union	Plymouth	47
Union Center	Nappanee	467
Union Grove	Muncie	74
Upper Fall Creek	Middletown	37
Wabash	Wabash	89
Wakarusa	Wakarusa	62
Walnut	Argos	143
Waterford Community	Goshen	80
Wawaka	Wawaka	52
West Eel River	Silver Lake	95
West Goshen	Goshen	233
West Manchester	North Manchester	45
White Branch	Hagerstown	60
Windfall	Windfall	43
Yellow Creek	Goshen	132

Church of the Brethren/Mennonite: DA

Iglesia Evangelica Emmanuel	South Bend	10

Consrv Grace Brethren

Elkhart	Elkhart	50
Lakeland Consrv	Warsaw	40
Lakeview Heights	Lagrange	7
Mishawaka	Mishawaka	128
Peru	Peru	136

Dunkard Brethren

Goshen	Goshen	20
Plevna	Plevna	60

Grace Brethren Churches

Berne	Berne	154
Clay City	Clay City	35
Columbia City	Columbia City	26
Community	Warsaw	272
Eagle Creek	Indianapolis	91
First	Fort Wayne	154
Flora	Flora	62
Fort Wayne	Fort Wayne	48
Goshen	Goshen	76
Indian Heights	Kokomo	75
Ireland Road	South Bend	74
Leesburg	Leesburg	58
New Albany	New Albany	24
North Kokomo	Kokomo	35
Northeast	Indianapolis	26
Osceola	Osceola	211
Sidney	Sidney	16
Winona Lake	Winona Lake	698

Old Brethren

Wakarusa	Wakarusa	110
Warren County	Williamsport	20

Old Brethren German Baptist

Deer Creek	Camden	50

Old German Baptist Brethren

Bachelor Run	Flora	226
Beech Grove	Pendleton	153
Deer Creek	Camden	144
Eel River	Silver Lake	90
Mexico	Mexico	76

Middle Fork	Rossville	226
North Fork	Prymont	184
North Manchester	North Manchester	192
Yellow Creek	Goshen	173

MENNONITE

Apostolic Christian Church of America

Bluffton	Bluffton	905
Bluffton North	Bluffton North	400
Francesville	Francesville	280
Indianapolis	Indianapolis	78
La Crosse	La Crosse	83
Leo	Leo	124
Milford	Milford	106
Remington	Remington	99
South Bend	South Bend	23
Valparaiso	Valparaiso	58
Wolcott	Wolcott	98

Bethel Mennonite Fellowship

Bethany	Millersburg	15
Canaan	Canaan	11
Mount Joy	Raglesville	44

Charity Christian Fellowship

Victory	Goshen	78

Church of God in Christ Mennonite

Southern Hills	Hardinsburg	52

Consrv Mennonite Conf

Cornerstone	Austin	48
First	Montgomery	200
Griner	Middlebury	286
Maple City Chapel	Goshen	220
Mount Joy	Goshen	106
Pine Ridge	Goshen	32
Roselawn	Shipshewana	117
Siloam Fellowship	Goshen	110
Sunrise	Harlan	151
Townline	Shipshewana	88

Consrv Mennonite Unaffiliated

Cuba	Grabill	88
Pleasant View	Montgomery	58

Evangelical Mennonite Church

Brookside	Fort Wayne	423
Evangelical	Berne	158
Evangelical	Grabill	164
Evangelical	Upland	201
Pine Hills	Fort Wayne	168
SonLight	Angola	72
Westwood	Woodburn	73

General Conf Mennonite Church

Eighth Street	Goshen	227
First	Berne	1119
First	Nappanee	90
Hively Avenue	Elkhart	103
Maplewood	Fort Wayne	181
Pleasant Oaks	Middlebury	158
Silverwood	Goshen	217
Topeka	Topeka	136

Independent Mennonite Congregations

Believers	Evansville	18
Butlerville	Butlerville	69
Good Shepherd	New Haven	60
Maple Grove	Topeka	152
New Covenant	Nappanee	30
New Wine	Bourbon	70
Open Door	Kouts	78

Tri-Lakes	Bristol	110

Mennonite Biblical Alliance

Lamb of God	Auburn	12
Living Water	Goshen	65
Pleasant Grove	Goshen	155
Shalom	Odon	10

Mennonite Church

Bean Blossom	Bean Blossom	53
Belmont	Elkhart	177
Benton	Benton	91
Berea	Cannelburg	128
Berkey Avenue	Goshen	157
Bethel	Odon	268
Bonneyville	Bristol	132
Burr Oak	Rensselaer	64
Carroll Community	Fort Wayne	40
Central	Fort Wayne	339
Church Without Walls	Elkhart	60
Clinton Brick	Goshen	127
Clinton Frame	Goshen	562
College	Goshen	1063
Communion	Goshen	107
East Goshen	Goshen	219
El Buen Pastor	Goshen	32
Emma	Topeka	303
Fairhaven	Fort Wayne	52
Fellowship	Bloomington	15
Fellowship of Hope	Elkhart	57
First	Fort Wayne	54
First	Indianapolis	180
First	Middlebury	447
Forks	Middlebury	176
Gospel Lighthouse	New Paris	25
Holdeman	Wakarusa	199
Hopewell	Kouts	198
House of Power	Elkhart	10
Howard-Miami	Kokomo	280
Hudson Lake	Hudson Lake	38
Kern Road	South Bend	179
Lake Bethel	Stroh	33
Maranatha	Nappanee	87
Marion	Howe	142
North Goshen	Goshen	201
North Leo	Leo	162
North Main Street	Nappanee	232
Olive	Elkhart	133
Parkview	Kokomo	78
Plato	Lagrange	68
Pleasant View	Goshen	232
Prairie Street	Elkhart	203
Providence	Montgomery	336
Restoration	South Bend	10
Roselawn	Elkhart	38
Shalom	Indianapolis	36
Shore	Shipshewana	343
Sunnyside	Elkhart	130
Valparaiso	Valparaiso	58
Walnut Hill	Goshen	113
Warsaw	Warsaw	29
Waterford	Goshen	392
Wawasee Lakeside	Syracuse	192
Yellow Creek	Goshen	508

Mennonite Church/General Conf: DC

Assembly	Goshen	108
Faith	Goshen	24
Fellowship	Lafayette	11
Morning Star	Muncie	24
Paoli	Paoli	70
Southside	Elkhart	95

Mennonite Unaffiliated Congregations

Martinsville	Martinsville	10
Milford Chapel	Milford	59
New Covenant	Nappanee	20
Rich Valley	Kokomo	40
Salem	New Paris	191
South Union	Nappanee	11
Toto	North Judson	15

Mid-West Mennonite Fellowship

Bethel Consrv	Nappanee	99
Fresh Start	Washington	67
Hillside	Shoals	12
North Liberty	North Liberty	38
Sandy Ridge	Nappanee	89

Nationwide Mennonite Fellowship Churcheses

Grace	Goshen	25

O. O. Mennonite Groffdale Conf

Blossers	Nappanee	61
Clearland	Wakarusa	48
Tippecanoe	Tippecanoe	41
Yellow Creek	Goshen	136

O. O. Mennonite Wenger/Weaver Group

Yellow Creek	Goshen	35

O. O. Mennonite Wisler Conf

Fairview	Nappanee	185
Southside	Mentone	40
Yellow Creek	Goshen	195

IOWA

AMISH

Beachy Amish

Leon Salem	Leon	68
Sharon Bethel	Kalona	106

O. O. Amish

Chariton East	Chariton	55
Chariton West	Chariton	55
Corydon	Corydon	55
Cresco	Cresco	55
East Middle	Hazelton	55
Edgewood	Edgewood	55
Kalona Community	Kalona	55
Middle	Bloomfield	55
Middle	Kalona	55
Middle	Milton	55
Middle East	Kalona	55
Middle North	Kalona	55
Middleburg	Kalona	55
North	Milton	55
Northeast	Bloomfield	55
Northeast	Hazelton	55
Northeast	Kalona	55
Northwest	Bloomfield	55
Northwest	Drakesville	55
Northwest	Fairbank	55
Northwest	Kalona	55
Pleasant Valley	Kalona	55
Redding	Redding	55

Riceville Middle	Riceville	55
Riceville North	Riceville	55
Riceville South	Riceville	55
Rockdale	Maquoketa	55
Seymour	Seymour	55
South	Bloomfield	55
South	Milton	55
South Central	Fairbank	55
Southeast	Hazelton	55
Southwest	Bloomfield	55
Southwest	Fairbank	55
Southwest	Kalona	55
Waukon	Waukon	55
West	Bloomfield	55

O. O. Amish Swartzentruber

Lamoni	Lamoni	50

BRETHREN

Brethren in Christ

Oak Park	Des Moines	29

Church of the Brethren

Ankeny	Ankeny	99
Brooklyn	Brooklyn	15
Dallas Center	Dallas Center	93
English River	South English	97
Fairview	Unionville	47
Iowa River	Marshalltown	107
Ivester	Grundy Center	170
Kingsley	Kingsley	20
Libertyville	Batavia	57
Maxwell	Maxwell	17
Monroe County	Avery	17
Mount Etna	Mount Etna	21
Ottumwa	Ottumwa	128
Panora	Panora	312
Panther Creek	Adel	203
Peace	Council Bluffs	70
Prairie City	Prairie City	183
Robins	Robins	38
Salem	Lenox	18
Sheldon	Sheldon	59
South Waterloo	Waterloo	337
Stover Memorial	Des Moines	67

Church of the Brethren: DA

Beaver	Beaver	30
First Baptist/Brethren	Cedar Rapids	38
Greene	Greene	40
Hammond Avenue	Waterloo	81
Hillcrest	Fredericksburg	235

Consrv Grace Brethren

Beaver Valley	Grimes	41
Leon	Leon	19

Dunkard Brethren

Dallas Center	Dallas Center	80

Grace Brethren Churches

Carlton	Garwin	81
Cedar Rapids	Cedar Rapids	64
Dallas Center	Dallas Center	50
Davenport	Davenport	35
Des Moines	Des Moines	25
Pleasant Grove	North English	20
Udell	Udell	4
Waterloo	Waterloo	398

O. O. River Brethren

Iowa District	Dallas Center	33

MENNONITE

Apostolic Christian Church of America

Burlington	Burlington	60
Elgin	Elgin	39
Garden Grove	Garden Grove	15
Iowa City	Iowa City	18
Lester	Lester	287
Oakville	Oakville	235
Pulaski	Pulaski	51
West Bend	West Bend	210

Charity Christian Fellowship

Zion	Wellman	24

Church of God in Christ Mennonite

Bloomfield	Bloomfield	35
Heartland	McIntire	59
Lime Springs	Lime Springs	68

Consrv Mennonite Conf

Fairview	Kalona	183
Mount Zion	Leon	22
New Boston	New Boston	17
Sunnyside	Kalona	155
Upper Deer Creek	Wellman	100

General Conf Mennonite Church

Ames	Ames	8

Mennonite Church/General Conf: DC

Bethel	Wayland	170
Casa de Oracion Emanuel	Davenport	57
Cedar Falls	Cedar Falls	35
Daytonville	Wellman	9
Des Moines	Des Moines	66
East Union	Kalona	245
Eicher Emmanuel	Wayland	60
Evangelical	Fort Dodge	72
First	Iowa City	267
Kalona	Kalona	307
Lower Deer Creek	Kalona	283
Manson	Manson	124
Muscataine	Muscataine	38
Peace	Burlington	19
Pleasant View	Mount Pleasant	113
Pulaski	Pulaski	124
Sugar Creek	Wayland	352
Washington	Washington	124
Wayland	Wayland	211
Wellman	Wellman	254
West Union	Parnell	305
Zion	Donnellson	135

Mennonite Unaffiliated Congregations

Bethany	Kalona	18
Salem	Keota	16

Nationwide Mennonite Fellowship Churches

Haven	Kalona	63

O. O. Mennonite Groffdale Conf

Cedar Valley	Charles City	65
Deerfield	Riceville	55

O. O. Mennonite Weaverland Conf

South Osage	Osage	40

KANSAS

AMISH

Beachy Amish

Arlington	Arlington	37
Cedar Crest	Hutchinson	143
Center	Hutchinson	140

New Order Amish

East Hutchinson	Hutchinson	55
West Hutchinson	Partridge	55

O. O. Amish

Middle	Haven	55
North	Garnett	55
North	Haven	55
South	Garnett	55
South	Haven	55
West	Hutchinson	55

BRETHREN

Brethren Church, The

Fort Scott	Fort Scott	23
Mulvane	Mulvane	44
New Heights Fellowship	Derby	32

Brethren in Christ

Abilene	Abilene	100
Crossroads	Salina	50
Rosebank	Hope	71
Zion	Abilene	118

Church of the Brethren

Buckeye	Abilene	46
Community	Hutchinson	120
Eden Valley	Saint John	69
Fellowship	Lenexa	10
First	Wichita	520
First Central	Kansas City	53
Fredonia	Fredonia	25
Garden City	Garden City	225
Independence	Independence	66
Lone Star	Lawrence	58
Maple Grove	Norton	50
McPherson	McPherson	449
Monitor	Conway	65
Mont Ida	Welda	38
Navarre	Navarre	20
Newton	Newton	39
Olathe	Olathe	53
Osage	McCune	133
Ottawa	Ottawa	67
Paint Creek	Redfield	25
Parsons	Parsons	50
Prairie View	Scott City	103
Quinter	Quinter	248
Salem Community	Nickerson	141
Scott Valley	Burlington	5
Topeka	Topeka	144
Trinity	Sabetha	30
Verdigris	Emporia	16
Washington	Washington	17
Washington Creek	Lawrence	58

Dunkard Brethren

Quinter	Quinter	78

Grace Brethren Churches

Portis	Portis	99
Wichita	Wichita	5

Old German Baptist Brethren

Big Creek	Quinter	84
Cedar Creek	Harris	180
Eight Mile	Ottawa	48
Sand Creek	Sawyer	88
Willow Springs	Baldwin City	81

MENNONITE

Apostolic Christian Church of America

Bern	Bern	179
Ft. Scott	Ft. Scott	31
Kiowa	Kiowa	39
Lamont/Gridley	Lamont/Gridley	46
Sabetha	Sabetha	165
Wichita	Wichita	38

Church of God in Christ Mennonite

Alexanderfeld	Hillsboro	55
Bethel	Greensburg	110
Cimarron	Cimarron	106
Dodge City	Dodge City	0
Eden	Burns	191
Emmanuel	Fredonia	123
Garden View	Halstead	119
Gospel	Moundridge	225
Grace	Halstead	262
Grant	Ulysses	197
Homeland	Montezuma	182
Lakin	Lakin	92
Living Hope	Ingalls	100
Lone Tree	Galva	439
Meridian	Hesston	185
Montezuma	Montezuma	278
Morning Star	Durham	113
Plains View	Plains	59
Salem	Copeland	201
Scott	Scott City	151
Sharon Springs	Sharon Springs	46
United Center	Galva	179
Zion	Inman	215

Consrv Mennonite Conf

Maranatha	Hutchinson	81
Plainview	Hutchinson	120

Evangelical Mennonite Brethren

Meade	Meade	140

Evangelical Mennonite Church

Cornerstone	Hutchinson	53
Grace	Newton	192
Sterling	Sterling	176

General Conf Mennonite Church

Alexanderwohl	Goessel	562
Bergthal	Pawnee Rock	94
Bethel	Inman	390
Bethel College	North Newton	709
Buhler	Buhler	351
Burrton	Burrton	88
Calvary	Liberal	52
Central Heights	Durham	48
Eden	Moundridge	788
Faith	Newton	383
First	Halstead	296
First	Hillsboro	334
First	Hutchinson	248
First	McPherson	210
First	Newton	701
First	Pretty Prairie	427
First	Ransom	102
First Christian	Moundridge	227
Goessel	Goessel	186
Grace Hill	Whitewater	208
Hanston	Hanston	24
Hoffnungsau	Inman	288

Hope	Wichita	179
Hopefield	Moundridge	77
Inman	Inman	146
Kingman	Kingman	181
Lorraine Avenue	Wichita	354
New Creation	Newton	50
Rainbow	Kansas City	178
Salina	Salina	60
Tabor	Newton	323
Trinity	Hillsboro	259
West Zion	Moundridge	250
Zion	Elbing	147

Independent Mennonite Congregations

Emmanuel	Meade	265
Emmaus	Whitewater	256
First	Burns	87
Garden	Hesston	133
Swiss	Whitewater	240

Manhattan Mennonite Church: GC/MB/MC

Manhattan	Manhattan	80

Mennonite Brethren

Buhler	Buhler	436
Community Bible	Olathe	129
Ebenfield	Hillsboro	232
First	Wichita	614
Garden Valley	Garden City	289
Good News	Marion	50
Hesston	Hesston	113
Hillsboro	Hillsboro	651
Koerner Heights	Newton	165
North Oak	Hays	90
Parkview	Hillsboro	263
Topeka	Topeka	149
Ulysses	Ulysses	114
United at the Cross	Wichita	26
Valleyview	Cimarron	110
Zoar	Inman	239

Mennonite Church

Argentine	Kansas City	21
Crystal Springs	Harper	21
Faith	South Hutchinson	57
Greensburg	Greensburg	95
Hesston	Hesston	590
Pleasant Valley	Harper	84
Protection	Protection	122
South Hutchinson	South Hutchinson	371
Spring Valley	Canton	33
Yoder	Yoder	174

Mennonite Church/General Conf: DC

Church of the Servant	Wichita	36
Faith	Montezuma	32
Fe y Esperanza	Montezuma	10
Inter-Mennonite	Hesston	204
New Hope	Lenexa	28
Peace	Lawrence	66
Shalom	Newton	133
Southern Hills	Topeka	92
Whitestone	Hesston	321

Mennonite Evangelical Churches

Evangelical	Copeland	33

Mid-West Mennonite Fellowship

Prairie	Hutchinson	27

Reinlaender Mennonite Church

Reinlaender	Sublette	78

KENTUCKY

AMISH
Amish Mennonite Unaffiliated
Monroe County	Mount Herman	70
Pleasant Ridge	Monticello	63

Beachy Amish
Casey	Liberty	53
Cedar Springs	Leitchfield	39
Deer Creek	Sebree	31
Franklin	Franklin	95
Hickory	Hickory	102
Plainview	Auburn	54
Providence	Franklin	95
Summersville	Summersville	24

New Order Amish
Crofton	Crofton	68
Marrowbone	Burkesville	32
North	Guthrie	60
Penchem	Guthrie	56
South	Guthrie	60

New Order Amish Fellowship
Guthrie	Guthrie	40

O. O. Amish
Center Point	Munfordville	55
Crab Orchard	Crab Orchard	55
Cub Run	Cub Run	55
East	Dunnville	55
East	Glasgow	55
Elk Horn	Merrimac	55
Forestville	Munfordville	55
Hillsboro	Hillsboro	55
Hopkinsville East	Hopkinsville	75
Hopkinsville West	Hopkinsville	75
Hudson	Hudson	55
Huston	Hustonville	55
Lewisburg	Lewisburg	55
Logsden Valley	Munfordville	55
Marion Northeast	Marion	55
Marion Northwest	Marion	55
Marion South	Marion	55
Marion West	Marion	55
North	Gradyville	55
Pembroke	Pembroke	75
Salem	Salem	55
Southwest	Gradyville	55
Springfield	Springfield	55
Three Springs	Hardyville	55
Trenton	Trenton	75
Upton	Upton	55
Waterloo Valley	Horse Cave	55
West	Dunnville	55
West	Glasgow	55

O. O. Amish Swartzentruber
Park City East	Park City	50
Park City West	Park City	50
Sonora	Sonora	50

BRETHREN
Brethren Church, The
Drushal Memorial	Lost Creek	24
Krypton	Krypton	35

Brethren in Christ
Beulah Chapel	Columbia	57
Bloomington Chapel	Columbia	80

Campbellsville	Campbellsville	38
Knifley	Knifley	18
Millerfields	Columbia	39

Church of the Brethren
Constance	Hebron	72
Flat Creek/Mud Lick	Manchester	168
Rock House	Hatfield	9
Wolf Creek	Laura	13

Grace Brethren Churches
Clayhole	Clayhole	25
Lexington	Lexington	5
Victory Mountain	Dryhill	57

MENNONITE
Church of God in Christ Mennonite
Fountain Run	Fountain Run	12
Murray	Murray	183

Consrv Mennonite Conf
Bowlings Creek	Altro	26
Buckhorn Creek	Rowdy	27
Caney Creek	Clayhole	37
Highland	Louisville	38
Lexington	Lexington	16
Panco	Oneida	28
Turners Creek	Talbert	48

Independent Mennonite Congregation
Wild Cat	Manchester	12

Mennonite Christian Fellowship
Mercer	Salvisa	28
Mount Carmel	Mount Carmel	99

Mennonite Church
Ridgeview	Morgantown	10
Talcum	Talcum	37
West Liberty	West Liberty	14

Mennonite Church/General Conf: DC
Harlan	Harlan	16

Nationwide Mennonite Fellowship Churches
Breckinridge	Stephensport	57
Faith Hills	Crockett	58
Hope Valley	Flat Gap	48
Valley View	Leburn	47

O. O. Mennonite Groffdale Conf
Cedar Hill	Liberty	92
Meadow Valley	Pembroke	118

O. O. Mennonite John Martin Group
Miller Valley	Elkton	24

O. O. Mennonite Noah Hoover Group
Oak Grove	Scottsville	120
Red Hill	Scottsville	70

O. O. Mennonite Reidenbach Group
Hoover	Fairview	32

O. O. Mennonite Stauffer Group
Stauffer	Elk Horn	37

O. O. Mennonite Unaffiliated
Christian Community	Holland	54
Vernon Community	Hestand	75

O. O. Orthodox Mennonite
Trigg County	Cerulean	21

Washington Franklin Mennonite Conf
Lincoln County	Crab Orchard	13
Pace's Creek	Manchester	41

LOUISIANA

BRETHREN
Church of the Brethren

Lake Charles	Lake Charles	90
Roanoke	Roanoke	81

MENNONITE
Church of God in Christ Mennonite

Delta	Transylvania	60
Highland	DeRidder	238

Mennonite Church

Amor Viviente	Metairie	180
Des Allemands	Des Allemands	121
Lighthouse	Buras	17
Native Christian	Gretna	15

MAINE

AMISH
Beachy Amish

Plain	Newport	12

BRETHREN
Church of the Brethren

Fellowship	Brunswick	23
Fellowship	Gardner	18
Lewiston	Lewiston	51

MENNONITE
Church of God in Christ Mennonite

Maple Grove	Bridgewater	3

Mennonite Church

Kennebec	Augusta	29

O. O. Mennonite Unaffiliated

Christian Community	Oakfield	19

MARYLAND

AMISH
Beachy Amish

Harmony	Millington	55

New Order Amish Fellowship

Oakland	Oakland	40

O. O. Amish

Cecil	Cecil	55
East	Mechanicsville	55
Middle	Mechanicsville	55
New Market	Charlotte Hall	55
North	Charlotte Hall	55
Ryceville	Mechanicsville	55

BRETHREN
Brethren Church, The

Gateway Fellowship	Hagerstown	37
Hagerstown First	Hagerstown	82
Linwood	Linwood	139
Saint James	Saint James	335

Brethren in Christ

Faith	Essex	29
Paramount	Hagerstown	115
Van Lear	Williamsport	53
Walkersville	Walkersville	55

Church of the Brethren

Asher Glade	Friendsville	119
Bear Creek	Accident	76
Beaver Creek	Hagerstown	112
Beaver Dam	Union Bridge	57
Bethesda	Grantsville	37
Broadfording	Hagerstown	225

Brownsville	Brownsville	370
Bush Creek	Monrovia	397
Cherry Grove	Grantsville	95
Community of Joy	Salisbury	20
Denton	Denton	85
Downsville	Downsville	41
Dundalk	Baltimore	52
Edgewood	New Windsor	125
Evergreen	Reisterstown	38
Fahrney-Keedy	Brownsville	25
Fairview	Cordova	124
Fairview	Table Rock	67
First	Baltimore	139
Flower Hill	Gaithersburg	52
Frederick	Frederick	1058
Friendship	Baltimore	192
Frostburg	Frostburg	109
Georges Creek	Lanaconing	34
Glade Valley	Walkersville	68
Good Shepherd	Silver Spring	36
Greenhill	Westover	84
Grossnickle	Myersville	181
Hagerstown	Hagerstown	395
Harmony	Myersville	46
Laughlin	Grantsville	36
Laurel Glen	Oakland	108
Living Stone	Cumberland	215
Locust Grove	Mount Airy	120
Long Green Valley	Glen Arm	147
Longmeadow	Hagerstown	94
Manor	Brownsville	110
Maple Grove	Grantsville	33
Meadow Branch	Westminster	233
Monocacy	Rocky Ridge	127
Myersville	Myersville	497
Oak Grove	McHenry	184
Oak Park	Oakland	190
Peach Blossom	Easton	209
Pine Grove	Oakland	95
Piney Creek	Taneytown	101
Pipe Creek	Union Bridge	70
Pleasant View	Burkittsville	217
Red Creek Bethel	Oakland	9
Ridgely	Ridgely	69
Sam's Creek	New Windsor	73
Sharpsburg	Sharpsburg	64
Stone Bridge	Hancock	59
Thurmont	Thurmont	147
Union Bridge	Union Bridge	255
University Park	Hyattsville	107
Welty	Smithsburg	159
Westernport	Westernport	175
Westminster	Westminster	327
Woodberry	Baltimore	79

Church of the Brethren/Mennonite: DA

Gortner Union	Oakland	31

Church of the Brethren: DA

United Christian	Columbia	86

Consrv Grace Brethren

Mill Run	Westernport	20

Dunkard Brethren

Swallow Falls	Oakland	28
Walnut Ridge	Taneytown	16

Grace Brethren Churches
Accident	Accident	20
Calvary	Hagerstown	65
Calvert County	Owings	312
Clinton	Clinton	388
Frederick	Frederick	113
Hagerstown	Hagerstown	533
Lanham	Lanham	177
Maranatha	Hagerstown	189
Valley	Hagerstown	99
Waldorf	Waldorf	625

Old German Baptist Brethren
Beaver Dam	Union Bridge	7

MENNONITE
Bethel Mennonite Fellowship
Salisbury	Salisbury	34

Consrv Mennonite Conf
Cherry Glade	Accident	265
Maple Glen	Grantsville	85

Cumberland Valley Mennonite Church
Lanes Run	Clear Spring	37
Mount Olive	Maugansville	80
Yarrowsburg	Brownsville	43

Eastern Pennsylvania Mennonite Church
Hopewell	Mount Airy	60
Mechanicsville	Mechanicsville	46

Keystone Mennonite Fellowship
Oakwood	Conowingo	12

Mennonite Biblical Alliance
Snow Hill	Snow Hill	44

Mennonite Christian Fellowship
Swanton	Swanton	54

Mennonite Church
Capital Christian	Laurel	77
Community	Hagerstown	17
Dargan	Sharpsburg	49
Dawsonville	Dawsonville	41
Ethiopian Evangelical	Baltimore	50
First	Columbia	15
Goshen	Laytonsville	27
Guilford Road	Jessup	32
Hebron	Hagerstown	56
Holly Grove	Westover	152
Mount Airy	Mount Airy	27
Mount Zion	Boonesboro	147
North Baltimore	Baltimore	41
North Side	Hagerstown	53
Ocean City	Ocean City	24
Victory Temple Community	Baltimore	30
Wilkens Avenue	Baltimore	55

Mennonite Church/General Conf: DC
Hyattsville	Hyattsville	138
Iglesia Completo	Hyattsville	102

Mennonite Unaffiliated Congregation
Dry Run	Swanton	90

Nationwide Mennonite Fellowship Churches
Hagerstown	Hagerstown	55

O. O. Mennonite Stauffer Group
Loveville	Loveville	170

Washington Franklin Mennonite Conf
Clear Spring	Clear Spring	90
Flintstone	Flintstone	50
Meadow View	Keedysville	77
Miller	Leitersburg	172
Paradise	Hagerstown	134
Pinesburg	Williamsport	67
Pondsville	Smithsburg	63
Reiff	Cearfoss	258
Stouffer	Smithsburg	144

MASSACHUSETTS
MENNONITE
Eastern Pennsylvania Mennonite Church
Mendon	Mendon	28

Mennonite Church
Chinese Grace	Malden	59
Chinese Saving Grace	Boston	127
Good Shepherd	Needham	34

Mennonite Church/General Conf: DC
Boston	Sommerville	52

Nationwide Mennonite Fellowship Churches
Westfield	Westfield	11

MICHIGAN
AMISH
Beachy Amish
Pilgrim	Nottawa	51

New Order Amish
Rosebush	Rosebush	45

O. O. Amish
Blanchard	Blanchard	55
Bloomingdale	Bloomingdale	55
Bronson-Orland	Bronson	55
California North	California	55
California Northwest	California	55
California South	California	55
California Southwest	California	55
Camden South	Camden	55
Cass City North	Cass City	55
Cass City South	Cass City	55
Clare East	Clare	55
Clare Middle	Clare	55
Clare Northwest	Clare	55
Clare West	Clare	55
Coral	Coral	55
Evart	Evart	55
Fremont	Fremont	55
Gladwin	Gladwin	55
Gladwin Middle	Gladwin	55
Graber	Camden	55
Graber East	Camden	55
Greenville	Greenville	55
Greenville	Greenville North	55
Hale	Hale	55
Hillsdale	Hillsdale	55
Holton	Holton	55
Homer	Homer	55
Hudson	Hudson	55
Manton	Manton	55
Marion	Marion	55
Marlette	Marlette	55
Marlette North	Marlette	55
Marlette South	Marlette	55
McBain	McBain	55
Newaygo North	Newaygo	55
Newaygo South	Newaygo	55
North	Charlotte	55

North	Coldwater	55
North Middle	Centerville	55
Northeast	Centerville	55
Northeast	Quincy	55
Northeast	Leonidas	55
Northwest	Coldwater	55
Northwest	Sturgis	55
Oscada East	Mio	55
Oscada Middle	Mio	55
Oscada West	Mio	55
Osseo	Osseo	55
Ossineke	Ossineke	55
Ovid North	Ovid	55
Ovid South	Ovid	55
Reading	Reading	55
Scottville	Scottville	55
Six Lakes	Six Lakes	55
South	Charlotte	55
South	Quincy	55
South	Vermontville	55
South Gladwin	Gladwin	55
South Middle	Burr Oak	55
South Middle	Centreville	55
Southeast	Centreville	55
Southwest	Centreville	55
Southwest	Montgomery	55
Stanwood	Stanwood	55
Stanwood Northwest	Stanwood	55
Stanwood West	Stanwood	55
Vestaburg	Vestaburg	55
West Ludington	Ludington	55

O. O. Amish Swartzentruber

Gladwin	Gladwin	50
Gladwin South	Gladwin	50

BRETHREN

Brethren Church, The

Matteson	Bronson	4

Brethren in Christ

Bethel	Merrill	28
Bethel Community	Cassopolis	10
Carland-Zion	Owosso	41
Lakeview	Goodrich	63
Leonard	Leonard	39
Mooretown	Sandusky	64

Church of the Brethren

Adrian	Adrian	22
Battle Creek	Battle Creek	37
Beaverton	Beaverton	95
Crystal	Vestaburg	36
Fairview	Blissfield	14
First	Drayton Plains	77
First	Flint	22
Hope	Freeport	100
Lakeview	Brethren	85
Lansing	Lansing	42
Marilla	Marilla	57
Midland	Midland	48
Muskegon	Muskegon	22
New Haven	New Haven	104
New Life	Mount Pleasant	62
Onekema	Onekema	129
Skyridge	Kalamazoo	67
Sugar Ridge	Custer	51
Sunfield	Sunfield	11

Trinity	Detroit	81
Zion	Prescott	50

Church of the Brethren/Mennonite: DA

Florence	Constantine	40
Shalom	Ann Arbor	33

Church of the Brethren: DA

First	Detroit	45
Woodgrove	Hastings	114

Consrv Grace Brethren

Calvary	Alto	124
Hastings Bible	Hastings	19
New Troy	New Troy	47
Niles	Niles	14
Ozark	Moran	32

Dunkard Brethren

Hart	Hart	51

Grace Brethren Churches

Lake Odessa	Lake Odessa	72
Lansing	Lansing	42

Old German Baptist Brethren

Scottville	Scottville	37

MENNONITE

Bethel Mennonite Fellowship

Pelkie	Pelkie	43

Charity Christian Fellowship

Manistee	Marilla	52

Church of God in Christ Mennonite

Mission	Harrison	0
Mount Calm	Carson City	137
Newark	Ithaca	228

Consrv Mennonite Conf

Bowne	Clarksville	58
Fairhaven	Sebewaing	105
Grace	Flint	40
Mount Morris	Mount Morris	20
National City	National City	24
North Wayne	Dowagiac	35
Pigeon River	Pigeon	216
Pineview	Vassar	48
Riverside	Turner	133
Riverview	White Pigeon	38

Evangelical Mennonite Church

Evangelical	Lawton	112
Good Shepherd	Adrian	45
Our Redeemer	Midland	74

General Conf Mennonite Church

Comins	Comins	100

Independent Mennonite Congregation

Firm Foundation	Centreville	60

Mennonite Church

Bethel	Ashley	116
Cedar Grove	Manistique	14
Coldsprings	Mancelona	59
Fairview	Fairview	425
Fellowship Center	Sturgis	44
Germfask	Germfask	34
Good News	Pinckney	9
Grace Chapel	Saginaw	68
Grand Marias	Grand Marias	8
Hilltop	Petoskey	15
Liberty	Liberty	22
Locust Grove	Burr Oak	239
Maple Grove	Gulliver	12
Maple River	Brutus	49

Menominee River	Menominee	30
Michigan Avenue	Pigeon	105
Midland	Midland	69
Naubinway	Naubinway	5
Ninth Street	Saginaw	42
Peace Community	Detroit	40
Pine Grove	Battle Creek	45
Rexton	Rexton	38
Salem	Waldren	81
Soo Hill	Escanaba	31
Stutzmanville Chapel	Harbor Springs	106
Wasepi	Centreville	50
Wayside	Brimley	26
Wildwood	Engadine	49

Mennonite Church/General Conf: DC

Ann Arbor	Ann Arbor	7
Community	Detroit	60
MSU Fellowship	East Lansing	26

Mennonite Unaffiliated Congregations

Calvary Chapel	Sturgis	130
Cherry Blossom	Kingsley	31
Faith	Hillsdale	50
Fellowship	Carson City	12
Pleasantview	Brethren	30

Mid-West Mennonite Fellowship

Consrv Fellowship	Mio	15
Grace Fellowship	Charlevoix	20
Seney	Seney	8
Shiloh	Constantine	12
Traverse Bay	Traverse City	23

Nationwide Mennonite Fellowship Churches

Fairview Consrv	Fairview	31

O. O. Mennonite Groffdale Conf

Vickeryville	Sheridan	27

O. O. Mennonite Wisler Conf

Bethany	Snover	108

Reformed Mennonite Church

Shelby	Shelby	30

MINNESOTA

AMISH

Beachy Amish

Believers	Grove City	82

O. O. Amish

Clearbrook	Clearbrook	55
Northwest	Preston	55
South	Bertha	55
Utica	Utica	55
Utica South	Utica	55
Wadena	Wadena	55
Wadena South	Wadena	55

O. O. Amish Swartzentruber

Canton	Canton	50
Granger	Granger	50
Harmony	Harmony	50
Long Prairie	Long Prairie	50
Northeast	Canton	50
Southeast	Canton	50

BRETHREN

Church of the Brethren

Lewiston	Lewiston	100
Open Circle	Burnsville	12
Root River	Preston	64
Worthington	Worthington	66

HUTTERITE

Schmiedeleut Hutterite

Altona	Henderson	55
Big Stone	Graceville	55
Elmendorf	Mountain Lake	55
Haven	Dexter	55
Heart Land	Lake Benton	55
Neuhof	Mountain Lake	55
Oakwood	Dexter	55
Spring Prairie	Hawley	55
Starland	Gibbon	55

MENNONITE

Apostolic Christian Church of America

Minneapolis	Minneapolis	47
Morris	Morris	300
Winthrop	Winthrop	55

Church of God in Christ Mennonite

Lake Haven	Starbuck	41

Consrv Mennonite Conf

Balsam Lake	Bovey	5
Cloverdale	Nashwauk	25

Evangelical Mennonite Brethren

Mountain Lake	Mountain Lake	180

Independent Mennonite Congregation

Gospel	Mountain Lake	190

Mennonite Brethren

Carson	Delft	52
Mountain Lake	Mountain Lake	84
New Hope	New Hope	95
Russian Evangelical	Brooklyn Park	250

Mennonite Church

Lake Region	Detroit Lakes	8
Leader	Leader	11
Point of Pines	International Falls	17
Strawberry Lake	Ogema	54

Mennonite Church/General Conf: DC

Bethel	Mountain Lake	456
Butterfield	Butterfield	48
Disciples	Duluth	6
Emmanuel	Roseville	41
Faith	Minneapolis	26
Fellowship	Rochester	22
First	Mountain Lake	150
Hilltop	Jackson	32
Immanuel	Delft	89
Lao Christian	Mountain Lake	35
Saint Paul	Saint Paul	15
United Hmong	Saint Paul	20

Mennonite Unaffiliated Congregations

Black River	Loman	21
Christian Life	International Falls	14
Kitichi Pines	Blackduck	52

Mid-West Mennonite Fellowship

Northwood	Little Fork	16
Prairie	Blooming Prairie	29

O. O. Mennonite Wisler Conf

Brooten	Brooten	24

MISSISSIPPI

AMISH

O. O. Amish Swartzentruber

Pontotoc	Randolph	40

BRETHREN
Old German Baptist Brethren

Leaf River	Mount Olive	9

MENNONITE
Church of God in Christ Mennonite

Brooksville	Brooksville	192
Clarksdale	Clarksdale	143
Leland	Leland	150
Okolona	Okolona	133
South Haven	Macon	194
West Point	West Point	95

Independent Mennonite Congregation

Fellowship of Hope	Macon	18

Mennonite Biblical Alliance

Faith	Crawford	54

Mennonite Church

Cornerstone	Macon	64
Grace	Quitman	9
Gulfhaven	Gulfport	141
Jubilee	Meridian	34
Nanih Waiya	Preston	42
Open Door	Jackson	24
Pearl River	Philadelphia	47

Mennonite Unaffiliated Congregations

Magnolia	Macon	118
Maranatha	Taylorsville	23
Mennonite Christian	Aberdeen	74

Pilgrim Mennonite Conf

Darbun	Darbun	43

MISSOURI

AMISH
Amish Mennonite

Moberly	Moberly	48
Olive Hill	Sedalia	115
Pleasant Grove	Vandalia	170
Pleasant View	Buffalo	220
Shelbyville	Shelbyville	57

Beachy Amish

Mint Hill	Linn	10
Pleasant View	Paris	22

O. O. Amish

Anabel	Anabel	55
Bethany	Bethany	55
Canton North	Canton	55
Canton South	Canton	55
Carrollton	Carrollton	55
Dixon	Dixon	55
Downing	Downing	55
East	Jamesport	55
East La Plata	La Plata	55
Humansville	Humansville	55
Kahoka	Kahoka	55
Licking	Raymondville	55
Middle	Jamesport	55
Middle East	Clark	55
Middle West	Clark	55
Mount Vernon	Mount Vernon	55
Mountain Grove	Mountain Grove	55
Nevada	Nevada	55
North Clear	Jamesport	55
North Windsor	Windsor	55
Northeast	Bowling Green	55
Northeast	Clark	55
Northwest	Clark	55
Northwest	Curryville	55
Northwest	Jamesport	55
Prairie Home	Prairie Home	55
Seymour C South	Seymour	55
Seymour East	Seymour	55
Seymour Middle East	Seymour	55
Seymour North	Seymour	55
Seymour Northeast	Seymour	55
Seymour South	Seymour	55
Seymour Southeast	Seymour	55
Seymour West	Seymour	55
South	Bowling Green	55
South Clear	Jamesport	55
South Windsor	Windsor	55
Southeast	Clark	55
Southwest	Clark	55
Spickard	Spickard	55
Stanberry	Stanberry	55
Unionville	Unionville	55
Verona	Verona	55
Verona South	Verona	55
West	Jamesport	55
West La Plata	La Plata	55
West Windsor	Windsor	55
Wheatland	Wheatland	55

O. O. Amish Swartzentruber

Grundy	Spickard	16

BRETHREN
Church of the Brethren

Bethany	Norborne	40
Broadwater	Essex	32
Cabool	Cabool	41
Carthage	Carthage	21
Deepwater	Deepwater	48
Farrenburg	New Madrid	32
Good Shepherd	Springfield	19
Greenwood	Mountain Grove	15
Messiah	Kansas City	167
Mineral Creek	Leeton	21
New Beginnings	Warrensburg	58
Osceola	Osceola	38
Peace Valley	Peace Valley	119
Rockingham	Hardin	40
Saint Joseph	Saint Joseph	53
Shelby County	Leonard	17
Spring Branch	Wheatland	33
Turkey Creek	Warsaw	8

Church of the Brethren/Mennonite: DA

Fellowship	Columbia	11

Dunkard Brethren

Grandview	Grandview	22

German Baptist Brethren

Jamesport	Jamesport	40

Old German Baptist Brethren

Walnut Creek	Knob Knoster	54

MENNONITE
Apostolic Christian Church of America

Kansas City	Kansas City	40
Lamar	Lamar	66
St. Louis	St. Louis	13
Taylor	Taylor	94

Bethel Mennonite Fellowship

La Monte	La Monte	68

Ozark	Seymour	119
Summersville	Summersville	60

Church of God in Christ Mennonite

Bethany	Rich Hill	140
Beulah	Versailles	154
Jamesport	Jamesport	56
Living Faith	Walker	88
Oak Ridge	Stover	91

Eastern Pennsylvania Mennonite Church

Versailles	Versailles	84
Warrensburg	Warrensburg	14

General Conf Mennonite Church

Bethel	Fortuna	213

Independent Mennonite Congregation

Redeemer of the World	Saint Louis	32

Mennonite Brethren

Summit	Lee's Summit	17

Mennonite Christian Fellowship

Bethel	Richmond	47
Fairview	Fairview	58
Golden City	Golden City	75
Locust Creek	Linneus	70
Maysville	Maysville	35
Spring River	LaRussell	77

Mennonite Church

Berea	Birch Tree	10
Bethesda	Saint Louis	62
Cornerstone	Hannibal	19
Cornerstone	Versailles	36
Evening Shade	Warsaw	32
Harrisonville	Harrisonville	245
Mount Pisgah	Leonard	51
Pea Ridge	Palmyra	41
Sycamore Grove	Garden City	158

Mennonite Church/General Conf: DC

Saint Louis	Saint Louis	64

Mennonite Unaffiliated Congregation

Rock Springs	Eldorado Springs	30

Mid-West Mennonite Fellowship

Spring Hill	Latham	15

Nationwide Mennonite Fellowship Churches

Grandin	Grandin	61

O. O. Mennonite Groffdale Conf

Clear View	Latham	190
Excelsior	Excelsior	135
Hopewell	Barnett	155

O. O. Mennonite John Martin Group

Morgan County	Versailles	40

O. O. Mennonite Noah Hoover Group

Rich Hill	Rich Hill	29

O. O. Mennonite Reidenbach Group

Nolt Church	Barnett	36

O. O. Mennonite Stauffer Group

Tunas	Tunas	114

O. O. Mennonite Weaverland Conf

Indian Creek	Memphis	150
Millport	Rutledge	162
North View	Arbela	130
Pleasant Hill	Latham	116

MONTANA

AMISH

New Order Amish

Mission	Saint Ignatius	18

O. O. Amish

Ashland-Forsyth	Ashland	30
Libby	Libby	45
Rexford	Rexford	55

BRETHREN

Church of the Brethren: DA

Big Sky	Froid	30

HUTTERITE

Dariusleut Hutterite

Ayers	Grassrange	45
Deerfield	Lewiston	45
East Malta	Malta	45
Flat Willow	Roundup	45
Fords Creek	Grassrange	45
Forty Mile	Lodge Grass	45
Gildford	Gildford	45
Kilby Butte	Roundup	45
King Ranch	Lewiston	45
Loring	Loring	45
North Harlem	Harlem	45
Spring Creek	Lewiston	45
Surprise Creek	Stanford	45
Turner	Turner	45

Lehrerleut Hutterite

Big Sky	Cut Bank	45
Big Stone	Sand Coulee	45
Birch Creek	Dupuyer	45
Camrose	Ledger	45
Cascade	Sun River	45
Duncan Ranch	Harlowton	45
Eagle Creek	Galata	45
East End	Havre	45
Fair Haven	Ulm	45
Glacier	Cut Bank	45
Glendale	Cut Bank	45
Golden Valley	Ryegate	45
Hartland	Havre	45
Hidden Lake	Cut Bank	45
Hilldale	Havre	45
Hillside	Sweet Grass	45
Kingsbury	Valier	45
Martinsdale	Martinsdale	45
Miami	Conrad	45
Milford	Wolf Creek	45
Miller	Choteau	45
Mountain View	Broadview	45
New Rockport	Choteau	45
Pleasant Valley	Belt	45
Pondera	Valier	45
Rimrock	Sunburst	45
Riverview	Chester	45
Rockport	Pendroy	45
Sage Creek	Chester	45
Seville	Cut Bank	45
Springdale	White Sulphur	45
Springwater	Harlowton	45
Twin Hills	Carter	45

MENNONITE

Evangelical Mennonite Brethren

Lustre	Lustre	85

Mennonite Brethren

Gospel	Wolf Point	56
Lustre	Lustre	94

Mennonite Church		
Coalridge	Coalridge	31
Mountain View	Kalispell	88
Red Top	Bloomfield	53
Mennonite Church/General Conf: DC		
Ashland	Ashland	9
Bethel	Wolf Point	59
Bethlehem	Bloomfield	74
Lame Deer	Lame Deer	45
White Chapel	Glendive	18
White River Cheyenne	Busby	60
Mennonite Unaffiliated Congregations		
Fairfield	Fairfield	12
Woodside	Corvallis	25

NEBRASKA
BRETHREN

Brethren Church, The		
Falls City	Falls City	69
Church of the Brethren		
Antelope Park	Lincoln	124
Bethel	Carleton	124
Enders	Enders	29
Holmesville	Holmesville	88
Grace Brethren Churches		
Beaver City	Beaver City	40
MENNONITE		
Church of God in Christ Mennonite		
Cedar Hills	Scotia	56
Golden Plains	Madrid	154
Mission	Friend	2
General Conf Mennonite Church		
Beatrice	Beatrice	152
First	Beatrice	244
Mennonite Brethren		
Faith Bible	Omaha	51
Henderson	Henderson	183
Iglesia Aqua Viva	Omaha	70
Millard	Omaha	73
New Life	Grant	90
Rolling Hills	Papillion	31
Mennonite Church/General Conf: DC		
Beemer	Beemer	138
Bellwood	Milford	241
Beth El	Milford	138
Bethesda	Henderson	1131
East Fairview	Milford	252
First	Lincoln	81
Milford	Milford	135
New Hope	Omaha	15
Northside	Omaha	16
Salem	Shickley	242
Wood River	Wood River	85
Mennonite Unaffiliated Congregation		
West Fariview	Beaver Crossing	56

NEW JERSEY
BRETHREN

Brethren Church, The		
First	Sergeantsville	8
Church of the Brethren		
Amwell	Stockton	124
Grace Brethren Churches		
Hope	Hope	32

Independent Brethren		
First	Baptistown	51
MENNONITE		
Eastern Pennsylvania Mennonite Church		
Vineland	Vineland	38
Hopewell Mennonite District		
Grace	Oxford	48
Mennonite Church		
Alpha	Alpha	48
City of Refuge	Vineland	32
Crossroads Community	Marlton	7
Faro Ardiente	Vineland	79
Friendship	Penns Grove	20
Garden Chapel	Dover	34
Manantial de Vida	Camden	25
New Life Covenant	Cardiff	65
Norma	Norma	36
Puerto de Sion	Trenton	70
Word Fellowship	Stratford	93

NEW MEXICO
AMISH

Amish Mennonite Unaffiliated		
Mimbres Valley	Mimbres	14
BRETHREN		
Brethren in Christ		
Navajo Chapel	Bloomfield	52
Sandia	Albuquerque	35
Church of the Brethren		
Clovis	Clovis	78
Tokahookaadi	Cuba	33
Dunkard Brethren		
Ant Hill	Cuba	8
Torrean Mission	Cuba	25
Grace Brethren Churches		
Cedar Hill Navajo	Counselor	25
Counselor	Counselor	27
Day Mesa	Day Mesa	11
First	Taos	150
MENNONITE		
Church of God in Christ Mennonite		
Mountain View	Albuquerque	10
Consrv Mennonite Conf		
Abundant Life	Albuquerque	65
Living Word	Albuquerque	25
Mennonite Church		
Carlsbad	Carlsbad	43
Mennonite Church/General Conf: DC		
Albuquerque	Albuquerque	27
Light of Life	Farmington	33
Nationwide Mennonite Fellowship Churches		
Belen	Belen	42
Farmington	Farmington	63

NEW YORK
AMISH

Beachy Amish		
Crystal Valley	Dundee	72
Northern Light	Henderson	31
Silver Lake	Perry	25
New Order Amish		
Lyndonville	Lyndonville	42
O. O. Amish		
Addison	Addison	55

Axeville East	Cattaraugus	55
Axeville West	Cattaraugus	55
Clyde	Clyde	55
Conewango East	Conewango Valley	55
Conewango West	Conewango Valley	55
East	Fort Plain	55
East	Rensselaer Falls	55
Fayette	Romulus	55
First Iron	Conewango Valley	55
Jasper	Jasper	55
Jasper North	Jasper	55
Jordanville	Jordanville	55
Lowville	Lowville	55
Mayville North	Dewittsville	55
Mayville South	Dewittsville	55
Newport	Fairfield	55
North	Belfast	55
North	Conewango Valley	55
North	Fillmore	55
North Clymer	Clymer	55
Northeast	Conewango Valley	55
Norwood	Norfolk	55
Ovid	Romulus	55
Ovid B	Romulus	55
Pope Road	Randolph	55
Prattsburg	Prattsburg	55
Sherman	Sherman	55
Snow Hill	Conewango Valley	55
South	Conewango Valley	55
South	Fillmore	55
South	Friendship	55
South Clymer	Clymer	55
West	Clymer	55
West	Conewango Valley	55
West	Fort Plain	55
Woodhull South	Woodhull	55

O. O. Amish Swartzentruber

East	Heuvelton	50
Middle	Heuvelton	50
North	Heuvelton	50
West	Heuvelton	50

BRETHREN

Brethren in Christ

Fellowship Chapel	Bronx	35
Ransom Creek	Clarence Center	29

Church of the Brethren

First	Brooklyn	178
Haitain First	Brooklyn	124

Consrv Grace Brethren

Saratoga Springs	Saratoga Springs	38

HUTTERITE

Bruderhof Communities

Catskill	Elka Park	200
Fox Hill	Walden	65
Maple Ridge	Ulster Park	225
Woodcrest	Rifton	240

MENNONITE

Apostolic Christian Church of America

Croghan-Naumburg	Croghan-Naumburg	55

Charity Christian Fellowship

Grace	Bainbridge	80
Philadelphia	Philadelphia	41

Church of God in Christ Mennonite

Finger Lakes	Auburn	20

Mission	New York City	9

Consrv Mennonite Conf

Carthage	Carthage	40
Croghan	Croghan	215
Naumburg	Castorland	429

Consrv Mennonite Conf/Mennonite Church: DA

Lowville	Lowville	260
Pine Grove	Glenfield	61

Eastern Pennsylvania Mennonite Church

Crystal Light	Croghan	60
Waterloo	Waterloo	69

Mennonite Biblical Alliance

Followers of Jesus	Brooklyn	35

Mennonite Brethren

Betania Telegu	Woodside	16

Mennonite Christian Fellowship

Madison	Madison	85

Mennonite Church

Alden	Alden	157
Believers	Brooklyn	35
Bethel	Amsterdam	13
Bethsaida Evangelical	Rochester	10
Clarence Center-Akron	Akron	168
Community	Corning	85
Ephesians	Manhattan	28
Ethiopian Evangelical	Manhattan	60
Evangelical Garifuna	Bronx	16
Evangelical Tabernacle	Brooklyn	30
First	Brooklyn	33
First	New Bremen	265
Friendship Community	Bronx	40
Grace	Schoharie	20
Harris Hill	Williamsville	17
Iglesia de Avivamiento	Queens	140
Iglesia Ebenezer	Bronx	27
Iglesia Valle de Jesus	Queens	25
Independence	Independence	43
Jesus	Addison	27
King of Glory	Bronx	98
Kossuth	Bolivar	16
North Bronx	Bronx	22
Pleasant Valley	Hammondsport	35
Redeeming Grace	Staten Island	36
Rhema	Lowville	55
Seventh Avenue	Manhattan	33
Shalom	Cattaraugus	12
Syracuse	East Syracuse	10
Watertown	Watertown	60
West Union	Rexville	87
Westside	Buffalo	35
Woodville	Woodville	74
York Corners	Wellsville	111

Mennonite Church/General Conf: DC

Amor Viviente	Brooklyn	150
Manhattan	Manhattan	28
Rochester Area	Rochester	18

Mennonite Church: DA

Immanuel	Flushing	109

Mid-Atlantic Mennonite Fellowship

Lakeland	Lakemont	26

Nationwide Mennonite Fellowship Churches

Hope	Lowville	32
Seneca	Romulus	38

Directory of Congregations

257

O. O. Mennonite Groffdale Conf
Benton	Penn Yan	280
Gravel Run	Dundee	170
Milo	Penn Yan	230
Rushville	Rushville	110

O. O. Mennonite Weaverland Conf
Fayette	Fayette	183
Maple View	Clyde	78
Pleasant Ridge	South Butler	156

Pilgrim Mennonite Conf
Phillips Creek	Belmont	32

NORTH CAROLINA
AMISH
New Order Amish
Union Grove	Union Grove	45
Yanceyville	Yanceyville	61

BRETHREN
Church of the Brethren
Brummetts Creek	Greenmountain	90
Eden	Eden	207
Fairview	Rocky Mount	122
Friendship	North Wilkesboro	82
Little Pine	Sparta	107
Living Faith	Concord	33
Maple Grove	Lexington	63
Melvin Hill	Green Creek	133
Mill Creek	Tryon	115
Mount Carmel	Sparta	32
New Haven	Sparta	29
Peak Creek	Laurel Springs	41
Saint Paul	Mount Airy	40
Shalom	Durham	44
Shelton	Mount Airy	160
Spindale	Spindale	167
Winston Salem	Fraternity	197

Grace Brethren Churches
Hope Community	Carey	76

MENNONITE
Charity Christian Fellowship
Believers	Cleveland	58
Believers	Spruce Pine	40

Church of God in Christ Mennonite
Lighthouse	Grifton	98

Mennonite Biblical Alliance
Foothills	Tryon	53
United Covenant	Etowah	20

Mennonite Brethren
Beechbottom	Newland	12
Boone	Boone	42
Bushtown	Lenoir	50
Darby	Ferguson	14
Laytown	Lenoir	56
West End	Lenoir	35

Mennonite Church
Asheville	Asheville	55
Bethel Christian	Sanford	102
Big Laurel	Creston	42
Fellowship of Christ	Rocky Mount	31
Greensboro	Greensboro	15
Hickory	Hickory	54
Jefferson	Jefferson	8
Meadowview	Lansing	33
Mountain View	Hickory	77

New Jerusalem	Robbins	26

Mennonite Church/General Conf: DC
Durham	Durham	32
Raleigh	Raleigh	73

Nationwide Mennonite Fellowship Churches
Hope	Pantego	69
Pine Ridge	Rutherfordton	60
Severn	Severn	30

NORTH DAKOTA
BRETHREN
Church of the Brethren
Cando	Cando	80
Pleasant Valley	York	37
Surrey	Surrey	33

HUTTERITE
Schmiedeleut Hutterite
Fairview	Lamour	55
Forest River	Fordville	55
Maple River	Fullerton	55
Spring Creek	Forbes	55
Sundale	Milnor	55
Willow Bank	Edgely	55

MENNONITE
Church of God in Christ Mennonite
Grafton	Grafton	98

Independent Mennonite Congregation
Salem	Munich	85

Mennonite Brethren
Harvey	Harvey	140
John's Lake	McClusky	5
Minot	Minot	57

Mennonite Church
Fairview	Surrey	39
Lakeview	Wolford	47

Mennonite Church/General Conf: DC
Casselton	Casselton	32
Swiss	Alsen	21

Mennonite Unaffiliated Congregations
Heartland	Mylo	9
Salem	Mylo	20

OHIO
AMISH
Amish Mennonite Unaffiliated
Haffley	Clark	8

Beachy Amish
Amana	Pattersonville	16
Antrim	Antrim	111
Bethel	Berlin	151
Bethesda	Plain City	100
Canaan	Plain City	106
Ebenezer	McConnelsville	61
Fryburg	Millersburg	38
Grace Haven	Winesburg	45
Haven	Plain City	130
Hicksville	Hicksville	43
Living Waters	Sugarcreek	15
Maranatha	Sugarcreek	109
Melita	Utica	75
Messiah	Millersburg	38
Minerva	Minerva	100
Peniel	Holmesville	75
Pleasant View	Hartville	70

Salem	Bakersville	57
Shiloh	Fredericksburg	61
Zion	Middlefield	41

New Order Amish

Berlin East	Berlin	60
Berlin Northeast	Berlin	60
Cherry Ridge	Sugarcreek	60
Danville East II	Danville	60
Deer Run	Sugarcreek	60
East	Rushsylvania	60
Elm Grove East	Fredericksburg	60
Highland	Leesburg	60
Kinsman	Kinsman	60
Martins Creek East	Millersburg	60
Martins Creek West	Millersburg	60
Middle	Belle Center	60
Mount Hope	Mount Hope	60
Salt Creek East	Fredericksburg	60
Salt Creek North	Wooster	60
Salt Creek South	Holmesville	60
Salt Creek West	Fredericksburg	60
Sharp Run North	Millersburg	60
Sugarcreek East	Sugarcreek	60
Union Valley West	Sugarcreek	60
Union Valley East	Sugarcreek	60
Walnut Creek East	Walnut Creek	60
Walnut Creek Lower	Walnut Creek	60
Walnut Creek Northwest	Walnut Creek	60
West	Belle Center	60
West Holmesville	Holmesville	60
Winesburg	Winesburg	60

New Order Amish Fellowship

Berlin	Berlin	48
Hartville	Uniontown	17
Mount Hope B	Mount Hope	60
Walnut Creek-Sugarcreek	Sugarcreek	46
Walhonding	Walhonding	40
Winesburg	Winesburg	42

O. O. Amish

Adamsville	Adamsville	60
Aldernick	Columbiana	60
Alpine East	Dundee	60
Alpine West	Dundee	60
Apple Creek East	Apple Creek	60
Apple Creek Northeast	Apple Creek	60
Apple Creek Southeast	Apple Creek	60
Apple Creek Southwest	Apple Creek	60
Apple Creek West	Apple Creek	60
Apple Creek West B	Apple Creek	60
Ashery East	Fredericksburg	60
Ashery Northeast	Fredericksburg	60
Ashery West	Fredericksburg	60
Baltic	Baltic	60
Baltic South	Baltic	60
Barrs Mills East	Sugarcreek	60
Barrs Mills Northeast	Sugarcreek	60
Barrs Mills Northwest	Sugarcreek	60
Barrs Mills South	Sugarcreek	60
Barrs Mills Southeast	Sugarcreek	60
Barrs Mills Southwest	Sugarcreek	60
Beaver	Beaver	60
Beechvale Northeast	Millersburg	60
Beechvale Southeast	Millersburg	60
Beechvale West	Millersburg	60

Becks Mills	Baltic	60
Becks Mills North	Millersburg	60
Becks Mills South	Millersburg	60
Bergholz	Bergholz	60
Berlin Middle East	Berlin	60
Berlin Southeast	Berlin	60
Bloomfield	North Bloomfield	60
Bremen	Bremen	60
Brinkhaven East	Danville	60
Brinkhaven West	Danville	60
Brush Run East	Sugarcreek	60
Brush Run West	Baltic	60
Bundysburg	Middlefield	60
Bundysburg Road Northwest	Middlefield	60
Bunker Hill	Millersburg	60
Bunker Hill East	Millersburg	60
Bunker Hill East B	Millersburg	60
Bunker Hill Middle East	Millersburg	60
Bunker Hill North	Millersburg	60
Bunker Hill Northeast	Millersburg	60
Bunker Hill Northwest	Millersburg	60
Bunker Hill Southeast	Millersburg	60
Burton	Burton	60
Burton Station	Middlefield	60
Burton-Windsor Rd.	Middlefield	60
Calmoutier	Fredericksburg	60
Calmoutier North	Fredericksburg	60
Calmoutier Southwest	Fredericksburg	60
Calmoutier West	Fredericksburg	60
Carr Road	Orrville	60
Carroll	Carrollton	60
Carroll II	Carrollton	60
Center Ridge	Fresno	60
Charm	Charm	60
Charm East	Charm	60
Charm North	Charm	60
Charm Northwest	Charm	60
Charm South	Charm	60
Cherry Valley	Dorset	60
Chesterhill	Chesterhill	60
Clark East	Millersburg	60
Clark West	Millersburg	60
Conneaut South	Conneaut	60
Danville East	Danville	60
Danville East II	Danville	60
Danville North	Danville	60
Danville West	Danville	60
Defiance County	Hicksville	60
DeGraff East	DeGraff	60
DeGraff West	DeGraff	60
Doughty Northeast	Millersburg	60
Doughty Northwest	Millersburg	60
Doughty Southeast	Millersburg	60
Doughty Southwest	Millersburg	60
East	Ashland	60
East Union	Orrville	60
East Union East	Orrville	60
East Valley West	Winchester	60
East Walnut Creek	Walnut Creek	60
Elm Grove	Fredericksburg	60
Fairview East	Millersburg	60
Fairview West	Millersburg	60
Farmerstown	Farmerstown	60

Farmerstown North	Farmerstown	60
Farmerstown South	Farmerstown	60
Farmerstown Southeast	Farmerstown	60
Farmerstown Southwest	Farmerstown	60
Farmerstown West	Farmerstown	60
Farmington East	West Farmington	60
Farmington North	West Farmington	60
Farmington Road	Burton	60
Farmington Southeast	West Farmington	60
Flat Ridge	Baltic	60
Flat Ridge East	Baltic	60
Flat Ridge Northwest	Millersburg	60
Flat Ridge South	Baltic	60
Frams Corner	Burton	60
Fredericksburg North	Fredericksburg	60
Fredericksburg West	Fredericksburg	60
Fryburg East	Millersburg	60
Fryburg West	Millersburg	60
Garrettsville	Garrettsville	60
Girdle Road	Middlefield	60
Girdle Road II	Middlefield	60
Glenmont	Brinkhaven	60
Hayes Corner	Middlefield	60
Hayes Corner East	Middlefield	60
Hayes Corner South	Middlefield	60
Hayes Corner West	Middlefield	60
Holmesville Middle North	Holmesville	60
Holmesville Middle West	Holmesville	60
Holmesville North	Fredericksburg	60
Holmesville Northeast	Holmesville	60
Holmesville Northwest	Holmesville	60
Holmesville Southeast	Holmesville	60
Holmesville Southwest	Holmesville	60
Honey Run	Millersburg	60
Hostetler East	Apple Creek	60
Hostetler Middle East	Apple Creek	60
Hostetler Middle West	Apple Creek	60
Hostetler West	Apple Creek	60
Huntsburg East	Huntsburg	60
Huntsburg Middle	Huntsburg	60
Huntsburg Northeast	Huntsburg	60
Huntsburg Northwest	Huntsburg	60
Huntsburg South	Middlefield	60
Huntsburg Southeast	Huntsburg	60
Huntsburg Southwest	Huntsburg	60
Huntsburg West	Huntsburg	60
Jeromesville	Jeromesville	60
Johnsons Corner Northeast	Huntsburg	60
Kansas Road	Orrville	60
Kenton Middle	Kenton	60
Kenton Northeast	Kenton	60
Kenton West	Kenton	60
Kidron Middle	Kidron	60
Kidron North	Kidron	60
Kidron Road East	Apple Creek	60
Kidron South	Kidron	60
Kinsman South	Kinsman	60
Knob View	Baltic	60
Laird Road	Middlefield	60
Lakeville East	Lakeville	60
Lakeville Middle East	Lakeville	60
Lakeville Southeast	Lakeville	60
Lakeville West	Lakeville	60
Lewisville East	Lewisville	60
Lewisville North	Lewisville	60
Lewisville South	Lewisville	60
Maysville East	Apple Creek	60
Maysville Northeast	Apple Creek	60
Maysville Northwest	Apple Creek	60
Maysville Southwest	Fredericksburg	60
Maysville West	Apple Creek	60
McKay	McKay	60
Meadow Brook	Millersburg	60
Mespo	Mesopotamia	60
Mespo Hill	Mesopotamia	60
Mespo Hill North	Mesopotamia	60
Mespo Hill Northeast	Mesopotamia	60
Mespo Hill Northwest	Mesopotamia	60
Mespo Hill South	Mesopotamia	60
Mespo Hill Southeast	Mesopotamia	60
Mespo West	Mesopotamia	60
Middle	Ashland	60
Middle East	Ashland	60
Middle East	Bellville	60
Middle East	West Union	60
Middle West	Fredericktown	60
Middlebourne	Middlebourne	60
Middlefield	Middlefield	60
Middlefield North	Middlefield	60
Middlefield North Middle	Middlefield	60
Middlefield Northeast	Middlefield	60
Middlefield Southeast	Middlefield	60
Middlefield West	Middlefield	60
Mill Creek	Millersburg	60
Millersburg West	Millersburg	60
Mount Eaton	Mount Eaton	60
Mount Eaton North	Mount Eaton	60
Mount Eaton South	Mount Eaton	60
Mount Eaton Southeast	Mount Eaton	60
Mount Eaton Southeast A	Dundee	60
Mount Eaton Southwest	Mount Eaton	60
Mount Hope East	Mount Hope	60
Mount Hope Middle	Mount Hope	60
Mount Hope Middle North	Mount Hope	60
Mount Hope North	Mount Hope	60
Mount Hope Northeast	Mount Hope	60
Mount Hope Northwest	Mount Hope	60
Mount Hope South	Mount Hope	60
Mount Hope Southeast	Mount Hope	60
Mount Hope Southeast 61B	Mount Hope	60
Mount Hope Southeast 73B	Mount Hope	60
Mount Hope Southwest	Mount Hope	60
Nauvoo	Middlefield	60
New Bedford East	Baltic	60
New Bedford Middle	Fresno	60
New Bedford North	Baltic	60
New Bedford Northeast	Baltic	60
New Bedford Southeast	Fresno	60
New Bedford Southwest	Fresno	60
New Bedford West	Baltic	60
Newcomb Road	Middlefield	60
Newcomb Road-Parkman	Parkman	60
North Girdle Road	Middlefield	60
North Mount Hope	Mount Hope	60

North Newcomb	Middlefield	60
North Old State	Middlefield	60
North Troy	Burton	60
North Troy East	Burton	60
Northeast	Bellville	60
Northeast	Nova	60
Northwest	Bellville	60
Northwest	Shiloh	60
Old State Road	Middlefield	60
Orrville Northeast	Orrville	60
Orrville West	Orrville	60
Orwell	Orwell	60
Parkman	Parkman	60
Parkman Middle	Parkman	60
Parkman North	Parkman	60
Parkman Northeast	Parkman	60
Patriot	Patriot	60
Patriot South	Patriot	60
Peebles	Peebles	60
Pierpont South	Pierpont	60
Salesville North	Salesville	60
Salesville South	Salesville	60
Sharp Run	Millersburg	60
Sharp Run East	Millersburg	60
Shreve South	Shreve	60
South	Parkman	60
South Burton	Middlefield	60
South Mespo	Mesopotamia	60
South Newcomb	Middlefield	60
Southeast	Ashland	60
Southeast	Fredericktown	60
Southeast	LaRue	60
Southeast	Parkman	60
Southwest	Ashland	60
Southwest	Fredericktown	60
Southwest	Navarre	60
Southwest	West Farmington	60
Southwest Maysville	Fredericksburg	60
Southwest West	West Farmington	60
Stutzman & Troyer	Apple Creek	60
Sugarcreek North	Sugarcreek	60
Sugarcreek South	Sugarcreek	60
Sugarcreek Stony Point	Sugarcreek	60
Townline North	Middlefield	60
Townline South	Middlefield	60
Trail North	Trail	60
Trail Northeast Annex	Trail	60
Trail Southeast	Trail	60
Trail West	Trail	60
Troy Northeast	Burton	60
Troy South	Burton	60
Troy Southeast	Burton	60
Troyer Ridge	Millersburg	60
Troyer Valley East	Sugarcreek	60
Troyer Valley West	Sugarcreek	60
Twin Creek	Baltic	60
Walnut Creek East	Walnut Creek	60
Walnut Creek North	Walnut Creek	60
Walnut Creek Northeast	Walnut Creek	60
Walnut Creek Upper North	Walnut Creek	60
Walnut Creek Upper South	Walnut Creek	60
Walnut Creek West	Walnut Creek	60

Weaver Ridge	Millersburg	60
West	Fredericksburg	60
West	Fredericktown	60
West	Greenwich	60
West Waterford	Fredericktown	60
Wheat Ridge East	West Union	60
Wheat Ridge West	West Union	60
Wilmot East Valley	Wilmot	60
Windsor	Middlefield	60
Windsor North	Orwell	60
Winesburg Middle	Winesburg	60
Winesburg North	Winesburg	60
Winesburg Northeast	Winesburg	60
Winesburg Northwest	Winesburg	60
Winesburg West	Winesburg	60

O. O. Amish Nebraska

Andover	Andover	60
Williamsfield	Williamsfield	60

O. O. Amish Swartzentruber

Albion	West Salem	50
Barnesville	Barnesville	50
East Middle	Homerville	50
Fountain Nook	Apple Creek	50
Fountain Nook II	Fredericksburg	50
Homerville	Homerville	50
Homerville Northwest	Homerville	50
Kidron	Kidron	50
Kidron East	Kidron	50
Lodi North Middle	Lodi	50
Maysville	Apple Creek	50
Maysville West	Fredericksburg	50
Middle	Apple Creek	50
Middle West	Homerville	50
Mount Eaton	Mount Eaton	50
North	Dundee	50
North Middle	Apple Creek	50
Northwest	Apple Creek	50
Peoli	Peoli	50
Peoli South	Peoli	50
Polk	Polk	50
Salt Creek East	Fredericksburg	50
South Middle	Dundee	50
Southeast	Dundee	50
Southeast	West Salem	50
Southwest	Fredericksburg	50
West	Fredericksburg	50
West Lebanon	Dalton	50
West Lebanon East	Navarre	50
West Lebanon North	Dalton	50
West Middle	Sullivan	50
Winesburg East	Winesburg	50
Wooster Ech	Wooster	50

BRETHREN

Brethren Church, The

Bryan First	Bryan	253
Columbus First	Columbus	49
First Brethren	Fremont	53
Garber	Ashland	52
Gratis First	Gratis	70
Gretna	Bellefontaine	152
Hillcrest	Dayton	14
Living Waters	Mansfield	0
Louisville Bible	Louisville	36
Louisville First	Louisville	124

Anabaptist World USA

262

New Lebanon	New Lebanon	212
Newark	Newark	33
North Georgetown	North Georgetown	140
Park Street	Ashland	479
Pleasant Hill First	Pleasant Hill	123
Smithville	Smithville	273
Smokey Row	Columbus	113
Trinity	North Canton	70
University	Ashland	27
Vineyard Community	Franklin	80
West Alexandria First	West Alexandria	244
Williamstown	Williamstown	35

Brethren in Christ

Amherst	Massillon	123
Ashland	Ashland	123
Beulah Chapel	Springfield	27
Christ Gospel	Ravenna	15
Dayton	Dayton	50
Fairview	Englewood	123
Gethsemane	New Carlisle	42
Highland	West Milton	95
Mission	Dayton	25
Northgate	Tipp City	24
Oak Hill	Wooster	38
Pleasant Hill	Pleasant Hill	67
Sippo Valley	Massillon	33
Valley Chapel	East Canton	48
Western Hills	Cincinnati	37

Church of the Brethren

Baltic	Baltic	127
Bear Creek	Dayton	204
Beavercreek	Beavercreek	129
Beech Grove	Hollansburg	109
Bellefontaine	Bellefontaine	76
Bethel	New Middletown	43
Black River	Spencer	44
Bradford	Bradford	236
Bristolville	Bristolville	107
Brookville	Brookville	310
Castline	Arcanum	371
Cedar Grove	New Paris	227
Center	Louisville	91
Charleston	Chillicothe	33
Chippewa	Creston	47
Cincinnati	Cincinnati	13
Circleville	Circleville	66
City	Ashland	200
Community	Brook Park	161
County Line	Harrod	354
Covington	Covington	354
Defiance	Defiance	42
Deshler	Deshler	11
Dickey	Ashland	124
Donnels Creek	North Hampton	502
Dupont	Dupont	423
Eagle Creek	Forest	65
East	Sugarcreek	65
East Chippewa	Orrville	377
East Dayton	Dayton	36
East Nimishillon	North Canton	57
Eastwood	Akron	156
Eaton	Eaton	832
Eden	Canton	133
Emmanuel	Huber Heights	63

Eversole	New Lebanon	130
First	Akron	65
First	Canton	66
Fostoria	Fostoria	30
Freeburg	Paris	66
Fruitful Vine	West Alexandria	0
Good Shepherd	Tipp City	0
Gratis	Gratis	34
Greenville	Greenville	269
Happy Corner	Clayton	301
Harris Creek	Bradford	69
Hartville	Hartville	344
Heatherdowns	Toledo	65
Kent	Kent	150
Lake Breeze	Sheffield	24
Lakewood	Millbury	159
Lick Creek	Bryan	122
Lima	Lima	63
Lower Miami	Dayton	72
Mack Memorial	Dayton	147
Mansfield	Mansfield	104
Maple Grove	Ashland	237
Marble Furnance	Peebles	8
Marion	Marion	59
Medina	Medina	37
Mohican	West Salem	108
Mount Pleasant	North Canton	168
New Carlisle	New Carlisle	334
New Philadelphia	New Philadelphia	65
North Bend	Danville	119
Oakland	Bradford	544
Olivet	Thornville	119
Owl Creek	Bellville	109
Painesville	Painesville	134
Painter Creek	Arcanum	85
Paradise	Smithville	82
Piqua	Piqua	145
Pitsburg	Arcanum	165
Pleasant Hill	Pleasant Hill	206
Pleasant View	Lima	142
Poplar Grove	Union City	23
Poplar Ridge	Defiance	158
Potsdam	Potsdam	445
Prices Creek	West Manchester	144
Prince of Peace	Kettering	200
Reading	Homeworth	52
Richland	Mansfield	56
Ross	Mendon	25
Salem	Englewood	449
Silver Creek	Pioneer	53
Springfield	Akron	207
Stonelick	Pleasant Plain	57
Stony Creek	Bellefontaine	71
Strait Creek	Peebles	4
Sugar Creek, East	Sugarcreek	65
Sugar Creek, West	Lima	208
Swan Creek	Wauseon	23
Trinity	Massillon	142
Trinity	Sidney	99
Trotwood	Trotwood	194
Troy	Troy	241
Union City	Union City	87
West Alexandria	West Alexandria	95
West Charleston	Tipp City	158

West Milton	West Milton	129
White Cottage	White Cottage	98
Woodworth	Youngstown	83
Zion Hill	Columbiana	127
Consrv Grace Brethren		
Ankenytown	Bellville	99
Community	Findlay	36
Coolville	Coolville	38
Englewood	Englewood	55
Findlay	Findlay	50
Fremont	Fremont	54
Galion	Galion	41
Mansfield	Mansfield	319
Mount Vernon	Mount Vernon	85
Newark	Newark	9
Orrville	Orrville	61
Spring Valley	Elyria	51
Sterling	Sterling	42
Trinity	Northwood	0
Tuscarawas	New Philadelphia	13
Vandalia	Vandalia	25
Dunkard Brethren		
Englewood	Englewood	51
Pleasant Ridge	Bryan	60
West Fulton	Wauseon	70
Grace Brethren Churches		
Akron	Akron	70
Ashland	Ashland	595
Basore Road	Dayton	315
Bowling Green	Bowling Green	36
Brookville	Brookville	200
Calvary	Dayton	30
Calvary	Kettering	28
Camden	Camden	20
Canton	Canton	198
Centerville	Centerville	101
Clayton	Clayton	115
Columbus	Columbus	1920
Community	West Alexandria	53
Community	West Milton	548
Cornerstone	Mansfield	38
Danville	Danville	16
Delaware	Delaware	161
East Side	Columbus	338
Ellet	Akron	144
First	Dayton	287
Fremont	Fremont	424
Friendship	Covington	71
Grace Community	Huber Heights	174
Homerville	Homerville	153
Lexington	Lexington	169
Licking County	Pataskala	99
London	London	20
Loveland	Cincinnati	52
Marion	Marion	50
Maumee Valley	Toledo	31
Middlebranch	Middlebranch	141
Millersburg	Millersburg	59
Minerva	Minerva	82
North Riverdale	Dayton	113
Northwest Chapel	Dublin	186
Norton	Norton	276
Pickerington	Pickerington	20
Powell	Powell	10

Rittman	Rittman	195
Rocky Ridge	Columbus	30
Shepherd's Grace	Medina	95
Southview	Ashland	115
Southwest	Columbus	100
Toledo	Toledo	23
Trotwood	Trotwood	130
Troy	Troy	52
Western Reserve	Macedonia	121
Woodville	Mansfield	134
Wooster	Wooster	925
Old Brethren		
Bradford	Bradford	30
Old German Baptist Brethren		
Ash Grove	Lima	114
Bear Creek	New Lebanon	49
Covington	Covington	159
Donnels Creek	North Hampton	71
Lower Twin	Camden	122
Maple Grove	New Carlisle	124
Oak Grove	Gettysburg	86
Painter Creek	Pitsburg	158
Palestine	Palestine	95
Prices Creek	Eldorado	148
Salem	Clayton	168
Shady Grove	Union City	54
Stillwater	Dayton	54
Sugar Grove	Covington	204
Upper Twin	Eaton	118
Wolf Creek	Brookville	151
O. O. German Baptists		
Arcanum	Arcanum	45
Bradford	Bradford	40
Covington	Covington	40
MENNONITE		
Apostolic Christian Church of America		
Akron	Akron	103
Columbus	Columbus	20
Junction	Junction	78
Latty	Latty	240
Mansfield	Mansfield	170
Rittman	Rittman	433
Sardis	Sardis	35
Smithville	Smithville	206
Toledo	Toledo	42
Charity Christian Fellowship		
Calvary	Dalton	65
Cambridge	Byesville	80
Faith	Berlin	75
Remnant	Bellville	69
Church of God in Christ Mennonite		
Homeworth	Homeworth	110
Rock of Ages	Apple Creek	174
Consrv Mennonite Conf		
Agape	Hilliard	72
Assembly	Fredericksburg	224
Bethany	Hartville	174
Calvary	Mount Eaton	58
Cornerstone	Hartville	135
Covenant	West Liberty	14
East Union	Orrville	209
Fairlawn	Apple Creek	113
Grace	Berlin	249
Hicksville	Hicksville	151

Johnsville	Johnsville	53
Light in the Valley	Sugarcreek	175
Maple Grove	Hartville	207
Maple View	Burton	116
Maranatha	Plain City	65
Mechanicsburg	Mechanicsburg	88
New Beginnings	Cincinnati	44
Open Door	Hartville	30
Pleasant View	Berlin	318
Shalom	London	74
Shiloh	Irwin	203
Turkey Run	Logan	28
United Dayspring	Millersburg	104

Consrv Mennonite Unaffiliated

Bethany	Holmesville	80
Faith Haven	Benton	68
Hebron	Hartville	23
Sharon	Sugarcreek	252
Zion Consrv	Millersburg	142

Evangelical Mennonite Church

Evangelical	Archbold	633
Evangelical	Wauseon	471
Forest Hills	Strongsville	29
Life Community	Hilliard	11
Oak Bend	Perrysburg	113
Solid Rock	West Unity	105

General Conf Mennonite Church

First	Bluffton	529
First	Sugarcreek	155
First	Wadsworth	111
Grace	Pandora	341
Saint John	Pandora	376
Salem	Kidron	215
Trenton	Trenton	138

Independent Mennonite Congregation

Ebenezer	Bluffton	490

Mennonite Biblical Alliance

Agape Assembly	Parkman	39
Fairhaven	West Salem	14
Mount Zion	Bladensburg	20
United Bethel	Plain City	286

Mennonite Christian Fellowship

Calvary	Mount Perry	83

Mennonite Church

Aurora	Aurora	206
Beech	Louisville	282
Berean	Youngstown	34
Berlin	Berlin	202
Bethel	Wadsworth	69
Bethel	West Liberty	186
Buen Pastor	Archbold	53
Central	Archbold	539
Chestnut Ridge	Orrville	121
Community	Bellefontaine	35
Community Christian	Thurman	10
Cornerstone	Plain City	68
Crown Hill	Rittman	120
Dayspring	Canton	65
Dove	Dalton	59
Emmanuel	Monclova	10
Fairpoint	Fairpoint	54
Family Outreach	Kalida	64
Fellowship Chapel	Vinton	52
First	Canton	52

Friendship	Bedford Heights	91
Gilead	Chesterville	70
Hartville	Hartville	532
Hillside	Jackson	23
Huber	New Carlisle	91
Inlet	Wauseon	30
Kidron	Kidron	784
Lafayette	West Lafayette	21
Lee Heights	Cleveland	382
Leetonia	Leetonia	116
Lockport	Stryker	437
Longenecker	Winesburg	148
Martins	Orrville	188
Martins Creek	Millersburg	242
Midway	Columbiana	179
Millersburg	Millersburg	153
Moorhead	Shreve	76
New Mercies	Burton	36
North Clinton	Wauseon	330
North Lima	North Lima	107
Northridge	Springfield	235
Oak Grove	West Liberty	164
Orrville	Orrville	253
Owl Creek	Beaver	21
Peace	Elyria	40
Pike	Elida	109
Pine Grove	Stryker	76
Pleasant View	North Lawrence	114
Primera Iglesia	Defiance	23
Primera Iglesia	Fremont	19
Saint Johns	Logan	22
Salem	Elida	99
Salem	Wooster	38
Sharon	Plain City	251
Smithville	Smithville	223
Sonnenberg	Kidron	262
South Union	West Liberty	89
Southside	Springfield	27
Springdale Chapel	Cincinnati	45
Stoner Heights	Louisville	49
Summit	Barberton	40
Tedrow	Wauseon	126
Toledo	Toledo	107
University Euclid	Cleveland	26
Walnut Creek	Walnut Creek	453
Wayside Chapel	Pedro	42
West Clinton	Pettisville	287
Wooster	Wooster	185
Zion	Archbold	465

Mennonite Church/General Conf: DC

Agora Fellowship	Columbus	20
Columbus	Columbus	147
Dover	Dover	30
Fellowship	Cincinnati	62
Jubilee	West Liberty	16
Lima	Lima	86
Oak Grove	Smithville	440

Mennonite Unaffiliated Congregations

Christian Brethren	North Lima	6
Crossroads	Andover	40
Flat Ridge	Newcomerstown	45
Gospel Haven	Millersburg	111
Shalom	Sugarcreek	10
Sharon	Elida	152

OKLAHOMA

Mid-West Mennonite Fellowship

Carbon Hill	Carbon Hill	30
Country View	Wilmot	71
Deeper Life	Plain City	44
Gospel Light	Trail	110
Hartville Consrv	Hartville	109
Pilgrim	Middlefield	28
Salem	Leetonia	110
Sonlight	Maysville	97

Nationwide Mennonite Fellowship Churcheses

Bethel	Apple Creek	43
Canaan	Zanesville	60
Glade Run	Kensington	40
Sharon	Columbiana	22
Valley View	Patriot	36

Ohio Wisler Mennonite Churches

County Line	Dalton	101
Maple Hill	Wadsworth	60
Mount Joy	Leetonia	110
Valley View	Dalton	85
Woodlawn	Greenwich	65

O. O. Mennonite Groffdale Conf

Blooming Glen	Shiloh	190
Springmill	Shiloh	150

O. O. Mennonite Stauffer Group

Bainbridge	Bainbridge	89

O. O. Mennonite Wisler Conf

Chester	Wooster	108
Pleasant View	Columbiana	120

Pilgrim Mennonite Conf

Mount Joy	Washingtonville	61

Reformed Mennonite Church

Bluffton	Bluffton	33
Marshallville	Marshallville	20
Wauseon	Wauseon	17

OKLAHOMA

AMISH

Beachy Amish

Zion	Thomas	46

O. O. Amish

Clarita	Coalgate	55
Northeast	Chouteau	55
Northwest	Chouteau	55
Southeast	Chouteau	55
Southwest	Inola	55

BRETHREN

Brethren in Christ

Bethany	Thomas	162
Oklahoma City	Oklahoma City	46
Red Star	Leedey	33

Church of the Brethren

Antelope Valley	Billings	169
Big Creek	Cushing	132
Enid	Enid	18
Frogville Fellowship	Fort Towson	21
Pleasant Plains	Aline	32
Thomas	Thomas	40

MENNONITE

Bethel Mennonite Fellowship

Grand Lake	Fairland	16

Charity Christian Fellowship

Poteau	Poteau	6

Church of God in Christ Mennonite

Cedar	Weatherford	26
Fairview	Fairview	167
Plainview	Chickasha	199
Pleasant View	Goltry	57

Consrv Mennonite Conf

Zion	Pryor	139

Consrv Mennonite Unaffiliated

Calvary	Paden	21

General Conf Mennonite Church

Bethel	Hammon	25
Bethel	Hydro	80
Deer Creek	Deer Creek	59
Eden	Inola	192
Fellowship	Stillwater	10
First	Clinton	87
Grace	Enid	140
Greenfield	Carnegie	25
Herald	Cordell	129
Indian	Seiling	45
Joy	Oklahoma City	16
Koinonia	Clinton	23
New Hopedale	Meno	177
Turpin	Turpin	100

Independent Mennonite Congregation

Zion	Canton	24

Kleine Gemeinde

Kleine Gemeinde	Boley	70

Mennonite Brethren

Adams	Adams	51
Balko	Balko	62
Bible	Cordell	97
Corn	Corn	421
Enid	Enid	277
Fairview	Fairview	550
Faith Bible	Lawton	68
Memorial Road	Edmond	87
Okeene	Okeene	44
Pine Acres	Weatherford	273
Post Oak	Indiahoma	53
Western Oaks	Bethany	45
Westport	Collinsville	437

Mennonite Church

Oak Grove	Adair	26
Pleasant View	Hydro	210

OREGON

BRETHREN

Brethren in Christ

El Monte Calvario	Salem	30
Pacific Highway	Salem	32
Redwood Country	Grants Pass	71

Church of the Brethren

Fruitdale Community	Grants Pass	42
Peace	Portland	60
Springfield	Springfield	41
Weston	Weston	117

Consrv Grace Brethren

Albany	Albany	12

Dunkard Brethren

Newberg	Newberg	7

Grace Brethren Churches

Walker Road	Beaverton	60

Anabaptist World USA

Old German Baptist Brethren

Dallas	Dallas	25

MENNONITE

Apostolic Christian Church of America

Portland	Portland	17
Silverton	Silverton	118

Church of God in Christ Mennonite

Evergreen	Scio	109

Independent Mennonite Congregations

Centro Cristiano Puente	McMinnville	20
Fairview	Albany	350
Iglesia Principe de Paz	McMinnville	45
New Hope	Lebanon	140
Sweet Home	Sweet Home	250
True Vine	McMinnville	255

Mennonite Brethren

Ammanuel Evangelical	Portland	30
Dallas	Dallas	75
Grants Pass	Grants Pass	51
Iglesia Cristiana	Hillsboro	47
Kingwood Bible	Salem	115
North Park	Eugene	51
Primera Ebenezer	Portland	55
Slavic Christian	Portland	500
Slavic Christian	Salem	250
Slavic Evangelical	Fairview	400

Mennonite Church/General Conf: DC

Albany	Albany	145
Calvary	Aurora	203
Eugene	Eugene	54
Fellowship	Corvallis	21
First	McMinnville	34
Grace	Dallas	119
Iglesia Pentacostas	Woodburn	75
Lebanon	Lebanon	240
Ministerios Restauracion	Oak Grove	10
Neighborhood	Logsden	35
Pacific Covenant	Canby	32
Peace	Portland	22
Plainview	Albany	43
Portland	Portland	205
Prince of Peace	Corvallis	120
River of Life	Sweet Home	82
Salem	Salem	122
Western	Salem	89
Zion	Hubbard	217

Mennonite Unaffiliated Congregations

Hopewell	Hubbard	100
Winston	Winston	45

Western Consrv Mennonite Fellowship

Brownsville	Brownsville	75
Grande Ronde	Cove	64
Harrisburg	Harrisburg	92
Payette Valley	Fruitland	34
Porter	Estacada	65
Sheridan	Sheridan	63
Tangent	Tangent	109

PENNSYLVANIA

AMISH

Amish Mennonite Unaffiliated

Community	Honey Brook	110
Spring Garden	Spring Garden	130

Beachy Amish

Gapview	Gap	90
Maple Grove	Hadley	20
Mine Road	Gap	160
Mountain View	Salisbury	194
Pequea	White Horse	92
Plainview	Guys Mills	33
Pleasant View	Belleville	133
Shade Mountain	Mifflin	82
Shady Grove	Mifflinburg	141
Shaver Creek	McAlveys Fort	31
Shekeinah	Middleburg	70
Summitview	New Holland	175
Valley View	Belleville	160
Washington County	Burgettstown	15
Weavertown	Ronks	267
Westhaven	New Holland	70

New Order Amish

Conneaut East	Conneautville	60
Conneaut West	Conneautville	60
Honey Brook	Honey Brook	60
Jamestown	Jamestown	60
Limeville	Gap	10
Townville	Townville	60

O. O. Amish

Ambrose North	Marion Center	55
Ambrose South	Marion Center	55
Ashville	Quarryville	75
Bart	Bart	75
Beaver Creek	Strasburg	75
Beaver Dam	Honey Brook	75
Belleville	Belleville	55
Belmont	Paradise	75
Berrysburg	Millersburg	75
Bird-in-Hand	Bird-in-Hand	75
Booneville	Loganton	75
Bradford	Rome	55
Britton Run East	Spartansburg	55
Britton Run Middle	Spartansburg	55
Britton Run West	Spartansburg	55
Brush Valley East	Rebersburg	75
Brush Valley West	Rebersburg	75
Buells Corner East	Spartansburg	55
Buells Corner North	Spartansburg	55
Buells Corner South	Centerville	55
Buena Vista	Gap	75
Byler East	Belleville	75
Byler West	Belleville	75
Byler West II	Belleville	75
Cains	Narvon	75
Cambridge	Narvon	75
Cattail	Gordonville	75
Centerville	Centerville	55
Centerville West	Centerville	55
Cherry Lane	Myerstown	75
Cherry Tree	Cherry Tree	55
Clintonville	Clintonville	55
Clintonville Middle	Clintonville	55
Clintonville West	Clintonville	55
Compass	Gap	75
Conestoga	Narvon	75
Cooperville	Christiana	75
Crawford West	Atlantic	55
Crossroad	Gratz	75

Congregation	Location	
Cumberland Valley	Newburg	75
Dayton	Dayton	55
Delta	Delta	75
Dornsife	Dornsife	55
East	Danville	75
East	Mercer	55
East	Myerstown	75
East	New Wilmington	55
East	Spring Run	55
East	Trade City	55
East Beaver Creek	Strasburg	75
East Centerville	Gordonville	75
East Cumberland Valley	Newburg	75
East Dauphin	Spring Glen	75
East Hatville	Gordonville	75
East Intercourse	Intercourse	75
East Nine Points	Christiana	75
East Nittany	Mill Hall	75
East Penns Valley	Aaronsburg	75
East Perry	Landisburg	75
East Salem	Mifflintown	55
East Smyrna	Christiana	75
East Wakefield	Wakefield	75
East Weavertown	Ronks	75
East White Deer Valley	Montgomery	75
East Witmer	Witmer	75
Edisonville	Strasburg	75
Elk Creek	Rebersburg	75
Emlenton	Emlenton	55
Enon Valley	Enon Valley	55
Fairfield	Peach Bottom	75
Fairmont	Quarryville	75
Fairview	Ronks	75
Fredonia	Fredonia	55
Gap	Gap	75
Greenland	Lancaster	75
Greentree	Christiana	75
Greentree	Quarryville	75
Guys Mills East	Guys Mills	55
Guys Mills Southwest	Guys Mills	55
Guys Mills West	Guys Mills	55
Hammer Creek A	Lititz	75
Hammer Creek B	Lititz	75
Harristown	Paradise	75
Hazen	Hazen	55
Homer City	Homer City	55
Homeville	Christiana	75
Indiana	Indiana	75
Iva	Paradise	75
Knox	Knox	55
Leola	Leola	75
Limeville	Gap	75
Lititz	Lititz	75
Little Nittany	Howard	75
Long Lane	Belleville	55
Lower	Belleville	55
Lower Middle	Belleville	55
Lower Middle	Meyersdale	55
Lower Millcreek	New Holland	75
Lower Pequea Gap	Gap	75
Mackeyville	Mill Hall	75
Mahoning	Smicksburg	55
Meadville	New Holland	75
Mechanics Grove	Quarryville	75
Mechanicsburg	Leola	75
Middle	Atlantic	55
Middle	Mercer	55
Middle	Punxsutawney	55
Middle	Salisbury	55
Middle	Smicksburg	55
Middle Kirkwood	Kirkwood	75
Middle North	New Wilmington	55
Middle North	Smicksburg	55
Middle South	Atlantic	55
Middle South	Smicksburg	55
Middle Southeast	Smicksburg	55
Millbach	Newmanstown	75
Mount Eden	Quarryville	75
Mount Joy	Mount Joy	75
Mount Pleasant	Quarryville	75
Mount Vernon	Gap	75
New Milltown	Intercourse	75
New Millwood	Gap	75
New Providence	New Providence	75
Newport	Gordonville	75
Nickel Mines	Paradise	75
Nipponese	Williamsport	75
Niverton	Salisbury	55
North	Atlantic	55
North	Mifflintown	55
North	Myerstown	75
North	New Wilmington	55
North	Newburg	75
North	Stoneboro	55
North	Trade City	55
North	Union City	55
North	Punxsutawney	55
North Annex	New Wilmington	55
North Beaver Creek	Strasburg	75
North Cream	Christiana	75
North Cumberland Valley	Newburg	55
North Drumore	Drumore	75
North Honey Brook	Honey Brook	75
North Intercourse	Intercourse	75
North Kinzers A	Kinzers	75
North Kinzers B	Kinzers	75
North Kirkwood	Kirkwood	75
North Linesville	Linesville	55
North Lower Pequea	Narvon	75
North Parkesburg	Parkesburg	75
North Spring Garden	Kinzers	75
North Union	Kirkwood	75
North Whitehorse	Gap	75
Northeast	Luthersburg	55
Northeast	New Wilmington	55
Northeast	Troutville	55
Northeast	Myerstown	75
Northeast Georgetown	Paradise	75
Northeast Groffdale B	New Holland	75
Northeast II	New Wilmington	55
Northeast Lower Millcreek	New Holland	75
Northeast Millcreek	Leola	75
Northeast Pequea	Narvon	75
Northumberland	Dornsife	75
Northwest	New Wilmington	55
Northwest	Reynoldsville	55
Northwest Groffdale	New Holland	75

Directory of Congregations

267

Northwest II	New Wilmington	55
Northwest Lower Pequea	Gordonville	75
Northwest Nine Points	Christiana	75
Nottingham	Nottingham	75
Oakland	Mifflintown	55
Oakland Mills	Oakland Mills	55
Oregon	Leola	75
Oxford	Oxford	75
Paradise	Paradise	75
Path Valley East	Dry Run	75
Path Valley Middle	Dry Run	75
Path Valley North	Dry Run	75
Path Valley South	Dry Run	75
Pocohantas	Meyersdale	55
Quarryville A	Quarryville	75
Quarryville B	Quarryville	75
Rebersburg	Rebersburg	75
Rocky Springs	Lancaster	75
Ronks	Ronks	75
Salisbury Heights	Gap	75
Sandy Hill	Coatesville	75
Sinking Valley	Tyrone	55
Smicksburg South	Smicksburg	55
Smicksburg West	Smicksburg	55
Smoketown	Smoketown	75
Soudersburg	Soudersburg	75
South	Linesville	55
South	Mercer	55
South	Mifflintown	55
South	New Wilmington	55
South	Newburg	75
South	Punxsutawney	55
South	Spring Run	55
South	Union City	55
South Beaver Creek	Quarryville	75
South Cream	Oxford	75
South Drumore	Drumore	75
South Georgetown	Christiana	75
South Greentree	Quarryville	75
South Hermitage	Narvon	75
South Honey Brook	Honey Brook	75
South Intercourse	Intercourse	75
South Kinzers	Kinzers	75
South Kirkwood	Oxford	75
South Middle Pequea	Gordonville	75
South Milroy	Reedsville	55
South Mount Vernon	Parkesburg	75
South New Providence	New Providence	75
South Spring Garden	Gap	75
South Union	Kirkwood	75
South Whitehorse	Gap	75
Southeast	Atlantic	55
Southeast	Volant	55
Southeast Groffdale	Gordonville	75
Southeast Lower Millcreek	Gordonville	75
Southeast Millcreek A	Ronks	75
Southeast Millcreek B	Ronks	75
Southwest	Atlantic	55
Southwest	New Wilmington	55
Southwest	Punxsutawney	55
Southwest Groffdale	Leola	75
Southwest Honey Brook	Honeybrook	75
Southwest Nine Points	Christiana	75
Southwest Upper Millcreek	Lancaster	75
Spartansburg East	Spartansburg	55
Spartansburg East II	Spartansburg	55
Spartansburg West	Spartansburg	55
Springs	Springs	55
Springville	Kinzers	75
Steelville	Christiana	75
Stoney Creek	Berlin	55
Strasburg	Strasburg	75
Stumptown Road	Bird-in-Hand	75
Sugar Grove North	Sugar Grove	55
Sugar Grove Middle East	Sugar Grove	55
Sugar Grove South	Sugar Grove	55
Sugar Grove West	Sugar Grove	55
Sugar Valley East	Loganton	75
Sugar Valley Middle	Loganton	75
Sugar Valley West	Loganton	75
Summit Mills	Meyersdale	55
Supplee	Honey Brook	75
Talmage	Talmage	75
Ulysses	Ulysses	55
Upper East	Allensville	55
Upper Middle	Belleville	55
Upper Middle	Meyersdale	55
Upper Middle Pequea	Ronks	75
Upper Millcreek	Leola	75
Upper Pequea	Ronks	75
Upper West	Allensville	55
Van Wert	Mifflintown	55
Vintage	Vintage	75
Volant	Volant	55
Wakefield	Wakefield	75
Washingtonville East	Washingtonville	55
Washingtonville West	Washingtonville	55
West	Atlantic	55
West	Milton	75
West	Myerstown	75
West	New Wilmington	55
West	Punxsutawney	55
West	Trade City	55
West Beaver Creek	Strasburg	75
West Centerville	Gordonville	75
West Conestoga	Narvon	75
West Cumberland Valley	Newburg	55
West Dauphin	Elizabethville	75
West Georgetown	Paradise	75
West Kirkwood	Kirkwood	75
West Lititz	Lititz	75
West Lower Millcreek	Ronks	75
West Lykens Valley	Millersburg	75
West Millcreek	Bird-in-Hand	75
West Nickel Mines	Paradise	75
West Nittany	Howard	75
West Penns Valley	Spring Mills	75
West Perry	Blain	75
West Perry B	Blain	55
West Smyrna	Christiana	75
West Upper Millcreek	Lancaster	75
West Weavertown	Bird-in-Hand	75
West Witmer	Witmer	75
White Deer Valley	Allenwood	75
Whitehall	Belleville	55
York	Delta	75

O. O. Amish Nebraska

Barrville	Barrville	55
Church Lane	Milroy	55
East	Milroy	55
East Milroy	Milroy	55
McClure	McClure	55
McClure II	McClure	55
Penn Valley	Woodward	55
Penn Valley II	Woodward	55
Reedsville	Reedsville	55
Reedsville West	Reedsville	55
Winfield	Winfield	55
Woodland Middle	Belleville	55
Woodland West	Reedsville	55

O. O. Amish Swartzentruber

Nicktown	Ebensburg	50

BRETHREN

Bible Brethren

Beaver Creek	Abbottstown	0
Mountain House	Carlisle	15

Brethren Church, The

Berlin	Berlin	113
Brush Valley	Adrian	149
Fairless Hills	Levittown	35
First	Mount Pleasant	55
Highland	Marianna	40
Johnstown Second	Johnstown	43
Johnstown Third	Johnstown	81
Main Street	Meyersdale	106
Masontown	Masontown	94
Pittsburgh First	Pittsburgh	28
Pleasant View	Vandergrift	85
Quiet Dell	Aleppo	3
Raystown	Marysville	36
Sarver	Sarver	40
Three Seasons Community	Berlin	0
Valley	Jones Mills	103
Vinco	Vinco	176
Wayne Heights	Waynesboro	49

Brethren Fellowship

Ephrata	Ephrata	35

Brethren in Christ

Air Hill	Chambersburg	197
Antrim	Chambersburg	454
Bethel Springs	Reinholds	18
Big Valley	Belleville	79
Blandburg	Blandburg	4
Blue Mountain	Roxbury	43
Bright Hope	Elizabethtown	60
Canoe Creek	Hollidaysburg	64
Carlisle	Carlisle	920
Cedar Grove	Mifflintown	261
Cedar Heights	Mill Hall	128
Center Grove	Three Springs	24
Central Community	Montgomeryville	23
Chambersburg	Chambersburg	307
Circle of Hope	Philadelphia	99
Clear Creek	Everett	90
Conoy	Elizabethtown	136
Coyler	Centre Hall	28
Cross Roads	Mount Joy	280
Crossroads Community	Lansdale	87
Cumberland Valley	Dillsburg	150
Dillsburg	Dillsburg	161

Eight Square Chapel	Hollidaysburg	17
Elizabethtown	Elizabethtown	548
Eschol	Eschol	9
Fairland	Cleona	240
Fairview	New Cumberland	63
Fairview Avenue	Waynesboro	184
Ferguson Valley	McVeytown	35
Five Forks	Waynesboro	526
Free Grace	Millersburg	183
Grantham	Grantham	432
Granville	Lewistown	26
Green Grove	Spring Mills	47
Green Spring	Newville	117
Hamilton Heights	Chambersburg	11
Hanover	Hanover	69
Harrisburg	Harrisburg	143
Harvest Community	Marietta	57
Hempfield	Lancaster	109
Hershey	Hershey	69
Hollowell	Waynesboro	234
Hummelstown	Hummelstown	59
Hunlock Creek	Berwick	27
Iron Springs	Fairfield	39
Jemison Valley	Westfield	136
Lancaster	Lancaster	263
Llewellyn	Llewellyn	38
Manheim	Manheim	368
Manor	Mountville	745
Marsh Creek	Downingtown	46
Marsh Creek	Howard	46
Martinsburg	Martinsburg	97
Mastersonville	Mastersonville	75
Mechanicsburg	Mechanicsburg	397
Messiah Village	Mechanicsburg	177
Millersville	Millersville	86
Montgomery	Mercersburg	135
Montoursville	Montoursville	33
Morning Hour	East Berlin	57
Mount Pleasant	Mount Joy	170
Mount Rock	Shippensburg	257
Mount Tabor	Mercersburg	131
Mountain Chapel	Breezewood	27
Mowersville	Newburg	51
New Covenant	Sellersville	96
New Guilford	Chambersburg	307
New Hope	Lansdale	155
New Joy	Akron	154
New Life	Middlesex	31
New Song	Mechanicsburg	26
Palmyra	Palmyra	129
Pathway Community	York	29
Peace Light	Gettysburg	45
Pequea	Lancaster	395
Perkiomen Valley	Collegeville	114
Pleasant Valley	Elliotsburg	23
Pleasant View	Red Lion	76
Redland Valley	York Haven	204
Refton	Refton	227
Roseglen	Duncannon	51
Saville	Ickesburg	47
Saxton	Saxton	17
Shermans Valley	Hopewell	26
Silverdale	Silverdale	149
Skyline View	Harrisburg	90

Directory of Congregations

269

Souderton	Souderton	197
South Mountain Chapel	Shippensburg	70
Speedwell Heights	Lititz	85
Spring of Hope	Altoona	21
Springhope	Schellsburg	24
Stowe	Stowe	48
Summit View	New Holland	106
Susquehana Valley	Selinsgrove	20
Tremont	Tremont	27
Wesley	Mount Holly Springs	33
West Shore	Enola	122
West Side	Chambersburg	53
Woodbury	Woodbury	15

Church of the Brethren

28th Street	Altoona	250
Akron	Akron	169
Albright	Roaring Spring	150
Alpha & Omega	Lancaster	63
Amaranth	Warfordsburg	41
Ambler	Ambler	118
Annville	Annville	429
Antietam Prices	Waynesboro	18
Arbutus	Johnstown	111
Aughwick-Germany Valley	Schellsburg	93
Bannerville	Milroy	119
Beachdale	Berlin	159
Bear Run	Mill Run	25
Bedford	Bedford	106
Beech Run	Mapleton Depot	78
Bellwood	Bellwood	157
Belvidere	York	30
Berkey	Windber	407
Bermudian	East Berlin	150
Bethel	DuBois	10
Bethel	Everett	115
Bethel	Farmington	137
Big Swatara	Harrisburg	47
Big Swatara, Hanoverdale	Hummelstown	186
Black Rock	Glenville	370
Blue Ball	Blue Ball	143
Brandts	Saint Thomas	130
Brothersvalley	Berlin	91
Buffalo Valley	Mifflinburg	208
Bunkertown	McAlisterville	201
Burnham	Burnham	110
Canaan	Gibbon Glade	93
Carlisle	Carlisle	193
Carson Valley	Duncansville	237
Center	Champion	62
Center Hill	Kittanning	318
Chambersburg	Chambersburg	672
Cherry Lane	Clearville	27
Chiques	Manheim	551
Claysburg	Claysburg	122
Clover Creek	Martinsburg	205
Cocalico	Denver	103
Codorus	Loganville	411
Conemaugh	Johnstown	164
Conestoga	Leola	296
Conewago	Hershey	219
Connellsville	Connellsville	60
Cornerstone	Lebanon	0
County Line	Champion	111
Coventry	Pottstown	297
Curryville	Curryville	134
Diehl's Crossroads	Martinsburg	53
Drexel Hill	Drexel Hill	128
Dry Run	Dry Run	45
Dunnings Creek	New Paris	139
East Calico	Reamstown	140
East Fairview	Manheim	371
East McKeesport	East McKeesport	31
Elbethel	Mount Pleasant	52
Elizabethtown	Elizabethtown	587
Ephrata	Ephrata	777
Everett	Everett	445
Fairchance	Fairchance	172
Fairview	Masontown	36
Fairview	Williamsburg	120
Faith Community	New Oxford	149
Falling Spring	Shady Grove	71
Farmers Grove	Honey Grove	9
First	Altoona	257
First	Harrisburg	276
First	Reading	294
First	Roaring Spring	622
First	York	487
Florin	Mount Joy	322
Free Spring	Mifflintown	113
Garrett	Garrett	28
Geiger	Friedens	203
Geiger Memorial	Philadelphia	42
Germantown	Philadelphia	78
Good Samaritan	Cranberry Township	85
Grace Christian	Upper Darby	25
Green Tree	Oaks	249
Greencastle	Greencastle	167
Greensburg	Greensburg	206
Greenville	Grampion	76
Hanover	Hanover	230
Harmonyville	Pottstown	71
Hatfield	Hatfield	83
Heidelberg	Reistville	123
Hempfield	East Petersburg	448
Hollidaysburg	Hollidaysburg	145
Holsinger	New Enterprise	158
Hooversville	Hooversville	49
Hostetler	Meyersdale	54
Huntsdale	Carlisle	135
Hyndman	Hyndman	27
Indian Creek	Harleysville	187
Indiana	Indiana	97
James Creek	Marklesburg	31
Jennersville	West Grove	50
Juniata	Altoona	60
Knobsville	McConnellsburg	54
Koontz	New Enterprise	56
Lake View Fellowship	East Berlin	32
Lampeter	Lampeter	308
Lancaster	Lancaster	685
Leamersville	Duncansville	204
Lebanon	Lebanon	263
Lewistown	Lewistown	123
Ligonier	Ligonier	116
Lititz	Lititz	620

Church of the Brethren/Mennonite: DA

Church of the Brethren: DA

Directory of Congregations

271

Brethren/Baptist	State College	484

Consrv Baptist Brethren

Frystown	Myerstown	55
Lititz	Lititz	75

Consrv Brethren

Millbach	Millbach	40

Consrv German Baptist Brethren

New Freedom	New Freedom	15

Consrv Grace Brethren

Aleppo	Aleppo	23
Brickerville	Lititz	75
Heritage Bible	Ephrata	12
Jenners	Jenners	0
Listie	Listie	103
Melrose Gardens	Harrisburg	84
North Buffalo	Kittanning	117
Reading	Stoystown	36
Washington	Washington	87

Dunkard Brethren

Bethel	Bethel	40
Clearville	Clearville	18
Lititz	Lititz	98
Mechanicsburg	Mechanicsburg	21
New Bethel	Bethel	35
Shrewsbury	Shrewsbury	62
Waynesboro	Waynesboro	35

German Seventh Day Baptist

Salemville	Salemville	55
Snow Hill	Waynesboro	18

Grace Brethren Churches

Altoona	Altoona	67
Bread of Life Fellowship	Denver	73
Chambersburg	Chambersburg	64
Community	Everett	92
Conemaugh	Conemaugh	45
Conococheague	Greencastle	23
Crossroads	Philadelphia	25
Echo Valley	Tremont	86
Elizabethtown	Elizabethtown	209
Ephrata Area	Ephrata	63
First	Altoona	50
First	Philadelphia	60
Gateway Community	Downingtown	10
Grace Community	Delmont	12
Greater Lancaster	Lancaster	81
Hope	Dillsburg	133
Hopewell	Hopewell	50
Ivywood Bible	Saxonburg	17
Johnstown	Johnstown	108
Kish Valley	Milroy	113
Laurel Mountain	Boswell	47
Leamersville	Duncansville	129
Lehigh Valley	Bethlehem	66
Lititz	Lititz	535
Manheim	Manheim	89
Martinsburg	Martinsburg	438
Meyersdale	Meyersdale	303
Myerstown	Myerstown	412
New Holland	New Holland	256
New Hope	Williamsport	4
New Life Community	Montgomeryville	10
Palmyra	Palmyra	78
Penn Valley	Telford	285
Pike	Johnstown	212

Riverside	Johnstown	272
Sherman's Valley	Blain	21
Singer Hill	Johnstown	157
Suburban	Hatboro	22
Summit Mills	Meyersdale	148
Susquehana	Wrightsville	91
Third	Philadelphia	27
Tiadeghon Valley	Avis	116
Tri-County	Royersford	20
Uniontown	Uniontown	127
Valley	Armaugh	70
Vicksburg	Hollidaysburg	115
Waynesboro	Waynesboro	147
West Kittaning	Kittaning	176
Willow Valley	Lancaster	123
York	York	103

Independent Brethren

Blue Rock	Waynesboro	38
Christ's Ambassador	Myerstown	90
Marsh Creek	Gettysburg	26
Oak Grove	Pine Grove	14

Old German Baptist Brethren

Antietam	Waynesboro	92
Browns Mill	Greencastle	139
Falling Spring	Chambersburg	196
Lancaster	Ephrata	74

O. O. River Brethren

Franklin District	Chambersburg	86
Horst Group	Chambersburg	109
Lancaster District	Mount Joy	83
Old Church	Saint Thomas	17

United Zion

Akron	Akron	96
Annville	Annville	26
Elizabethtown	Elizabethtown	86
Ephrata	Ephrata	231
Haaks	Newmanstown	36
Hahnstown	Ephrata	42
Mission	Lebanon	25
Moonshine Township	Lebanon	31
Palmyra	Palmyra	93
Reinholds	Reinholds	55
Stevens	Stevens	62

HUTTERITE

Bruderhof Communities

New Meadow Run	Farmington	230
Spring Valley	Farmington	180

MENNONITE

Apostolic Christian Church of America

Philadelphia	Philadelphia	33

Charity Christian Fellowship

Charity	Leola	290
Christian Light	Bedford	80
Emmanuel	Wyalusing	10
Hope	Lebanon	40

Church of God in Christ Mennonite

Fleetwood	Fleetwood	97
Living Faith	Shippensburg	73
Morning Star	Mifflinburg	89
Rock Haven	Belleville	128

Consrv Mennonite Conf

Crenshaw	Crenshaw	6
Locust Grove	Belleville	344
Mountain View	Reedsville	104

Oak Dale	Salisbury	103

Cumberland Valley Mennonite Church

Burns Valley	Doylesburg	42
Rowe	Shippensburg	87
Strasburg	Chambersburg	117

Eastern Pennsylvania Mennonite Church

Antrim	Greencastle	83
Bairs Codorus	York	25
Bernville	Bernville	57
Bethel	Quarryville	103
Blue Rock	Millersville	118
Centerville	Martindale	165
Churchtown	Carlisle	28
Conestoga Drive	Lancaster	55
Culbertson	Chambersburg	85
Danville	Danville	112
Denver	Denver	121
Dohner	Lebanon	76
French Creek	Cambridge Springs	64
Goodwill	Thompsontown	56
Hartleton	Hartleton	116
Hegins Valley	Hegins	65
Honey Brook	Honey Brook	94
Indian Creek	Telford	64
Latimore	York Springs	50
Little Mountain	Fredericksburg	70
Millerstown	Millerstown	38
Miners Village	Cornwall	71
Mountain View	Mount Holly Springs	70
New England Valley	Tamaqua	41
Pleasant View	Mount Joy	29
Rheems	Rheems	56
Richland	Richland	96
Simmontown	Gap	63
Texter Mountain	Robesonia	76
Valley View	Stevens	113
White Oak	Manheim	181
Woodbury	Woodbury	65

General Conf Mennonite Church

Bethel	Lancaster	133
Comunidad de Amor	Philadelphia	89
Cornerstone	Mifflintown	68
Deep Run West	Perkasie	240
East Swamp	Quakertown	446
Eden	Schwenksville	111
Emmanuel	Reinholds	148
Fairfield	Fairfield	48
First	Allentown	101
First	Huntington Valley	35
Germantown	Philadelphia	107
Good Samaritan	Holland	80
Grace	Lansdale	332
Hereford	Bally	161
Indian Valley	Harleysville	171
Lower Skippack	Skippack	233
Pine Grove	Bowmansville	218
Richfield	Richfield	360
Roaring Spring	Roaring Spring	20
Saucon	Coopersburg	72
Second	Philadelphia	63
Springfield	Quakertown	94
United	Quakertown	137
Upper Milford	Zionsville	148

Zion	Souderton	628

Hope Mennonite Fellowship

Garbers	Menges Mill	36
Muddy Creek	Fivepointville	79
Port Royal	Port Royal	36
Schaefferstown	Schaefferstown	158

Hopewell Mennonite District

Fellowship	Spring City	33
Good Shepherd	Adamstown	50
Hope Community Fellowship	Phoenixville	20
Hopewell	Elverson	327
Hopewell	Pottstown	136
Hopewell	Telford	57
Immanuel	Manheim	30
Living Hope	Reading	20
LOVE Christian Fellowship	Birdsboro	32
New Life Christian Fellowship	Bernville	40
Petra	New Holland	284

Independent Mennonite Congregations

Bethany House	Jenkintown	10
Bridgeport	Lancaster	10
Evangelical	Masontown	80
Holiness Missionary	Philadelphia	12
House of the Lord	Lancaster	12
Living Faith	Harleysville	96
New Covenant	Manheim	30
New Hope	Coatesville	21
Vineyard	Stevens	20

Keystone Mennonite Fellowship

Blandon	Blandon	25
Bradford	Bradford	18
Cross Roads	Richfield	80
East District	Watsontown	108
Fairview	Reading	92
Faith	Stevens	224
Living Water	Stevens	42
Lock Haven	Lock Haven	15
Marietta	Marietta	49
Myerstown	Myerstown	88
Oak Shade	Quarryville	37
Rawlinsville	Rawlinsville	50
Tidings of Peace	York	19
Valley	Rebersburg	28
Womelsdorf	Womelsdorf	55

Mennonite Biblical Alliance

Bethel	Cochranton	44

Mennonite Christian Fellowship

Emmanuel	Saint Thomas	51
Gospel Light	McVeytown	74
Hillsdale	Hillsdale	28
Pilgrim	Cochranton	55
Pine Grove	Pine Grove	20
Somerset	Somerset	42

Mennonite Church

Abundant Life Chinese	Philadelphia	50
Agape	Williamsport	130
Allensville	Allensville	249
Allentown	Allentown	25
Alsace Manor	Temple	26
Ambler	Ambler	82
Anabaptist Fellowship	Lancaster	0

Andrews Bridge	Christiana	21
Arca de Salvacion	Philadelphia	68
Ark Bible	Boyertown	47
Bally	Bally	191
Barrville	Barrville	85
Bart	Bart	143
Beaver Run	Turbotville	32
Beaverdam	Corry	128
Bender	Pen Argyl	128
Bethany	East Earl	215
Bethel	Gettysburg	97
Bethel	Warfordsburg	42
Bible Fellowship	Morris	40
Birch Grove	Port Allegany	33
Black Oak	Warfordsburg	33
Blainsport	Rheinholds	137
Blooming Glen	Blooming Glen	680
Blossom Hill	Lancaster	44
Blough	Holsopple	109
Bossler	Elizabethtown	124
Bowmansville	Bowmansville	291
Boyer	Middleburg	68
Boyertown	Boyertown	131
Buffalo	Lewisburg	147
Byerland	Willow Street	92
Calvary	Morris Run	14
Cambridge	Honey Brook	59
Canan Station	Altoona	45
Canton	Canton	405
Carpenter	Talmage	149
Carpenter Park	Davidsville	185
Cedar Grove	Greencastle	300
Cedar Hill	Elizabethtown	35
Cedar Street	Chambersburg	111
Chambersburg	Chambersburg	134
Chestnut Hill	Columbia	114
Christ the King	Lancaster	139
Christian Community	Manchester	30
Christian Fellowship	Lebanon	49
Christian Life	Philadelphia	37
Christiana	Christiana	59
Church of the Servant	Langhorne	85
Churchtown	Churchtown	62
Coatesville	Coatesville	25
Columbia	Columbia	27
Community	Bethlehem	38
Community	Milton	184
Community Chapel	Marietta	104
Conestoga	Morgantown	257
Cornerstone	Altoona	39
Cornerstone	Exton	26
Cornerstone	Mountaintop	49
Covenant	Lancaster	13
Covenant	Lansdale	120
Cristo es la Respuesta	Harrisburg	32
Deep Run East	Perkasie	340
Delaware	Thompsontown	54
Derry	Danville	34
Diamond Street	Philadelphia	40
Diller	Newville	60
Downing Hills	Downingtown	30
Doylestown	Doylestown	210
East Chestnut Street	Lancaster	263
East Hanover	Palmyra	15
East Petersburg	East Petersburg	317
El Buen Pastor	Lancaster	85
Elizabethtown	Elizabethtown	199
Ephrata	Ephrata	338
Erb	Lititz	158
Erisman	Manheim	243
Ethiopian Evangelical	Philadelphia	15
Fairview	Waynesboro	160
Fellowship	Quarryville	20
Finland	Pennsburg	109
First	Johnstown	46
First Deaf	Lancaster	155
Forest Hills	Leola	340
Fountain of Life	Middletown	69
Franconia	Franconia	715
Frazer	Frazer	156
Frederick	Frederick	65
Gehman	Adamstown	95
Gingerichs	Lebanon	244
Good	Elizabethtown	78
Goodville	Goodville	94
Grace	Manheim	66
Green Terrace	Wernersville	34
Groffdale	Leola	267
Habecker	Mountville	87
Halifax	Halifax	44
Hammer Creek	Lititz	271
Hampden	Reading	44
Hernley	Manheim	125
Herr Street	Harrisburg	28
Hershey	Kinzers	124
Hersteins	Schwenksville	82
Hess	Lititz	116
Hinkletown	Ephrata	384
Home	Lancaster	0
Hope Community	Fleetwood	80
Hopewell	Reading	65
House of the Lord	Liberty	64
Iglesia Ebenezer	Bethlehem	25
Indiantown	Ephrata	127
James Street	Lancaster	236
Kapatiran Christian	Berwyn	40
Kauffman	Manheim	56
Kaufman	Holsopple	119
Kennet Square	Kennet Square	32
Kingview	Scottdale	133
Kinzer	Kinzers	63
Krall	Schaefferstown	60
Lakeview	Susquehana	54
Landis Valley	Lancaster	114
Landisville	Landisville	293
Laurel Street	Lancaster	71
Lauver	Cocolamus	58
Lichty	East Earl	130
Life Fellowship	Conestoga	39
Lighthouse	Upland	134
Line Lexington	Line Lexington	219
Lititz	Lititz	189
Living Faith	Shippensburg	111
Living Hope	Forksville	20
Living Hope	Millersville	10
Living Stones	Peach Bottom	108
Living Word	Fleetwood	82
Locust Lane	Harrisburg	54

Lost Creek	Oakland Mills	185
Love Truth Chinese	Philadelphia	35
Luz de Faro	Chester	41
Luz de Salvacion	Lebanon	33
Luz Verdadera	Reading	77
Lyndon	Lancaster	51
Manbeck	Beaver Springs	35
Manheim	Manheim	64
Maple Grove	Atglen	225
Maple Grove	Belleville	284
Maple Grove	New Castle	33
Maranatha Family	Nazareth	55
Marion	Marion	161
Martindale	Martindale	412
Martinsburg	Martinsburg	136
Masontown	Masontown	91
Masonville	Washington Boro	100
Mattawana	Mattawana	83
Meadville	Kinzers	35
Mechanic Grove	Quarryville	94
Meckville	Bethel	88
Media	Oxford	94
Mellinger	Lancaster	387
Mercersburg	Mercersburg	109
Methacton	Norristown	105
Metzler	Ephrata	300
Mill Run	Altoona	62
Millersville	Millersville	95
Millport	Leola	150
Millwood	Gap	62
Mount Joy	Mount Joy	358
Mountain View	Trout Run	25
Mountville	Mountville	175
Mount Pleasant	Paradise	47
Mount Vernon	Oxford	187
Nanticoke	Nanticoke	40
Neffsville	Neffsville	532
New Beginnings	Bristol	49
New Community	Berwyn	17
New Danville	New Danville	211
New Holland	New Holland	175
New Holland Spanish	New Holland	56
New Life	Bernville	50
New Life	East Athens	26
New Life	Ephrata	110
New Life	Norristown	108
New Life	Somerset	20
New Mercies	Philadelphia	54
New Providence	New Providence	84
Newlinville	Coatesville	27
Nickel Mines	Paradise	117
Old Road	White Horse	134
Oley	Oley	73
Otelia	Mount Union	47
Oxford Circle	Philadelphia	40
Palabra de Vida	Philadelphia	0
Palo Alto	Pottsville	75
Paradise	Paradise	277
Parkesburg	Parkesburg	68
Peace Chapel	Harrisburg	22
Perkasie	Perkasie	117
Perkiomenville	Perkiomenville	124
Philadelphia Cambodian	Philadelphia	180
Pilgrims	Ephrata	44

Pittsburgh	Pittsburgh	36
Plains	Lansdale	241
Pleasant View	Chambersburg	125
Pond Bank	Chambersburg	61
Praise Center	Eddystone	50
Praise Center	South Avis	56
Providence	Collegeville	41
Red Run	Denver	100
Ridgeview	Gordonville	452
Rissers	Elizabethtown	95
River Corner	Conestoga	72
River of God	Easton	155
Roca de Salvacion	Lancaster	10
Rock Hill	McConnellsburg	16
Rockhill	Telford	154
Rockville	Belleville	123
Rockville	Honey Brook	207
Rocky Ridge	Quakertown	124
Roedersville	Pine Grove	39
Rohrerstown	Rohrerstown	70
Rossmere	Lancaster	86
Salam Fellowship	Wyncote	20
Salem	Shelly	92
Salem Ridge	Greencastle	142
Salford	Harleysville	487
Sandy Hill	Coatesville	167
Schubert	Schubert	52
Scottdale	Scottdale	145
Shady Pine	Willow Hill	80
Shalom	East Greenville	29
Shiloh	Reading	22
Slate Hill	Camp Hill	165
Souderton	Souderton	668
South Christian Street	Lancaster	97
South Philadelphia Vietnamese	Philadelphia	20
South Seventh Street	Reading	53
Springs	Springs	332
Spruce Lake	Canadensis	30
Stahl	Johnstown	106
Stauffer	Hershey	32
Steel City	Bethlehem	97
Steelton	Steelton	82
Stony Brook	York	110
Strasburg	Strasburg	192
Strickler	Middletown	28
Stumptown	Bird-in-Hand	312
Sunnyside	Conneaut Lake	50
Sunnyside	Lancaster	110
Susquehanna	Selingsgrove	40
Swamp	Quakertown	195
Thomas	Holsopple	131
Towamencin	Kulpsville	174
University	State College	71
University Fellowship	Millersville	25
Upper Skippack	Skippack	118
Valley View	Spartansburg	118
Vietnamese Gospel	Souderton	32
Village Chapel	New Holland	81
Vincent	Spring City	181
Way of Life	Philadelphia	10
Way Through Christ	Chester	0
Weaver	Johnstown	77
Weaverland	Weaverland	573

Welsh Mountain	New Holland	28
West End	Lancaster	20
West Franklin	Monroeton	20
Wheelerville	Wheelerville	19
Whitehall	Whitehall	47
Willow Street	Willow Street	246
Witmer Heights	Lancaster	101
Word of Joy	Royersford	59
Zion	Birdsboro	85
Zion	York	129
Zion Covenant	Chambersburg	100

Mennonite Church/General Conf: DC

Akron	Akron	413
Community	Lancaster	177
West Philadelphia	Philadelphia	88
West Swamp	Quakertown	320

Mennonite Unaffiliated Congregations

Beaver Springs	McClure	53
Beth El	Belleville	108
Cornerstone	Ephrata	80
Faith Builders	Guys Mills	31
Followers of Jesus	Lancaster	35
Haycock	Quakertown	52
Lansdale	Lansdale	70
Mount Hope	Manheim	88
New Covenant	Ephrata	197
North Lebanon	Lebanon	57
Shippensburg	Shippensburg	72

Mid-Atlantic Mennonite Fellowship

Bairs-Hostetters	Littlestown	111
Blue Ball	Blue Ball	146
Fair Haven	Myerstown	98
Lebanon Valley	Mount Aetna	83
Millmont	Millmont	161
Mountain View	McConnellsburg	51
New Haven	Lititz	122
Open Door	Adamstown	63
Pleasant Valley	Ephrata	175
Refton	Refton	31
Shalom	Watsontown	35
Sharon	Lebanon	114
Sixth Street	Philadelphia	7
Strodes Mills	Strodes Mills	50
Union Valley	Ulster	26

Mid-West Mennonite Fellowship

Pleasant View	Cochranton	85

Nationwide Mennonite Fellowship Churches

Bethel	Mount Pleasant Mills	68
Blooming Valley	Blooming Valley	45
Blue Mountain	Lynnville	27
Grace	Ephrata	70
Meadow Green	Three Springs	47
New Bethlehem	New Bethlehem	42
Royers	Myerstown	62
Spring Valley	Fayetteville	46
Stony Fork	Stony Fork	52
Stoughstown	Newville	46

O. O. Mennonite Groffdale Conf

Bowmansville	Bowmansville	360
Center	Kutztown	165
Churchtown	Churchtown	345
Clearfield	Shippensburg	160
Conestoga	Ephrata	170
Fleetwood	Fleetwood	145
Groffdale	Leola	390
Martindale	Martindale	395
Martinsburg	Martinsburg	145
Meadow View	Shippensburg	90
Millway	Lititz	85
Mountain View	Mifflinburg	275
Muddy Creek	Denver	255
New Enterprise	New Enterprise	95
New Holland	New Holland	270
Piney Creek	Martinsburg	100
Shippensburg	Shippensburg	170
Spring Grove	Terre Hill	160
Vicksburg	Vicksburg	210
Weaverland	East Earl	395

O. O. Mennonite John Martin Group

House Church	Bowmansville	13

O. O. Mennonite Reidenbach Group

Family Meetings	Ephrata	12
House Church	Bowmansville	30
House Church	New Holland	25
House Church I	Ephrata	21
House Church II	Ephrata	20
Limestone	Milton	61
Reidenbach	Ephrata	86
West Reidenbach	Ephrata	38

O. O. Mennonite Stauffer Group

Indiana County	Indiana	27
Pallas	Mount Pleasant Mills	135
Pike	Ephrata	283
Riverview	Port Treverton	155
Upper District	Port Treverton	110

O. O. Mennonite Unaffiliated

Aaron Martin Church	Port Treverton	24
Brubaker Church	Port Treverton	110
Martin Weaver Church	Ephrata	11
Pike Weaver Church	Ephrata	33

O. O. Mennonite Weaverland Conf

Bethel	Bethel	189
Bowmansville	Bowmansville	137
Churchtown	Churchtown	138
Clearview	Manheim	239
County Line	Meiserville	75
Fairmount	Quarryville	95
Fairview	Myerstown	235
Groffdale	Leola	322
Lime Rock	Lititz	210
Martindale	Martindale	231
Martin's	Myerstown	217
Meadow Valley	Ephrata	418
Millbach	Millbach	146
Milltown	Alinda	89
Mount Zion	Myerstown	280
Mountain View	Lebanon	180
Oakville	Newville	70
Pequea	Gordonville	180
South Hinkletown	Ephrata	163
Springville	Ephrata	332
Walnuttown	Walnuttown	105
Weaverland	East Earl	209

O. O. Orthodox Mennonite

Orthodox	Port Treverton	6

Pilgrim Mennonite Conf

Blue Ridge	Newville	72
Calvary	Chambersburg	49
Chapel	Hereford	29
Elm Street	Lebanon	110
Lake View	North East	44
Leola	Leola	49
Providence	Grantville	64
Shade Mountain	Mount Pleasant Mills	103
Shirksville	Jonestown	97
Swatara	Myerstown	140

Reformed Mennonite Church

Longeneckers	Strasburg	83
Middlesex	Carlisle	30
Waynesboro	Waynesboro	14

United Mennonite

House Meeting	Chambersburg	5
House Meeting	Lancaster	12

Washington Franklin Mennonite Conf

Friend's Cove	Rainsburg	35
Waynecastle	Waynesboro	152

York-Adams Mennonite Churches

Hanover	Hanover	92
Hersheys	Thomasville	31
Kralltown	East Berlin	71
Mummasburg	Gettysburg	57
North Hartman Street	York	15

PUERTO RICO

BRETHREN

Church of the Brethren

Cristo el Senor	Vega Baja	61
Cristo Nuestra Paz	Yahuecos	45
de Rio Prieto	Rio Prieto	55
Iglesia Cristiana	Villa Prades	0
Iglesia Cristo Misionera	Caimito	59
Iglesia de los Hermanos	Castaner	89
Pueblo de Dios	Manati	19

MENNONITE

Caribbean Mennonite Conf

Betel	Arecibo	60
El Buen Pastor	Hatillo	40
Iglesia Evangelica	Lares	16
Manantial de Vida	Sabana Hoyos	28
Roca de Salvacion	Coamo	54

Mennonite Church

Aibonito	Aibonito	66
Banta Arriba	Aibonito	9
Bayamon	Bayamon	56
Betania	Aibonito	70
Cayey	Cayey	35
Coamo	Coamo	75
La Plata	La Plata	35
Palo Hincado	Barranquitos	39
Ponce	Ponce	41
Summit Hills	San Juan	36

Mennonite Unaffiliated Congregation

Guavate	Caguas	30

Southeastern Mennonite Conf

Followers of Christ	Anasco	3
Fountain of Life	Barceloneta	2

SOUTH CAROLINA

AMISH

Beachy Amish

Calvary	Blackville	43
Cold Springs	Abbeville	140
Cross Hill	Cross Hill	33

BRETHREN

Church of the Brethren

Travelers Rest	Travelers Rest	53

Grace Brethren Churches

Aiken	Aiken	131
Anderson	Anderson	40

MENNONITE

Consrv Mennonite Conf

Dayspring	Batesburg	12

Mennonite Biblical Alliance

Shiloh	Due West	62

Mennonite Church

Anderson	Anderson	27
Cornerstone	Charleston	31

Mennonite Unaffiliated Congregations

Fair Play	Fair Play	67
New Holland	New Holland	47
Pickens	Pickens	38
Whispering Pines	Honea Path	115

South Atlantic Mennonite Conf

Barnwell	Blackville	82

SOUTH DAKOTA

HUTTERITE

Schmiedeleut Hutterite

Blumengard	Faulkton	55
Bon Homme	Tabor	55
Brentwood	Faulkton	55
Cedar Grove	Platte	55
Claremont	Claremont	55
Clark	Raymond	55
Clearfield	Delmont	55
Cloverleaf	Howard	55
Deerfield	Ipswich	55
Evergreen	Faulkton	55
Fordham	Carpenter	55
Glendale	Frankfort	55
Graceville	Winfred	55
Grass Land	Westport	55
Grass Ranch	Kimball	55
Greenwood	Delmont	55
Hillcrest	Garden City	55
Hillside	Doland	55
Huron	Huron	55
Hutterville	Stratford	55
Jamesville	Utica	55
Lakeview	Lake Andres	55
Long Lake	Wetonka	55
Maxwell	Scotland	55
Mayfield	Willow Lake	55
Millbrook	Mitchell	55
Millerdale	Miller	55
New Elm Springs	Ethan	55
Newdale	Elkton	55
Newport	Castlewood	55
Oak Lane	Alexandria	55
Orland	Montrose	55

Anabaptist World USA

278

Pearl Creek	Iroquois	55
Pembrook	Ipswich	55
Plainview	Leola	55
Platte	Platte	55
Pleasant Valley	Flandreau	55
Pointsett	Estelline	55
Riverside	Huron	55
Rockport	Alexandria	55
Roland	White	55
Rosedale	Mitchell	55
Rustic Acres	Madison	55
Spink	Frankfort	55
Spring Lake	Arlington	55
Spring Valley	Wessington Springs	55
Sunset	Britton	55
Thunderbird	Faulkton	55
Tschetter	Olivet	55
Upland	Artesian	55
White Rock	Rosholt	55
Wolf Creek	Olivet	55

MENNONITE

Church of God in Christ Mennonite

Faith	Iroquois	139
Rolling Plains	Ward	17

Evangelical Mennonite Brethren

Marion	Marion	50

Independent Mennonite Congregations

Bethesda	Marion	90
Hutterthal	Carpenter	230
Mount Olivet	Huron	195

Keystone Mennonite Fellowship

Olive Branch	Cherry Creek	8

Mennonite Brethren

Bethel	Yale	179
Bethesda	Huron	303
Bible Fellowship	Rapid City	143
Emmanuel	Onida	44
Grace Bible	Gettysburg	93
Lakota Gospel	Porcupine	25
Lincoln Hills	Sioux Falls	101
Salem	Freeman	143
Silver Lake	Freeman	74

Mennonite Church/General Conf: DC

Bethany	Freeman	239
Emmanuel	Doland	130
Fellowship	Brookings	2
Friedensberg	Avon	83
Good Shepherd	Sioux Falls	74
Hutterthal	Freeman	236
New Hutterthal	Bridgewater	92
Salem	Freeman	434
Salem-Zion	Freeman	386
Sermon on the Mount	Sioux Falls	29
Zion	Bridgewater	85

TENNESSEE

AMISH

Amish Mennonite Unaffiliated

Cumberland	Altamont	50
Finger	Finger	42
Hardin County	Olivehill	25
Marshall County	Lewisburg	31
Moore County	Lynchburg	30
Rock Springs	Wildersville	35

Beachy Amish

Belvidere	Belvidere	72
Bethel	Cottage Grove	55
Calvary	Cottage Grove	50
Mount Zion	Deer Lodge	62
Whiteville	Whiteville	62

O. O. Amish

Carroll	Huntington	55
Hickman	Nunnelly	55
McKenzie	McKenzie	55

O. O. Amish Swartzentruber

East	Ethridge	50
East Lawrenceburg	Lawrenceburg	50
Middle	Ethridge	50
Middle East	Ethridge	50
North	Summertown	50
Northwest	Ethridge	50
South	Ethridge	50
West	Ethridge	50

BRETHREN

Brethren in Christ

Center Hill	Smithville	24
De Rossett	De Rossett	65
Pomeroy Chapel	Smithville	48
Rolling Acres	McMinnville	116

Church of the Brethren

Cedar Grove	Rogersville	32
Erwin	Erwin	65
First	Bristol	31
French Broad	White Pine	156
Hawthorne	Johnson City	102
Jackson Park	Jonesborough	134
Johnson City	Johnson City	58
Knob Creek	Johnson City	34
Limestone	Limestone	11
Midway	Surgoinsville	18
Mountain Valley	Greeneville	82
Nashville	Nashville	8
New Hope	Jonesborough	86
Petersons Chapel	Erwin	29
Pleasant Grove	Red Hill	34
Pleasant Hill	Blountville	34
Pleasant Valley	Jonesborough	128
Pleasant View	Jonesborough	24
Trinity	Blountville	102

Consrv Grace Brethren

Telford	Telford	66

Grace Brethren Churches

Johnson City	Johnson City	24

MENNONITE

Apostolic Christian Church of America

Nashville	Nashville	9

Charity Christian Fellowship

Grace	Woodbury	72
Pilgrim	Monterey	50

Church of God in Christ Mennonite

Cumberland Mountain	Monterey	58
Pleasant View	Lobelville	52

Mennonite Christian Fellowship

Berea	Rutherford	33
Greene County	Greeneville	55
Mount Moriah	Crossville	72
White County	Sparta	63

Mennonite Church

Concord	Knoxville	27
Harmony	Nashville	37
Knoxville	Knoxville	40
Rainbow	Mountain City	38

O. O. Mennonite Unaffiliated

Cane Creek	Pleasantville	42
Christian Community	Cookeville	16
Christian Community	Decatur	28
Russell Creek	Lobelville	53

Reformed Mennonite Church

House Church	Oakland	8

TEXAS
AMISH

Amish Mennonite Unaffiliated

Grandview	Grandview	53

Beachy Amish

Faith	Lott	24
Grace	Bastrop	77

O. O. Amish

Beeville	Beeville	6
Gonzales	Gonzales	8
Moran	Cisco	6

BRETHREN

Church of the Brethren

Faith Center	Whitehouse	7
Falfurrias	Falfurrias	33
Nocoma	Nocoma	77
Pampa	Pampa	50
Waka	Waka	58

Grace Brethren Churches

Longview	Longview	81
McAllen	McAllen	17

MENNONITE

Apostolic Christian Church of America

Zapata	Zapata	7

Charity Christian Fellowship

Maranatha	Melissa	27

Church of God in Christ Mennonite

Country Side	Dalhart	73
El Campo	El Campo	86
Farwell	Farwell	98
Red River Valley	Detroit	91
Southern Hope	Victoria	22
Texhoma	Texhoma	55
Texline	Texline	176
West Haven	Brookston	53

Consrv Mennonite Conf

Abundant Life	San Antonio	35
Fountain of Life	San Antonio	73

Eastern Pennsylvania Mennonite Church

Grays Prairie	Scurry	54

Evangelical Mennonite Mission Conf

Gospel	Seminole	216

General Conf Mennonite Church

Iglesia Cristiana	Dallas	35

Mennonite Brethren

Donna	Donna	16
Grulla	La Grulla	130
Iglesia de Gracia	Garciasville	10
Iglesia Evangelica	Laredo	15
La Joya	La Joya	40
Lull	Edinburg	20

McAllen	McAllen	12
Mission	Mission	36
Nueva Vida	Palmview	12
Pharr	Pharr	10
United	Premont	8

Mennonite Church

Calvary	Mathis	120
Casa de Oracion	Alamo	42
Good News	San Juan	32
Iglesia del Cordero	Brownsville	85
New Jerusalem	Edinburg	25
Perryton	Perryton	43
Primera	Harlingen	86
Prince of Peace	Corpus Christi	54
Tabernacle de Fe	Mathis	27

Mennonite Church/General Conf: DC

Austin	Austin	40
Communidad de Esperanza	Dallas	25
Hope Fellowship	Waco	14
Houston	Houston	51
Luz del Evangelio	Dallas	30
Peace	Dallas	89
San Antonio	San Antonio	55

Mennonite Evangelical Churches

Evangelical	Paris	37
Seminole	Seminole	179

Old Colony Mennonite

Old Colony	Seminole	407

Reinlaender Mennonite Church

Reinlaender	Seminole	387

UTAH
MENNONITE

Mennonite Brethren

South Mountain	Draper	23

Nationwide Mennonite Fellowship Churches

Northern Utah	Willard	20

VERMONT
BRETHREN

Church of the Brethren

Genesis Fellowship	Putney	52

Consrv Grace Brethren

Irasburg	Irasburg	40

Grace Brethren Churches

Island Pond	Island Pond	44

MENNONITE

Eastern Pennsylvania Mennonite Church

Wolcott	Wolcott	25

Independent Mennonite Congregation

Andover	Andover	81

Mennonite Church

Bethany	Bridgewater Corners	26
Taftsville	Taftsville	58

VIRGINIA
AMISH

Beachy Amish

Faith	Catlett	50
Faith Mission	Free Union	80
Farmville	Farmville	41
Gospel Light	Charlottesville	25

Kempsville	Virginia Beach	62
Mount Zion	Stuarts Draft	27
Oak Grove	Aroda	99
Pilgrim	Stuarts Draft	171

O. O. Amish

Abingdon	Abingdon	12
Charlotte	Charlotte Court House	65
Gretna	Gretna	55
Walker Mountain	Pearisburg	36
White Gate	Pearisburg	36

BRETHREN

Brethren Church, The

Bethlehem	Harrisonburg	62
Grace Community	Winchester	0
Liberty	Woodstock	27
Maurertown	Maurertown	148
Mount Olive	McGaheysville	320
Port Republic	Cross Keys	7
Saint Luke	Woodstock	126
Waterbrook	Edinburg	101

Brethren in Christ

Adney Gap	Callaway	14
Bethel	Hillsville	110
Calvary	Accomac	17
Community of Faith	Roanoke	68
Highland Park	Dublin	86
Lynchburg	Lynchburg	34
Ridge View	Roanoke	36
Winchester	Winchester	16

Church of the Brethren

Antioch	Rocky Mount	370
Antioch	Woodstock	123
Arbor Hill	Staunton	76
Arlington	Arlington	97
Barren Ridge	Staunton	258
Bassett	Bassett	221
Beaver Creek	Bridgewater	14
Bethany	Boones Mill	72
Bethel	Arrington	86
Bethel	Broadway	170
Bethlehem	Boones Mill	134
Blue Ridge	Blue Ridge	163
Blue Ridge Chapel	Waynesboro	215
Boones Mill	Boones Mill	97
Bridgewater	Bridgewater	697
Briery Branch	Dayton	350
Burkesfork	Willis	29
Calvary	Winchester	213
Cedar Bluff	Boones Mill	105
Cedar Grove	Brandywine	60
Cedar Grove	Mount Jackson	54
Cedar Grove	Ruckersville	69
Cedar Run	Broadway	88
Central	Roanoke	231
Charlottesville	Charlottesville	199
Chimney Run	Warm Springs	139
Christiansburg	Christiansburg	196
Cloverdale	Cloverdale	222
Collinsville	Collinsville	138
Columbia Furnace	Woodstock	190
Copper Hill	Copper Hill	349
Coulson	Hillsville	363
Cumberland	Clintwood	145

Daleville	Daleville	160
Damascus	Criders	162
Dayton	Dayton	227
Dranesville	Herndon	131
Duncans Chapel	Willis	70
Elk Run	Churchville	44
Emmanuel	Danville	63
Emmanuel	Mount Solon	234
Evergreen	Stanardsville	142
Ewing	Ewing	21
Fairview	Endless Caverns	111
Fairview	Floyd	49
Fairview	Mount Clinton	114
Ferrum	Ferrum	32
First	Danville	72
First	Harrisonburg	521
First	Pulaski	100
First	Roanoke	214
First	Rocky Mount	132
Flat Rock	Forestville	119
Forest Chapel	Crimora	151
Free Union	Free Union	77
Fremont	Fremont	47
Front Royal	Front Royal	168
Garbers	Harrisonburg	98
Germantown Brick	Rocky Mount	273
Good Shepherd	Blacksburg	41
Green Hill	Salem	110
Greenmont	Harrisonburg	325
Grottoes	Grottoes	101
Henry Fork	Rocky Mount	220
Hiner	McDowell	37
Hiwassee	Hiwassee	37
Hollins Road	Roanoke	149
Hollywood	Fredericksburg	116
Hopewell	Hopewell	45
Ivy Farms	Newport News	160
Jeters Chapel	Vinton	162
Jones Chapel	Martinsville	145
Keezeltown	Keezeltown	150
Knight's Chapel	Barboursville	52
Laurel Branch	Floyd	71
Leakes Chapel	Stanley	280
Lebanon	Mount Sidney	168
Lighthouse	Boones Mill	48
Linville Creek	Broadway	213
Little River	Goshen	123
Lowman Valley	Marion	77
Luray	Luray	135
Lynchburg	Lynchburg	81
Madison	Brightwood	80
Manassas	Manassas	427
Mason's Cove	Salem	95
Meadow Mills	Middletown	75
Melrose	Harrisonburg	105
Middle River	New Hope	260
Midland	Midland	212
Mill Creek	Port Republic	436
Monte Vista	Callaway	81
Montezuma	Dayton	421
Moscow	Mount Solon	163
Mount Bethel	Dayton	288
Mount Bethel	Eagle Rock	39
Mount Herman	Bassett	176

Mount Joy	Buchanan	51
Mount Lebanon	Barboursville	25
Mount Olivet	Timberville	148
Mount Pleasant	Harrisonburg	154
Mount Union	Bent Mountain	82
Mount Vernon	Waynesboro	106
Mount Bethel	Linville	65
Mount Bethel	Luray	86
Mountain Grove	Fulkes Run	218
Mountain Grove Chapel	Dyke	26
Mountain View	McGaheysville	0
New Bethel	Chatham	188
New Covenant	Chester	39
New Hope	Stuart	153
Newport	Shenandoah	112
Nineven	Hardy	51
Ninth Street	Roanoke	252
Nokesville	Nokesville	316
Oak Grove	Roanoke	249
Oak Grove, South	Rocky Mount	114
Oak Hill	Fort Valley	88
Oakton	Vienna	157
Oronoco	Buena Vista	49
Palmyra Fellowship	Edinburg	29
Parkway	Mabry Mill	16
Peters Creek	Roanoke	214
Pine Grove	Linville	55
Pine Ridge	Earlysville	134
Pleasant Hill	Grottoes	88
Pleasant Valley	Alum Ridge	119
Pleasant Valley	Weyers Cave	352
Pleasant View	Mount Jackson	80
Pleasantdale	Daleville	22
Poages Mill	Roanoke	295
Pound River	Clintwood	24
Red Hill	Roanoke	80
Red Oak Grove	Floyd	148
Rileyville	Stanley	65
Round Hill	Toms Brook	80
Rowland Creek	Marion	19
Rummet Run	Bridgewater	81
Saint Paul	Mount Airy	40
Salem	Stephens City	66
Sangerville	Bridgewater	88
Saunders Grove	Moneta	71
Selma	Selma	26
Shiloh	Stanardsville	44
Smith Mountain Lake	Moneta	31
Smith River	Stuart	160
Snow Creek	Boones Chapel	109
Staunton	Staunton	402
Stone	Buena Vista	179
Stonewall	Floyd	29
Stony Creek	Bayse	103
Summerdean	Roanoke	227
Timberville	Timberville	223
Topeco	Floyd	313
Trinity	Luray	52
Trinity	Troutville	122
Trout Run	Wardensville	25
Troutville	Troutville	95
Valley Pike	Mauretown	249
Vinton	Vinton	98
Wakefield Chapel	Hopewell	54

Wakeman's Grove	Edinburg	299
Walker's Chapel	Mount Jackson	101
Walnut Grove	Damascus	49
Waynesboro	Waynesboro	407
West	Richmond	151
White Hill	Stuarts Draft	418
White Rock	Willis	90
Williamson Road	Roanoke	376
Woodbridge	Woodbridge	115

Church of the Brethren: DA

Brethren Christian Uniting	Virginia Beach	118
Terrace View	Forest	44

Consrv Brethren

Central Plains	Palmyra	40

Dunkard Brethren

Dayton	Dayton	10

Grace Brethren Churches

Alexandria	Alexandria	27
Blue Ridge	Winchester	118
Boones Mill	Boones Mill	20
Clearbrook	Roanoke	76
Covington	Covington	81
Fairlawn	Radford	65
First	Buena Vista	192
Garden City	Roanoke	92
Ghent	Roanoke	177
Lighthouse	Salem	43
Patterson Memorial	Roanoke	158
Richmond	Richmond	134
Riner	Riner	74
Troutville	Troutville	20
Washington Heights	Roanoke	100
Winchester	Winchester	95

Old German Baptist Brethren

Mountain View	Rocky Mount	125
Oak Hill	Rocky Mount	196
Peters Creek	Roanoke	122
Pigg River	Rocky Mount	105

MENNONITE

Consrv Mennonite Conf

Dayspring	Catlett	36
Providence	Virginia Beach	38

Cornerstone Mennonite Church

Albermarle	Port Republic	18
Augusta	Waynesboro	189
Rockingham	Harrisonburg	1244

General Conf Mennonite Church

Richmond	Richmond	31

Mennonite Biblical Alliance

Blue Ridge	Madison	10
Calvary	Harrisonburg	55
Oak Hill	Cumberland	23

Mennonite Church

Beldor	Elkton	42
Bethel	Broadway	60
Big Spring	Rileyville	47
Broad Street	Harrisonburg	26
Buenas Nuevas	Arlington	30
Calvary	Hampton	1040
Charlottesville	Charlottesville	42
Christiansburg	Christiansburg	36
Community	Harrisonburg	171
CrossRoads	Timberville	31

Directory of Congregations

281

Dayton	Dayton	155
Dove	Chesapeake	20
Faith	South Boston	23
Family of Hope	Harrisonburg	12
First	Richmond	79
Gospel Hill	Fulks Run	80
Grace	Linville	45
Greenmonte	Stuarts Draft	89
Harrisonburg	Harrisonburg	545
Hebron	Fulks Run	73
Hilderbrand	Waynesboro	22
Huntington	Newport News	128
Immanuel	Harrisonburg	98
Landstown	Virginia Beach	164
Lindale	Harrisonburg	284
Lynside	Lyndhurst	58
Morning View	Singers Glen	77
Mount Clinton	Mount Clinton	105
Mount Jackson	Mount Jackson	57
Mount Pleasant	Chesapeake	261
Mount Vernon	Grottoes	58
Mountain View	Waynesboro	114
Northern Virginia	Vienna	57
Park View	Harrisonburg	386
Powhatan	Powhatan	129
Providence	Newport News	50
Rehoboth	Schuyler	15
Ridgeway	Harrisonburg	166
Shalom	Harrisonburg	18
Springdale	Waynesboro	184
Staunton	Staunton	42
Stephens City	Stephens City	96
Stuarts Draft	Stuarts Draft	92
Trissels	Broadway	112
Valley View	Criders	72
Vietnamese	Falls Church	72
Warwick River	Newport News	203
Waynesboro	Waynesboro	196
Weavers	Harrisonburg	279
Williamsburg	Williamsburg	68
Woodland	Bayse	28
Word of Life	Norfolk	28
Zion	Broadway	245
Zion Hill	Singers Glen	104

Mennonite Unaffiliated Congregations

Bethel	Gladys	87
Floyd County	Floyd	25
Living Faith	Harrisonburg	70
Lucas Hollow	Stanley	10
Timberville	Timberville	45

Nationwide Mennonite Fellowship Churches

Pilgrim	Amelia	122
Pleasant Valley	Dayton	26

O. O. Mennonite Virginia Conf

Oak Grove	Dayton	198
Pleasant View	Dayton	138
Riverdale	Dayton	90

O. O. Mennonite Weaverland Conf

Mount Pleasant	Dayton	136

O. O. Mennonite Wenger/Weaver Group

Oak Grove	Dayton	163
Pleasant View	Dayton	110

Southeastern Mennonite Conf

Bank	Dayton	127

Bethany	Dayton	61
Bethesda	Broadway	42
Ebenezer	South Boston	45
Front Royal	Front Royal	23
McGaheysville	McGaheysville	41
Mount Herman	Stanardsville	55
Peake	Hinton	64
Pike	Harrisonburg	94
Rawley Springs	Rawley Springs	48

WASHINGTON
AMISH
O. O. Amish

Springdale	Springdale	27

BRETHREN
Church of the Brethren

Community	Salkum	73
Covington Community	Kent	108
Ellisforde	Tonasket	86
Larchmont Community	Tacoma	30
Olympic View	Seattle	268
Outlook	Outlook	26
Richland Valley	Mossyrock	76
Whitestone	Tonasket	33

Church of the Brethren: DA

Columbia-Lakewood	Seattle	49
Community	Lacey	148
Sunnyslope	Wenatchee	113
Wenatchee	Wenatchee	160

Consrv Grace Brethren

Spokane Valley	Spokane	18

Grace Brethren Churches

Community	Goldendale	51
Friendship	Vancouver	20
Grandview	Grandview	80
Harrah	Harrah	70
Iglesia de Los Hermanos	Mabton	33
Kent	Kent	137
Mabton	Mabton	89
Maple Valley	Maple Valley	28
Seattle	Seattle	30
Sunnyside	Sunnyside	205
Toppenish	Toppenish	57
Yakima	Yakima	40

Old German Baptist Brethren

Cascade Valley	Ellensburg	85
Columbia River	Pasco	107

HUTTERITE
Dariusleut Hutterite

Marlin	Marlin	30
Schoonover	Odessa	30
Spokane	Reardon	30
Stahl	Ritzville	30
Warden	Warden	30

MENNONITE
Charity Christian Fellowship

Manna	Ellensburg	30

Church of God in Christ Mennonite

Columbia River	Othello	87
Rainbow Valley	Tonasket	19

Independent Mennonite Congregations

C. C. P. M. de Vida Eterna	Warden	50
Columbia Basin	Ephrata	14

Mennonite Brethren

Bethel Ethiopian	Seattle	40
Birch Bay	Blaine	135
Community	Bellingham	94
Good News	Ferndale	147
Korean	Seattle	30
Light of the Gospel Slavic	Spokane	100
Pilgrim Evangelical	Vancouver	500
Pilgrim Slavic	Spokane	205
Slavic	Bellingham	500
Slavic Missionary	Seattle	201
Washington Central Korean	Federal Way	60

Mennonite Church/General Conf: DC

Evergreen	Bellevue	52
Menno	Ritzville	149
Seattle	Seattle	132
Shalom	Spokane	22
Spring Valley	Newport	70
Trinity Taiwanese	Federal Way	20
Warden	Warden	57

Mennonite Unaffiliated Congregation

New Hope	Everett	11

Western Consrv Mennonite Fellowship

Pine Grove	Colville	36

WEST VIRGINIA

AMISH

O. O. Amish

Ohio River	Letart	24
Reedy	Reedy	8

BRETHREN

Brethren Church, The

Cameron	Cameron	39
Gatewood	Fayetteville	12
Mathias	Mathias	59
Oak Hill	Oak Hill	110
White Dale	Terra Alta	8

Brethren in Christ

Bunker Hill	Bunker Hill	102

Church of the Brethren

Allensville	Hedgesville	84
Bean Settlement	Rockoak	43
Beaver Run	Burlington	144
Bethel	Petersburg	122
Bethlehem Fellowship	Fort Seybert	32
Boyer	Boyer	7
Brake	Petersburg	211
Brick	Maysville	40
Brookside	Aurora	46
Capon Chapel	Levels	43
Cedar Grove	Brandywine	60
Circle of Love	Buckhannon	43
Clifton Mills	Bruceton Mills	41
Crab Orchard	Crab Orchard	133
Crab Run	Mathias	157
Durbin	Durbin	49
Elkins	Elkins	78
Fellowship	Martinsburg	153
Friends Run	Franklin	82
Glady	Elkins	14
Goshen	Canaan	27
Harman	Harman	47
Harness Run	Burlington	22

Harpers Chapel	Moorefield	40
Hazleton	Hazleton	47
Johnsontown	Hedgesville	131
Jordan Run	Jordan Run	65
Kelly Chapel	Rada	65
Keyser	Keyser	220
Knobley	Martin	107
Maple Spring	Eglon	108
Mathias	Mathias	280
Moler Avenue	Martinsburg	175
Moorefield	Moorefield	493
Mount Carmel	Milam	30
Mount View	Lost City	39
Mount Zion	Meadowville	54
Mountain Dale	Hazleton	0
Mountain Grove	Thomas	10
Mountain View	Bunker Hill	232
New Dale	Baker	99
New Hope	Dunmore	73
North Fork	Cherry Grove	100
Oak Dale	Scherr	134
Oak Grove	Ridgeley	12
Oakvale	Oakvale	35
Old Furnance	Ridgeley	81
Olean	Gold Bond	20
Onego	Onego	68
Petersburg Memorial	Petersburg	163
Pine Grove	Arborvale	55
Pleasant Hill	Fairmont	18
Pleasant Valley	Troy	6
Pleasant View	Fayetteville	43
Pocohontas	Green Bank	102
Romney	Romney	54
Rough Run	Maysville	55
Salem	Brandonville	77
Sandy Creek	Bruceton Mills	143
Sandy Ridge	Franklin	28
Shady Grove	Brandonville	55
Shiloh	Kasson	62
Smith Chapel	Bluefield	28
Smith Creek	Franklin	62
South Mill Creek	Mozer	50
Spruce Run	Linside	166
Sugarland	Parsons	22
Sunnyside	New Creek	246
Tearcoat	Augusta	361
Thorn Chapel	Moyers	17
Trout Run	Wardensville	25
Valley Bethel	Bolar	21
Valley River	Junior	17
Walnut Grove	Moorefield	129
White Pine	Purgitsville	47
Wiley Ford	Wiley Ford	157

Church of the Brethren/Mennonite: DA

Morgantown	Morgantown	101

Church of the Brethren: DA

Terra Alta	Terra Alta	7

Consrv Grace Brethren

Community	Parkersburg	22

Dunkard Brethren

Ridge	Ridgeley	12

Grace Brethren Churches

First	Grafton	102
Parkersburg	Parkersburg	62

Rosemont	Martinsburg	89
Old German Baptist Brethren		
Spruce Run	Linside	34
MENNONITE		
Mennonite Christian Fellowship		
Gap Mills	Gap Mills	69
Mennonite Church		
Crest Hill	Wardensville	10
Lambert	Belington	26
Mathias	Mathias	62
Philippi	Philippi	20
Pleasant Grove	Fort Seybert	9
Riverside	Harman	28
Salem	Baker	38
Mennonite Unaffiliated Congregation		
Believers	Petersburg	26
Southeastern Mennonite Conf		
Boyer Hill	Bartow	16
Brushy Run	Onego	38
North Fork	Seneca Rocks	28

WISCONSIN
AMISH
Amish Mennonite

Pleasant Valley	Muscoda	89
New Order Amish		
Spencer	Spencer	81
Stratford	Stratford	38
O. O. Amish		
Athens	Augusta	55
Augusta Northeast	Augusta	55
Augusta South Middle	Augusta	55
Augusta Southeast	Augusta	55
Augusta Southwest	Augusta	55
Augusta West	Augusta	55
Beetown	Beetown	55
Bloomington	Bloomington	55
Bonduel	Bonduel	55
Bonduel Annex	Bonduel	55
Brodhead	Brodhead	55
Chaseburg	Chaseburg	55
Chetek	Chetek	55
Clayton	Clayton	55
Clearlake	Clearlake	55
East	Cashton	55
East	Durand	55
Edgar	Edgar	55
Elkhart Lake	Elkhart Lake	55
Fennimore	Fennimore	55
Gilman	Gilman	55
Granton East	Granton	55
Granton Northeast	Granton	55
Granton Southeast	Granton	55
Granton West	Granton	55
Greenwood	Greenwood	55
Hillpoint	Hillpoint	55
Hillsboro Middle	Hillsboro	55
Hillsboro Northeast	Hillsboro	55
Hillsboro Southeast	Hillsboro	55
Hillsboro West	Hillsboro	55
Ironton East	LaValle	55
Ironton West	Cazenovia	55
Kingston Northeast	Kingston	55
Kingston Northwest	Kingston	55

Kingston South	Kingston	55
Kingston Southeast	Kingston	55
Kingston Southwest	Kingston	55
Livingston	Livingston	55
Loganville	Loganville	55
Lookout	Lookout	55
Marion	Marion	55
Middle	Cashton	55
Middle South	Cashton	55
Middle West	Westby	55
Milan	Milan	55
Milladore	Milladore	55
Mondovi Middle	Mondovi	55
Mondovi West	Mondovi	55
New Auburn	New Auburn	55
New Glarus	New Glarus	55
New Holstein	New Holstein	55
North	Wilton	55
North Center	Wilton	55
Northeast	Medford	55
Northeast	Norwalk	55
Northside	Blair	55
Northwest	Cashton	55
Northwest	Medford	55
Oakfield	Oakfield	55
Oconta	Oconta	55
Owen-Unity	Owen	55
Portage North	Amherst	55
Portage South	Amherst	55
Readstown I	Readstown	55
Readstown II	Readstown	55
Rising Sun	Rising Sun	55
Saint Cloud	Elkhart Lake	55
South	Curtiss	55
South	Westby	55
South	Wilton	55
Southeast	Kendall	55
Southside	Blair	55
Taylor	Taylor	55
Valley	Wilton	55
Valley East	Ontario	55
Valley West	Cashton	55
Wautoma East	Wautoma	55
Wautoma West	Wautoma	55
West	Cashton	55
West	Wilton	55
Wulff Valley	Mondovi	55
O. O. Amish Swartzentruber		
Liberty Pole	Liberty Pole	50
Loyal North	Loyal	50
Loyal South	Loyal	50
Viroqua	Viroqua	50
BRETHREN		
Brethren in Christ		
New Vision	Waukesha	47
Church of the Brethren		
Rice Lake	Rice Lake	12
Stanley	Stanley	66
German Baptist Brethren		
Athens	Athens	70
Old German Baptist Brethren		
Redstone Valley	Elroy	55

WISCONSIN

MENNONITE
Charity Christian Fellowship
Gospel Light	Richland Center	91

Church of God in Christ Mennonite
Barron	Barron	105
Gospel	Almena	157
Hillcrest	Barron	93

Consrv Mennonite Unaffiliated
Sheldon Consrv	Sheldon	39

Eastern Pennsylvania Mennonite Church
Owen	Owen	54

Mennonite Church
Exeland	Exeland	16
Sand Lake	Stone Lake	15
South Lawrence	Glen Flora	70

Mennonite Church/General Conf: DC
Madison	Madison	44
Maple Avenue	Waukesha	39

Mennonite Unaffiliated Congregations
Grace	Stone Lake	23
Sparta	Sparta	23
The Sheepfold	Wausau	28
Wayside	Conrath	15

Mid-West Mennonite Fellowship
Bethany	Stratford	22
Buck Creek	Richland Center	53
Northwoods	Hayward	72

Nationwide Mennonite Fellowship Churches
Athens	Athens	70
Augusta	Augusta	72
Oak Ridge	Redgranite	33
Pleasantview	Brodhead	15
Shiloh	Tony	55
Thorp	Thorp	65
Unity	Unity	53

O. O. Mennonite Groffdale Conf
Longwood	Longwood	170
Meadow Brook	Withee	90
Plattville	Plattville	13
Sunny Ridge	Curtiss	190

O. O. Mennonite Weaverland Conf
Pine Grove	Granton	144
Fennimore	Fennimore	22

WYOMING

BRETHREN
Brethren Church, The
Cheyenne	Cheyenne	76

MENNONITE
Nationwide Mennonite Fellowship Churches
High Prairie	Carpenter	34

Directory of Congregations

285

GENERAL
INDEX

A

Acculturation, 55, 129, 132
Affiliation, 14
African-American, 14
Agriculture, 78, 95, 108, 170
Alabama, 177
Alaska, 177
Almanac (Raber's). *See New American Almanac*
Alsace, 23
American Evangelicalism, 44, 126
Amish
    beliefs, 69
    history, 26-7, 120, 209
    population and membership count, 32,
      34-5, 67, 75-6, 142
    publications, 210
    values, 72
Amish-related groups. *See* Group Index: Amish
Amish settlements
    Adams County, IN, 67, 150
    Allen County, IN, 67, 150
    Elkhart-Lagrange, IN, 72
    Holmes County, OH, 63, 69, 148-50
    Lancaster County, PA, 70, 142
    Mifflin County, PA, 68, 149
Ammann, Jakob, 27
Anabaptist
    beliefs, 23, 42-52
    definition of, 21
    history, 21, 42, 129-30, 141, 209
    movement, 12-3, 25, 43, 46, 50, 213
    sympathizers, 22, 27, 64
    vision, 24
Anabaptists, types of
    anarchists, 26
    ethnic, 64
    general, 64
    mystics, 22
    population and membership count, 12,
      14-5, 32-5, 133-4, 143
    publications, 209
    radicals, 21-6, 214
    spiritualists, 22
Annual Conference (Brethren), 82-3, 86, 217

Apostolic Christian Church of America, 14. *See
    also* Group Index: Mennonites
Arizona, 37, 39, 178
Arkansas, 178
Arnold, Eberhard, 101
Ashland College, 86
Ashland Theological Seminary, 86, 121
Ashland University, 119-20
Asian American, 14
Assimilation, 46
Assimilation, degrees of
    general, 15
    traditional, 15, 55-6, 58, 61-2, 104,
      130, 154
    transformational, 15, 58, 60-2, 104,
      117, 130, 154
    transitional, 15, 56, 58-60, 130, 155
Association of Brethren Caregivers. *See*
    National Association
Ausbund, 42, 74
Austerlitz, 24
Austria, 25-26
Automobiles. *See* Technology

B

Baptism
    adult, 75
    age of, 15, 44, 75
    beliefs and practices, 82-5
    believers, 21, 24, 29, 43
    general, 40, 73, 75, 80-1, 86, 88, 107, 115
    infant, 21, 44
Baptists, 141
Barn raising, 47. *See also* Mutual aid
Beliefs. *See* Anabaptist, beliefs; Confession of
    faith; *see also under* Amish; Brethren;
    Hutterite; Mennonite
Believers church, 31
Believers Church Bible Commentary, 128
Believers Church Conferences, 128
Bethany College, 121
Bethel College, 119
Blackboard Bulletin, The, 126
Bluffton College, 119
Bonhoeffer, Dietrich, 46

general, 14, 76, 100, 129-30, 132, 155
high school, 76
higher, 81, 108, 110, 120-2, 131
theological, 121-2
Egly, Henry, 161
Elderly, 73
Electricity. *See* Technology, electricity
Elizabethtown College, 119
Episcopalian, 64
Ethnicity. *See* Immigration; Mennonite immigrants
Evangelical United Brethren, 141
Evangelical Visitor. See Visitor
Evangelism. *See* Missions
Excommunication, 42, 46, 60, 75. *See also* Church, discipline; Shunning

F

Family Life, 126
Family size, 15, 72, 75, 94, 130, 134
Farming. *See* Agriculture
Feetwashing. *See* Footwashing
Fellowship, definition of, 14, 67
Flag, 52
Florida, 39, 89, 182
Footwashing, 27, 133
"Free" church, 31, 43
Freedom. *See* Religious freedom
Friends. *See* Quakers
Fresno Pacific University, 119
Froehlich, Samuel, 158
Fruits of the Spirit, 44, 46

G

Gelassenheit, 46, 97-8
Gender roles, 130, 132
General Assembly, 117
Georgia, 182
German Swiss ethnicity. *See* Mennonite imigrants, Swiss German
Germantown, 30, 41
Germany, 13, 21, 26, 28
Gibb, Donald, 93
Global Mission Partnerships, 124
Global Women's Project, 126
Goshen College, 119, 142
Government, 21, 51, 60-1, 99
Grace College, 119
Grace Theological Seminary, 86
Group(s)
defined, 32-3
size, 34
Growth. *See* Population and membership count, *under* Amish; Brethren; Hutterite; Mennonite

H

Haiti Missions, 123
Hauerwas, Stanley, 64
Hawaii, 39, 183
Healthcare agencies. *See* Institutions, church-related
Heifer Project International, 118
Hesston College, 119
Historic Peace Churches, 48, 127
Historical libraries, 124-5
Hoffman, Melchior, 26
Holdeman, John, 159
Holy Spirit, 23, 29, 44
Homosexuality, 115, 117, 128, 132. *See also* Brethren-Mennonite Council for Lesbian and Gay Concerns
Hoover, Noah, 168
Hungary, 25
Hutter, Jacob, 24
Hutterite
beliefs, 92-3, 97-9, 102-3
Chronicle, the Hutterite, 25, 42, 98
history, 24-5, 93, 101, 211
movement, 24
population and membership count, 33, 35, 92
publications, 211
Hutterite-related groups. *See* Group Index: Hutterite
Hymnal: A Worship Book, 127

I

Idaho, 183
Identity, 37, 39, 41-2, 70-1, 84, 135-6, 141
Illinois, 80, 106, 112, 184
Immigration, 12-3, 30-1, 111-5
Indiana, 36, 39, 67, 70, 72, 75, 81-2, 87, 106, 108, 119, 121, 123, 184
Individual conscience, 31, 52, 55, 62, 83, 135
Individualism, 61, 72, 79, 97, 103
Individualistic, 59
Industry. *See* Business
Information centers
Amish, 210
Brethren, 210
Mennonite, 211
Institutions, church-related, 118, 120, 125
Integration (MC-GC), 114, 123
Intergroup cooperation, 127-8
Internet. *See* Technology, computer; World Wide Web
Iowa, 75, 113, 185

J

Juniata College, 119

New American Almanac, 142-3, 227
New York, 75, 108, 112, 195
Nickolsburg, 24
Nonconformity. *See* Separation from the world
Non-creedal, 45, 83-4, 86
Nonresistance. *See* Peacemaking
North America, 23
North Carolina, 79, 196
North Dakota, 25, 31, 80, 115, 197

O
Occupation(s), 14, 131-2
Ohio, 35-6, 39, 63, 69-70, 75, 81-2, 86-7, 89, 106, 108, 110, 119, 148, 197
Oklahoma, 31, 198
Old Order groups, definition of. *See* Assimilation, traditional
Old Order Wisler Mennonite Conference, 147
Old Testament, 43
On Earth Peace Assembly, 126
Ordination of women, 60-1, 110, 132, 164
Ordnung, 67, 72, 75, 108
Oregon, 123, 199
Organizations. *See* Institutions, church-related

P
Palatinate, 23
Parachurch agencies. *See* Institutions, church-related
Patriotism, 52
PAX (Peace) Program, 49
Peacemaking, 13, 24, 29, 31, 48, 51, 61, 83, 126, 131, 137
Pennsylvania, 30, 36, 40-1, 68, 70, 75, 79, 81-2, 87, 89, 106-8, 119-20, 123, 130, 200
Persecution, 22, 24, 26, 29-31, 52, 98
Photography. *See* Technology, photography
Pietism, 79, 88, 91, 119
    general, 55
    radical, 13, 29-30, 79, 83
Plymouth Brethren, 141
Poland, 23
Political involvement, 48, 52, 56, 61-2, 111, 126, 131
Political office, holding, 60-2
Population and membership count. *See* Amish; Brethren; Hutterite; Mennonite
Prarieleut. *See* Group Index: Hutterite
Presbyterian, 64
Privacy, 73
Private property, 66, 103
Protestant Reformation, 21, 29
Puerto Rico, 12, 158, 201

Q
Quakers, 13, 48, 141

R
Radical Pietism. *See* Pietism, radical
Radios. *See* Technology, radios
Reformation. *See* Protestant Reformation
Reformed churches, 29
Relations with outsiders, 54
Religious freedom, 12, 52
Religious ritual. *See* Ritual
Retreat centers. *See* Institutions, church-related
Revolutionary War, 48
Rhode Island, 32
Riedemann, Peter, 25, 92
Ritual, 57
Romania, 25
Russian Mennonites. *See* Mennonite immigrants, Dutch Russian

S
SERRV, 125
Schism. *See* Conflict
Schmiedeleut. *See* Group Index: Hutterite
Schools. *See* Education
Schwarzenau Brethren, 217. *See also* Brethren history
Scripture, use of, 21, 23, 43, 46, 136, 164
Self-examination, 46
Separation from the world, 51, 54, 98-9, 101, 110
Separation of church and state, 110
Sermon on the Mount, 102
Service ministries, 49, 85, 124-5
Shunning, 28, 46, 68, 111, 159. *See also* Church, discipline
Simons, Menno. *See* Menno
Social issues, 61-2
Social justice, 51, 61, 126, 131
Social mobility, 63-64
Society of Brothers. *See* Bruderhof Communities
South Carolina, 79, 202
South Dakota, 25, 31, 80, 92, 115, 202
Suffering. *See* persecution
Sunday school, 59, 69-70, 108-9, 127, 136, 148
Swiss Brethren, 23, 26, 47
Swiss German ethnicity. *See* Mennonite immigrants, Swiss German
Switzerland, 26

T
Tabor College, 119
Taxes, 100
Technology

ANABAPTIST
GROUP INDEX

Amish

Amish Mennonite, 66-7, 70, 142, 144, 147, 159
Amish Mennonite Unaffiliated, 144, 147
Beachy Amish, 63, 66-7, 70, 142, 144, 147, 165
New Order Amish, 64, 66-7, 69, 142, 144, 148
New Order Amish Fellowship, 70, 144, 148
Old Order Amish, 57, 64, 66-8, 142, 144, 148, 150, 164
Old Order Amish Andy Weaver, 68, 144, 149
Old Order Amish Byler, 68, 144, 149
Old Order Amish groups, 35
Old Order Amish Nebraska, 68, 144, 149
Old Order Amish Renno, 68, 144, 150
Old Order Amish Swartzentruber, 68, 142, 144, 150
Old Order Amish Swiss Groups, 67, 144, 150
Old Order Amish Troyer, 68, 144, 150

Brethren

Bible Brethren, 144, 150
Brethren Church, The, 35, 61, 79, 81, 86, 88, 119-21, 123, 144, 151-2
Brethren Community Fellowship, 144, 151
Brethren Fellowship, 144, 151
Brethren Revival Fellowship, 85, 144, 152
Brethren in Christ, 35-6, 45, 61, 63, 79, 89, 119-21, 123, 127, 134, 144, 151, 156, 175
Church of the Brethren, 35-6, 49, 61, 63, 79, 82, 84, 119-21, 124-5, 127, 132, 134, 144, 150-4, 174-5
Church of the Brethren/Mennonite: Dual Affiliated, 144, 153
Church of the Brethren: Dual Affiliated, 144
Church of the Brethren: Other Affiliated, 152
Conservative Baptist Brethren, 144, 153
Conservative Brethren, 144, 153
Conservative German Baptist Brethren, 144, 153
Conservative Grace Brethren Church, 86, 144, 153
Dunkard Brethren, 88, 124, 144, 153-4

Fellowship of Grace Brethren Churches, 81
German Baptist Brethren, 13, 29, 144, 151, 154
German Seventh-Day Baptists, 144, 154
Grace Brethren Churches, Fellowship of, 35, 61, 63, 79, 86, 119, 121, 123, 134, 144, 154
Independent Brethren, 144, 155
Old Brethren, 144, 153, 155
Old Brethren German Baptists, 87, 145, 155
Old German Baptist Brethren, 57, 63, 79, 81, 87, 120, 123, 145, 155-6
Old Order German Baptists, 87, 145, 156
Old Order River Brethren, 89, 124, 145, 156
Smaller Groups, Independent Congregations, 35
United Zion, 89, 145, 156

Hutterite

Bruderhof. *See* General Index: Bruderhof Communities
Dariusleut, 25, 92-3, 145, 157
Lehrerleut, 25, 92-3, 145, 157
Prairieleut, 25
Schmiedeleut, 25, 92-3, 145, 157

Mennonite

Apostolic Christian Church of America, 14, 35, 106-7, 145, 158
Bethel Mennonite Fellowship, 145, 158
Caribbean Mennonite Conference, 145, 158
Charity Christian Fellowship, 107, 145, 158-9
Church of God in Christ (Holdeman) Mennonite, 145, 159
Church of God in Christ Mennonite, 35, 105, 110, 145, 159
Conservative Mennonite Conference, 145, 159-60, 164
Conservative Mennonite Unaffiliated, 145, 160, 166
Cornerstone Mennonite Churches, 145, 160
Cumberland Valley Mennonite Church, 145, 160

ABOUT THE AUTHORS

Donald B. Kraybill has authored, co-authored, and edited more than fifteen books on Anabaptist groups, including *The Upside-Down Kingdom* (1990), which received the national Religious Book Award; *The Riddle of Amish Culture* (2001), a standard reference for understanding social change among the Amish; and *The Amish Struggle with Modernity* (1994). He edited the award-winning *The Amish and the State* (1993) and co-authored *Mennonite Peacemaking: From Quietism to Activism* (1994), and *Amish Enterprise: From Plows to Profits* (1995). He co-edited *Building Communities of Compassion: Mennonite Mutual Aid in Theory and Practice* (Herald Press, 1998). His most recent book, coauthored with Carl F. Bowman, is *On the Backroad to Heaven: Old Order Hutterites, Mennonites, Amish, and Brethren* (Johns Hopkins University Press, 2001).

Kraybill holds a Ph.D. in sociology and is Professor of Sociology and Anabaptist Studies at Messiah College in Pennsylvania, where he previously served as provost. Prior to that he directed The Young Center for Anabaptist and Pietist Studies at Elizabethtown (Pa.) College. He has served in various leadership roles in the Mennonite Church and the Church of the Brethren.

Donald and his wife, Frances, are members of the Elizabethtown (Pa.) Church of the Brethren.

C. Nelson Hostetter graduated from Messiah Academy and Junior College (Grantham, Pa.), then earned a bachelor's degree in sociology from Goshen (Ind.) College. He pursued advanced studies at a variety of institutions, including the Institute of Behavioral Science at the University of Colorado (Boulder) and the Institute of Emergency Preparedness at the University of Southern California (Los Angeles). Hostetter is the compiler of *Anabaptist Mennonites Nationwide, USA* (Masthof Press, 1997).

During World War II, he served four years in Civilian Public Service in Virginia, Florida, Michigan, and Puerto Rico. Hostetter has served as coordinator of the Western Ohio Mennonite Disaster Service Unit and as the executive coordinator for Mennonite Disaster Service in the United States, Canada, and the Caribbean. In recent years he has served as a volunteer consultant for Church World Service National Disaster Response and as a staff person for several interchurch disaster relief efforts: the Pennsylvania Catholic Conference, the Pennsylvania Council of Churches, the Kentucky Council of Churches, and the West Virginia Council of Churches. He has led disaster response workshops for the Church of the Brethren, the Brethren in Christ, the Mennonite Church, and other denominations.

Nelson and his wife, Esther, are members of the Akron (Pa.) Mennonite Church.